REVIEW C

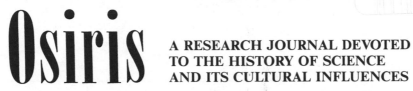 **A RESEARCH JOURNAL DEVOTED TO THE HISTORY OF SCIENCE AND ITS CULTURAL INFLUENCES**

EDITORIAL OFFICE
DEPARTMENT OF HISTORY AND SOCIOLOGY OF SCIENCE
UNIVERSITY OF PENNSYLVANIA
215 SOUTH 34TH STREET
PHILADELPHIA, PENNSYLVANIA, 19104-6310, USA

SUGGESTIONS FOR CONTRIBUTORS TO OSIRIS

OSIRIS is now devoted to thematic issues, conceived and compiled by guest editors.

1. Manuscripts should be **typewritten** or processed on a **letter-quality** printer and **double-spaced** throughout, including quotations and notes, on paper of standard size or weight. Margins should be wider than usual to allow space for instructions to the typesetter. The right-hand margin should be left ragged (not justified) to maintain even spacing and readability.

2. Bibliographic information should be given in **footnotes** (not parenthetically in the text), typed separately from the main body of the manuscript, **double-** or even **triple-spaced,** numbered consecutively throughout the article, and keyed to reference numbers typed above the line in the text.

   a. References to **books** should include author's full name; complete title of the book, underlined (italics); place of publication and publisher's name for books published after 1900; date of publication, including the original date when a reprint is being cited; page numbers cited. *Example:*

   [1]Joseph Needham, *Science and Civilisation in China,* 5 vols., Vol. I: *Introductory Orientations* (Cambridge: Cambridge Univ. Press, 1954), p. 7.

   b. References to articles in **periodicals** should include author's name; title of article, in quotes; title of periodical, underlined; year; volume number, Arabic and underlined; number of issue if pagination requires it; page numbers of article; number of particular page cited. Journal titles are spelled out in full on first citation and abbreviated subsequently. *Example:*

   [2]John C. Greene, "Reflections on the Progress of Darwin Studies," *Journal of the History of Biology,* 1975, *8*:243–273, on p. 270; and Dov Ospovat, "God and Natural Selection: The Darwinian Idea of Design," *J. Hist. Biol.,* 1980, *13*:169–174, on p. 171.

   c. When first citing a reference, please give the title in full. For succeeding citations, please use an abbreviated version of the title with the author's last name. *Example:*

   [3]Greene, "Reflections" (cit. n. 2), p. 250.

3. Please mark clearly for the typesetter all unusual alphabets, special characters, mathematics, and chemical formulae, and include all diacritical marks.

4. A small number of **figures** may be used to illustrate an article. Line drawings should be directly reproducible; glossy prints should be furnished for all halftone illustrations.

5. Manuscripts should be submitted to OSIRIS with the understanding that upon publication **copyright** will be transferred to the History of Science Society. That understanding precludes OSIRIS from considering material that has been submitted or accepted for publication elsewhere.

OSIRIS (ISSN 0369-7827) is published once a year.

Subscriptions are $39 (hardcover) and $25 (paperback).

Address subscriptions, single issue orders, claims for missing issues, and advertising inquiries to *Osiris,* The University of Chicago Press, Journals Division, P.O. Box 37005, Chicago, Illinois 60637.

Postmaster: Send address changes to *Osiris,* The University of Chicago Press, Journals Division, P.O. Box 37005, Chicago, Illinois 60637.

Osiris is indexed in major scientific and historical indexing services, including *Biological Abstracts, Current Contents, Historical Abstracts,* and *America: History and Life.*

Research Schools
Historical Reappraisals

Edited by Gerald L. Geison and Frederic L. Holmes

A RESEARCH JOURNAL
DEVOTED TO THE HISTORY OF SCIENCE
AND ITS CULTURAL INFLUENCES
SECOND SERIES   VOLUME 8   1993

RESEARCH SCHOOLS: HISTORICAL REAPPRAISALS

Cover: One research school in action: William Henry Perkin, Jr., and colleagues in the laboratory (courtesy of the Librarian, Museum of the History of Science, University of Oxford).

One touchstone in the historiography of research schools: Justus Liebig's laboratory at Giessen. From J. P. Hofmann, Das Chemische Laboratorium der Ludwig-Universität zu Giessen *(Heidelberg, 1842). Courtesy of the Edgar Fahs Smith Memorial Collection in the History of Chemistry, Special Collections, Van Pelt–Dietrich Library, University of Pennsylvania.*

Preface

AFTER THE RESPONSE to the first five volumes of *Osiris* had proved the success of the journal, particularly of its thematic numbers, the editor and editorial board articulated a policy that members of the board would take an active role in identifying and organizing future thematic volumes. Their involvement was intended to assure that, over the long term, the successive themes chosen would reflect issues of critical importance widely distributed through the many subfields and modes of enquiry that constitute the history of science. The present volume is one of the early outcomes of that policy.

One member of the then editorial board, Gerald Geison, had played a major part in defining scientific research schools as a fruitful subject for historical examination, and his book *Michael Foster and the Cambridge School of Physiology* provided an exemplary study of a specific instance. I had made one or two minor contributions to the topic. Together we volunteered to bring together a group of scholars whose current work either dealt explicitly with the formation and activities of research schools or could be readily adapted to treatment in terms of research schools.

The original group, which included most but not all of the final contributors to the volume, produced initial drafts of their papers in the fall of 1990. These papers were circulated among the group and became the basis for a day-long workshop held on 1 December of that year at the Section of History of Medicine of the Yale University School of Medicine. The sustained intensity of the discussions that centered on each of the papers was a memorable experience for those who participated. During that long day we not only debated many issues raised in the individual papers, but questioned deeply the sources and meaning of our common subject, the research school as a historical entity.

The workshop discussions have left significant traces on the revised versions of each of the papers presented there. (The authors who were invited to join the project subsequent to the workshop received copies of the manuscripts of those who were there.) The impact is most marked on the three "interpretative studies." In particular, the remarkable opening article by John Servos can be viewed as a probing response to some of the central questions raised on that occasion.

The studies included in this volume collectively affirm that, despite the problems of definition and scope that surface prominently in them, the nature of research schools has already proved a major opportunity for cogent historical exploration. The volume also suggests, however, that despite the recent proliferation of publications that refer to research schools, to which Servos draws attention, the surface of a vast field has been touched only lightly so far. To elucidate the functions and characteristics of research schools in all the complexity, diversity, and diffuseness of boundaries that they display will require historical treatments on a grand scale. To follow at a deep level the intimate internal interactions that take place between leaders and followers, mentors and students, senior and junior associates, investigators and their institutional supporters will require densely detailed accounts. To depict the manifold external interactions with the wider scientific communities, including rival research schools, against which the distinctive profiles of a school must be measured will require great breadth of historical vision.

The isolation of generalizable themes such as the formation of research schools is effective in bringing innovative historical approaches into focus; but we should also keep in mind that as historians we aim to integrate such themes into studies defined by the contours of time and place. Not all important contributions to the theme of the research school will be explicitly organized around that concept. In this regard we can point to no more powerful model than John Heilbron and Robert Seidel's recent book *Lawrence and His Laboratory.* This magisterial treatment of the pre–World War II development of the laboratory in which the cyclotron was born integrates many thematic elements into a compelling story. The phrase *research school* does not appear within its long narrative. Heilbron and Seidel have nevertheless provided, among many other things, one of the most comprehensive accounts of the emergence of a twentieth-century research school yet to appear. It is a sterling example of the scope and scale on which we will have to work in order to realize the promise that this theme holds for us.

A volume of compact articles, such as this one, can thus provide only samples of the rewards that larger studies may bring. We hope that the volume offers enticing vistas of the historical landscape that such studies might occupy.

Frederic L. Holmes
1 March 1992

INTERPRETATIVE ISSUES

Research schools, though useful "units of analysis" (see page 228), are not unambiguous ones. Below: August Kékulé, although he "freed himself from the spirit of the school" (see page 4), went on to found his own. Courtesy of the Edgar Fahs Smith Collection. Left: Friedrich Kohlrausch also founded a school, but its distinctiveness was diluted once he published a textbook incorporating its practices (see page 28). Courtesy of the Chemical Heritage Foundation, Philadelphia.

Research Schools and Their Histories

By John W. Servos[*]

FEW ARTICLES have had greater impact on historians of modern science during the past twenty-five years than J. B. Morrell's "The Chemist Breeders: The Research Schools of Liebig and Thomas Thomson." Most of the papers in this volume of *Osiris* offer explicit homage to Morrell; all take his categories and questions as a point of departure. These papers constitute, in turn, a small fraction of a thriving literature devoted to the study of scientific research schools and their influence.[1] Morrell himself may not have created a "research school" in a narrow sense, since few of those scholars who share this interest have actually worked with him; but he helped launch a school in a broader sense—a tradition of thought and work directed toward the exploration of a subject that was inadequately treated by earlier scholars. In Morrell's case, this means the study of those laboratory-based research groups that have played important roles in the recent development of science.

This article will treat the provenance of the notion of research schools and the question of why this category has proved attractive to many historians of science. It will do so by attending to the ways in which historians and scientists have used the terms *school* and *research school.*

To outsiders, our clan can sometimes seem obsessed with words and their roots. Terms like *impetus* and *force* are the subjects of impressive scholarship, and rightly so. By tracing the development of such words, we gain some insight into the concepts and unarticulated assumptions of their users. Like other fields, ours has a history studded with examples of words and phrases that have, sometimes quickly and sometimes slowly, infiltrated our language and become organizing principles for investigation. Some have acquired special connotations because of their use within our field, and others have been borrowed from outside. A short list might include *paradigm, discourse, professionalization,* and *rhetoric.*

Historians generally have limited patience for studies of their own vocabulary.

[*] Department of History, Amherst College, Amherst, Massachusetts 01002.
Work on this article was partially supported by the National Science Foundation (Grant # BIR-8922464).

[1] See J. B. Morrell, "The Chemist Breeders: The Research Schools of Liebig and Thomson," *Ambix,* 1972, *19*:1–46. Gerald L. Geison reviews literature published before 1980 in his "Scientific Change, Emerging Specialties, and Research Schools," *History of Science,* 1981, *19*:20–40. Perusal of the most recent volume of *Isis Current Bibliography* reveals about a dozen titles that refer to scientific research schools, although the count must radically underestimate the size of the literature on the topic. Joseph S. Fruton, e.g., in *Contrasts in Scientific Style: Research Groups in the Chemical and Biochemical Sciences* (Philadelphia: American Philosophical Society, 1990), prefers the term *research groups* for laboratory-based circles of teachers and students (see his note, pp. 1–2). The notes and bibliography of Fruton's valuable book supply many references to recent writings on research schools.

Better, most feel, to get on with the task at hand and leave such ruminations to the future. From time to time, however, it is good to pause and think about the origins and meaning of the words we use, and perhaps there is no better occasion for such reflection than the appearance of a volume, such as this one, that is organized around a fashionable phrase. By so doing we may not only learn something of the history of the phrase itself, but also understand better the origins of our historical consciousness of the institutions that the phrase describes, the nature of the project that engages students of those institutions, and the strengths and limitations of that project.

Although the expression *research school* seems so useful and right as to have had a venerable history, its frequent use in recent scholarship seems to have no parallel in earlier times, either among historians or scientists themselves. Of course, the unadorned term *school* has seen much service. Aside from its ordinary brick and mortar meaning, it has long been applied to groups, sometimes but not always teachers and disciples, that are united by the possession of common doctrine, method, or style (e.g., "the school of Aristotle" or "the Cartesian school"). While scientists sometimes use the word in such neutral ways, they also deploy it as a derogatory term. Such usage was especially common in the decades around the turn of the century, although not confined to that period. Groups deemed to have an unreasoned commitment to some pet theory or doctrine were labeled, usually by their critics, "schools." The *Jahresbericht* of Justus Liebig and Hermann Kopp differed from that of J. J. Berzelius, wrote T. E. Thorpe, because "it was to be done impartially, and with no special reference to any set of dogmas or particular school of chemical thought." The school of Wilhelm Ostwald, according to Henry E. Armstrong, regarded "all unbelievers as heretics worthy of the stake," commanded the "obedience of scientific youth," and could censor criticism since "[a]ll the major channels of communication and most of the minor are secured by the high priests of the cult."[2]

Membership in a school could impair objectivity; it could also close imaginations. Had August Kekulé "been shortsighted enough to accept the assistantship which Liebig offered him," Francis R. Japp wrote, he "might have gone on producing research work cut to a single pattern . . . and so on to the end of the chapter." But "Kekulé always emphasised the necessity for getting rid of preconceptions due to early training. 'Free yourselves from the spirit of the school,' he said; 'you will then be capable of doing something of your own.' " By choosing to work with other master chemists, Kekulé liberated himself from a potentially oppressive regime and found the freedom to express his creative genius. In his words, "Originally a pupil of Liebig, I had become a pupil of Dumas, Gerhardt, and Williamson: I no longer belonged to any school."[3]

Prolonged immersion in a "school" could inhibit budding genius; polemics between the leaders of "schools" could waste energy and effort; the hegemony of a single "school" could impede progress—the literature of nineteenth-century sci-

[2] T. E. Thorpe, "The Life Work of Hermann Kopp," in *Memorial Lectures Delivered before the Chemical Society, 1893–1900* (London: Gurney & Jackson, 1901), p. 780; and Henry E. Armstrong, quoted by R. G. A. Dolby, "Debates over the Theory of Solution: A Study of Dissent in Physical Chemistry in the English-Speaking World in the Late Nineteenth and Early Twentieth Centuries," *Historical Studies in the Physical Sciences (HSPS)*, 1976, 7:297–404, on pp. 346, 387.

[3] Francis R. Japp, "Kekulé Memorial Lecture," in *Memorial Lectures,* pp. 99, 98.

ence is replete with cautionary tales about such dangers. At the same time, contemporary observers were not blind to certain advantages that schools offered. Whatever the implications for the creative development of their students or the conceptual advance of their disciplines, scientists who founded schools made capital contributions to industrial progress and national prestige. Thus Henry Armstrong praised "the Hofmann school" for contributing to the progress of industry by training technical chemists, and J. M. Crafts lauded Adolphe Wurtz and Charles Friedel for fashioning a "school . . . bound together by a common regard and by community of view," that "became an important factor in the nation's progress."[4]

Among those scientists and observers of science who used the term *school* in the nineteenth and early twentieth centuries, none was fonder of it than that Scottish polymath John Theodore Merz. His *History of European Thought in the Nineteenth Century,* still unsurpassed for scope, deploys the term promiscuously to describe the tightly focused schools of research of German laboratories, the intellectual affinities of individuals linked by association with a particular university or by citizenship in a single city or nation, and traditions of thought that span centuries, national boundaries, and linguistic groups. Members of his "schools" might look to common masters, but they might also simply share common interests, or ideas, or methods, or styles of thought. Thus we find references to Berzelius's "school of chemistry," to the "Berlin school of medicine," to "the modern English school" of biology "headed by Darwin," and to the "Scotch school of philosophy."

Like many of his contemporaries, Merz saw hazards in schools:

> At the time when the mathematical and physical sciences were leading the way in France, and gradually forcing their way into Germany, most of the universities in the latter country had one or more representatives of that new and apparently promising school which termed itself the "Philosophy of Nature." The trammels of this school had to be shaken off by those who . . . took up the cause of the exact or mathematical sciences.

But such passages are rare in Merz. He was far more impressed with the school's capacity to extend the influence of exceptional leaders by undertaking "to finish what the master has begun, to carry his ideas into far regions and outlying fields of research, or to draw their remoter consequences." Especially important here were the laboratory-based schools of German-speaking central Europe:

> Wherever the progress of learning and science requires a large amount of detailed study inspired by a few leading ideas, or subservient to some common design and plan, the German universities and higher schools supply a well-trained army of workers, standing under the intellectual generalship of a few great leading minds. Thus it is that no nation in modern times has so many *schools of thought* and learning as Germany, and none can boast of having started and carried through such a large number of gigantic enterprises, requiring the co-operation and collective application of a numerous and well-trained staff. The university system, in one word, not only teaches

---

[4] Henry E. Armstrong, "Notes on Hofmann's Scientific Work," *ibid.,* pp. 637–638, 640; and J. M. Crafts, "Friedel Memorial Lecture," *ibid.,* p. 993.

knowledge, but above all it teaches *research*. This is its pride and the foundation of its fame.[5]

Scientists like Liebig and Friedrich Wöhler, Johannes Müller, and J. E. Purkyně might deploy different ideas and methods, but all were enrolled in a progressive movement and all were contributing to the advance of exact science. Britain, with its tradition of intense individualism, had much to learn from these continental examples, although Merz could not resist noting that individualism, too, had its virtues: "Minds like Newton and Faraday, full of new life, but modestly content with deepening and strengthening their secluded vigour, refrained from boastful publicity or ostentatious parade, working for all ages rather than for a special school or a passing generation." Even this celebrant of the "school of research" (a phrase Merz may have coined) salted his enthusiasm for the institution with some of the reservations of his contemporaries.[6]

Nineteenth-century scientists thus were ambivalent about the associations of students and teachers that we commonly call research schools. While recognizing their efficiency in transmitting technique, they found it hard to reconcile their methods with widely held notions about the norms and values of science and the workings of creative genius. Schools might train, but could they educate or liberate? That is, could they ever foster among students imagination and independence of mind?

This ambivalence, so common in the generations that created the first research schools, finds echo in the writings of historians, sociologists, and philosophers of science of the mid-twentieth century. Even those scholars who were instrumental in focusing attention on the community structure of science, most notably Derek J. de Solla Price, Diana Crane, and Thomas S. Kuhn, treated "schools" with reserve, not to say disdain.

Price was concerned, first and foremost, with the ways in which social arrangements and institutions adjust themselves to the problems posed by the expansion of the population of scientists and the growth of scientific knowledge. In an argument familiar to most historians of science, he contended that research scientists can keep up with the work of a community of other scientists limited to perhaps a hundred or so individuals and that invisible colleges form naturally as a consequence. These colleges are composed of individuals who exchange preprints and reprints, attend conferences and meetings together, and share research questions and techniques. Although Price borrowed the term *invisible college* from the seventeenth century, the groupings that best illustrated his idea were the informal networks of twentieth-century science that form and reform around such institutions as the Rochester Conference for fundamental particle studies. Such institutions, Price suggested in a closing flourish, have supplanted associations of "the great professor with his entourage of graduate students, the sort of thing for which Rutherford or Liebig are well known. The great difference here is that the apex of the triangle is not a single beloved individual but an invisible college; its locale is not a dusty attic of a teaching laboratory but a mobile

---

[5] John Theodore Merz, *A History of European Thought in the Nineteenth Century,* Vol. I, *Scientific Thought* (London: Blackwood, 1904; New York: Dover, 1965), pp. 204, 250, 167.

[6] *Ibid.,* pp. 205, 278 (quotations). See also, e.g. p. 167.

commuting circle of rather expensive institutions."[7] Schools and invisible colleges perform similar functions in Price's view, since both serve to subordinate young, inexperienced, or unimaginative scientists (who constitute the great majority) to leaders with more wisdom and talent. Invisible colleges, however, are more effective at the job, at least in a world of telephones and jet planes, since they give research groups the capacity to respond more quickly to changing methods and ideas.

Kuhn, influenced perhaps by scientists' usage, adopted "school" to describe groups that, although engaged in the study of the same parts of nature, cannot agree on fundamentals. In the first edition of *The Structure of Scientific Revolutions,* he relegated such schools to the prehistory of science. Maturity comes to a science when the anarchy of the schools is supplanted by the orderly puzzle solving of "communities" that share allegiance to certain fundamental methods and concepts. In his essays of the early 1970s Kuhn modified this position, suggesting that "there are schools in the sciences, communities, that is, which approach the same subject from incompatible viewpoints. But they are far rarer there than in other fields; they are always in competition; and their competition is usually quickly ended."[8] Whether Kuhn did irreparable harm to his original concept of "normal science" by such qualification is less important, from the present standpoint, than that he continued to treat schools as something of an embarrassment in mature sciences. Philosophers, artists, and sociologists may be analyzed in terms of their affiliations with schools, but scientists are best viewed as members of other kinds of communities, especially disciplines or specialties and, at a lower level, invisible colleges. If schools exist in a mature science, they are fleeting associations whose rivalries exist only within the larger and more enduring frameworks of common belief and association. While endorsing research into the social structure of science, Kuhn exhibited little enthusiasm for the school as a focal point of such inquiry.

Crane accorded a much more important role to research groups built around master and students than Price or Kuhn, all the while denying the appropriateness of the word *school* to describe them. "Solidarity groups," she suggested, coalesce around influential teachers who recruit and socialize new members, define the important problems for research in their specialties, and interact with members of other solidarity groups through "communication networks" or invisible colleges. As in schools, membership in solidarity groups implies some allegiance to a common "point of view." But these solidarity groups should not be confused with schools since "a school is characterized by the uncritical acceptance on the part of disciples of a leader's idea system. It rejects external influence and validation of its work. By creating a journal of its own, such a group can bypass the criticism of referees from other areas." Members of solidarity groups are capable of criticizing one another's ideas and interact with the members of other solidarity groups through invisible colleges. Schools, by contrast, are insular and intolerant of dissent. They, she added in a note, are like religious sects, which "break away from the church and build separate organizations,

---

[7] Derek de Solla Price, *Little Science, Big Science* (New York: Columbia Univ. Press, 1963), p. 90.

[8] Thomas S. Kuhn, *The Structure of Scientific Revolutions,* 2nd ed. (Chicago: Univ. Chicago Press, 1970), p. 177.

emphasizing aspects of doctrine or policy that they believe have been ignored or misinterpreted by the church. The religious sect is a relatively closed system that resists external influences rather than attempting to adapt to them. Members who deviate from orthodox views on any issue are quickly expelled." Like Kuhn, Crane reserves the term *school* for those associations which do not measure up as being truly scientific.[9]

The contrast between these earlier references to schools, many of which amount to sneers, and more recent studies of research schools, many of which are celebratory, is striking. Insofar as the shift can be followed on paper, it commenced in 1969, with the publication of Owen Hannaway's review of Maurice Crosland's *The Society of Arcueil*. In this shrewd notice Hannaway argued that the illustrious *savants* who congregated in the country home and laboratory of C. L. Berthollet are best viewed not as a circle of influential individuals nor as a society of scientific peers but rather as "a school" in which the relationship between Berthollet and his associates "was that of master and pupils." Echoes of an earlier ambivalence about schools were present. "The research problems the apprentices worked on," Hannaway wrote, "were grounded in the work of their seniors, and their conclusions were frequently influenced by their mentors' prejudices." Nevertheless, Hannaway was more concerned with the role of such schools in the "professionalization of science in the nineteenth century" than with any limitations they might place on individual expression. Here, Hannaway suggested, the principal significance of the Society of Arcueil may have been as a model and inspiration for the young Liebig—a model, that is, of "a research school."[10]

The expression had not been much used between the time of Merz and Hannaway's review, but references to research schools proliferated quickly in the early 1970s. Especially noteworthy were Jerome R. Ravetz's provocative and wide-ranging *Scientific Knowledge and Its Social Problems,* Morrell's study of Liebig and Thomson, and Robert Fox's article on the rise and fall of Laplacian physics.[11] All made the research school a central category in their analyses, all cited Hannaway's review as the source of the expression, none felt the compulsion to apologize for its use. The old word *school* could almost be said to have been rehabilitated by modifying it with the word *research*. It is worth inquiring into the reasons for the sudden popularity of this expression and asking whether its growing use was merely an accident of fashion or denotes a more fundamental change in the way historians viewed science.

Of these questions, the first is perhaps the easiest to answer, and it may best be approached by considering the factors that recommended the most influential of these essays, that of Morrell, to historians of science. When published in 1972, Morrell's paper found a receptive audience among readers concerned to make the history of science more sensitive to social context, more comparative, and more fully historical. It is customary to invoke the name of Thomas Kuhn when dis-

[9] Diana Crane, *Invisible Colleges: Diffusion of Knowledge in Scientific Communities* (Chicago: Univ. Chicago Press, 1972), pp. 34–35, 87 (quotations).

[10] Owen Hannaway, review of Maurice Crosland, *The Society of Arcueil: A View of French Science at the Time of Napoleon I,* in *Isis,* 1969, *60*:578–581, on p. 581.

[11] Jerome R. Ravetz, *Scientific Knowledge and Its Social Problems* (New York: Oxford Univ. Press, 1971); and Robert Fox, "The Rise and Fall of Laplacian Physics," *HSPS,* 1974, *4*:89–136.

cussing these trends, and not without cause.[12] By undermining claims about the importance of some inflexible "scientific method" and attributing the special success of science to peculiar features of its social organization (albeit not to schools), Kuhn's *Structure of Scientific Revolutions* offered historians of science a powerful justification for studying the institutions in which science was done. His habit of seeking patterns through the consideration of scientific ideas separated by time and place, a method not unknown to historians of science but more natural to colleagues in philosophy, emboldened others to think more comparatively about the past. And while his essay was less an example of historical scholarship than a reflection on its uses, *Structure* offered historians of science a persuasive rationale for putting aside whiggish concerns about questions of priority, precursors, and the validity of scientific ideas of the past—concerns that had long sidetracked the inquiries of historians, amateur and professional alike. His essay preached a humility about the present and respect for the past that is essential to sensitive historical inquiry.

With or without Kuhn, however, historians were gravitating toward study of the social institutions of science. This movement reflected political and social forces far larger than the history of science: the resurgence of traditions of scholarship inspired by Marx, the remarkable growth of social history and sociology during the 1950s and 1960s, and changes in the recruitment and education of historians of science that attenuated their links with the sciences and strengthened their links with history. Perhaps most important, however, were the efforts to open up the science of the nineteenth and twentieth centuries to historical study. The size, complexity, and technicality of modern science posed formidable challenges to historical research and even more daunting obstacles to historical teaching. It seemed possible to discover thematic unities in the science of earlier eras without egregious simplification and to convey those themes to students with modest backgrounds in science and mathematics. Modern science resisted such treatment. To be sure, historians could offer students epilogues of sorts to the Scientific Revolution by picking their targets carefully. A few topics in modern science could even be treated in some depth. The history of evolutionary biology, so long as it does not press too far into genetics, embryology, or debates over systematics, offers one such example. But the prospects of writing a history of modern science serviceable in undergraduate classrooms or even graduate courses appeared dim—at least if such synthetic efforts took as their model the books that served historians of ancient and medieval science or the Scientific Revolution so well. It seemed even less plausible to think that such syntheses, if produced, could ever appeal to "general" historians or others outside the profession.

As Kathryn Olesko points out so skillfully in her contribution to this volume and elsewhere, the demands of the classroom shape traditions of research, and this is as true in the history of science as it is in the sciences themselves. The real genius of Morrell's essay was, I would suggest, that it constituted an example of how modern science could be handled in ways that are both historically sensitive and eminently teachable. And in doing so, it suggested avenues by which much

---

[12] See, e.g., Roy Porter, "The History of Science and the History of Society," in *Companion to the History of Modern Science,* ed. R. C. Olby, G. N. Cantor, J. R. R. Christie, and M. J. S. Hodge (London: Routledge, 1990), p. 38.

additional research into and teaching about modern science might be organized into similar form.

Morrell's organizing principle, of course, was the research school—an institution that flourished in the universities and research institutes of the nineteenth and twentieth centuries, an institution that depends on patrons, regular infusions of students, a ready supply of problems solvable in limited time by predictable methods, reliable means of reaching readers, and leaders capable of directing efforts along profitable lines. Nonspecialists could take from Morrell's concise account a sense of how Liebig's science differed from its antecedents and recognize in his description of the research school an institutional form still extant. Specialists recognized in his article categories that promised utility in the analysis of all kinds of laboratory science, assertions that could easily be turned into questions when deployed in other contexts, and appealing associations with other bodies of literature.

Indeed, although much of his article consisted of an exposition of the careers of Liebig and Thomson, Morrell missed few opportunities to link his inquiry with emerging themes in the history of science. His description of Liebig as a successful entrepreneur and his laboratory as a "knowledge factory" reverberated among readers familiar with recent studies of business leadership. His suggestion that "Big Science began at Giessen in the early 1840s" suggested continuities between Liebig's laboratory and the industrial-scale science of the twentieth century. His decision to contrast Liebig with a British contemporary brought his inquiry into relation with the question of national styles in science and more particularly with the issue of why Germany seized leadership in most branches of laboratory science in the nineteenth century. His reference to the role of research schools in "the expansion of specialization" raised questions about the emergence of new disciplines. His attention to the role of the technique of combustion analysis at Giessen and his interest in the routine behavior of his subjects seem prescient in view of recent efforts to take laboratory practice seriously. His emphasis on the role of charismatic leadership and personal discipleship in the transmission of craft knowledge linked his work to Michael Polanyi's writings on the tacit component of knowledge. Small wonder that many historians of science have made research schools a focal point of investigation during the past twenty years. Their study has offered many sorts of students of modern science a common port of entry and departure.

It has also been a safe harbor for those historians, which is to say most historians of science, who felt uneasy with extreme forms of idealism or social determinism and with dogmatically internalist or externalist approaches to historical analysis. The research schools of Liebig and Thomson, as depicted by Morrell, were shaped by "intellectual, institutional, technical, psychological and financial circumstances." Their success or failure could not be reduced to the presence or absence of some one essential ingredient; their study demanded that attention be paid to student populations and account books, to research apparatus and journals, to group dynamics and individual psychology, to the research programs of individuals and the intellectual traditions of their communities, to university politics and the goals of patrons. Without polemic or jargon, and without making an exhaustive survey of these circumstances, Morrell presented readers with a wonderful sketch of how cognitive, social, and material factors interacted to generate different levels of success in the efforts of his historical actors. While opening many doors, he closed none.

Morrell's influence on later writers testifies to the enduring power of eclectic forms of history to excite imaginations. Many historians of science have come to think of research schools as elemental to modern science. They are the vehicles by which knowledge, especially tacit knowledge, is transmitted. As such they may play a role in the development and preservation of national and regional styles in science. They are natural units within universities and certain other institutions for scientific research. They are the collectives that exploit and articulate the ideas of their individual members. They compete with one another for patronage, for space in journals, for students, for prestige, and for influence in disciplines. They are the wombs within which new concepts and methods develop and, sometimes, new specialties. Larger aggregates, such as the science faculties of universities and disciplines, may be resolved into these elements; individual scientists in many fields find full opportunity for expression only within them.

How does this view of the research school differ from that which earlier writers endorsed? The differences appear to be threefold. First, and perhaps most important, recent work suggests that conflict is far more important to the normal processes of science than earlier observers were willing to allow. Our scientific specialties frequently embrace schools that can hold incompatible views of what constitute proper questions, methods, and answers. As Steven Turner's essay in this volume shows so elegantly, members of such schools can even speak different languages. And rival schools may coexist, not peacefully, for decades and even generations. The work of the past two decades, while drawing some inspiration from Kuhn, has undermined part of his thesis. Conflict is not so easily segregated from consensus in the history of science as his model suggests, a point that David Kushner makes explicitly in his contribution on George Darwin and geophysics.

Nor can recent work sit in perfect comfort alongside that of Price and Crane. Like Kuhn, they stressed the cooperativeness of scientists and minimized conflict. Scientists may bring different viewpoints to the invisible colleges in which they participate, but they subordinate their differences in the interest of achieving the rewards of membership in larger communities. The invisible colleges described by Price and Crane surely exist, yet recent studies of research schools suggest that they are not so much devices for regimenting atomistic scientists (Price) nor networks for connecting generally cooperative solidarity groups (Crane) as arenas in which members of rival schools compete.[13] Dominance of such networks may confer prestige and resources on one or another school, but such dominance often eludes any single group.

A second shift in the assumptions governing the way historians view research schools (and, indeed, schools more generally) is that during the past twenty years they have tended to apply different normative standards to their subjects than did earlier writers. Instead of viewing manifestations of interestedness among scientists as infractions of the methods or moral code of science, recent writers tend to

---

[13] Such a picture emerges from historical studies of research schools but is best captured by Bruno Latour and Steve Woolgar in *Laboratory Life: The Social Construction of Scientific Facts* (Beverly Hills, Calif.: Sage, 1979).

accept such behavior as normal and inevitable. Value judgments, when ventured at all, are now directed toward evaluating the fruitfulness of different lines of inquiry. These evaluations sometimes reflect the influence of Imre Lakatos and his effort to appraise research programs as "progressive" or "degenerative" on the basis of their capacity to generate novel predictions and theories.[14] The conceptual categories of the philosopher of science are augmented and complicated a good deal, however, by historians. Not only must successful research schools promote ideas that are reasonably coherent and fecund; they must also be effective in recruiting students, mobilizing material resources, and propagating their message. As in Darwinian natural selection or economic competition, the factors making for success are complex and context-specific. Indeed, the very same factors that may lead to prosperity in one setting can be liabilities in others.

Third, unlike earlier observers, writers of the past twenty years have been little troubled by any dichotomy between originality and "schooling." They typically see no necessary conflict between training and education, between the acquisition of proficiency in some body of ideas and techniques and the vigorous expression of creative energy. The capacity to be inventive cannot be taught like multiplication tables, but under the proper regime it can be cultivated. Indeed, many recent studies have stressed the importance of rigorous apprenticeships in the development of exceptional creative talent.[15] These may entail the transmission of a kind of craft knowledge of the fine points of laboratory technique or of the subtleties of mathematical analysis. But perhaps even more important may be the broader lessons that proven research scientists may impart—lessons about where to look for questions, how to phrase them, and how to apportion the scarcest of resources, time. As Joel Hagen points out in his contribution to this volume, not every research director, or would-be research director, proves an effective model for students. But the frequency with which eminent scientists emerge from the laboratories of other eminent scientists belies any suggestion that "schooling" dulls imagination. Tightly focused research schools may turn out hacks, but they also turn out highly original scientists and do so with regularity. By stressing the role of apprenticeship in the creative work of science, recent studies of research schools have contributed to that broader demystification of genius which has been an important theme in the modern history of science.

Consideration of the changing fortunes of the word *school* reveals to us how much the history of science has changed in the last twenty years. Perhaps it is appropriate to conclude by asking if recent work on the history of research schools can withstand the same sort of scrutiny that we apply to our historical subjects. Can the study of research schools, that is, still move us forward in our study of the

[14] Imre Lakatos, "Falsification and the Methodology of Scientific Research Programmes," in *Criticism and the Growth of Knowledge,* ed. Lakatos and Alan Musgrave (Cambridge: Cambridge Univ. Press, 1970), pp. 91–196.

[15] See, e.g., Fruton, *Contrasts in Scientific Style* (cit. n. 1); Robert G. Frank, Jr., "American Physiologists in German Laboratories, 1865–1914," in *Physiology in the American Context, 1850–1940,* ed. Gerald L. Geison (Bethesda, Md.: American Physiological Society, 1987), pp. 11–46; and Jack Morrell's essay in this volume. Historians were not the first to explore this subject; see Robert K. Merton's 1968 essay, "The Matthew Effect in Science," in *The Sociology of Science: Theoretical and Empirical Investigations* (Chicago: Univ. Chicago Press, 1973), pp. 452–453.

history of modern science? The essays collected in this volume suggest that there is a future, although they also reveal some of the difficulties and limitations of organizing historical research around research schools. Such studies do not have boundaries as clear and unambiguous as do the lives of scientists or the histories of institutions that are coincident with physical or legal structures. Several contributors have difficulty fitting their materials to the category; most find it necessary to stretch or qualify it. But such discomfort is hardly unusual. Historians have long encountered similar difficulties with such categories as *class* and *elite*. Demarcation problems may be discouraging, but they need not be fatal. Indeed, as several of the essays here collected demonstrate, efforts to compare the tightly focused and laboratory-based research schools of a Liebig or a Michael Foster with looser confederations of scientists can result in useful and important insights. Whether Kushner's George Darwin or Turner's Hermann Helmholtz led research schools is moot; but surely we see them more clearly for being able to compare them and their circles with communities that come closer to meeting Geison's now-canonical definition of the research school as "small groups of mature scientists pursuing a reasonably coherent programme of research side-by-side with advanced students in the same institutional context and engaging in direct, continuous social and intellectual interaction."[16]

In a more general sense, work on research schools must lead historians to demarcation problems, since, as Geison pointed out a decade ago, the study of the schools cannot be entirely severed from investigation of the individuals that compose them and the larger networks through which they interact.[17] On the one side their study merges with biography; on the other with the histories of disciplines, universities, traditions of thought, and even national styles of science. Far from being a liability, however, this situation is advantageous, since it gives the historian license to move freely from consideration of the largely private realm of creative effort to the more public arena of justification and persuasion.

More troubling than any problem of demarcation are three issues associated with the basic assumptions of recent work on research schools. The first is the growing tendency to discount the role of consensus in scientific conduct. That conflict and competition exist and are normal parts of science can hardly be denied, but are they as pervasive as recent literature suggests? Historians thrive on conflict. Not only does it give us the opportunity to study individuals, ideas, and institutions under stress, when their strengths and weaknesses become most apparent, but it also affords us much-prized elements of drama. Research schools, with their entrepreneurial leaders and ambitious disciples and their webs of personal loyalties and enmities offer conflict-minded historians ample material. But to what extent does our instinct for the good story dictate our choice of topics and color our picture of scientists' behavior? We tend to see in the past that which we seek. Were we to look harder for harmony and cooperation among research schools, would we find it? Need a recognition of the importance of "schools" in science imply adversarial relations among those schools as a correlate?

A second question grows out of the criteria that historians use to evaluate research schools. We no longer accuse those who backed the wrong horse of crimes

[16] Geison, "Scientific Change" (cit. n. 1), p. 23.
[17] *Ibid.*, p. 35.

against science, but we continue to judge some scientists and their schools successes and others failures. It is right and proper, and perhaps inevitable, to do so. Even if we are reluctant to offer an opinion as to whether so-and-so's work was "any good," we must ascertain and explain the judgments made of that work by our subject's contemporaries. But as critics of Lakatos's writings have pointed out, evaluating the fruitfulness of research programs is a tricky business, and judgments of the success or failure of research schools often entail such evaluations.[18] The normative standards we apply to our subjects may be different from those applied by our predecessors, but they may be no more secure.

The third question arises from the recent inversion of the old relationship between originality and schooling. We have abandoned myths of heroic genius by linking the fulfillment of creative potential to apprenticeship in research schools. But have we demystified genius or simply substituted one form of mystification for another? Olesko rightly criticizes those who would wrap an impenetrable cloak around the acquisition of research skills. When we say that research schools are efficient at breeding creative scientists because they are effective in transmitting tacit knowledge of craft skills from masters to disciples, are we not obscuring precisely what needs to be illuminated?

Schools teach. Or so the theory goes. But what? Any parent will know that it can be difficult, sometimes depressingly so, to discern what Johnny learns by attending school. And anyone who has sat at both ends of the classroom will know that what teachers seek to transmit is not always what students receive, a point made recently by Lisa Rosner in her fine book on medical education at Glasgow.[19] What do research schools teach?

My own suggestion, for what it is worth, is that tacit knowledge of technique constitutes but a small part of what masters transmit to their disciples in such institutions. Far more important may be the guidance that they offer on the problem-structure of their disciplines and the enthusiasm and inspiration to persevere that some inspire through informal exchanges and example.[20] In the end we may find that such hard-to-specify knowledge (if such it should be called) can indeed be conveyed by routes other than personal contact. A textbook, for example, that is suffused with the persona of its author may be able to stand in for personal contact; one thinks of James D. Watson's *Molecular Biology of the Gene* or Richard Feynman's *Lectures on Physics.* But few scientists have such powerful personalities as Watson or Feynman or such facility at written expression. Far more numerous are those whose power to enliven their subjects extends little further than the laboratory bench or classroom, but who, within those precincts, show a remarkable ability to identify, groom, and inspire talent.[21] Be this as it may, Olesko's challenge is ignored only at our peril. Until the question of what is

[18] See, e.g., Thomas S. Kuhn's comments in "Reflections on My Critics," in *Criticism and the Growth of Knowledge,* ed. Lakatos and Musgrave (cit. n. 14), pp. 239–241, 256–259.

[19] Lisa Rosner, *Medical Education in the Age of Improvement* (Edinburgh: Edinburgh Univ. Press, 1991), p. 2.

[20] See the sources cited in note 15 above.

[21] E.g., Franz Hofmeister, Michael Foster, and Arthur A. Noyes: see Fruton, *Contrasts in Scientific Style* (cit. n. 1); Gerald L. Geison, *Michael Foster and the Cambridge School of Physiology: The Scientific Enterprise in Late Victorian Society* (Princeton, N. J.: Princeton Univ. Press, 1978); and John W. Servos, *Physical Chemistry from Ostwald to Pauling: The Making of a Science in America* (Princeton, N. J.: Princeton Univ. Press, 1990).

taught in research schools is more fully addressed, claims about their significance to modern science rest on incomplete foundations.

Despite these formidable difficulties, the study of research schools seems likely to remain a vitally important part of our effort to explore the history of modern science. These institutions are simply too important to the cognitive and social history of the enterprise and offer too many advantages as integrative vehicles to fall into historical neglect. And although recent changes in the social organization of certain sciences have led to new kinds of interactions among scientists, research schools have not disappeared.[22] "As the competition for funding and fame becomes ever fiercer among molecular biology laboratories," a recent issue of *Science* tells us, "conversation among colleagues often turns to questions of style: What manner of lab is best for producing good science and staying competitive? . . . Must large labs sacrifice creativity for efficiency? How many people and research projects can one investigator manage? Under what conditions might a lab director lose track of the papers to which he is signing his name—risking becoming party to fraud, misconduct . . . or just plain embarrassment?"[23]

The study of laboratory-based research schools, it would seem, offers rewards not only to those whose primary concern is the past, but also to those whose eyes are on the present and future.

[22] See Peter Galison, *How Experiments End* (Chicago: Univ. Chicago Press, 1987), pp. 275–276.
[23] Marcia Barinaga, "Laboratories of the Famous and Well-Funded," *Science,* 1991, *252*:1776.

Tacit Knowledge and School Formation

By Kathryn M. Olesko[*]

ALL SCHOOLS have pedagogic elements. The intellectual and investigative
cohesiveness of a school is achieved by different avenues; all involve some
form of training. Although possessing individual scientific styles, members of a
school have learned, to a greater or lesser degree, to think and practice in like-
minded ways. This holds for both main types of scientific schools: the research
schools that have been at the center of historical inquiry for some time, and the
more traditional schools associated initially with master-pupil relationships and
later with more formal educational settings that only recently have attracted historical attention. Schools at centers of learning or institutions of higher education
often exist by virtue of strong and well-defined training programs that successfully convey distinctive methods of scientific practice and judgment capable of
distinguishing their participants from other investigators in the same discipline.
Research schools, in contrast, often rely on more informal means of normalizing
the investigative practices and mental habits of its members; apprenticeship
under or imitation of older members, collaboration with peers, assistantships in
research, and internal works-in-progress sessions are but a few of the social means
whereby practitioners learn to be like one another. Creating a certain number of
commonalities and sustaining them above a critical threshold are so important in
a school that schools can neither form nor continue to exist without some mechanisms for instruction and reinstruction.

A key process in forming a school is transmitting craft skills of investigation
from colleague to colleague, from master to pupil. Until recently, the process of
skill transmission was notoriously ill defined, understood as one that took
place largely unconsciously, by imitation, experience, emulation. This received
understanding—based more on presumption and intuition than on actual empirical studies, either historical or sociological, of science pedagogy—shrouded the
acquisition of skills in secrecy by classifying it as tacit knowledge: inarticulable
and therefore invisible to the historical eye. Recently, however, historical studies
of science pedagogy have suggested that the domain of tacit knowledge may be
considerably smaller than hitherto assumed; while sociological studies of skill acquisition have argued that an element of tacitness remains in laboratory techniques even as they are rationalized and codified, and furthermore that this
tacitness is desirable for the production of innovation.[1] The historical and socio-

---

[*] Department of History, Georgetown University, Washington, D.C. 20057-1058.
[1] For historical studies see, e.g., Graeme Gooday, "Precision Measurement and the Genesis of Physics Teaching Laboratories in Victorian Britain," *British Journal for the History of Science,* 1990,
23:25–51; and Kathryn M. Olesko, *Physics as a Calling: Discipline and Practice in the Königsberg*

© 1993 by The History of Science Society. All rights reserved. 0021-1753/93/8401-0002$01.00

logical approaches to skill acquisition do not contradict one another; for historical studies of science pedagogy have not argued that all of scientific practice is
codified, only that a considerable portion of it is, including parts of those areas
formerly thought most immune to explicit codification, such as data analysis.

Tacit knowledge is thus a strategic historiographic locus for understanding
school formation. So is its opposite, explicit knowledge. Sociologists of science
use a variety of terms to designate knowledge and skills that are explicit, including rationalized, codified, coherent, standardized, routine, "ready-made," and
stabilized. Explicit techniques and knowledge are articulable and generally ex-
hibit great similarity from practitioner to practitioner. Both tacit and explicit
knowledge explain how behavior is constrained in a scientific school; these constraints shape the identity of the school. The purpose of this essay is twofold: first,
to raise questions about how historians have hitherto viewed skill and knowledge
acquisition in school formation; and second, to suggest ways in which the pedagogic element in school formation can be reexamined so as to recast the role of
tacit and explicit knowledge and practices in it.

I. TACIT KNOWLEDGE AND SCHOOL FORMATION

Historians of scientific schools have acknowledged the pedagogic element in
them. Gerald L. Geison's influential and oft-quoted definition of a scientific
school incorporates its function as an agent of advanced instruction. He defines a
school as "small groups of mature scientists pursuing a reasonably coherent program of research *side-by-side* with *advanced students* in the same institutional
context and engaging in direct, continuous social and intellectual interaction."
Geison furthermore emphasizes that a director must help new recruits make the
transition "from learning to independent research." Jerome Ravetz assigns a
strong causal role to the pedagogic element in school formation: "The character of
scientific work done by the graduates of different sorts of research schools will *inevitably* reflect their training."[2] Marxist historiography of scientific schools, with
its greater sensitivity to the fine distinctions that must be made when discussing
the social organizations of modern society, assigns a prominent role to the pedagogic element. In a volume on scientific schools that has been influential in eastern European literature but is only now entering the West, Valerij Borisovič
Gasilov lists, as the first of thirty-five definitions of a scientific school, "a method
or a system of teaching, instruction, diffusion of knowledge, transmission of
knowledge, from teacher to pupil." In the same volume A. M. Cukerman warns,

Seminar for Physics (Ithaca, N.Y./London: Cornell Univ. Press, 1991) (neither Gooday nor I explicitly
address the nature of tacit knowledge). For sociological studies see Kathleen Jordan and Michael
Lynch, "The Sociology of a Genetic Engineering Technique: Ritual and Rationality in the Performance of the 'Plasmid Prep,' " in *The Right Tools for the Job: At Work in Twentieth-Century Life Sciences,* ed. Adele E. Clarke and Joan H. Fujimura (Princeton, N.J.: Princeton Univ. Press, 1992); and
Jordan and Lynch, "The Mainstreaming of a Molecular Biological Tool: A Case Study of a New Technique," in *A Sociology of a New Technology,* ed. Graham Button (London: Routledge & Kegan Paul,
in press).
[2] Gerald L. Geison, "Scientific Change, Emerging Specialties, and Research Schools," *History of
Science,* 1981, *9*:20–40, on p. 23 (emphasis added); and Jerome R. Ravetz, *Scientific Knowledge and
Its Social Problems* (New York: Oxford Univ. Press, 1971), p. 100 (emphasis added).

though, that "the idea of a scientific school cannot be reduced to a purely formal teacher-pupil relationship" because of the wide variation in how students absorb and apply what is taught. But he still admits that it must have an educative function if it is to transmit a director's "way of thinking."[3]

Empirical studies of research schools have generally considered active engagement in research to be the means whereby the craft skills of investigation, especially experimental investigation, are transmitted. Hence Geison identifies as Michael Foster's "single most important contribution" to the formation of the Cambridge school of physiology "his steadfast care and feeding of the research ethos," which Foster accomplished by teaching an evolutionary approach to physiological phenomena and by transmitting by example certain tools and methods, all suited for treating problems linked to his study of the heartbeat, which became the center of gravity of the school's investigations. In his study of the Munich school of metabolism, Frederic L. Holmes views the school's formation largely through the contours of the research programs and the visions of its leaders; thus, "participation of the younger members in the research activity" of the school's leader became simultaneously "training for future independent work."[4] Other similar examples could be cited.[5] To date the literature on research schools has in general emphasized the dominant qualities of a director's research style as the principal resource of the school's craft skills of investigation, which are learned largely by imitation and experience.

But how, exactly, does that imitation and experience occur? The exact process is never fully articulated, although the factors facilitating imitation and experience are. Factors such as effective leadership, a well-equipped laboratory, and an environment conducive to early participation in research figure prominently in such descriptions. This lacuna is less the result of the lack of suitable source materials, it seems, than of the powerful (and often unacknowledged) influence upon historical analysis of certain older sociological and philosophical approaches to *how* scientists learn the art of investigation. Here Michael Polanyi's notion of *tacit knowledge* has exerted considerable influence, despite the debatable nature of his evidence (he draws less upon the history or practice of science than upon other social and cultural activities, such as music and sport) and despite his at-times unconvincing style of presentation (key definitions are sometimes presented as tautologies).

---

[3] Valerij Borisovič Gasilov, "Analyse der Interpretation des Terminus 'wissenschaftliche Schule,'" in *Wissenschaftliche Schulen,* 2 vols., ed. Semem R. Mikulinsky *et al.* (Berlin: Akademie-Verlag, 1977–1979), Vol. I, pp. 291–321, on p. 294; and A. M. Cukerman, "Die Denkweise des Leiters—Ein bestimmender Faktor für die Bildung einer wissenschaftlichen Schulen," *ibid.,* pp. 429–436, on p. 429.

[4] Gerald L. Geison, *Michael Foster and the Cambridge School of Physiology: The Scientific Enterprise in Late Victorian Society* (Princeton, N. J.: Princeton Univ. Press, 1978), p. 359 (see also pp. 224–235); and Frederic L. Holmes, "The Formation of the Munich School of Metabolism," in *The Investigative Enterprise: Experimental Physiology in Nineteenth-Century Medicine,* ed. William Coleman and Holmes (Berkeley/Los Angeles: Univ. California Press, 1988), pp. 179–210, esp. pp. 180 (quotation), 202–206.

[5] See, e.g., Leo J. Klosterman, "A Research School of Chemistry in the Nineteenth Century: Jean Baptiste Dumas and his Research Students," *Annals of Science,* 1985, *42*:1–40 (Part I), 41–80 (Part II), esp. pp. 6–7, 21, 29; and James A. Secord, "The Geological Survey of Great Britain as a Research School, 1839–1855," *History of Science,* 1986, *24*:223–275, esp. p. 262 (although the pedagogic element is not as prominent in this school as in the others mentioned).

Polanyi's fundamental premise is that scientists engaged in investigation, especially of the experimental sort, act according to rules that are only partially specifiable. Language, according to Polanyi, does not possess the power to articulate all that a scientist learns or does; "Rules of art can be useful," he claims, "but they do not determine the practice of an art; they are maxims which can serve as a guide to an art only if they can be integrated in the practical knowledge of the art." Polanyi's belief that the craft skills of science are tacitly learned and known and largely inarticulable has had profound consequences in the study of skill learning, including in scientific schools, because it has often prefigured the historiographic categories used for thinking through such studies. Polanyi writes that "an art which cannot be specified in detail cannot be transmitted by prescription, since no prescription for it exists. It can be passed on only by example from master to apprentice. This restricts the range of diffusion to that of personal contacts, and we find accordingly that craftsmanship tends to survive in closely circumscribed local traditions."[6] Within Polanyi's framework the way in which the craftwork of science has been approached in the empirical study of scientific schools—by focusing on the research style of the master or leader—obtains its methodological justification.

Polanyi's ideas and their methodological implications find expression in the writings of other seminal thinkers. Ludwik Fleck's *Genesis and Development of a Scientific Fact,* not well known in the West until after the publication of Polanyi's book, also supported the notion that the "technical skills required for any scientific investigation" cannot be "formulated in terms of logic."[7] In an important and influential chapter, "Science as Craftsman's Work," Ravetz too asserts that the craft work of science is inaccessible, tacit, and unconscious, and hence incapable of being "specified in a formal account" and unable to surpass the simplest level of description. His ideas display an uncanny similarity to Polanyi's: he believes that tacit knowledge of craft skills is transmitted "largely through the close personal association of master and pupil"; that it is "learned entirely by imitation and experience" but perhaps "without any awareness"; and that it is an important element in the creation of scientific schools.[8] It has been largely Ravetz's discussion of tacit knowledge that has inspired historians to identify it as a subject worthy of investigation, despite its presumed unspecifiable character. Martin Rudwick has called for historians "to recover what . . . a network of individuals . . . held *tacitly* in common." Pertinent to present concerns, Geison has suggested that schools could be used fruitfully to understand "the transmission of 'tacit' knowledge in the actual 'craft' of science."[9]

Despite the optimism of Rudwick and Geison, Polanyi's philosophy of tacit knowledge qua historiographic strategy is in several respects problematic. The goal of scientific practice is creativity; yet Polanyi maintains that the learning of

[6] Michael Polanyi, *Personal Knowledge: Towards a Post-Critical Philosophy* (Chicago: Univ. Chicago Press, 1958), pp. 50 (see also pp. 49, 53–63), 53.

[7] Ludwik Fleck, *Genesis and Development of a Scientific Fact,* trans. Fred Bradley and Thaddeus J. Trenn (Chicago: Univ. Chicago Press, 1979), p. 35.

[8] Ravetz, *Scientific Knowledge* (cit. n. 2), pp. 75, 76, 102–106, quoting from pp. 75, 103.

[9] Martin J. S. Rudwick, *The Great Devonian Controversy: The Shaping of Scientific Knowledge Among Gentlemanly Specialists* (Chicago: Univ. Chicago Press, 1985), p. 10; and Geison, "Scientific Change" (cit. n. 2), p. 36.

craft skills necessitates the denial of the self in favor of submission to authority. "To learn by example," he writes, "is to submit to authority."[10] Polanyi's scientist works, paradoxically, entirely within tradition. Polanyi's insistence on the unconscious and inarticulate nature of craft skills denies the possibility that scientists or even novices can examine their thinking and practice in consciously critical and self-reflexive ways, and thus strips them of one of the most powerful mental techniques that Western intellectuals have exercised since the Reformation. Ravetz, in contrast, recognizes that there must be a balance between blind indoctrination and the cultivation of a critical perspective, but he still acknowledges that learning the craft skills of science is largely a conservative process.[11] The relatively closed nature of tacit knowledge is also apparent in sociological studies of craft skills. Although acknowledging that skills must be rationalized to a certain extent to be learned—thereby placing skills and knowledge in an arena where changes and permutations could occur—such studies still make local styles a matter of learning tacitly the inarticulable techniques that others already know.[12]

The broader historiographic implications of tacit knowledge—not in what it implies *should* be investigated, but in what *cannot* be examined under its aegis—are most problematic and troublesome. The presumed inarticulable nature of the tacit knowledge of craft skills helped to ground the historical view of school formation (and even more generally of scientific practice and initiation into it) in mystery and secrecy, so that historians depict the school as operating much like an early modern guild. This view of tacit knowledge became a framework for historical investigation and interpretation: it determined beforehand how the crucial intellectual and social processes of skill, knowledge, and even value acquisition were configured. School formation in particular came to be viewed as dependent upon a limited number of readily explicit factors, such as the research style of a school's leader. A low priority was assigned to examining in fine detail such matters as the means by which school members learned from one another or, in the case of educationally based scientific schools, even the content of science courses and laboratory exercises that helped shape school members to begin with; for the skills and values of scientific practice were presumed unspecifiable. Thus the actual mechanisms for acquiring skills and values central to the formation of a school fell outside the domain of direct historical investigation. Labeled tacit a priori, the process of acquiring craft skills and their values, as it took place in the school, remained invisible to the historical eye.

Despite the existence of pertinent sources, little has been done to specify what *must* be tacitly learned and what *can be* acquired by more explicit or formal means, especially in the pedagogic settings in which schools sometimes took hold. Ravetz does cite "pitfalls"—places where the investigative procedure could go especially wrong—as a special instance where instruction in laboratory exercises must be explicitly given. He seems, however, to consider this an unusual instance of articulation because he drew attention to the fact "that the formal training of scientists has generally been carried on without any recognition of the craft character of scientific work." "Explicit precepts," Ravetz warns, "are insufficient,"

[10] Polanyi, *Personal Knowledge* (cit. n. 6), p. 53.
[11] Ravetz, *Scientific Knowledge* (cit. n. 2), p. 96.
[12] See, e.g., Jordan and Lynch, "Sociology of a Genetic Engineering Technique" (cit. n. 1).

useful "only in the context of the solution of sophisticated *technical* problems."[13] Recent sociological studies have not gone much further, identifying explicit precepts with routine practices, tacit ones with the "secrets" of performing a practice correctly.[14]

In general, assuming that craft skills are a form of tacit knowledge foreclosed even studying both the abstract body of knowledge and practical exercises that constituted science education, including the pedagogic element in school formation, and the sources (such as lecture and laboratory exercise notebooks of students, assistants, and professors) that could assist both in differentiating tacit and explicit knowledge and in defining the realm over which the latter rules. These are challenging issues in the study of scientific schools, not only because a deeper study of science teaching and learning could diminish the realm of the tacit, but also because if it is found that what is taught does not fully coincide with the dominant themes, topics, and techniques of a leader's research, the entire historiographic tradition of defining the pedagogic element of a school primarily in terms of the imitation and adaptation of the *research* example set by its leader could collapse.

II. THE PEDAGOGIC ELEMENT IN SCHOOL FORMATION: GERMAN CASES

Teaching and its relationship to research have not, however, been ignored in the literature on scientific schools. The way in which Michael Foster assembled physiological knowledge for teaching, by assigning a prominent role to evolutionary principles, influenced the research work of his students. Frederic L. Holmes has examined the near fusion of teaching and research in Justus Liebig's Giessen laboratory, where a well-known school of chemistry took shape. In the Königsberg seminar for physics, where by several contemporary accounts a school of physics took shape, a minor technique in Franz Neumann's research—exact experiment and the determination of constant and accidental errors—became a dominant theme in his science pedagogy, which strongly influenced the protocol and style of his students' investigations.[15] In each of these cases, however, it was not primarily research but rather teaching that shaped the character of the school. Foster actually published little; Liebig's early laboratory did not have as strong ties to his research as did his later laboratory; and what Neumann's students considered indispensable techniques in physical investigation were not readily apparent in Neumann's research.

As these examples and several others in this volume amply testify, leading centers of science education in nineteenth-century Germany are strategic and rich cases for reexamining the role of tacit knowledge in school formation. The eighteenth-century German university generally lacked the institutional conditions for close social and intellectual interaction between professors and students because lecture courses dominated university learning. Although new pedagogic techniques, such as exercises that applied what had been learned, appeared by the end of the century, classes were by and large run in traditional ways. In the

---

[13] Ravetz, *Scientific Knowledge,* pp. 102, 99, 102, 103 (emphasis added).

[14] Jordan and Lynch, "Sociology of a Genetic Engineering Technique."

[15] Geison, *Michael Foster* (cit. n. 4); Frederic L. Holmes, "The Complementary of Teaching and Research in Liebig's Laboratory," *Osiris,* 1989, 5:121–164; and Olesko, *Physics as a Calling* (cit. n. 1).

early nineteenth century new pedagogic methods and new forums for learning science—exercise sessions, seminars, teaching laboratories, and, by the end of the century, full-fledged institutes—fostered such strong cognitive and affective bonds between professors and students that distinctive styles of scientific practice became associated with local settings. About one of those new forums for teaching and learning, the seminar, Wilhelm Schrader wrote that it allowed for the continuity of leadership that produced a clearly defined work discipline (*Arbeitszucht*) and a solid working tradition (*Arbeitsüberlieferung*).[16] The close personal relationship resulting from such bonding is evident in the moving affective language used in correspondence, in the mythical stories and mystical images that grew up around educational experiences, in the indistinct boundary between the public institutional space of education and the private domestic sphere of the professor's home life, and in the ease with which moral qualities became affixed to the performance of scientific work.

The intellectual bonding that took shape in these forums depended on a strong pedagogic element that eventuated in shared characteristics of scientific thinking and practice. The complicated and creative nature of pedagogic activity in the natural sciences at the beginning of the nineteenth century made these new and intimate forums ideal breeding grounds for schools. The novelty of schools is apparent in the lexicon entries *Schule* and *wissenschaftliche Schule* from the first half of the century.[17] At that time natural philosophers were working out the pedagogic definition of the scientific disciplines; students were collaborators in that process, making known what worked in the classroom and what did not. The distinct identity of schools was aided by the insular nature of these new forums where well-defined curricula—local pedagogic definitions of the natural sciences —took shape. Students learned to apply scientific methods in practical exercises. These exercises as well as the proto-investigations based on them helped to shape the students' identities as scientific practitioners, to create a sense of community among them, and to form schools whose intellectual coherence and cohesiveness largely resulted from the efficacy of science pedagogy.

Because teaching and research coexisted in the German university—and were equally strong—the meaning of the term *school* took several forms in German settings in the nineteenth century. At one end of the spectrum were research schools of the type created by Justus Liebig at Giessen in chemistry, by Carl Ludwig at Leipzig in physiology, by Wilhelm Wundt at Leipzig in psychology, and by August Böckh at Berlin in philology. Each of these schools had strong, distinctive, and innovative programs of instruction, but their distinguishing mark was the outstanding research productivity of their members.

Yet the term *school* was also used to describe educational settings where little research was done but where intense systematic teaching, often culminating in no more than organized practical exercises that broke down the elements of research methodologies into smaller problems, took place. Hence the physicist Gustav Kirchhoff could claim that as a result of his cooperation with the mathematician

---

[16] Wilhelm Schrader, "Ueber akademische Seminare," *Lehrproben und Lehrgänge aus der Praxis der Gymnasien und Realschulen,* 1899, *60*:1–19, on p. 18.

[17] C. Friedrich, "Wissenschaftliche Schule in der Pharmacie: Teil I," *Pharmacie,* 1988, *43*:274–277, on p. 274.

Leo Koenigsberger as codirector of Heidelberg University's mathematico-physical seminar in the brief period between 1870 and 1874, "a mathematico-physical school has been built at our university, which is our pride and joy."[18] That there are no other references to a school of physics at Heidelberg does not diminish the importance of Kirchhoff's remark, which underscores the fact that special educational settings, such as the seminar, gave rise to schools whose origins and constitution we as historians have still insufficiently examined. Schools were also viewed in more personal terms, as desirable professional accomplishments, even before the goals of recent institutional and pedagogic reforms had been completely realized. The mathematician Carl Jacobi, anxious to trade his position at Königsberg for another, wrote to the Prussian minister of education in 1835 that he wanted to go to Bonn University, where he believed that he could found a school.[19] Significantly, the strength of Jacobi's school—at Königsberg, after all, not Bonn—was partially founded on his teaching, which he used as a vehicle for working through his research interests.

As Alan Rocke emphasizes in his article on Hermann Kolbe's school of chemistry in this volume, the power of science pedagogy to produce strong intellectual bonding should not be underestimated. Rocke's description of Kolbe's teaching and leadership at Marburg and Leipzig illustrates the factors that shape schools in educational settings: close personal contact between professors and students; the relaxation, periodically at least, of lines of intellectual authority between professors and students; a strong emphasis on practical laboratory work, completed in a graduated fashion; the assistance of the guiding hand of a master, but also the sense that independence is cultivated; self-instruction and even the articulation by the student of the techniques guiding scientific practice; and finally the explicit portrayal of steps in an investigative procedure. Schools based at educational institutes, such as Kolbe's, inculcated techniques, values, and styles of interpretation and judgment until they became overriding precepts guiding scientific investigation, shaping the student's image of scientific knowledge. At the advanced level, in research, a strong belief in a school's techniques and ideas could lead to bitter controversy, as Steven Turner demonstrates for the case of the Helmholtz-Hering exchange over visual perception. But even before the upper levels of scientific practice were reached, the distinctive character of a school could guide behavior in unusual ways.

The application of what was learned could be taken to extremes. Ravetz, for instance, discusses the case of a student in Wilhelm Wundt's Leipzig institute who doctored his data so as not to contradict the expectations of Wundt's school. Robert Frank notes how crestfallen Carl Ludwig was when a student in his Leipzig physiological institute, realizing the effect of a disturbance in his apparatus, reversed his conclusion (which had been achieved initially by "rigging" the apparatus) so that it no longer supported Ludwig's views.[20] It was difficult to extract oneself from such influence and bonding. In turning down Franz Neumann's

[18] Gustav Kirchhoff to Emil du Bois-Reymond, 27 Sept. 1874, quoted in Emil Warburg, "Zur Erinnerung an Gustav Kirchhoff," *Die Naturwissenschaften,* 1925, *13*:205–212, on p. 211.

[19] Leo Koenigsberger, *Carl Gustav Jacob Jacobi* (Leipzig: Teubner, 1904), pp. 173–174.

[20] Ravetz, *Scientific Knowledge* (cit. n. 2), pp. 96n–97n; and Robert G. Frank, Jr., "American Physiologists in German Laboratories, 1865–1914," in *Physiology in the American Context, 1850–1940,* ed. Gerald L. Geison (Bethesda, Md.: American Physiological Society, 1987), pp. 11–46, on p. 35.

invitation to habilitate in physics at Königsberg in 1861, Oskar Emil Meyer couched his decline in missionary terms. "Since the beginning of your instruction," he explained, "I was guided by the notion that I would be trained as an apostle of your gospel in the world. I cannot give that up now because you have appointed me deacon of your congregation." With embarrassment Meyer admitted that had he gone to Königsberg he would only have been able to lecture from notes he had taken in Neumann's courses. Yet buried deep in his letter was also a fear that, had he gone to Königsberg, "evil" people would say that he could not do anything without first seeking Neumann's advice.[21] Like the students of Wundt and Ludwig, Neumann's exhibited a distinctive investigative style. But that style's dependency upon strictly tacit knowledge is debatable; for in these examples, as well as those taken from other German schools, students could, if pressed, *self-consciously* call upon the skills and values that defined the school by referring back to the educational experiences, elementary or advanced, that had shaped them.[22]

Strong instructional programs, however, did not always lead to school formation. For example, by all accounts Robert Bunsen had an extremely good program of instruction at Heidelberg, was an effective and inspiring teacher (especially in conveying the craft skills of chemistry), and supervised dozens of research projects undertaken by students in his laboratory, many of which were published. Yet contemporary observers did not identify Bunsen as having established a school. As to why, it appears that the methods and problems undertaken at Heidelberg were just not sufficiently distinct enough from those elsewhere in Germany to justify the epithet "school," the identity of which rests at least in part on perceived differences between its practices and those elsewhere. One might therefore ask of Bunsen's program whether the generalization or broad appeal of the skills it conveyed vitiated school formation. The intellectual profile of Bunsen's example and other similar negative cases demands deeper historical examination in order to enhance our understanding of the pedagogic element in the formation and character of schools.

III. EXPLICIT, NOT TACIT: DATA ANALYSIS IN GERMAN SCHOOLS OF PHYSICS

Of special interest to the history of schools and the role of the pedagogic element and tacit knowledge in them are German schools of physics in the nineteenth century. When he took over the editorship of the prestigious *Annalen der Physik* in 1890, Gustav Wiedemann identified three schools that had shaped German physics in the middle decades of the nineteenth century. Wiedemann used the term "school" in a broad sense, meaning something akin to "school of thought," but one with a permanent institutional base, a distinct investigative style (especially in the use of quantitative techniques), and a coherent instructional program. The first school, centered at Berlin University under Gustav Magnus, was largely experimental in character and drew its conceptual and methodological inspiration from chemistry. The second and third combined mathematical and experimental

[21] Oskar Emil Meyer to Franz Neumann, 21 Nov. 1861, Franz Neumann Nachlaß, 53.IIA: Briefe von Schülern, Niedersächsische Staats- und Universitätsbibliothek, Handschriftenabteilung.

[22] See Olesko, *Physics as a Calling* (cit. n. 1), for examples of the affective bonding between Neumann and his students and of the characteristics of this school's style.

methods and were more strongly influenced by the exact experimental methods of astronomy. These schools appeared at Göttingen University under Wilhelm Weber and at Königsberg University under Franz Neumann. Of the two, Wiedemann viewed the Königsberg school of physics as having cultivated a stronger mathematical orientation.[23]

The demographic constitution of these German schools of physics cannot be defined as rigorously as that of research schools because instruction was the primary function of the institutes associated with each school, and hence research productivity alone cannot be used as a reliable guide to either membership in or the identity of the school. In broad terms, however, the most productive school was Magnus's, where from the 1840s to 1870 some eighty investigations issued from his Berlin laboratory; before 1870 student publication at Göttingen and Königsberg combined did not equal that at Berlin.[24] Although Weber's and Neumann's research interests and styles were resources for the courses and practica each offered, at neither location was physics instruction completely dominated by the dictates of a research agenda. The schools at Göttingen and Königsberg created their identities not from research but from teaching programs, and specifically from that part of their teaching that concerned quantification.

At Königsberg and Göttingen, especially at the latter, the large domain of explicit knowledge passed on to students lay in instructional programs in exact experimental physics, particularly in areas that Polanyi and Ravetz consider to be most immune to articulation and explicit codification, and therefore to constitute a hard core of tacit knowledge: techniques of measurement and data analysis, including the values and judgments exercised in their use. The process of going from instrument readings to the magnitudes that appear in formulas, Polanyi argues, "rests on an estimate of observational errors which cannot be definitely prescribed by a rule." Tacit knowledge, according to Polanyi, guides the scientist in computing those errors in order to move from experiment to theory. But, because "no strict relationship" exists between measured and reduced data, the process of data reduction, Polanyi argues, "remains . . . indeterminate."[25] Ravetz too views data analysis as a craft skill, but one much more intricate: "The simple judgment of the 'soundness' of data is a microcosm of the complex of accumulated social experience and judgments which go into scientific endeavor." Hence the well-known and common phenomenon of apparently similar sets of data being accepted by one researcher yet rejected by someone in the same field but from a different school, using different techniques. Craft knowledge is in Ravetz's view

[23] Gustav Wiedemann, "Vorwort," *Annalen der Physik*, 1890, *39*:ix–xii, on pp. x–xi, esp. p. xi. Wiedemann's delineation of schools was confirmed by other contemporary observers, and not only those who had affiliations with either of these schools. See e.g., C. Voit, "Franz Ernst Neumann," *Sitzungsberichte der math.-physikal. Classe der k. b. Akademie der Wissenschaften zu München*, 1896, *26*:338–343, on p. 339.

[24] A. W. Hoffmann, "Zur Erinnerung an Gustav Magnus," *Berichte der Deutschen Chemischen Gesellschaft*, 1870, *3*:993–1101, on pp. 1099–1101. Additional investigations not mentioned by Hoffmann are cited in A. Guttstadt, *Die Anstalten der Stadt Berlin für die öffentliche Gesundheitspflege und für den naturwissenschaftlichen Unterricht: Festschrift dargeboten den Mitgliedern der 59. Versammlung Deutscher Naturforscher und Aerzte von den städtischen Behörden* (Berlin: Stuhr, 1886), p. 140.

[25] Polanyi, *Personal Knowledge* (cit. n. 6), p. 19. See also his discussion of spurious results (p. 53) and self-regulating instruments (p. 20).

even needed to decide "which sort of functional relation is represented by the dis-
crete set of points" obtained through measurement, thus making the graphical
analysis of data a matter of deploying techniques and judgments tacitly learned.[26]

The cases of Göttingen and Königsberg indicate, however, that not only was
data and error analysis more explicit at these locations than either Polanyi or
Ravetz would seem to allow, but also that styles in data and error analysis differ-
entiated practitioners, including novices, in each school. Owing to the richness
and variety of its sources, including notebooks of practical measuring problems
assigned to students, Göttingen's program is especially revealing of the ways in
which esoteric techniques were made explicit not only for instructional purposes,
but also for actual research in physics.[27] For the most part, professors directed
practical laboratory exercises; but they also allowed advanced students to teach
beginners, thereby weakening the strict hierarchy customarily associated with
German institutes. Weber modeled Göttingen's practical measuring exercises, at
both the beginning and the advanced levels, largely on his and Carl Friedrich
Gauss's geomagnetic research, which strongly shaped the Göttingen organization, style, and approach for decades.[28]

The type of measurement in Göttingen's exercises was one in which precision
was achieved largely through the perfection of instruments, as had been done in
the geomagnetic work. Trials were generally thin; corrections for errors were embodied in instruments; and precision was described in terms like "a truly mathematical precision," "a microscopic precision," and "a precision that leaves
nothing to be desired."[29] What Polanyi, Ravetz, and others considered the prime
example of tacit knowledge—techniques of measurement and data analysis—was
made explicit in instruction. Student notebooks indicate that instructors delineated how instruments and their errors should be handled. A key term was *relia-
bility.* To call an instrument reliable meant that the instrument had been
perfected as much as possible so as to minimize the analytic computation of constant (or systematic) errors. All corrections were thus, in a sense, embodied in the
material perfection of the instrument so that the measurements in themselves, before being worked over, possessed a "fineness" (*Feinheit*) they might not have had

[26] Ravetz, *Scientific Knowledge* (cit. n. 2), pp. 76–77, 81–84, 88–91, 93, quoting from pp. 82, 84.

[27] These sources include reports for the Göttingen mathematico-physical seminar, where most of
the practical exercises were held, student notebooks from the seminar, and Friedrich Kohlrausch's instructional notebooks, which include exercises and student assignments kept while he was the assistant for practical exercises between 1866 and 1870. See Königliches Universitäts-Curatorium zu
Göttingen, Akten betr. die Einrichtung eines mathematisch-physikalischen Seminars (1850–1883),
Universitätsarchiv Göttingen, 4/Vh/20; Wilhelm Weber Nachlaß, Nr. 21: Seminar-Vorlesungen in
Nachschrift v. K. Hattendorff, and Hermann Wagner Nachlaß, Nr. 6: Vorträge von Wilhelm Weber
über verschiedene Gegenstände der mathematischen Physik, gehalten im physikalischen Seminar der
Georgia Augusta, 1860–63, both in Niedersächsische Staats- und Universitätsbibliothek, Hand-
schriftenabteilung; and Friedrich Kohlrausch, Tagebücher Nrs. 2500 and 2601, Sondersammlungen,
Deutsches Museum, Munich.

[28] Wilhelm Weber to Colonel Sabine, 20 Feb. 1845, rpt. in *Wilhelm Weber's Werke,* 6 vols., ed.
Königliche Gesellschaft der Wissenschaften zu Göttingen (Berlin: J. Springer, 1892–1894), Vol. II,
pp. 274–276; and reports of the Göttingen mathematico-physical seminar, 1850–1870, Universitätsarchiv Göttingen, 4/Vh/20.

[29] See such sources as the Göttingen seminar reports; C. F. Gauss to Wilhelm Olbers, 2 Aug. 1832,
C. F. Gauss Nachlaß, Niedersächsische Staats- und Universitätsbibliothek, Handschriftenabteilung;
and especially the remarks about precision and accuracy made in *Resultate aus den Beobachtungen
des magnetischen Vereins im Jahre 1836–41,* 6 vols., ed. C. F. Gauss and W. Weber (Göttingen:
Dieterich, 1837–1838; Leipzig: Weidemann, 1839–1843).

if less attention had been paid to refining instruments. Possessing such faith in their data, students more easily represented it in idealized images, such as maps or graphs, much in the same way that Gauss and Weber had used in their geomagnetic results. For the crucial area of data analysis, notebooks indicate that Weber instructed students to deal with "outliers" in a way consistent with the instrument-orientation of his exercises. In cases where the instrument was not yet properly calibrated (initial measurements) or where the calibration wore off (final measurements), students were told to eliminate data. Good data was thus tied to the perfect operating state of the instrument.[30]

It may seem self-evident that outliers should be eliminated, but it was not. Exercises that placed a higher value on the analytic determination of accidental errors by the method of least squares, such as those at Königsberg, taught students to retain all (or almost all) data. Hence at Königsberg precision was tied to the probability assessments in the method of least squares; results based on observations were believed not to possess mathematical certainty; and the analytic determination of both constant and accidental errors, not the perfection of instruments, was regarded as the best way to purify data.[31] Students at Göttingen, by contrast, questioned the ability of least squares to account for errors in the data. The material- or instrument-oriented approach to data practiced at Göttingen was enhanced by keeping practical applications in view in laboratory exercises, a custom not observed at Königsberg.[32] The practical purposes of the Göttingen exercises meant that an exact analysis of the data itself was less useful, because when a useful result was needed quickly, one just did not have the time to engage in elaborate and complex computations like those required in least squares. Göttingen's pragmatic program of physics instruction thus remained relatively immune to the excessive skepticism concerning data and theory construction that was, at times, so crippling at Königsberg.

That Wiedemann and others could identify a school at Göttingen only for the middle decades of the nineteenth century is significant. Between 1866 and 1870 Friedrich Kohlrausch codified Göttingen's practical exercises. In 1870 he published a textbook of practical physics based on those exercises.[33] An explicit statement of the research values and techniques that had guided the school of physics at Göttingen, his textbook focused more on instruments than on data. It advocated using least squares only to establish the overall limits of error, and deemed the exhaustive analytic determination of constant errors "too laborious." Kohlrausch's textbook was accepted very quickly and on a wide scale throughout Germany, establishing a uniformity of practical exercises in physics hitherto not seen. But its popularity vitiated the maturation of the Göttingen school into what Joseph Fruton has called a "research group."[34] Although fine distinctions in

[30] Weber Nachlaß, Nr. 21, and Wagner Nachlaß, Nr. 6 (both cit. n. 27).

[31] Olesko, *Physics as a Calling* (cit. n. 1).

[32] Seminar reports, Universitätsarchiv Göttingen, 4/Vh/20. Practical applications included problems from navigation, geodesy, mine surveying, telegraphy, sacchirimetry, and medicine.

[33] Kohlrausch, Tagesbücher Nrs. 2500 and 2601 (cit. n. 27); and Friedrich Kohlrausch, *Leitfaden der praktischen Physik* (Leipzig: Teubner, 1870).

[34] Joseph Fruton, "Contrasts in Scientific Style: Emil Fischer and Franz Hofmeister, Their Research Groups, and Their Theory of Protein Structure," *Proceedings of the American Philosophical Society,* 1985, *129*:313–370; and Fruton, "The Liebig Research Group: A Reappraisal," *ibid.,* 1988, *132*:1–66.

experimental styles based on approaches to measurement continued to characterize differences between schools of physics until early in the twentieth century, the
only schools that could realistically take shape were those that contrasted sharply
with Kohlrausch's general practices, such as the school of August Kundt. Hence
the experimental physicist Friedrich Paschen could remark in 1925 that "as an assistant to [Wilhelm] Hittorf, I had the opportunity to learn what was insufficiently
emphasized in the school of Kundt: namely to make precision measurements as
they were done by [Victor Henri] Regnault." Kundt's school rejected not only precision measurement of the Göttingen type but also the kind of rigorous computation of errors that had been practiced earlier at Königsberg.[35]

So we are left with somewhat of a paradox. The explicit codification of practices, including those of data analysis, helped to create a school at Göttingen. But
the widespread popularity of the Göttingen style, following Kohlrausch's publication of its characteristic practices in his textbook, diluted the distinctiveness of
the school's identity. From the beginning it had been the explicit statement, rendered in instruction, of exact experimental practices that had been so important
in shaping the identity of the school. Students exhibited the same preference for
instrument perfection over error analysis in their research that had been evident
in their practical exercises. *Pace* Ravetz and Polanyi, craft knowledge of the sort
associated with data and error analysis was not entirely ineffable.

IV. CONCLUSION: A SCHOOL'S SUCCESS

As Rocke argues here for the case of Kolbe, tacit knowledge cannot be entirely
eliminated from school formation; "cookbook knowledge" and precepts cannot
guide scientific practice completely. In fact, prior to the codification of the
Göttingen school's practices in Kohlrausch's textbook, residual tacit practices
did remain a part of the school's operation. Most of these tacit practices were
found in the execution of geomagnetic measurements proper, as when Kohlrausch supervised advanced students in them, rather than in other types of exercises and projects involving precision measurement. The failure of the Göttingen
school to mature and to sustain a distinct identity after the appearance of
Kohlrausch's textbook, however, can be attributed in large part to the inability
of the school to maintain a distinct identity in the context of the widespread dis-
semination of its practices. The case of Göttingen physics, as well as others like
it, suggests that a more nuanced understanding of the domains of the tacit
and the explicit, as well as the boundaries between them, is essential for understanding not only the formation of scientific schools, but also more generally
the formation of the scientist.

The burden of this brief essay has been that overemphasizing the role of tacit
knowledge in school formation has entailed ignoring a key factor in school formation: learning by explicit precept. As the cases described in this volume illustrate,
the precepts and assumptions guiding a school's operation can be self-consciously

[35] Friedrich Paschen, "Antrittsrede," *Sitzungsberichte der Preußischen Akademie der Wissenschaften, Phil.-hist. Klasse,* 1925, pp. cii–civ, on p. cii. Paschen could not, in fact, have chosen a more con-
tentious example of precision measurement. Regnault's measurements were accepted at Göttingen,
but at Königsberg were considered flawed for their inadequate consideration of certain experimental
errors. See Olesko, *Physics as a Calling* (cit. n. 1), pp. 297–298, 378–386.

deployed in arguments, debates, and controversies only when they are articulable, and hence explicit. In his article on the Helmholtz-Hering controversy in this volume, for instance, Steven Turner demonstrates the importance of a special set of explicitly recognizable characteristics, linguistic differences, in the definition and operation of a school as well as in scientific controversy. Explicit knowledge, such as these linguistic differences, lies at the basis not only of controversy between schools, but also of the identity, productiveness, and even continuity of a school. What the pedagogic element in school formation makes clear, however, is that a delicate balance must be maintained. If too much is made explicit in the scientific practice of a school, as when Kohlrausch codified Göttingen's practices in his textbook, then either a school will not form or an existing one will neither mature nor be sustained. A school's success thus depends on keeping some secrets, but neither too many nor too few.

National Styles? French and English Chemistry in the Nineteenth and Early Twentieth Centuries

By Mary Jo Nye*

COGNITIVE AND SOCIAL STYLES do exist in science. Style plays a role in the emergence and perpetuation of scientific ideas, institutions, and ideologies. Style is invoked in order to explain success or failure of individual, institutional, and national scientific endeavors and to account for scientific creativity.[1]

In a recent article in *Science,* the journalist Robert Crease writes of the selection process for experiments to be implemented in the Superconducting Super Collider: "Three groups, each headed by a man with a distinctly different style, were competing for two slots in which to build a half-billion dollar instrument." The "Polish-born, French-raised American" George Trilling is "confident and avuncular," "amiable and well-regarded," with a bureaucratic style; Samuel C. C. Ting is "authoritarian," "like a general reviewing his troops," building "ever bigger versions of the same basic detector"; and Michael Marx is "less precisely dressed than the others," "but far more aggressive than his rivals, hammering home" the argument that his group's detector is a new design especially tailored to the SSC.[2]

Crease shows no hesitation in using the notion of style, but the word is now under scrutiny by anthropologists, literary critics, and historians. Discussions of style have been closely knit with the notion of national style or tradition—as in Crease's analysis. Art historians have used the term widely in this way since J. J. Winckelmann interpreted Greek artistic style as an expression of the Greek way of life. "Greek" and "Italian" styles—taken as the reflections and expressions of

* Department of the History of Science, 601 Elm, Room 622, University of Oklahoma, Norman, Oklahoma 73019-0315.

** Research for this paper (and for the larger project that includes this material) was supported by the National Endowment for the Humanities (Grant #RH-20758-86), the National Science Foundation (Grant #DIR-8911578), and the University of Oklahoma's Research Council and Faculty Summer Research Fellowship program.

[1] See Mary Jo Nye, "Scientific Decline: Is Quantitative Evaluation Enough?" *Isis,* 1984, *75*:697–708; and, on creativity, Jacques Hadamard, *An Essay on the Psychology of Invention in the Mathematical Field* (Princeton, N. J.: Princeton Univ. Press, 1945). For a perceptive account of contrasting English and American views of French medical science, see also John H. Warner, "The Idea of Science in English Medicine: The 'Decline of Science' and the Rhetoric of Reform, 1815–1845," in *The Birth of Modern British Medicine, 1760–1840,* ed. Roger French and Andrew Wear (London: Routledge, in press).

[2] Robert Crease, "Choosing Detectors for the SSC," *Science,* 1990, *250*:1648–1650.

Greek and Italian culture—have long enjoyed privileged positions in the history of art and architecture. But the belief that an "ideal" style defines a privileged position against principles or behaviors that become demarcated as anomalous, abnormal, and "other" has recently attracted criticism. The notion of style can express nationalism, chauvinism, and racism. Postmodernist literary critics have attacked the concept of *genre* on similar grounds. " 'Do,' 'Do not' say 'genre.' . . . [A]s soon as genre announces itself, one must respect a norm, one must not cross a line of demarcation, one must not risk impurity, anomaly, or monstrosity," notes Jacques Derrida.[3] These ideas about style and national style also influence discussions of scientific style.

I. NATION, STYLE, SCHOOL

In his early twentieth-century history of nineteenth-century science, the Germanophile Scottish engineer J. T. Merz suggested that national styles that had existed at the beginning of the nineteenth century were waning as science was becoming more international and scientists were becoming less isolated from one another than in the past. But S. S. Schweber still finds national styles among physicists in the 1930s and 1940s, noting that European emigré physicists altered their styles of doing science to suit their new American environments. According to Schweber, Eugene Wigner's approach to quantum physics became less abstract, more closely tied to experimental findings, and more model-oriented at Princeton than it had been in Austria and Germany.[4]

Dominique Pestre suggests that after 1945 American emphasis on describing, calculating, and predicting—"getting the numbers out"—became an international style in cooperative big physics ventures like CERN. The success of the American approach in quantum physics led to the "marginalization of De Broglie's school" and the quick loss of influence of Copenhagen physics after 1950.[5] This identification of one national style with an international style at the expense of "De Broglie's school" and the Copenhagen school links the concepts of

[3] Johann J. Winckelmann, *Geschichte der Kunst des Altertums* (Dresden: Waltersche Buchhandlung, 1764). See Anna Wessely, "Transposing 'Style' from the History of Art to the History of Science," *Science in Context,* 1991, 4:265–278, on pp. 265–266; and Jacques Derrida, "The Law of Genre," trans. Avital Ronell, *Glyph,* 1980, 7, rpt. in *Critical Inquiry,* 1980, 7:55–81, on pp. 56–57, cited in Marjorie Perloff, ed. *Postmodern Genres* (Norman: Univ. Oklahoma Press, 1988), p. 4. On the history of style see Ernst Gombrich, "Style," *International Encyclopedia of the Social Sciences,* pp. 353–361; and Gombrich, *Norm and Form: Studies in the Art of the Renaissance* (London: Phaidon, 1966).

[4] John Theodore Merz, *A History of European Thought in the Nineteenth Century* (1904–1912), 4 vols, Vol. I, *Scientific Thought* (New York: Dover, 1965); and S. S. Schweber, "The Empiricist Temper Regnant: Theoretical Physics in the United States, 1920–1950," *Historical Studies in the Physical Sciences,* 1986, 17:55–98. For a discussion of American scientific style see Nathan Reingold, "National Styles in the Sciences: The United States Case," in *Human Implications of Scientific Advance,* ed. E. G. Forbes (Edinburgh: Edinburgh Univ. Press, 1978), pp. 163–173. On "style" in the biological sciences see Jonathan Harwood, "National Styles in Science: Genetics in Germany and the United States between the World Wars," *Isis,* 1987, 78:390–414.

[5] Dominique Pestre, "From Revanche to Competition and Cooperation: Physics Research in Germany and France," paper given at the conference "Society in the Mirror of Science: The Politics of Knowledge in Modern France," 30 Sept.–1 Oct. 1988, University of California, Berkeley; and Pestre, "Vers un modèle de relations scientifiques radicalement nouveau: Le cas des physiciens allemands et français après 1945," in *Frankreich und Deutschland: Forschung, Technologie, und industrielle Entwicklung im 19. und 20. Jahrhundert,* ed. Yves Cohen and Klaus Manfrass (Munich: Beck, 1990), pp. 130–141.

national style and research school. By focusing on the analytic unit of the research school, the historian can understand more fully the origin and perpetuation of the idea of scientific style, including the ascription of "national style" to a
way of doing science. Styles are exemplified in individuals' work, but their perpetuation, if not their origin, lies in scientific traditions passed on through formally
institutionalized schools—for example, universities—and through informally
constituted "schools," which include "research schools."

The term *research school* itself requires explication. Gerald Geison's 1981
essay defines it as largely identical to a "research group": a small group of "mature
scientists pursuing a reasonably coherent programme of research side-by-side
with advanced students in the same institutional context and engaging in direct,
continuous social and intellectual interaction." Building on studies by Jack
Morrell, John Servos, Maurice Crosland, Robert Fox, Gerald Holton, and Owen
Hannaway, Geison restricts his analysis to "laboratory-based research schools."
As in Joseph Fruton's focus on the *group,* Geison's characterization of *school* emphasizes its local nature and its strictly enumerable membership.[6]

I use the term *research school* in a broader sense that allows for a school of individuals to be linked through a network of institutions and generations. This
broadening of the strict definition recognizes the process in which a school's identity becomes diluted by the generalization of its style over separate locales and
generations—a process Kathryn Olesko describes elsewhere in this volume.

As John Servos and Steven Turner note, also in this volume, the word *school* in
the nineteenth century often carried a pejorative meaning, in which schools were
associated with controversy and polemics. This attitude is not surprising, since
the struggle against scholasticism and the skeptical schools of the seventeenth
century was by no means forgotten in the early nineteenth century. In a century
characterized by political struggle toward republicanism, subservience to disciplinary "masters" could be viewed as a vestige of the old tyrannies of scholasticism
and clericalism. Yet, in a century characterized by increasing nationalism, the
successes of an influential scientist and his "school" could be seen alternatively as
a matter of national glory or national threat.

The shift from a pejorative to a positive connotation for the word, as well as the
conflation of the individual or local school with the national school, can easily be
illustrated. In 1839, for example, Jean-Baptiste Dumas's local rival Jules Pelouze
complained that Dumas was using the "theory of substitutions to elevate himself
to the position of Chef de l'Ecole of the new organic chemistry." Since Dumas
held appointments singly or simultaneously at six Parisian institutions during
1824–1868 and used his position within the Ministry of Public Education to
place twenty-four of his twenty-nine research associates in teaching positions
throughout France, it is easy to see how "Dumas's school" slowly became synony-

⁶ Gerald L. Geison, "Scientific Change, Emerging Specialties, and Research Schools," *History of
Science,* 1981, *19*:20–40, on p. 23; Joseph S. Fruton, "Contrasts in Scientific Style: Emil Fischer and
Franz Hofmeister: Their Research Groups and Their Theory of Protein Structure," *Proceedings of the
American Philosophical Society,* 1985, *129*:313–370; Fruton, "The Liebig Group: A Reappraisal,"
ibid., 1988, *132*:1–66; and Fruton, *Contrasts in Scientific Style: Research Groups in the Chemical and
Biological Sciences* (Philadelphia: American Philosophical Society, 1990). See also Michael N. Keas,
"The Structure and Philosophy of Group Research: August Wilhelm von Hofmann's Laboratory Re-
search Program in London (1845–1865)" (Ph.D. diss., Univ. Oklahoma, 1992).

mous not only with "Parisian" but with "French" chemistry. In a study of Dumas's research school, Leo Klosterman details the use of these conflated terms by Dumas's contemporaries.[7]

In 1868 Adolphe Wurtz broadened the definition of the French school beyond Dumas to include Auguste Laurent and Charles Gerhardt: "The basic lines [of the substitution theory] are indelibly drawn, and it was the French school that drew them." Wurtz further enlarged the argument to claim that "chemistry is a French science. It was founded by Lavoisier, of immortal memory." Regarding his own research school, Wurtz wrote the Minister of Public Education that nineteen prominent chemists had worked in his laboratory at the Faculty of Medicine, including two Englishmen; that 210 memoirs had been published from the laboratory since 1853; and that to find another example of such activity, one would have to turn to the "school formed by Liebig at Giessen."[8]

In view of the intense scientific and nationalist rivalries that existed during the nineteenth and early twentieth centuries, we should not be surprised to see scientists using the language of national styles and national stereotypes. I shall now sketch some typical characterizations of national styles among late nineteenth-century French and English scientists, examine some of the institutionalized traditions that were the realities behind the stereotypes, and then investigate the applicability and inculcation of these stereotyped styles in two distinct research schools in chemistry, which I call the Ecole Normale and the Manchester schools of the 1920s. I conclude with comments about the role played by research schools in creating or continuing traditions of national scientific styles.

II. CONTRASTING ELEMENTS IN NATIONAL STYLES:
THE DICHOTOMY BETWEEN ABSTRACT AND CONCRETE

In some ways Pierre Duhem and Ernest Rutherford make a peculiar pairing, but they appear to have held the same opinions about the conceptual styles they took to be characteristic of English and Continental scientists. In a passage from his memorable characterization of the electrical theories of Michael Faraday, James Clerk Maxwell, and Oliver Lodge, Duhem wrote:

> Two electrically charged bodies are before us, and the problem is to give a theory of their mutual attractions or repulsions. The French or German physicist . . . will by an act of thought postulate in the space outside these bodies that abstraction called a material point and, associated with it, that other abstraction called an electric charge. He then tries to calculate a third abstraction: the force to which the material point is subjected . . . [with] clarity, simplicity, and order. The same does not hold for an

[7] Dumas, quoted in F. L. Holmes, *Claude Bernard and Animal Chemistry* (Cambridge, Mass.: Harvard Univ. Press, 1974), p. 77. See also Leo J. Klosterman, "A Research School of Chemistry in the Nineteenth Century: Jean-Baptiste Dumas and His Research Students," *Annals of Science,* 1985, *42*:1–80; on pp. 4–5, notes 12–13.

[8] Adolphe Wurtz, "Histoire des doctrines chimiques depuis Lavoisier" (1868), trans. in Henry Watts, *History of Chemical Theory* (London: Macmillan, 1869); and Wurtz to Minister of Public Education, 27 May 1868, File #F¹⁷21890 (Charles Adolphe Wurtz), Archives Nationales de France, Paris. For an account of the Liebig-Dumas rivalry, see F. L. Holmes, "Justus von Liebig," *Dictionary of Scientific Biography,* ed. Charles C. Gillispie, Vol. VIII (New York: Scribners, 1973), pp. 332–342; and Holmes, "Justus Liebig and the Construction of Organic Chemistry," paper given at the Beckman Center Conference on Modern Chemistry, Philadelphia, May 1990.

Englishman. . . . These abstract notions of material points, force, line of force, and equipotential surface do not satisfy his need to imagine concrete, material, visible, and tangible things.[9]

We know something of Rutherford's views on national styles through his witticisms and jokes passed down by admiring colleagues and students. There is the story P. M. S. Blackett reports of Wilhelm Wien's explaining to Rutherford (in 1910) that Newton was wrong in the matter of relative velocity, which is "not the sum of the two velocities $u + v$, but . . . the expression according to Einstein must be divided by $(1 + uv/c^2)$." Wien added, "But no Anglo-Saxon can understand relativity;" to which Rutherford replied, "No, they have too much sense." Again according to Blackett, Rutherford claimed he was struck at the 1911 Solvay Physics Congress in Brussels "by the fact that continental people do not seem to be in the least interested to form a physical idea as a basis of Planck's theory. They are quite content to explain everything on a certain assumption and do not worry their heads about the real cause of a thing. I must, I think, say that the English point of view is much more physical and much to be preferred."[10]

The tenacity of the stereotype of pragmatic, concrete English thinking in contrast to esoteric, abstract Continental reasoning is striking. If we construct a tentative list of elements of French style in physical science, especially for chemistry in the late nineteenth century, it must begin with the characterization articulated by Duhem and Rutherford. The goal of scientific explanation among French scientists was a finely crafted theory of generalized abstractions, expressed in rigorous mathematics. Where mathematical theory was yet premature, then scientific explanation must consist in classification and reasoning by analogy. In contrast, English scientists pragmatically used visual models and a kind of mathematical thinking typical of applied and engineering science.[11] Let us call this first dichotomy "abstract versus concrete" and examine it by way of examples.

The abstract-concrete dichotomy has a basis in the pedagogical traditions in the two countries. In France, the best-known scientists at the turn of the twentieth century were graduates of the Ecole Polytechnique and the Ecole Normale Supérieure. Nearly all ambitious *lycée* students trained themselves for the mathematical hurdles of the competitive examinations determining entry to the Ecole Polytechnique and Ecole Normale ("Normale Sup"). Nowhere did mathematics have more prestige than in France. As Léon Brillouin said in 1962, every ambitious young man wanted to do the purest sort of mathematics; and he also wanted to do it "because all the committees for the examinations were composed of pure

[9] Pierre Duhem, *The Aim and Structure of Physical Theory,* trans. Philip P. Wiener (New York: Atheneum, 1974), on pp. 69–71. For Duhem's less generous characterization of German science see Duhem, *La science allemande* (Paris: Hermann, 1915); and Duhem, "Quelques réflexions sur la science allemande," *Revue des Deux Mondes,* 1915, *25*:657–686.

[10] P. M. S. Blackett, "Memories of Rutherford," in *Rutherford at Manchester,* ed. J. B. Birks (London: Heywood, 1962), pp. 102–113, on pp. 111–112.

[11] On nineteenth-century English, German, and French scientific styles see Merz, *Scientific Thought* (cit. n. 4). For "concrete" versus "abstract" stereotypes and their perpetuation in differing educational systems see Eda Kranakis, "Social Determinants of Engineering Practice: A Comparative View of France and America in the Nineteenth Century," *Social Studies of Science,* 1989, *19*:5–70. On the different approaches of the French and the English to geometry in the nineteenth century see Joan L. Richards, *Mathematical Visions: The Pursuit of Geometry in Victorian England* (San Diego, Calif.: Academic Press, 1988).

mathematicians." When Brillouin entered the Sorbonne around 1910, there was no chair of applied mathematics. Students like Brillouin, who were inclined toward physical theory rather than toward experimental physics, were advised to go directly into pure mathematics.[12] Not until 1958 did the predoctoral *agrégation* examination have separate sections on physics and chemistry.[13] As a consequence, most chemists had a thorough grounding in mathematics.

In England, in contrast, mathematical training was intense only for that small number of students preparing for the mathematical tripos at Cambridge University. A high proportion of the successful first and second wranglers shucked college-day mathematics for the bar or politics. Many physicists and most chemists were not educated at Cambridge or, for that matter, at Oxford, so that education in the physical sciences in England was far less intertwined with mathematical training than in France.[14]

Even those who did well in the tripos did not continue to practice pure mathematics with the single-minded dedication of many of their French colleagues. J. J. Thomson is well known for a scientific style described by the historian David Topper "reason[ing] by means of images" in constructing a mechanical picture of nature. But it was not always so. Thomson's college career began at Owens College, Manchester, in 1870. He entered Trinity College, Cambridge, in 1876. He was second wrangler in the mathematical tripos, and his treatise on vortex rings won him the Adams Prize. When G. F. Fitzgerald advised Henry Armstrong on possible authors for a lecture on the subject of vortex atoms in connection with theories of matter, electricity, the ether, and chemistry, Fitzgerald mused, "If J. J. Thomson would only condescend to come down out of his mathematics, he could do it very well." By the mid 1890s Thomson had made the descent.[15]

In France the chemistry of the late nineteenth century was dominated by the opposed figures of Adolphe Wurtz and Marcellin Berthelot. While Wurtz supported chemical atomism and the adoption of atomic weights, Berthelot defended the use of equivalent combining proportions and opposed the drawing of structural formulae. Although he stopped writing water as HO instead of H_2O in 1891, Berthelot still wrote benzene as $C_2H_2(C_2H_2)(C_2H_2)$ in 1898, and there is not the least use of structural formulae in his discussions of isomerism in a 1901 text on hydrocarbons. But these two French chemists, like most of their contemporaries, agreed on the need to use structural formulae and apparent molecular models with great caution, with even Wurtz noting that "these formulas . . . do not give any indication on the form of the molecule in space."[16] Again, Auguste Laurent

[12] Interview of Léon Brillouin by P. P. Ewald, G. Uhlenbeck, T. S. Kuhn, and Mrs. Ewald, New York, 29 March 1962, Archives for the History of Quantum Physics, University of California, Berkeley.

[13] Raymond Dulou and Albert Kirrmann, "Le Laboratoire de Chimie de l'Ecole Normale Supérieure; Notes historiques," *Bulletin de la Société des Amis de l'Ecole Normale Supérieure,* Sept. 1973, *54* (issue *hors série*), p. 4.

[14] See P. M. Harman, ed., *Wranglers and Physicists: Studies on Cambridge Physics in the Nineteenth Century* (Manchester: Univ. Manchester Press, 1985). On institutions in metropolitan London see Robert Bud and Gerrylynn K. Roberts, *Science versus Practice: Chemistry in Victorian Britain* (Manchester: Univ. Manchester Press, 1984).

[15] David Topper, "To Reason by Means of Images: J. J. Thomson and the Mechanical Picture of Nature," *Annals of Philosophy,* 1980, *37*:30–57; and G. F. Fitzgerald to H. E. Armstrong, 28 Nov. 1888, Armstrong file, Imperial College Archives. See also the quotation from S. S. Hough, on Henri Poincaré and George Darwin, in David Kushner's article in this volume, on p. 207.

[16] Adolphe Wurtz, *Introduction à la théorie atomique* (Paris: Baillière, 1879), p. 255. See also Albert

proposed a three-dimensional model in 1837 for thinking about the "nucleus" of organic molecules and the substitution of radicals into organic molecules, but his model may best be thought of as an application of geometric reasoning to chemical problems. The same can be said of the tetrahedron model of carbon advanced by J. H. van't Hoff and Achille Le Bel in 1874.

For the most part, it was British and German chemists who introduced highly visual and cartoon-like representations for molecules and the valence bond during the nineteenth century. Among these chemists were Archibald Couper, Alexander Crum Brown, Josef Willbrand, Josef Ladenburg, and Auguste Kekulé. In England John Dalton had introduced wooden molecular models and enjoyed great success with them at lecture demonstrations both for public audiences and for students.[17] However, German chemists seemed to have more misgivings than their English colleagues. Only once did Kekulé actually use what Hermann Kolbe ridiculed as Kekulé's "sausage formulas," in a textbook of 1861.[18]

Many English chemists leaned strongly on visualization, but not all: Henry Armstrong was one exception. Armstrong was well known in British scientific circles for avoiding pictorial imagery and model building in chemistry. A like-minded soul, the older Oxford professor of chemistry Benjamin Brodie, commended him in 1874: "I am glad to see that none of the various forms of 'pictorial chemistry' has found favour with you, but that you have adhered to the simple equational method of expressing results." The dominant position was exemplified by the model-minded physicist Oliver Lodge, who admonished Armstrong, "I think . . . that you are trying to be *too* conservative, though some conservatism on the part of a chemical leader is useful and desirable."[19]

There are other exceptions to the modeling and pictorial rule, among them William Henry Perkin, Jr., about whom it was said that he "never paused to consider the underlying mechanism of organic chemical reactions," and for whom changes in structural formulas sufficed as explanation.[20] But what complicates these exceptions to the rule is the German education of these English chemists. Did a stint in the German laboratories develop some caution that tempered an English penchant for visual models? Armstrong, a pupil of Edward Frankland's at the Royal College of Chemistry in London, spent five academic terms at Leipzig

Kirrmann, "La naissance des formules moléculaires en chimie organique," *L'actualité chimique,* Jan. 1974, No. 1, pp. 45–49; and Mary Jo Nye, "Berthelot's Anti-Atomism: A 'Matter of Taste?' " *Ann. Sci.,* 1981, *38*:585–590.

[17] See Bert Ramsay, "Molecules in Three Dimensions," *Chemistry,* 1974, *47*(1):6–9, *47*(2):6–11; and Ramsay, *Stereochemistry* (London: Heyden, 1981).

[18] Auguste Kekulé, *Lehrbuch der organischen Chemie,* Vol. I (Erlangen: Enk, 1861), discussed in Aaron Ihde, *The Development of Modern Chemistry* (New York: Harper & Row, 1964), pp. 305–306. On these representations see O. Theodor Benfey, *From Vital Force to Structural Formulas* (1964, 1975) (Philadelphia: Beckman Center for the History of Chemistry, 1992).

[19] Benjamin Brodie to H. E. Armstrong, 25 Feb. 1874, and Oliver Lodge to Armstrong, 21 Sept. 1908; both Armstrong file, Imperial College Archives. Armstrong was professor of chemistry at Central Technical College (later Imperial College) in London from 1884 to 1911; see J. Vargas Eyre, *Henry Edward Armstrong, 1848–1937: The Doyen of British Chemists and Pioneer of Technical Education* (London: Butterworths, 1958).

[20] Robert Robinson, *Memoirs of a Minor Prophet: Seventy Years of Organic Chemistry* (Amsterdam/London: Elsevier, 1976), p. 27. See also the article by Jack Morrell in this volume.

studying with Kolbe, who heaped abuse on Kekulé's images of sausages and aromatic rings. Perkin studied under both Wilhelm Wislicenus and Adolf von Baeyer, as did many other English chemists. Thus styles linked to traditions and institutions are complicated in the English case by a German, and sometimes a French, connection.[21]

III. FURTHER CONTRASTING ELEMENTS IN NATIONAL STYLES

The dichotomy "abstract-concrete" defines only one set of characterizations of differences in style between French and English physical science. Other sets we might add are individualistic versus cooperative; fragmented versus focused; urbane versus Puritan; chauvinistic versus touristic; and classical versus contemporary.

Regarding the first two dichotomies, French scientists, taught to admire pure mathematics, may have developed more individualistic styles than the English. Martin Klein has argued, with respect to J. Willard Gibbs, that mathematicians tend to work in greater isolation than do other scientists.[22] If this is the case, emphasis on mathematical genius may have led French scientists to value individual and independent endeavor especially. During the course of the nineteenth century, there was less of the kind of cooperation that had characterized Lavoisier's investigations at the Arsenal or the meetings of the Berthollet-Laplace group at Arcueil.[23]

A distinction must be made, however, between the French and the English variants of "individualism," one rooted in the French tradition of bureaucracy and professionalism, the other in the English tradition of liberalism and amateurism. Here the English stand apart from both French and German scientists, who made further distinctions among themselves. Significantly, one of A. W. Hofmann's German students reported that Hofmann had not been satisfied with his English students while directing the Royal College of Chemistry in London, because he thought their "individualism" made them unsuitable "for the establishment of a scientific school in the German sense." Although both English and French scientists admired many aspects of the organization of German science, they shared Hippolyte Taine's doubts, following a trip to Germany in 1867, about transplanting German "regimentation" into French (or English) scientific life.[24] The fear of regimentation, at its worst, fostered an uncooperative individualism in France, in

[21] See B. N. Clark, "The Influence of the Continent upon the Development of Higher Education and Research in Chemistry in Great Britain during the Latter Half of the Nineteenth Century," Ph.D. diss., Univ. Manchester, 1979); and Paul R. Jones, "The Strong German Influence on Chemistry in Britain and America," *Bulletin for the History of Chemistry,* 1989, 4:3–7.

[22] Martin Klein, discussion following "Work in Progress: Theoretical Physics at Leyden in the 1920s," colloquium, 6 May 1988, Harvard University. Gibbs usually is taken to be the exception to the rule that nineteenth-century American science was utilitarian and pragmatic.

[23] F. L. Holmes, *Lavoisier and the Chemistry of Life: An Exploration of Scientific Creativity* (Madison: Univ. Wisconsin Press, 1985); and Maurice Crosland, *The Society of Arcueil: A View of French Science at the Time of Napoleon I* (Cambridge, Mass.: Harvard Univ. Press, 1967).

[24] C. A. von Martius, introduction to A. W. Hofmann, *Chemische Erinnerungen aus der Berliner Vergangenheit,* 2nd ed. (Berlin, 1918), p. 12, quoted in Jeffrey Johnson, "Hierarchy and Creativity in Chemistry, 1871–1914," *Osiris,* 1989, 5:214–240, on p. 224; and Taine, quoted in Theodore Zeldin, *France, 1848–1945* (Oxford: Oxford Univ. Press, 1973–1977), Vol. I, p. 117.

contrast to the tradition of "self-help" which, at its best, led to cooperative individualism in England.

The fragmentation of effort in France resulted not only from the isolationism of French individualism, but from the concentration of ambitious scientists in Paris and the practice there of *cumul,* or multiple appointments. Parisian scientists tended to accumulate independent positions—for example, at the Faculté de Pharmacie, the Ecole Centrale des Arts et Manufactures, and the *lycée*-level Ecole de Sèvres—so that their time was divided among several institutions, their efforts spread thin, and their research dispersed among several subjects simultaneously. Dominique Pestre has noted that this tendency persisted into the 1920s and 1930s, with many physicists pursuing a gamut of different scientific subjects rather than a specialized research program.[25]

English scientists tended to associate with only one institution at a time, whether at Oxford, Cambridge, or London or one of the redbrick universities. There was disgruntlement at Cambridge when James Dewar ended up spending most of his time in London.[26] Sociability and cooperation were valued. In England the expectation developed by the 1860s, based on a hybrid German-English model, that laboratory directors would spend time with students and research associates in the laboratory.

Henry Roscoe, for example, a student of Robert Bunsen's in the 1850s, directed teaching and research laboratories at Manchester from 1857 to 1885. He devised a system combining the Oxbridge tutorial tradition and the German professorial system. He was careful to give each of his students at Manchester personal attention, rather than just to walk through the laboratory.[27] This continued to be the style of instruction and research at Manchester under Roscoe's successors Harold Baily Dixon and Arthur Lapworth. In contrast, Berthelot's French students found that he paid them little attention, as was also the director's practice in the Ecole Normale chemical laboratory under Henri Sainte-Claire Deville during 1851–1881 and under his successors Henri Jules Debray, Alphons Alexandre Joly, and Désiré J. B. Gernez during 1881–1904.[28]

It was a matter of concern to English chemists that German practices seemed to be changing by the century's end. Writing his father from Berlin in 1900, Edward Frankland Armstrong complained that van't Hoff worked in his personal laboratory and never sought out students; when the students wanted to speak to van't Hoff, "We send the boy in to make an appointment. Thus my work is to some considerable extent self-help and reliance." The younger Armstrong, like other observers of German chemistry around 1900, also complained that the German students' doctoral research had become merely routine synthesis: "The preparation of ethyl, butyl, propyl, hexyl, etc. derivatives . . . and the assistant gives de-

[25] Dominique Pestre, "Y-a-t-il une physique à la française entre les deux guerres?" *Recherche,* 1985, *16*:998–1005, on p. 1003. Notoriously, A. J. Balard simultaneously held three *chairs* of chemistry at Parisian institutions in the mid-nineteenth century.

[26] W. H. Mills, "Schools of Chemistry in Great Britain and Ireland; VI: The University of Cambridge," *Journal of the Royal Institute of Chemistry,* 1953, *77*:423–431, 467–473, on p. 469.

[27] Robert H. Kargon, *Science in Victorian Manchester: Enterprise and Expertise* (Baltimore: Johns Hopkins Univ. Press, 1977), p. 179.

[28] Dulou and Kirrmann, "Laboratoire de Chimie de l'Ecole Normale Supérieure" (cit. n. 13), p. 11. On Berthelot see Jean Jacques, *Berthelot: Autopsie d'un mythe* (Paris: Belin, 1987).

tailed orders."[29] Thus the "style" of German chemistry had changed, according to foreign observers.

Moving to the next dichotomy, one can argue that French scientists pursued a more cosmopolitan and urbane style of living than most of their English colleagues and were less affected by what is often called the "Protestant work ethic." French scientists tended to become involved in politics to a degree uncharacteristic for English (or German) scientists because the Académie des Sciences had frequent ties with governmental advisory bodies and nearly all scientific positions were civil service positions that could be influenced by powerful figures well placed in government posts.[30]

Americans abroad who, like the English, sought to complete their training in physics or chemistry on the continent, often felt intimidated by urban, cosmopolitan Paris and were much more at ease in Germany's small university towns. Indeed, as provincial sciences faculties became better funded and equipped around 1900, even some French scientists chose to remain in provincial institutions, in part because there were fewer distractions from laboratory research than in Paris.[31]

By the end of the nineteenth century, particularly in the redbrick universities, English scientists seem to have been more likely to overwork themselves than their French counterparts, particularly those in Paris. French laboratories closed down several months out of the year, and in many nothing went on in the evening.[32] Similarly, as Jack Morrell notes in his essay in this volume, the older English universities remained bastions for gentlemen, and Oxford's tradition of athletic activities for undergraduates between lunch and teatime prevented Perkin from putting into practice Baeyer's regime of ten continuous laboratory hours from 8 A.M. to 6 P.M.

A clearer contrast between English and French scientific styles lies in the dichotomy between tourism and chauvinism. English scientific education was more international, especially before 1917, when Oxford instituted a D.Phil. degree for the first time.[33] As mentioned earlier, many English chemists studied a year or two in Germany before completing their doctoral and postdoctoral researches. Armstrong and the younger Perkin were typical, as was their teacher Edward Frankland, who in 1847 had accompanied the young Hermann Kolbe to Marburg and studied for three months in Bunsen's laboratory. Frankland returned to Germany, both to Marburg and Giessen, during 1848–1849, following an exciting and bewildering arrival in Paris in June of 1848 as revolution unfolded in the streets. He managed to hear a few lectures by Dumas and Edouard Fremy, but not

[29] Edward Frankland Armstrong to H. E. Armstrong, 11 Feb. 1900, [summer 1900], Armstrong file, Imperial College Archives.

[30] See Charles C. Gillispie, *Science and Polity in France at the End of the Old Regime* (Princeton, N.J.: Princeton Univ. Press, 1980); and Harry Paul and Terry Shinn, "The Structure and State of Science in France," *Contemporary French Civilization*, 1981/2, 6:153–193.

[31] See Henry Blumenthal, *American and French Culture, 1800–1900: Interchange in Art, Science, Literature, and Society* (Baton Rouge: Louisiana State Univ. Press, 1975); and Mary Jo Nye, *Science in the Provinces: Scientific Communities and Provincial Leadership in France, 1860–1930* (Berkeley/ Los Angeles: Univ. California Press, 1986), on Paul Sabatier, pp. 151–152, and Victor Grignard, p. 185.

[32] See Nye, *Science in the Provinces*, p. 122.

[33] J. C. Smith, "The Development of Organic Chemistry at Oxford," typescript, 2 pts., MSS A.6, A.7, Pt. I, p. 51, Robert Robinson Papers, Royal Society of Chemistry, London.

to work with them. In contrast, hardly any French physicists or chemists studied abroad as students; one exception at the turn of the century was Paul Langevin, who spent a year at Cambridge. In his history of organic chemistry at Oxford, J. C. Smith notes that there was a great mixture of ages and nationalities among the twenty research students at Oxford's Dyson Perrins laboratory in the 1920s and 1930s but never, until 1947, a French student.[34]

Finally, one can contrast French "classicism" with what may be called British "contemporism." As Robert Fox has demonstrated, after the Restoration French scientists stressed the importance of carefully crafted lectures that presented scientific knowledge, whether physics, chemistry, or other natural sciences, as a deductively derived or hierarchically classified logical structure. Even in the early 1900s, as Edmond Bauer recalled, physics was taught at the Sorbonne in a very old-fashioned, "classical" way.[35] Mechanics, optics, acoustics, and heat were at its heart; electricity and magnetism were presented as developed by André-Marie Ampère, with little or no attention to Maxwell. Historical introductions provided confidence in the logical unfolding and structural beauty of scientific understanding.

Education in the physical sciences in England appears instead to have been more nearly geared to capturing students' interest and imagination and to introducing students immediately to new theories and experiments. In recalling the honors physics course at Manchester around 1908, the physicist Harold R. Robinson noted that students began practically full-time research in their third year. They were expected to write a paper on modern physics, especially radioactivity. "This scheme of undergraduate training left wide gaps in our knowledge of important sections of classical physics," he noted, but "physics . . . was a living and growing science." There was not much respect among many English scientists for "old" science. Nevil Sidgwick, whose biting sarcasms amused or chagrined colleagues and students, commented on the appropriateness of the name "Old Chemistry Department" for the inorganic chemistry building at Oxford: "Soddy does teach *old* chemistry."[36]

An important reason for emphasis on novelty and change within the English chemical tradition, in contrast to the preference for classical form and structure in France, lies in the fact that French chemists during the nineteenth century gained prestige from association with "academic" values and pure science, whereas English chemistry was more clearly and openly allied with practical in-

[34] *Sketches from the Life of Edward Frankland,* [ed. Margaret Nanny West and Sophie Jeanette Colenso] (London: Spottiswoode, 1902), pp. 455–480; and Smith, "Development of Organic Chemistry" (cit. n. 33), Pt. II, p. 46.

[35] Robert Fox, "Scientific Enterprise and the Patronage of Research in France, 1800–1870," in *The Patronage of Science in the Nineteenth Century,* ed. Gerald L'E. Turner (Leyden: Noordhoof, 1976), pp. 9–51, on pp. 19–24; and Edmond Bauer, interview by T. S. Kuhn and T. Kahan, 8 Jan. 1963, session 1, Archives for History of Quantum Physics.

[36] H. R. Robinson, "Rutherford: Life and Work to the Year 1919, with Personal Reminiscences of the Manchester Period," in *Rutherford at Manchester,* ed. Birks (cit. n. 10), pp. 53–86, on p. 68; and Sidgwick, quoted in Smith, "Development of Organic Chemistry" (cit. n. 33), Pt. II, p. 3. Rajkumari Williamson has found that examination questions in physics at Manchester took up X rays and radioactivity immediately following their discovery and investigation: paper delivered at joint meeting of the British Society for the History of Science and the History of Science Society, July 1988, University of Manchester.

terests.[37] This situation began to change in France around 1900 with the creation of schools and institutes of applied science in the provinces and in Paris.

Nevertheless, prestige continued to be associated with pure mathematics and pure science, especially in the fifteen to seventeen science faculties throughout France, each with a chair in physical sciences or chemistry. As Terry Shinn has demonstrated, the curriculum and research at the Ecole de Chimie et de Physique in Paris after its founding became gradually less applied and specialized and more general, mathematical, and theoretical, in order to enhance its prestige and fulfill the aims of its directors Albin Haller and Paul Langevin.[38]

If differences in national style can indeed be identified for French and English science in the nineteenth and early twentieth centuries, these differences surely manifest themselves in particular research schools in the two countries. Let us turn now to brief, but systematic, résumés of some of the work and traditions characteristic of two important schools of chemistry, one at the Ecole Normale Supérieure and the other at Manchester over a circumscribed period of time, namely the 1920s.[39]

IV. THE MANCHESTER SCHOOL IN THE 1920s

The terms "Ecole Normale" and "Manchester" "schools" of chemistry refer here to two distinctive traditions in chemical education, research agendas, and methodologies characteristic of several generations of chemists concerned with *theories* of organic reaction mechanisms while teaching or studying at the Ecole Normale Supérieure or the University of Manchester. The chemical laboratory of the Ecole Normale Supérieure was directed for five decades in the nineteenth century by Deville or his pupils, who concerned themselves little with organic chemistry, reaction mechanics, or general theories. In 1904, however, Robert Lespieau inaugurated a new tradition at the laboratory, which he directed until 1934, becoming in 1921 the only chair holder in France in theoretical chemistry, as "professeur de théories chimiques." Particularly given the so-called positivist bias in French chemistry against the introduction of physical atomism and physical mechanisms into late nineteenth-century chemical theory, the history of Lespieau's avowedly "theoretical" school of chemistry helps delineate styles and practices among specific, nationally distinct schools within the wider field of theoretical chemistry.

Just as "Ecole Normale School of Chemistry" here refers to a specific, but extended group who practiced what later came to be called physical organic chemis-

[37] See Bud and Roberts, *Science versus Practice* (cit. n. 14); and Colin A. Russell, *Science and Social Change in Great Britain and Europe, 1700–1900* (London: St. Martin's Press, 1983).

[38] Terry Shinn, "Des sciences industrielles aux sciences fondamentales: La mutation de l'Ecole supérieure de physique et de chimie (1882–1970)," *Revue Française de Sociologie*, 1981, *22*:167–182. Under the Napoleonic reorganization scheme, each science faculty was required to maintain four professors—one each for differential and integral calculus, rational mechanics and astronomy, physical sciences, and natural history. See Nye, *Science in the Provinces* (cit. n. 31); and Harry W. Paul, *From Knowledge to Power: The Rise of the Science Empire in France, 1860–1939* (Cambridge: Cambridge Univ. Press, 1985).

[39] For a fuller treatment of these two schools see Mary Jo Nye, "Chemical Explanation and Physical Dynamics: Two Research Schools at the First Solvay Chemistry Conferences, 1922–1928," *Ann. Sci.,* 1989, *46*:461–480; and Nye, *From Chemical Philosophy to Theoretical Chemistry: Dynamics of Matter and Dynamics of Disciplines, 1800–1950* (Berkeley/Los Angeles: Univ. California Press, in press).

try at the Ecole Normale, so "Manchester School of Chemistry" for the purposes of this essay refers to chemists educated or teaching at Manchester over some decades who interested themselves in theories of organic reactions and underlying mechanisms, including the application to organic chemistry of physical ideas and instrumentation. This school has a longer history than the one in Paris, its tradition beginning with Frankland's tenure at Owens College in the 1850s. The focus here is the period of the 1920s.[40]

The University of Manchester was a locus to which chemists immigrated and from which they emigrated to new locations during the late nineteenth and early twentieth centuries. Arthur Lapworth was an influential figure in this school, holding chairs in organic and physical chemistry in turn. A student of Henry Armstrong's at the Central Technical School in South Kensington, London, in the late nineteenth century, Lapworth had revealed himself early to be an independent-minded investigator. It was said that he refused to show Armstrong his Ph.D. thesis, remarking, "It is my work and I have no intention of changing it."[41]

Lapworth's fellow students at Central Technical included Thomas Martin Lowry, who in 1920 became the first professor of physical chemistry at Cambridge, and William J. Pope, who taught at the Manchester Municipal School of Technology before becoming professor of chemistry at Cambridge in 1908. Lapworth left London for the University of Manchester in 1904, where he taught inorganic and physical chemistry. He succeeded William Henry Perkin, Jr., in the chair of organic chemistry in 1913 when Perkin was appointed to Oxford. Lapworth returned to teaching physical and inorganic chemistry in 1922 in order to place Robert Robinson in Manchester's organic chemistry professorship.

Robinson first came to Manchester as an undergraduate student in 1902 and returned as a professor during 1922–1928. When he accepted an appointment at Oxford in 1930, he found three other ex–Manchester faculty members on the staff: Edward Hope, Wilson Baker, and John C. Smith. The Dyson Perrins Laboratory had familiar features, since its builders had completed the Morley Laboratory at Manchester.[42] At Oxford, as at Manchester, Robinson's principal investigations lay in the chemistry of natural products, particularly the synthesis of alkaloids, and it was for this work that he was awarded the Nobel Prize in 1947. Yet in his memoirs Robinson wrote that he considered the development of an electronic theory of reaction mechanisms "my most important contribution to knowledge."[43]

As an undergraduate and graduate student at Manchester, Robinson became a protégé and then a close friend of Lapworth. His other teachers included Perkin, H. B. Dixon, G. H. Bailey, Chaim Weizmann (later president of Israel), and Jocelyn F. Thorpe, who, Robinson said, made two new substances every day.[44] Thorpe became professor of organic chemistry at Imperial College in 1913, where his most distinguished student was Christopher Ingold.

In the decade before World War I, as afterwards, Manchester was a lively center for both chemistry and physics. A physics colloquium on Friday afternoons in

[40] Kargon, *Science in Victorian Manchester* (cit. n. 27), p. 212.
[41] As reported by Ida Smedley and quoted in Robinson, *Memoirs* (cit. n. 20), p. 69.
[42] Smith, "Development of Organic Chemistry" (cit. n. 33), Pt. I, p. 18; Pt. II, p. 3.
[43] Robinson, *Memoirs* (cit. n. 20), p. 184.
[44] Robinson, *Memoirs*, p. 66.

1908 attracted a strong following, including some chemists. Robinson came to know Ernest Rutherford and to admire him greatly.[45] The Manchester chemists interested themselves in theories of ions and atoms. Despite his mentor Armstrong's vehement opposition to Svante Arrhenius's theory of dissociation and ionization, Lapworth extended the notion of ions to hydrocarbon chemistry in 1901, with a hypothesis that atoms became polarized within molecules, for example, in cyanohydrin formation and bromination substitutions.[46]

$$H_2C=C-C=CH_2 \atop | \quad \quad |$$
$$H \quad \quad H$$

$$H_2C-C=C-CH_2 \atop | \quad | \quad | \quad |$$
$$Br \quad H \quad H \quad Br$$

butadiene   **1,4 addition product**

Figure 1. 1,4 Addition in butadiene

One of the most interesting problem areas in organic chemistry lay in reactions of compounds that contain alternating double bonds, the so-called conjugated systems. Perkin, who had been a fellow student with Johannes Thiele in Munich, may have transmitted to Lapworth and Robinson at Manchester a special interest in Thiele's conceptual treatment of problems like 1,4 addition in butadiene, which Thiele explained by using notions of residual affinity and partial valence supplementary to principal valence (see Figure 1). Alfred Werner had a different notion of chemical affinity, which he believed was spread over the combining surface of a carbon atom and subject to fractionation, so that the alpha carbon (the carbon atom adjacent to the principal functional group, e.g., the left-hand C in $-C-CO_2H$) might become a seat of residual affinity and thus of reactivity.[47]

While teaching in Sydney during 1912–1915, Robinson began to work out ideas on reaction mechanisms, allowing partial valences in conjugated systems to derive from normal valences. He returned to England to teach at Liverpool, and in a lively and long correspondence, he and Lapworth speculated on how to apply polar and electron ideas in chemistry, pursuing especially the approaches already begun by J. J. Thomson and others. They developed the idea that partial dissociation of molecules causes a slight internal polarization, leading to the formation or disappearance of valences.[48]

In 1920 Lapworth and Robinson published independent memoirs. Lapworth

[45] See H. R. Robinson, "Rutherford" (cit. n. 36), pp. 72–73; and Robert Robinson, *Memoirs,* pp. 67–69.

[46] Arthur Lapworth, "A Possible Basis of Generalization of Intramolecular Changes in Organic Compounds," *Journal of the Chemical Society (London): Transactions,* 1898, *73:*445–459; and Lapworth, "The Form of Change in Organic Compounds and the Function of the α-Meta Orientating Groups," *ibid,* 1901, *79:*1265–1284. See also Martin D. Saltzmann, "Arthur Lapworth: The Genesis of Reaction Mechanism," *Journal of Chemical Education,* 1972, *49:*750–752.

[47] Discussed in Robert Robinson, "Quelques aspects d'une théorie électrochimique du mécanisme des réactions organiques," Institut International de Chimie Solvay, *Rapports et discussions relatifs à la constitution et la configuration des molécules organiques: Quatrième Conseil de Chimie tenue à Bruxelles du 9 au 14 avril 1931* (Paris: Gauthier-Villars, 1931), on p. 423; and Robinson, "The History of Electronic Theories of Organic Reactions" (typescript), Robinson Papers, The Royal Society.

[48] Robinson, "Quelques aspects," p. 424.

Figure 2. Robinson's schema for the internal dynamics of a molecule

gave what he called "alternating" polarity the primary role in initiating and determining the course of reaction, with the influence of a "key-atom" extending over a long hydrocarbon chain if double bonds are present. Robinson identified the activation of molecules with the rearrangement of valences "most probably synonymous with changes in position of electrons" so that the active molecules are polarized and contain partially dissociated valences. In 1921 Robinson and Lapworth's approach was directly influenced by Irving Langmuir's lecture before a joint meeting of the physics and chemistry sections at a meeting of the British Association for the Advancement of Science in Edinburgh. Robinson instantly saw the importance of the electron valence theory, first developed in 1916 and 1919 by G. N. Lewis and Irving Langmuir, and he incorporated it into a paper of 1922, coauthored with W. O. Kermack of the Royal College of Medicine in Edinburgh.[49]

Robinson added the movement of electron pairs to the idea of internal and alternating polarity. As in his earlier correpondence with Lapworth, he represented the internal dynamics of an active molecule by arrows, implying the movement of electrons in the double bond (see Figure 2). Robinson later recalled Henry Armstrong's reaction to his pictorial representations of alternating single and double bonds in a chain of carbon atoms and to the schemas representing electron shifts or bond shifts with curved arrows. No one, Armstrong said, "would hang him in chains, conjugated or otherwise. The symbol [Robinson] introduced to illustrate electron displacement . . . was dismissed wittily by Armstrong—'a bent arrow never hit the mark.' "[50]

Lapworth and Robinson continued working on reaction mechanisms for six years, and Robinson regularly taught these ideas to his advanced students at Manchester. The theory was characterized by visual imagery and useful graphic

[49] See Martin D. Saltzmann, "Sir Robert Robinson—A Centennial Tribute," *Chemistry in Britain,* June 1986, pp. 543–548; Saltzmann, "The Robinson-Ingold Controversy: Precedence in the Electronic Theory of Organic Reactions," *J. Chem. Ed.,* 1980, *57*:484–488; and J. Shorter, "Electronic Theories of Organic Chemistry: Robinson and Ingold," *Natural Products Reports: A Journal of Current Developments in Bio-organic Chemistry,* 1987, *4*:61–66. The 1920 papers are Arthur Lapworth, "Latent Polarities of Atoms and Mechanism of Reaction, with Special Reference to Carbonyl Compounds," *Memoirs and Proceedings of the Manchester Literary and Philosophical Society,* 1919/20, *64*(3):1–16; and Robert Robinson, "The Conjugation of Partial Valencies," *ibid., 64*(4):1–14. See also W. O. Kermack and Robert Robinson, "An Explanation of the Property of Induced Polarity of Atoms and an Interpretation of the Theory of Partial Valencies on an Electronic Basis," *J. Chem. Soc.,* 1922, *121*:427.

[50] Robert Robinson, introduction in Eyre, *Henry Armstrong* (cit. n. 19), pp. ix–x; and Robinson, "Quelques aspects" (cit. n. 47), p. 437. For a detailed account of the development of these ideas and their applications by Robinson in the synthesis of natural products, see Jennifer Seddon [Curtis], "The Development of Electronic Theory in Organic Chemistry" (honours thesis in chemistry, St. Hugh's College, Oxford, 1972).

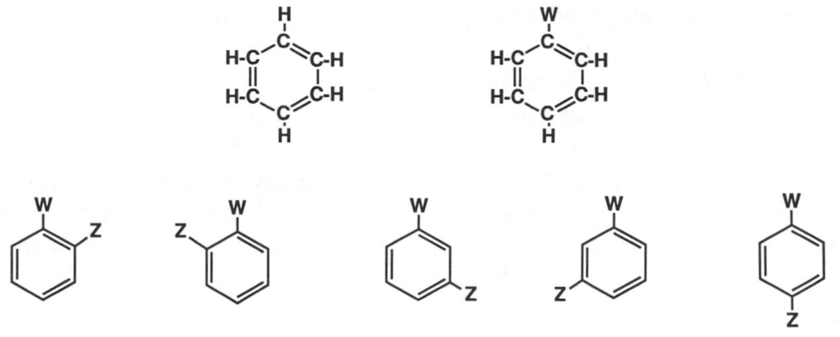

1, 2 or ortho   **1, 3 or meta**   **1, 4 or para**

Figure 3. *Aromatic substitution patterns*

devices, like the curved arrow and noughts and crosses, which helped predict the course of reaction, especially for *ortho, meta,* and *para* disubstitutions in aromatic rings (see Figure 3). In the late 1920s and 1930s Christopher Ingold developed a larger theory rooted in the Lapworth-Robinson scheme. His new terms *electrophilic* and *nucleophilic* caught on, as did his $\delta+$, $\delta-$ notation for partial or fleeting charge, confirming the usefulness of the Manchester approach.[51]

The Manchester school of organic chemistry, like earlier generations of English chemists, was oriented toward visual imagery and pictorial simplicity that led to practical results.[52] Yet it did not rely on methods of physical instrumentation tied to thermodynamics and spectroscopy. Robinson's research groups were particularly inattentive to such methods. Recalling his arrival at Robinson's Dyson Perrins laboratory in 1933, Alexander Todd noted the dearth of polarimeters, spectrometers, and other equipment ordinary in the Frankfurt laboratory of Walther Borsche, which he had just left. "Robinson was like his teacher and predecessor Perkin in having little interest in gadgets—he was firmly attached to the degradative and synthetic methods of classical organic chemistry and was slow to adopt such things as ultra-violet and, later, infra-red spectroscopy as aids in structural work."[53]

V. THE ECOLE NORMALE SCHOOL IN THE 1920s

In 1921 Robert Lespieau held the first chair at the Sorbonne for "chemical theories." From 1904 onward, his Ecole Normale laboratory was a meeting place for chemists and physicists. Lespieau encouraged his students to follow lectures and research developments associated with Jean Perrin's Sorbonne laboratory for physical chemistry, including Perrin's work on energy conditions of chemical

[51] Robinson, "Quelques aspects," p. 436, and discussion following the paper, pp. 490–501, on p. 492. See Christopher K. Ingold, "Principles of an Electronic Theory of Organic Reactions," *Chemical Reviews,* 1934, *15*:225–274.

[52] On Thomas Lowry's use of models and visual way of thinking, see C. B. Allsop and W. A. Waters, "Thomas Martin Lowry," in *British Chemists,* ed. Alexander Findlay and William Hobson Mills (London: The Chemical Society, 1947), pp. 402–418, on pp. 405, 408, 413.

[53] Alexander Todd, *A Time to Remember: The Autobiography of a Chemist* (Cambridge: Cambridge Univ. Press, 1983), p. 27.

activation. Lespieau welcomed physicists to his laboratory and introduced his own students to techniques for studying cryoscopy, diamagnetism and paramagnetism, as well as spectroscopy, including Raman spectroscopy, for which he had great enthusiasm.[54] One of his students, Maurice Bourguel, was among the first in France to lecture on the usefulness of Raman spectroscopy for determining chemical identity and demonstrating the individuality of particular functional groups.[55] Lespieau also directed his students to André Job's research on reaction mechanisms. Job delivered lectures on the electronic theory of valence—the first such lectures in France—during 1922–1925 for students specializing in chemistry at the Ecole Normale.

Job's lectures, Perrin's and Job's discussions of chemical activation by radiation, and guest lectures given by Thomas Lowry at the Paris Chemical Society during 1924–1925 led two of Lespieau's students, Charles Prévost and Albert Kirrmann, to develop a generalized ionic theory of organic reaction mechanisms, which they published in two articles in 1931 and 1933. In the first article Prévost and Kirrmann identified their theory with recent work of Perrin's: ionization, they said, is the atomistic interpretation of chemical activation. "Our ionized molecule is the activated molecule of Jean Perrin. Organic ionization needs an exterior contribution of energy which is not needed in Arrhenius's theory of ionization of salts." The fundamental hypothesis of their memoir is identical to Lowry's almost a decade earlier: "The reactions of organic chemistry are reactions of ions."[56]

Prévost and Kirrmann attempted to attain a general theory of the elementary process of organic reaction, distinguishing what they called "synionic," or tautomerism, from "metaionie," a production of metaionic forms of a compound that cannot be isolated. Intramolecular ions, they stressed, are short-lived and separately undetectable; there is an ionizing *tendency*, not an ionized *state*.[57] But despite the long and detailed, carefully structured presentation in the memoir, it was not judged favorably by what its authors subsequently called the "Anglo-Saxon school" of chemists. The Prévost-Kirrmann memoir was rigorous and general, but it offered nothing new.[58]

[54] Dulou and Kirrmann, "Laboratoire de Chimie de l'Ecole Normale" (cit. n. 13), pp. 8–11; and Jules Guéron and Michel Magat, "A History of Physical Chemistry in France," *Annual Review of Physical Chemistry,* 1971, *22*:1–25, on pp. 4–6.

[55] In 1928 Chandrasekhara Raman discovered the effect that carries his name. Bourguel gave a lecture on the subject at the Paris Chemical Society on 27 May 1932, one week before his death from prolonged illness: Maurice Bourguel, "Applications de l'effet Raman à la chimie organique," *Bulletin de la Société Chimique de France,* 1933, *53*:469–505.

[56] Charles Prévost and Albert Kirrmann, "Essai d'une théorie ionique des réactions organiques," *Bull. Soc. Chim. France,* 1931, *49*:194–243, 1309–1368, on pp. 197, 196. See also Prévost and Kirrmann, "La tautomérie anneau-chaine, et la notion de synionie," *ibid.,* 1933, *53*:253–260; Lowry, "Intramolecular Ionisation in Organic Compounds," *Transactions of the Faraday Society,* 1923, *19*:487–496; and Lowry, "Applications in Organic Chemistry of the Electronic Theory of Valency," *ibid.,* pp. 485–487.

[57] Prévost and Kirrmann, "Essai d'une théorie ionique," pp. 224, 197. See also Charles Prévost, *Notice sur les titres et travaux scientifiques* (Paris: Société d'Editions d'Enseignement Supérieure, 1967), where Prévost's autobiographical remarks include the comment, "Like most of the students leaving the *classes de spéciales,* I thought I had a vocation as a mathematician" (p. 7).

[58] British and American chemists have rarely cited Prévost's and Kirrmann's work on "synionie"; nor is there mention of French contributions to theories of reaction mechanisms in the most influential text on the subject, Christopher K. Ingold's *Structure and Mechanism in Organic Chemistry* (Ithaca, N.Y.: Cornell Univ. Press, 1953).

The second unsuccessful line of attack on chemical mechanics was Perrin's radiation hypothesis. Perrin first broached it around 1912, but it became considerably bolder by the 1920s: "The essential mechanism of all chemical reaction is . . . to be sought in the action of light upon atoms." This was not a singularly French theory, but had its enthusiasts elsewhere, including the physical chemist William McCullagh Lewis at Liverpool.[59]

The idea had roots in Arrhenius's formula for molecular "activity," or the probability of transformation of a molecule at temperature T, where the probability is $k = Se^{-a/RT}$, with a being quantity of energy, S a constant for a given molecule, and R the gas-law constant. Perrin and his colleagues, including Job, pointed to the significance of a as the energy from ambient radiation which moves a molecule from a stable to a transition "critical" state.[60] Perrin based his theory on what he claimed to be a law of chemical mechanics for unimolecular reactions, whereby the average life of a molecule at a given temperature is independent of the frequency of collisions. This independence, it turns out, does not exist, and the theory is wrong. But it was enormously appealing to Perrin and his colleagues in the Ecole Normale tradition because of its apparently simple mathematical elegance, its expression in terms of energy requirements, and the possibility of deriving its statement from a quantum condition.[61]

VII. RESEARCH SCHOOLS: CONFIRMATION OR CREATION OF "NATIONAL" STYLES?

The approaches of the Ecole Normale and the Manchester research schools to the problem of reaction mechanisms and chemical activation seem to confirm in a general way the abstract-visual and classical-contemporary dichotomies for French and English chemical traditions and institutions.

In the development of theories about reaction mechanisms and activation in the 1920s, the Manchester school led the way with imaginative, visually graphic mechanisms based in ideas of corpuscular motions. The Ecole Normale school of chemistry tended to avoid visual, corpuscular imagery in favor of more generalized and abstract systems based firmly in empirical descriptions of ionization or radiation. Some French chemists later expressed bitterness at the domination of the field by Americans and Britons, contrasting French chemistry with the Anglo-Saxon school, which Prévost characterized as "from the beginning, sacrific[ing] descriptive chemistry, the solid part, to 'up-to-date' theoretical chemistry, which is less definitely established." Contemporism and bold theories in scientific

---

[59] See Jean Perrin, *Atoms,* trans. D. L. Hammick, 2nd Eng. ed. (New York: Van Nostrand, 1923), p. 104; and Perrin, "Matière et lumière," *Annales de Physique,* 1919, *11*:1–108, substantially unchanged in "Radiation and Chemistry," trans. H. Borns, *Trans. Faraday Soc.,* 1921/2, *17*:546–575. See also Nye, "Chemical Explanation and Physical Dynamics" (cit. n. 39); and M. Christine King and Keith J. Laidler, "Chemical Kinetics and the Radiation Hypothesis," *Archives for History of Exact Sciences,* 1984, *30*:45–86.

[60] See André Job, "Mécanismes chimiques," in *Formes chimiques de transition,* ed. J. Perrin and G. Urbain (Paris: Société d'Editions Scientifiques, 1931), pp. 125–164.

[61] Dissatisfaction with the radiation hypothesis helped revive the collision hypothesis of chemical activation, especially urged by F. A. Lindemann and developed by Cyril Hinshelwood, both at Oxford. See Cyril Hinshelwood, *The Kinetics of Chemical Change in Gaseous Systems,* 2nd ed. (Oxford: Clarendon, 1929); and King and Laidler, "Chemical Kinetics and the Radiation Hypothesis" (cit. n. 59), pp. 69–73.

pedagogy were anathema to Prévost: he told one of his students at her thesis defense in 1958, "Madame, if I have any reproach for you, it is that you know too well the modern theories."[62]

What most chemists outside France found especially valuable in the work of the French school in the 1920s were their contributions in updated classical fields closely related to physics and physical chemistry: the measurements of diamagnetism by Paul Pascal, the studies of absorption spectra by Pauline Ramart-Lucas, and the researches on photochemistry by Alfred Louis Berthould and on colloids by Pierre Girard. In general, as Dominique Pestre has argued, it was in various kinds of spectroscopy, including Raman spectroscopy, that French scientists made steady and significant contributions all throughout the early twentieth century and interwar period.[63]

At first glance, the chauvinistic-touristic dichotomy may not appear to fit by the 1920s, partly because of the breakdown of English relations with German universities. Lowry, Lapworth, and Robinson were wholly trained in England. But the English did continue to travel, now setting off for American universities in response to inquiries from Americans like G. N. Lewis for names of "bright young men" who might want to study abroad.[64]

English chemists probably also burned the midnight oil more frequently than their Ecole Normale colleagues. At least one English chemist, Lowry, not only held to a Protestant work ethic, but preached on Sundays in a Methodist pulpit. At Manchester, Robinson worked in the laboratory in the wee hours of the morning alongside other "nightbirds" like D. L. Chapman and Ida Smedley.[65] Again, comparing the careers of Prévost and Ingold, one of Prévost's protégés commented that, while Prévost's laboratory research in no way approached Ingold's in quantity, it excelled in intellectual depth and critical acumen. Furthermore, Prévost and his colleagues knew how to live a good, full life and did not work interminably in the laboratory like Ingold and his group.[66] These remarks may point to a real difference in style, or idealized style, between English and French chemistry in the late nineteenth and early twentieth centuries, certainly between the Manchester and Paris groups.

French chemistry laboratories did become more oriented toward cooperative research by the 1920s, certainly at the Ecole Normale and at the provincial universities of Nancy, Toulouse, and Lyon.[67] Yet fragmentation of time and talents persisted, especially in the City of Light.

The love of abstract mathematics still was to distinguish the new generation of

[62] I am grateful to Mme Micheline Charpentier-Morize for this anecdote, communicated by letter, 16 Jan. 1991. See also Charles Prévost, "La valence et l'enseignement," *L'Information Scientifique,* 1951, 6:14–18, on p. 16.

[63] See, e.g., the papers and discussions in the Solvay chemistry conferences, 1922–1931, cited in Nye, "Chemical Explanation and Physical Dynamics" (cit. n. 39); and Dominique Pestre, *Physique et physiciens en France, 1918–1940* (Paris: Editions des Archives Contemporains, 1984), pp. 89–90.

[64] G. N. Lewis to F. G. Donnan, 21 March 1912, F. G. Donnan Letters, Box #1 (1906–1913), Archives, University College London.

[65] On French laboratories see Victor Grignard to Albert Ranc, spring 1935, rpt. in Roger Grignard, *Centenaire de la naissance de Victor Grignard, 1871–1971* (Lyon: Audin, 1972), plate xlvii. On the British side see Allsop and Waters, "Lowry" (cit. n. 52), pp. 402–403; and Robert Robinson, *Memoirs* (cit. n. 20), p. 37.

[66] Conversation with Constantin Georgoulis, at Paris, Université de Paris–Jussieu, 11 June 1987.

[67] See Nye, *Science in the Provinces* (cit. n. 31), Chs. 2, 4, 5.

theoretical chemists in France from those in England, if we are to believe remarks in correspondence between the English theoretical chemists C. A. Coulson and H. C. Longuet-Higgins. Coulson and Longuet-Higgins were leaders in developing a wave-mechanical interpretation for the kinds of problems the Manchester School treated qualitatively and pictorially. But they were cautious, lest French scientists develop a theoretical chemistry too abstract and nonphysical in nature. Commenting on a recent paper by a French colleague, Longuet-Higgins gave voice to a difference still perceived to exist in physical-chemical style between English and French theorists: the French paper, he said, was so far removed from reality that "I really feel that when theory becomes as introspective as this, it is time to call a halt."[68]

For the Ecole Normale and Manchester research schools, we can conclude that there were real differences in practitioners' approaches to chemical problems and in their judgments about the features of an acceptable chemical theory. These differences may be characterized as divergences in style that result from formal education, informal apprenticeship, tacit understanding, and emulation of the manners and mores of the *maître* or *Vater* figure. The passing on of such "style" is not accidental. It is enforced by formal lectures and examinations, provision of tools and instruments, institutional rewards, and scientific meetings and conversations.

In the late nineteenth century, following the recognition by England and France of Germany's new economic and military power, English and French scientists consciously gauged strengths and weaknesses of their social institutions and their intellectual cultures against each other and especially against Germany, explicitly defining what they would and would not compromise in English and French traditions as they understood them. Masters and disciples working in institutional groups, research schools, and long-lived traditions consciously reassessed and defined their values and methods, created and recreated their hagiography, and enhanced their reputations and standing in the discipline at large by the claim of perpetuating, or combatting, not a personal, but a national scientific style.

When Charles Prévost referred to the "Anglo-Saxon school" of chemistry and enumerated its weaknesses, the name of his rival Christopher Ingold was the unspoken synonym of "Anglo-Saxon." Identifying Ingold by the term "Anglo-Saxon" carried with it the implicit antinomy of identifying Prévost with "French," thereby creating or reinforcing for Prévost and the research school based at the Ecole Normale Supérieure a greater prestige than it might otherwise have enjoyed. "Prévost's school" thus became the "French school," regardless of rivals to his views and his school within France. Further study of research groups and research schools can help refine the parameters of the word *style* and the circumstances under which a single school, or a network of schools, defines for a time a "national style."

[68] H. C. Longuet-Higgins to C. A. Coulson, 31 May 1950, C. A. Coulson Manuscript Collection, Duke Humfrey's Library, New Bodleian Library, Oxford. I am grateful to Hugh Christopher Longuet-Higgins for permission to quote from his letter. Professor Longuet-Higgins became the second scientist to hold the chair of theoretical chemistry at Cambridge University, succeeding John Lennard-Jones in 1954. After holding the chair of theoretical physics at King's College, Charles Coulson became the first chairholder in theoretical chemistry at Oxford University in 1973.

CASE STUDIES:
LABORATORY SCIENCES

Figure 1. Top left: *Hermann Kolbe in a pen-and-ink drawing of 1880 by Ferdinand Justi, from a photograph of about 1860. Courtesy of Bildarchiv Foto Marburg, Erbengemeinschaft Justi.* Top right: *The Deutsches Haus in Marburg, home of Kolbe's institute during 1851–1865* (photo by A. J. Rocke). Bottom: *The Chemical Institute of the University of Leipzig, about 1908. From* Festschrift zur Feier des 500jährigen Bestehens der Universität Leipzig *(Leipzig: Hirzel, 1909).*

Group Research in German Chemistry: Kolbe's Marburg and Leipzig Institutes

By Alan J. Rocke*

I N THE RESEARCH SCHOOL LITERATURE of the last quarter century, the field of chemistry has not been neglected. The list of subjects hitherto examined, even when confined to nineteenth-century European chemists and excluding physiological chemists and biochemists, includes at least Claude-Louis Berthollet, Thomas Thomson, Justus Liebig, Jean-Baptiste Dumas, Adolf Baeyer, and Emil Fischer.[1] Some justification might therefore be expected for offering another case study in this category, namely, the groups led by the organic chemist Hermann Kolbe at the Universities of Marburg (1851–1865) and Leipzig (1865–1884).

More than a decade ago Gerald Geison noted that sociologists often prefer to examine social networks in emerging specialties as a technique for studying the development of science, whereas historians of science are drawn more to the subject of research schools. He urged the advantages of the latter approach, not least because the study of group research could elucidate the character of such emerging specialties themselves, and conceptual change in general, more effectively than the sociological "network" models.[2] In fact, as Geison also noted, most case studies of research schools by historians have been directed toward the process

* Program in History of Technology and Science, Case Western Reserve University, Cleveland, Ohio 44106.

I gratefully acknowledge grants supporting this research from the National Endowment for the Humanities and the Ohio Board of Regents. For kind assistance and permission to publish from manuscript materials, I thank Vieweg Verlag, Wiesbaden; Mr. and Mrs. Raven Frankland and Professor Colin Russell, Edward Frankland microfilmed papers, Milton Keynes; Handschriftenabteilung, Bayerische Staatsbibliothek, Munich; Sondersammlungen, Deutsches Museum, Munich; Hessisches Staatsarchiv, Marburg; and Universitätsarchiv, Leipzig.

[1] See Maurice Crosland, *The Society of Arcueil: A View of French Science at the Time of Napoleon* (Cambridge, Mass.: Harvard Univ. Press, 1967) (Berthollet); J. B. Morrell, "The Chemist Breeders: The Research Schools of Liebig and Thomas Thomson," *Ambix,* 1972, *19*:1–46; F. L. Holmes, "The Complementarity of Teaching and Research in Liebig's Laboratory," *Osiris,* 1989, *5*:121–164; L. J. Klosterman, "A Research School of Chemistry in the Nineteenth Century: Jean Baptiste Dumas and His Research Students," *Annals of Science,* 1985, *42*:1–80; and Joseph Fruton, *Contrasts in Scientific Style: Research Groups in the Chemical and Biological Sciences* (Philadelphia: American Philosophical Society, 1990), Chs. 2 (Liebig), 4 (Baeyer), 5 (Fischer). The career of W. H. Perkin, Jr., is treated in Morrell's essay in this volume, but it fell mostly in the early twentieth century.

[2] Gerald Geison, "Scientific Change, Emerging Specialties, and Research Schools," *History of Science,* 1981, *19*:20–40.

and character of emerging disciplines, hybrid fields, or the assimilation of revolutionary developments in a discipline.

The cases mentioned above are typical in this regard. Berthollet's group research was conducted in the first generation after Lavoisier and helped to establish a new model for chemicophysical investigation.[3] Thomson was one of the earliest elaborators of chemical atomism, and his research program was designed largely to support this emerging theory. Along with Jacob Berzelius, Liebig and Dumas were founders of the theory and practice of organic chemistry. Baeyer and Fischer represent almost inverse instances, but ones no less relevant to the subject of emerging disciplines. Both men were active until World War I, long after the apogee of classical organic chemistry had been reached; consequently, they can be viewed as representatives of an older generation amidst the rising stars of physical and physical-organic chemistry. It may be further remarked that "research school" subjects in areas other than nineteenth-century European chemistry also appear to have been chosen largely for their relevance to emergent disciplines and communities—examples include Enrico Fermi in nuclear physics, and A. A. Noyes and W. D. Bancroft in American physical chemistry.[4]

Unlike all of these, Kolbe spent his entire career in a well-established discipline, pursuing relatively standard scientific goals by means of widely accepted techniques; indeed, his career nicely brackets the high point of classical organic chemistry of the late nineteenth century. Although there is much yet to be learned from studying bifurcations in the growth of science, it ought not to be forgotten that most scientific investigations are carried out under the aegis of established research traditions. The Kolbe case has some real advantages in this respect, holding promise for a fuller understanding of what Thomas Kuhn calls "normal science."

Kolbe offers a second benefit. Although his thirty-three-year academic career had a certain disciplinary stability, it was almost evenly divided chronologically between two locations; thus it offers an advantageous natural structure for a comparative look at the two research groups he led at different sites and periods. Even more interesting, the transition year for the two periods, 1865, was an eventful one throughout the German Confederation. Bismarck was then scheming to expand Prussian power at the expense of Austria (a development that was soon to lead to the founding of the Empire), and the German states were in the midst of an industrial revolution. In chemistry, 1865 was the year in which August Kekulé proposed his theory of aromatic compounds, which became at once the centerpiece of the structural theory of organic compounds and the scientific key to the understanding of many of the most significant substances used in industry. An increasingly widespread realization that chemical science was relevant for industry was one of several factors that produced an extraordinary increase in the scale and visibility of German academic chemistry. Palatial chemical institutes were

---

[3] In addition to Crosland, *Society of Arcueil* (cit. n. 1), see also Robert Fox, "The Rise and Fall of Laplacian Physics," *Historical Studies in the Physical Sciences,* 1974, *4*:89–136.

[4] See Gerald Holton, "Fermi's Group and the Recapture of Italy's Place in Physics," in his *The Scientific Imagination: Case Studies* (Cambridge: Cambridge Univ. Press, 1978), pp. 155–198; and John Servos, *Physical Chemistry from Ostwald to Pauling: The Making of a Science in America* (Princeton, N.J.: Princeton Univ. Press, 1990).

built by several German states in the course of the 1860s, and enrollments blossomed throughout the country.

Because German chemical science, technology, and education were all in vigorous ferment just at the time Kolbe transferred to Leipzig, comparing his group research in 1851–1865 to that of 1865–1884 illuminates the evolution of the field at a critical time. Furthermore, there are good reasons for distinguishing two Marburg periods, 1851–1858 and 1859–1865, thus making a tripartite analytical structure. In sum, this case examines not a *bifurcation* between disciplines but an *inflection point* within an established discipline, an approach that has not yet been much used.[5]

Finally and most centrally, I will argue that my case highlights certain intrinsic difficulties whenever the "research school" approach is used for studies of conceptual influence and intellectual genealogy, and whenever too exclusive attention is focused on institutional as opposed to cognitive elements. Such problems have been studied in the past, but their severity has perhaps been insufficiently appreciated.

I begin with background describing something of Kolbe's personal life, his scientific education, and indirect mentors; I proceed to devote attention to his career trajectory. I then examine his group research and pedagogy in the two locations and conclude with some general and summary observations.

I. THE EDUCATION OF HERMANN KOLBE

Kolbe was born in 1818 in a small village just outside Göttingen in the Kingdom of Hanover; his father was a Lutheran pastor, his mother the daughter of a professor of anatomy at the nearby university.[6] As a student at Göttingen, in 1841 he became one of Friedrich Wöhler's earliest advanced research students. In the following year Wöhler procured for him a position as assistant to Robert Bunsen at Marburg in Electoral Hesse, and it was there that he earned his doctoral degree. In 1845–1847 Kolbe had a stint as an assistant of Lyon Playfair in London before he was hired as editor by a prominent scientific publisher, Eduard Vieweg in Brunswick. Due chiefly to Bunsen's influence, he entered on an academic career in 1851, when he succeeded his mentor at Marburg. Kolbe thus became *Ordinarius* at the relatively young age of thirty-two, without ever having passed through the usual stages of *Privatdozent* or *Extraordinarius*. His sudden rise was aided by some truly remarkable research he had done in Marburg and London—the "Kolbe electrolysis" reaction, cyanide substitution and hydrolysis, and a total synthesis of acetic acid—in the process isolating, as he thought, several hydrocarbon "radicals."

---

[5] Fruton, *Contrasts in Scientific Styles* (cit. n. 1), distinguished between his protagonists' different sites of activities, but he did not attempt to make such a distinction a basis for analysis. Servos, *Physical Chemistry*, goes much further in examining the evolution of the discipline as a function of place and time, for instance in following Noyes from MIT to Caltech, but the book focuses on the hybrid character of the field as it grew to maturity.

[6] Many biographical and science-historical details in this article are derived from A. J. Rocke, *The Quiet Revolution: Hermann Kolbe and the Science of Organic Chemistry* (Berkeley/Los Angeles: Univ. California Press, in press). See also Hermann Ost, "Hermann Kolbe: Ein Lebensbild," *Westermann illustrierte deutsche Monatshefte,* 1885, *30*:118–133; and Ernst von Meyer, "Zur Erinnerung an Hermann Kolbe," *Journal für Praktische Chemie,* 1885, *138*:417–466.

From his student days on, Kolbe had close ties with all four of the founders of post-Enlightenment German chemistry: Wöhler, Bunsen, Liebig, and Berzelius. Wöhler and Bunsen had been his teachers, and both remained good collegial friends ever after. Liebig was Wöhler's best friend and the dean of German chemists; he was Kolbe's idol and enthusiastic patron, especially in his later years. Berzelius was a formative influence for three of these men; after 1840 he had a troubled relationship with Liebig, but Wöhler, Bunsen, and Kolbe all revered him, and he returned their high regard. Berzelius also dominated in the realm of theory. From a basis in electrochemistry and chemical atomism he had developed a powerful set of theories of chemical composition. Simply put, the Berzelian program consisted in schematically resolving molecular formulas (i.e., molecules) into paired components thought to possess opposite electrical charges; for inorganic compounds these components were often elements or simple constituents such as sulfur trioxide, whereas for organic compounds these were thought to be more complex (often hydrocarbon) radicals. Wöhler and Bunsen—and after them Kolbe—faithfully followed this electrochemical-dualist or "radical" program. Wöhler and Bunsen accepted the Berzelian program without qualms, in large part because of their strong antitheoretical and proexperimentalist biases.

Liebig was different. During the 1830s and 1840s French chemists such as Dumas, Auguste Laurent, and Charles Gerhardt developed an alternative theoretical program by investigating hundreds of novel reactions involving the substitution by chlorine of the hydrogen in organic compounds. These chemists wished to replace electrochemical dualism with a more holistic substitutionist view, where arrangements of atoms within the molecule were at least as important as their identities. This program became known as the "type" theory (or theories). Liebig fought bitterly with the French, but the dialogue led him at least to heterodoxy as regards dualism. Berzelius viewed heterodoxy as heresy, and this was one of the sources of the estrangement between the two men. Partly because of the emotional strain of these disputes, in 1840 Liebig ostentatiously and sincerely— one may question whether successfully—forswore theoretical pursuits for the rest of his life.

As professor in Marburg, Kolbe continued to devote himself to the Berzelian program in organic chemistry, which by that time had suffered some distinct reverses at the hands of the French. He had acquired magnificent training in practical operations by the best teachers of his generation; moreover, unlike his immediate mentors—and following his mentors at one remove, Liebig and Berzelius—he had a passionate interest in theory. As far as pedagogy is concerned, a new model of how to carry out practical instruction in scientific institutes in German universities had been recently created, which Kolbe followed enthusiastically.

This model appeared first in Liebig's Giessen laboratory in the mid to late 1830s, and in Wöhler's and Bunsen's labs in Göttingen and Marburg by around 1840.[7] The earlier pattern had been to offer laboratory instruction to a handful of

[7] For details see, e.g., Holmes, "Liebig's Laboratory" (cit. n. 1); Morrell, "Chemist Breeders" (cit. n. 1); William Coleman and F. L. Holmes, eds., *The Investigative Enterprise: Experimental Physiology in Nineteenth-Century Medicine* (Berkeley/Los Angeles: Univ. California Press, 1988); and Rocke, *Quiet Revolution,* Ch. 1.

elite students on the basis of the institute director's personal patronage. Liebig pioneered the idea of broadly based practica offered not only to professionalizing chemists, but also to students of pharmacy, medicine, technology, agriculture, cameralistics, and even the humanities. New student clienteles were located, and enrollments mushroomed. Such courses now were fully institutionalized, by appearing in the published course lists and carrying a standard fee. Increasingly the new model required new resources of money, space, and manpower, but it also provided many benefits: increased income for the director, a number of skilled hands for performing his research, higher prestige for the universities, and a large supply of superbly trained scientists for state and society.

II. KOLBE AT MARBURG

When Kolbe arrived in Marburg, the once-proud university was undernourished and unhealthy.[8] University, town, and state were all narrow-minded and provincial, and a political crisis in Electoral Hesse had just reached the boiling point. The crisis further eroded the standing of the university—total enrollment declining by 1859 to the shocking level of 216. During these years Kolbe was having his own troubles. He was seriously underpaid, and his institute budget was inadequate. His response was to engage in vitriolic but fruitless battles both with the ministry and with collegial oversight committees. He sank deeper into personal debt, and at the same time his health began to suffer, culminating in a severe rheumatic ailment (in 1857–1858) that made him an invalid for many months. He struggled with depression. Perhaps worst of all, his research program was not thriving, and he was attracting few students.

One of his chief difficulties was that he had thrown in his lot with the "copula" interpretation of organic acids and bases, a Berzelian *pis aller* devised in the late 1830s to accommodate the new evidence and arguments of the type theorists. Kolbe zealously pursued the idea for many years, and it gained a few other temporary adherents—such as A. W. Hofmann and Edward Frankland—but not particularly enthusiastic ones. Hofmann cheerfully abandoned it in 1849 when he discovered that the copula formula for aniline was irremediably inconsistent with some of its reactions, and Frankland offered what he regarded as a definitive refutation of copulas in the same paper in which he enunciated a form of the law of atomic valence (1852). The defections of these two men were particularly worrisome to Kolbe, for they were his two closest collegial friends, and both had been hitherto theoretically "correct," safely within the Berzelian orbit. Wöhler, Bunsen, and Liebig all shunned theory altogether, Berzelius himself had died in 1848, and so Kolbe began to feel isolated in his defense of the true faith.

Worse was to come. In 1850–1852 Alexander Williamson and Charles Gerhardt introduced a series of novel reactions connected with an ingenious argument that excluded (as they claimed) any but type-theoretical explanations. By 1854 it seemed clear that many in the European chemical community agreed. Not only those in the homelands of the "typist" movement, France and England, but

---

[8] On Electoral Hesse and its university see Karl Demandt, *Geschichte des Landes Hessen,* 2d ed. (Kassel: Bärenreiter, 1972); and Christoph Meinel, *Die Chemie an der Universität Marburg seit Beginn des 19. Jahrhunderts* (Marburg: Elwert, 1978).

even German chemists in the heartland of radical theory were converting. Hofmann and (German-educated) Frankland were but the vanguard; a new generation of promising chemists, such as August Kekulé, Emil Erlenmeyer, Lothar Meyer, and Adolf Baeyer, began declaring themselves. Virtually the entire chemical faculty at Giessen became converts shortly after Liebig transferred to Munich (1852): Heinrich Will (Liebig's actual successor), Hermann Kopp, and Adolf Strecker, all fine mid-career chemists. Kolbe continued to resist, but his arguments became ever weaker, even in his own estimation. The pressure brought by collegial friends and by a mass of new evidence for the type theory ultimately became irresistible, and Kolbe finally capitulated.

In conjunction with Frankland, Kolbe developed his version of the type theory from 1857 to 1859, applying it particularly to carbon and incorporating his friend's valence law. The heart of the "carbonic acid theory," as he called it, was to view all organic molecules as derived from substitution in carbonic acid; in a passage written late in 1858 and published early in 1859, he explicitly declared carbon to be *vieratomig,* or tetravalent.[9] Kolbe was aware that others were also applying type and valence ideas to carbon. Above all, his principal rival Kekulé had already published his "theory of atomicity of the elements" in 1857–1858, a set of ideas that soon thereafter became known as "structure theory." Kekulé's and Kolbe's theories were similar, but they were not identical. Kolbe sought to provide a certain electrochemical-radical character in his theory, hence he was reluctant to aver that atoms could form bonds to each other—and certainly not carbon atoms to other carbon atoms, the heart of Kekulé's theory. Rather, it was *radicals* that were the active entities, and they must cohere in *some* sort of electrochemical fashion. Moreover, Kolbe affirmed that there was a strict hierarchy of constituent radicals in every compound, only one of them being the molecule's "fundamental radical." This view seems quite different from the directed non-electrochemical valence bonds of the structuralists, but in most cases structural and Kolbean formulas could be mutually translated with little loss of operational meaning. After 1860, virtually all observers—students, friends, and foes of Kolbe alike—considered him to be a structural chemist. Kolbe himself turned apoplectic at any such suggestion.

Equipped with what proved to be a powerful new theory, he applied it energetically after 1858 to a wide range of problems in organic chemistry—especially elucidating the "constitutions" of compounds and synthesizing natural products and novel organic substances. His most signal successes (in 1859) were a prediction of the existence of "pseudoalcohols" (what shortly became known as secondary and tertiary alcohols), and an interpretation, backed by new experiments, of the constitutions of malic, tartaric, and succinic acids. The predicted alcohols were soon synthesized by others, and no less an authority than Liebig proclaimed Kolbe's constitutional ideas on the acids as "triumphs" and "gems," even though Liebig himself had recently defended a different view.[10]

---

[9] Hermann Kolbe, *Ausführliches Lehrbuch der organischen Chemie,* Vol. 1 (Brunswick: Vieweg, 1854–1860), p. 740.

[10] Kolbe's "carbonic acid theory," with these predictions and interpretations in them, appeared first in the fascicles of his textbook (*ibid.*), but most accessibly and cogently in his famous article "Über den natürlichen Zusammenhang der organischen mit den unorganischen Verbindungen," *Annalen der Chemie und Pharmacie,* 1860, *113*:293–332.

These activities were but the tip of the iceberg. The field of organic chemistry quite suddenly became at once hectic, fruitful, and competitive—both exhilarating and a bit bewildering for participants. Just to use one numerical measure, in 1860 there were about three thousand well-characterized substances in the chemical literature; this number had grown steadily during the preceding several decades, with a consistent doubling period of about twenty years. But around 1860 the trend suddenly accelerated, so that the doubling time decreased to about nine years. It has remained so ever since.[11] The difference was valence and structure theory, which provided powerful tools aiding investigation and synthesis of organic compounds. Kolbe and his students rode high in the water in these years, putting out papers at a great clip. The same was true for Kekulé, Erlenmeyer, Baeyer, the Russian A. M. Butlerov, and other structuralists.

Kolbe was, however, senior to all of these leading chemists, not only in the sense of being somewhat older, but also in that he had already made a name for himself in the 1840s. He was also the only one of them to maintain substantive theoretical connections with the earlier chemical traditions. With the single exception of Hofmann, whom most everyone considered to have inherited Liebig's mantle and who was already regarded as the rising dean of German chemists, Kolbe thus became known in the early 1860s as the most eminent of the younger generation of chemists. In a real sense he was the father of resolved molecular formulas and the founder of synthetic organic chemistry.

III. KOLBE AT LEIPZIG

Eminence translates into demand for services. Hofmann was particularly in demand, holding (or reserving for himself) from 1863 to 1867 no fewer than four posts at three different universities (the Royal College of Chemistry, Bonn, and two successorships at Berlin). Yet another position came free at Leipzig in the spring of 1865. Hofmann was triply out of reach, and so the call came for Kolbe, who promptly accepted. When in 1867 Hofmann finally released the Bonn chair, Kolbe was again called, but declined; Kekulé then accepted the Bonn offer.

Leipzig was a large old university in the heart of vigorously industrializing Saxony, but it had fallen into neglect and decay.[12] An aggressive minister of culture named Paul von Falkenstein improved the university's fortunes during the 1860s in a fashion that can only be described as spectacular. In the face of local resistance he called the best scholars available, subdividing positions into new specialties when necessary and paying whatever salaries were required. Given the academic politics of the day, each new call in the scientific and medical disciplines meant the construction of an elaborate new building to serve as the new professor's institute, and Falkenstein, his sovereign, and their legislature spared no expense.

As late as 1861 in Marburg Kolbe was earning only 700 thalers; he was hired in

[11] Otto Krätz, "Der Chemiker in den Gründerjahren," in Der Chemiker im Wandel der Zeiten, ed. E. Schmauderer (Weinheim: Verlag Chemie, 1973), pp. 259–284, on pp. 269–270. Krätz gives only aggregate numbers, from which I have calculated the stated doubling times.

[12] Franz Eulenburg, Die Entwicklung der Universität Leipzig in den letzten hundert Jahren (Leipzig: Hirzel, 1909); and Rektor und Senat der Universität Leipzig, ed., Festschrift zur Feier des 500 jährigen Bestehens der Universität Leipzig (Leipzig: Hirzel, 1909).

Figure 2. *Kolbe's lecture theater at Leipzig, 1872. Courtesy of the Deutsches Museum, Munich.*

Leipzig at 2,000. When construction was completed in 1868, Kolbe acquired the best-designed, most modern, and by far the largest laboratory in Germany. Hofmann's palatial new labs at Bonn and Berlin could accommodate 60–70 *Praktikanten* each; Kolbe could accept 130 at a time. More students also meant more income; instead of around 600 thalers per year in student fees, as in Marburg, in Leipzig he could count on nearly ten times as much. As he had at Marburg, Kolbe proved to be an attractive lecturer and laboratory instructor in Leipzig, and soon even the huge capacity of his new lab was strained beyond its limits. Mostly for political reasons, in 1872–1874 Kolbe accepted 170 *Praktikanten* per semester—still far fewer than attempted to register!—but thereafter returned to the nominal capacity. Kolbe's stock soared, both locally and beyond. He was made *Geheimrat,* and nearly received the call to succeed Liebig at Munich in 1874.

Kolbe had certainly come up in the world, and in a hurry. What factors produced this fabulous success story? Kolbe himself ascribed it principally to his success as a teacher and scientist, and to some degree he was correct. However, other factors were also important. All the universities of the German Empire were booming in the early 1870s, and none more so than the University of Leipzig; between 1871 and 1873 alone its enrollment increased by nearly half, to close to three thousand students. After 1868 Kolbe had the largest and most modern chemical institute in Germany to serve as a draw. Even so, other institute directors at major universities were experiencing similar growth. Moreover, even in the era of one *Ordinarius* per institute Kolbe had a degree of monopoly on the teaching of chemistry in Leipzig that was rare in Germany.

Figure 3. *Kolbe's teaching laboratory at Leipzig, 1872. Courtesy of the Deutsches Museum, Munich.*

In general Kolbe's research projects in Leipzig represent a smooth continuation of those in Marburg: examples include the prediction and production of novel aliphatic isomers, especially secondary and tertiary alcohols and acids, and the synthesis of natural products. More prominent in Leipzig were experimental investigations connected with theoretical issues involving aromatic compounds, for Kolbe was much concerned after 1866 to weaken or disprove Kekulé's popular benzene theory—the "show horse" of structure theory, as Kolbe appropriately put it. (Such attempts at falsifying Kekulé's brainchild were spectacularly unsuccessful.) One important field largely new to Leipzig and forming the topic of dozens of his students' dissertation projects was organosulfur compounds. Included in this group were studies of aliphatic and aromatic sulfides, sulfates, sulfonic acids and esters, sulfinic acids and esters, and other organic sulfonyl and sulfoxyl compounds. In the process scores of new substances were discovered, including the first members of entirely new classes of compounds, such as the dialkyl sulfones, dialkyl sulfoxides, and nitroalkyls. One of the leading ideas motivating this research was Kolbe's conviction, *contra* Kekulé, that the valence of an element was not constant, but rather could vary—and indeed, the novel organosulfur compounds named include substances containing divalent, tetravalent, and hexavalent sulfur. The last field that deserves mention is a long series of investigations after 1873 on the preservative and antiseptic properties of salicylic acid.

Nearly all of this large body of research was scientifically important; however, little of the work done after around 1870 opened up new, theoretically significant opportunities. The most exciting topics elsewhere in Germany—positional isomerism in the aromatic field, synthetic methods, structure determinations, and, after 1876, stereochemistry—all were outgrowths of the classical structure theory that Kolbe abhorred. Simply stated, in the 1840s and 1850s Kolbe had been a principal founder of the investigation of "constitutions" of organic compounds; in the 1860s he was easily able to keep pace with the leaders of the field and to make substantial contributions; but after 1870 the contemporary significance of his work declined dramatically.

This decline was partly connected with Kolbe's personal passions. From his student days Kolbe had an intense visceral disgust for excessive use of hypothesis, and he regarded the most outrageous sinners in this regard to be members of the French school and others who thought they could specify spatial arrangements of atoms. Structural chemistry developed from—and in—precisely this direction, with the enormously popular fields of positional aromatic isomerism and, slightly later, stereochemistry. A return of ill health, the deaths of close friends and family members, the return of serious depression now connected with clear signs of paranoia and virulent xenophobia, the war with France, and the failures of many of his scientific programs turned Kolbe after about 1870 into a bitter and vindictive man. Even his close friends began to describe him as "monomaniacal" and "peculiar." Equipped with his own proprietary journal, the *Journal für Praktische Chemie,* Kolbe spent his days pursuing a holy crusade for the truth (as he saw it), or venomous and spiteful vituperation (as most of the collegial community considered it). By the time of his death in 1884, he had succeeded only in alienating himself from nearly everyone in the community.

IV. PEDAGOGY

Kolbe's teaching was from the first very successful. His letters suggest that he put a great deal of energy and thought into his lectures and practica, and the students responded favorably. Jacob Volhard, a Giessen Ph.D. who worked with Kolbe in summer semester 1862, described the Marburg lab as an ordinary-sized low-ceilinged room (it was about 25 by 35 feet), crammed with twelve to fifteen workers, each with his own charcoal fire as well as alcohol lamp. It was intolerably hot, crowded, and confined; usually filled with noxious vapors; and possessed no ventilation, running water, or gas. And yet, Volhard added, he and all his former labmates looked back on their Marburg years with nothing but fondness.[13]

Kolbe was an enthusiastic follower of Liebig's style of instruction, but faulted Liebig for not going far enough and not remaining completely consistent with his guiding ideas.[14] He agreed with Liebig that chemistry must be taught in the same

[13] D. Vorländer, "Jacob Volhard," *Berichte der Deutschen Chemischen Gesellschaft,* 1912, *45*:1855–1902, on p. 1865.
[14] The following discussion is based on Kolbe's report (8 Oct. 1863) to the Marburg University Senate on the activities of the Chemical Institute, *305a.* A IV, c. ε 1, Nr. 12, Hessisches Staatsarchiv, Marburg (a transcript is printed in Meinel, *Chemie an der Universität Marburg* [cit. n. 8], pp. 435–438, and Kolbe revised the report to form part of the introduction to his *Das chemische Laboratorium der Universität Marburg* [Brunswick: Vieweg, 1865], pp. 17–28); on Kolbe's final report to his ministry, 5 July 1865, 305n., Nr. 1045, *ibid.* (transcript printed in Meinel, pp. 438–444); on Hermann Kolbe, *Das chemische Laboratorium der Universität Leipzig* (Brunswick: Vieweg, 1872), pp. xxxiv–xlvi; on Ernst von Meyer, *Lebenserinnerungen* (n.p., n.d., ca. 1918), pp. 27–30; and on Ost, "Kolbe" (cit. n. 6), pp. 128–129.

way to all students, whether future professionals or students of ancillary fields; that it must be theoretically based but also firmly grounded in experimental practice; that the overall goal must be to teach the student to "think chemically"; that the laboratory must be as much a pedagogical as a research institution; and that advanced students must be considered vital scholarly collaborators. No lab manual was employed, however, as at Giessen. Instead, close personal supervision demonstrated to each *Praktikant* the methods of careful observing, recording, and understanding of every reaction, by which he was gradually led essentially to write his own manual. Kolbe and his assistant would carefully examine and critique each student's annotations, allowing nothing to remain unclear. The goal was total immersion in phenomena, so that the student truly absorbed into mind and soul the essence of every observation and operation. Like Bunsen (and unlike Liebig), Kolbe spent much time with beginners, letting his assistants spend more of their time with advanced students.

Kolbe thought this combination of intensive personal supervision and self-instruction was twice as efficient as the Giessen pattern, so that by the middle of the second semester of lab work most students were ready for the next stage. After about one semester of quantitative analysis, the student was put to work for a few weeks making organic preparations. Finally, the student was taught organic elemental analysis. At this point, typically after three semesters, the student would be assigned the task of studying a classic chemical paper chosen by the professor and directed to repeat the work or to make a small variation in it. Kolbe thought that this was the best way to induct students into proper scientific method and writing as practiced by the masters of the field. Kolbe would then suggest a small original project, often motivated by his current theoretical interests, that the student could work through essentially independently. From this point on the student was invited to make his own way through the scientific thickets. Depending on a variety of circumstances, Kolbe might or might not continue to direct the work of the student closely. But in any case, having passed through a two-year chemical novitiate, the student was regarded and treated as an independent worker and was invited to spend around forty-five hours per week in the lab rather than eight. Any publications of the student's work appeared under the student's own name, or as a collaboration if warranted.

Kolbe was proud of the excellent esprit de corps and exceptional diligence of his students, a spirit that was in evidence in both Marburg and Leipzig. This seems not to have been an idle boast. Concerning the late 1860s Henry Armstrong reminisced:

> Kolbe's laboratory, in those days, afforded wonderful opportunities. About a dozen of us were doing advanced work, in preparation for the Degree—seeking independence. Each had his *Arbeit*—his definite problem—in view, as his chief aim in life: we were all proud of being called on to show that we could do something. This was the distinctive feature of the German system. At most two or three had themes from the Professor—the rest were carrying out ideas of their own; the work was, therefore, varied. Whatever suggestion we made to Kolbe, he never discouraged us; his habit was to grasp the lapels of his coat, then to reply: "Try it, try it." We disputed with him constantly before the blackboard, often for hours together, nearly always taking exception to his theoretical views—but without his being offended. And we constantly

compared notes together. Each of us, therefore, was interested in the solution of a whole series of problems.[15]

Volhard's report from 1862, cited above, is consistent with this picture. Similarly, V. V. Markovnikov, who studied with Kolbe in Leipzig in 1866–1867, wrote to A. M. Butlerov, then professor at Kazan: "Kolbe was especially attentive to all the workers, and, contrary to expectations, he did not behave like a commanding general at all. On the contrary, he was very glad to discuss and argue, and I have already succeeded several times in locking horns with him. He himself often approached and asked me how one should understand formulas which were not written by his method."[16]

Kolbe emphasized: "In my laboratory I allow everyone who maintains his chemical convictions—which I respect—to continue working in his own direction, and am pleased whenever he obtains the expected results."[17] However intolerant Kolbe may have been to the differing views of colleagues at other universities, he was always indulgent and broad-minded with his own students. Without exception, his students loved him for it.

V. THE MARBURG RESEARCH GROUP

Given one assistantship by the University of Marburg, Kolbe initially filled the position with little-known chemists; later there followed the much more capable Rudolf Schmitt (1857–1861) and Eduard Lautemann (1861–1865). *Praktikanten* and guest workers from the Marburg period included Adolph Claus, Wilhelm Gerland, Carl Graebe, Peter Griess, Ludwig Mond, and Jacob Volhard; foreign students included Frederick Guthrie, Alexander Crum Brown, E. T. Chapman, N. A. Menshutkin, Maxwell Simpson, and A. M. Zaitsev. The paucity of students in the early and mid 1850s was a source of frustration for Kolbe, who had more ideas for research projects than he had skilled hands available to him. This problem was solved after 1858, when conditions improved markedly, enrollments rose, and eventually Kolbe was given permission to expand the laboratory.[18]

Kolbe's career had an uncharacteristically sharp inflection at the year 1858. Let us look first at some rough-and-ready numerical measures of the size and research productivity of the Marburg research group, comparing Kolbe's first seven and a half years (from his arrival in May 1851 until late 1858) with the following year and a half (from the beginning of 1859 until the middle of 1860) (see Table 1). To provide further reference points for comparison we also use data from Bunsen's lab at Marburg during the five years before Kolbe's arrival (1846–1851) and average enrollment figures for the university as a whole.

[15] Harold Hartley, quoting Armstrong without reference, in *Studies in the History of Chemistry* (Oxford: Clarendon Press, 1971), pp. 219–220.

[16] A. F. Plate, G. V. Bykov, and M. S. Eventova, *Vladimir Vasil'evich Markovnikov: Ocherk zhizni i deiatel'nosti, 1837–1904* (Moscow: Izdatel'stvo Akademii Nauk SSSR, 1962), p. 30, quoting from a letter from Markovnikov to Butlerov, no date cited. The translation is that of H. M. Leicester, "Controversies on Chemical Structure from 1860 to 1870," in *Kekulé Centennial,* ed. O. T. Benfey (Washington, D. C.: American Chemical Society, 1966), pp. 13–23, on p. 21.

[17] Kolbe, *Das chemische Laboratorium Leipzig* (cit. n. 14), p. xlviii.

[18] Meinel, *Chemie an der Universität Marburg* (cit. n. 8), pp. 83–119, 470–472, 480–486, 524–528.

Table 1. Research Productivity in Marburg

	Bunsen, 1846–1851	Kolbe, 1851–1858	Kolbe, 1859–1860
Average semester enrollments			
Of *Praktikanten* in lab	22	14	12
In chemistry lecture course	25	21	13
Of chemistry majors	13	4	0–1
At university overall	263	243	233
Papers published			
By lab director	10	4	6
Collaboratively	1	0	4
By students alone	16	10	9
Total	27	14	19
Aggregate intensive measures			
Papers per year by lab director	2	0.5	4
Total papers per year	5.4	1.9	12
Papers per *Praktikant* per year[a]	0.25	0.14	1

NOTE: Data for this table are taken from the numbers and information in Christoph Meinel, *Die Chemie an der Universität Marburg seit Beginn des 19. Jahrhunderts* (Marburg: Elwert, 1978), pp. 471–472, 522–525.

[a] This figure is based not on the number of papers authored by *Praktikanten,* but rather on the total number of papers per year produced by the institute as a whole divided by the average number of *Praktikanten.* This manner of accounting sidesteps the tricky question of authorship to give a rough intensive measure of research productivity for the entire group.

During the fourteen years examined here there was a gradual decline both in the prestige of the university and in its overall enrollment; nonetheless, compared to the other changes we are measuring, the decline is small enough—on the order of 10 percent—that this factor may be neglected. The sizes of classes and numbers of majors indicate that throughout the entire period the popularity of chemistry at Marburg declined. Factors independent of intrinsic merit operating at least in the 1850s must have been Kolbe's relative youth and lack of reputation in comparison with his predecessor.

As far as research productivity is concerned, Bunsen's later years in Marburg were quite successful, considering the time and place. Such was not the case with Kolbe's early Marburg period. In rough terms, he published personally a fourth as often as Bunsen had; his lab as a whole produced a third the annual number of papers; and even after his smaller number of *Praktikanten* is taken into account, per capita productivity was half Bunsen's. His own research and that of his school was, to put it bluntly, moribund.

This situation was transformed starting at the end of 1858. In the ensuing eighteen months his personal productivity was eight times what it had been, and that of his research group increased by a factor of seven. The transition between these periods was razor-sharp. In the fall of 1858 his lab was suddenly bursting with activity (if not with students), and in the last week of that year and the first of 1859 he wrote or edited seven contributions by him or his students or both; they were published as a group in the March 1859 number of the *Annalen der Chemie und*

Pharmacie.[19] In the course of 1859 he wrote five new papers solo and one with a student and edited three more by students. Three additional papers came out of his lab by the middle of 1860. Although I have not tabulated the data for the next five years—his last in Marburg—Kolbe managed to maintain close to the same impressive level of productivity of this remarkable eighteen-month period. This activity made him internationally famous; it led to his calls to Leipzig in 1865 and to Bonn in 1867 (the latter refused).

Even superficial examination of the numbers in the table above suffices to show that the explosive transformation was not facilitated by any increase in numbers of students at his disposal; in fact, the numbers continued to decline. He reached simultaneously a low point in numbers and a high point in excitement in March 1860, when he wrote to Eduard Vieweg that his carbonic acid theory had opened inviting prospects of discovery: "If only I had more hands," he cried, "that is, more capable students, who could help me to exploit this treasure trove before others use it." That semester he had but six auditors in his lecture, thirteen at various levels of competence in his practicum, and no chemistry majors at all. Seven months later he wrote Vieweg again, using identical phrases. He said he had been trying to exploit his theory for almost two years, with the help of some very good students, but distressingly small numbers of them.[20]

Were these students, admittedly smaller in number, nonetheless sufficiently better in *quality* than those he had in his early years in Marburg to explain the great break? Let us attempt at least an impressionistic qualitative comparison of the two periods.[21] During the early Marburg period (1815–1858) he taught one man who would later be regarded as a master chemist, Peter Griess (1829–1888), and three others who could be fairly described as good journeyman chemists, Wilhelm Gerland (ca. 1829–ca. 1905), the Englishman Frederick Guthrie (1833–1886), and the Irishman Maxwell Simpson (1815–1902). For two semesters in 1855/56 the future industrialist Ludwig Mond (1839–1909) studied in Kolbe's classroom and laboratory, but he was only sixteen at the time and left no traces in publications or in Kolbe's correspondence. It is probable that his subsequent study with Bunsen at Heidelberg had greater influence on him. During the period of Kolbe's sudden burst of activity in 1859–1860 he had a very capable young man in his lab who later made a successful academic career at the Dresden Technische Hochschule, Rudolf Schmitt (1830–1898). Another worker, quite productive but probably in the "journeyman" category, was Eduard Lautemann, about whom little is known. Adolf Claus (1840–1900), later a prominent structuralist, studied with Kolbe from 1858 and worked in the lab in 1859/60 before transferring to Göttingen; he was a tyro at the time and there is no evidence that he did any significant research at Marburg. Since the second period is much shorter than the first, an unequivocal ranking of the quality of the cast of charac-

[19] Hermann Kolbe to Eduard Vieweg, 24, 29 Dec. 1858, 5 Jan. 1859, letters 145, 146, 147, Kolbe file, 311K, Vieweg Verlag archive, Wiesbaden (hereafter **311K, Vieweg archive**); and *Annalen Chem. Pharm.,* 1859, *109*:257–304.

[20] Kolbe to Vieweg, 15 March 18[60] (incorrectly dated to 1856), 16 Oct. 1860, letters 116, 160, 311K, Vieweg archive; and Meinel, *Chemie an der Universität Marburg* (cit. n. 8), p. 472.

[21] The following information is based on a variety of direct and indirect sources, including Kolbe correspondence, publications, standard biographical reference works, and records in the Hessisches Staatsarchiv (esp. 305a. A IV, b. 2, Nr. 65 and 68; 305a. II Nr. 11; and acc. 1902/8).

ters before and after 1858 is difficult, but on the whole Kolbe had no better student material to work with in 1859–1860 than he did before this time, and as we have seen, he had fewer of them. In sum, we cannot explain the change by looking at the students.

Another candidate explanation for the transformation is the influence of external events. I have mentioned the illness that plagued Kolbe during virtually all of 1857 and the first half of 1858. During this period Kolbe's frustration was intensified by his physical inability, after he had written a short prospectus of his carbonic acid theory in December 1856, to substantiate it by experimental efforts. A mineral-water cure at Wiesbaden in late spring 1858 made him vigorous and healthy again; his return to Marburg on 16 June marks the precise point when he began to generate a prolific research program. Before 1857 he had been reasonably healthy, but a number of other problems had tended to interfere with his scientific productivity: courtship, marriage, and founding a family; money troubles; rancorous collegial disputes; and efforts to make as rapid progress as possible on his voluminous textbook and other writing projects.

But external events cannot provide anything approaching a full explanation. After 1858, as before, he was much occupied with his textbook, which was still far from complete, and with disputes with colleagues and acquaintances. Until August 1861 he was still making the same miserable salary he had accepted in 1851, and ministerial support for his laboratory continued to be so miserly that in the fall of 1860 he had to spend his own money to support it. His health, although improved, was still not good, and he continued to be afflicted by at least annual attacks of severe rheumatism, as well as regular influenzas and grippes. His mental health was also not good after 1858; throughout 1860 and 1861, for instance, he complained to Vieweg of an irritated nervous condition and deep depressions, and his letters suggest symptoms of a persecution complex and paranoia.[22] In August 1861 his wife suffered an attack of typhus, and her life hung in the balance for the better part of a year. She had another infection in 1865 that threatened her life for several months.

There is also strong presumptive evidence that publications as late as the middle of 1858 by Kekulé, Charles Adolphe Wurtz, and others influenced the formulation of the definitive version of his theory in that year. One might even conjecture that the medically enforced idleness in Wiesbaden of May–June 1858, complained of bitterly in a letter to Vieweg,[23] gave Kolbe the time to read and ponder the recent literature in a more relaxed fashion than would otherwise have been possible.

I have gone through this examination of candidate causes for the great break in order to support the thesis that the most obvious explanation for the change, the acquisition by 1858 of an extremely powerful theory that was absent before this time, stands virtually alone in importance. The difficulties with which Kolbe had to contend were as great during the years just after 1858 as before this time. But

[22] Kolbe to Vieweg, 15, 24 Oct. 1859, 3, 9 April, 16, 22 Oct. 1860, 8, 15 July 1861, letters 152, 153, 156, 157, 160, 161, 170, 172, 311K, Vieweg archive; and Kolbe to Liebig, 16 April 1860, Liebigiana IIB, Kolbe letter 5, Bayerische Staatsbibliothek, Munich.
[23] Kolbe to Vieweg, 29 May 1858, letter 138, 311K, Vieweg archive.

he had the principal prerequisite for productive research—a good new theory—
and that made all the difference.

This new research activity eventually exerted a very positive effect on Kolbe's
enrollments. From an average of twelve students per semester in Kolbe's practica
of 1859/60, the numbers increased to an average of twenty-two during the years
1860–1865; average attendance at lectures increased in the same period from
thirteen to nineteen; and chemistry majors increased from almost none to around
nine per semester. During this time the average total student enrollment at
Marburg increased only about 2 percent.[24] These changes came none too soon for
Kolbe. Despite his pleasure in his scientific success, Kolbe thought that given the
political situation and the reputation of the despised prime minister H. D.
Hassenpflug, no one wanted to come to Marburg. Foreign students, the real mark
of success, were only rarely present.[25]

If Kolbe's great break as far as research is concerned occurred in 1858–1860,
the analogous break as far as students are concerned came in summer semester
1862. Classroom enrollment and total numbers of *Praktikanten* were still about
the same, but now he had five real chemistry majors as well as a number of advanced workers in the lab, including several with the doctorate. In addition to
Schmitt and Lautemann, there were present Bunsen's former student Carl
Graebe (1841–1927), who stayed just that one semester and never officially ma-
triculated; Jacob Volhard (1834–1910), a former student of Will and Kopp at
Giessen, who had served as assistant successively to Bunsen, Liebig, and
Hofmann before his arrival in Marburg; and the Scots chemist Alexander Crum
Brown (1838–1922), who had studied with the English Liebigians William
Gregory at Edinburgh and Lyon Playfair at London, but who had also been
strongly even if indirectly influenced by Frankland, Kekulé, and Wurtz.

Kolbe also began to attract a steady stream of Russian chemists. The first to
come, once more in summer 1862, was Konstantin Zaitsev (or in German trans-
literation, Saytzeff); the following semester he was joined by his subsequently far
more famous brother Aleksandr Mikhailovich Zaitsev (1841–1910). In spring
1863 three new Russians arrived, and in the following year came three more; in
Kolbe's last semester in Marburg Nikolai Aleksandrovich Menshutkin (1842–
1907) studied with him. Butlerov, then at Kazan, where many of these newcomers
had studied, must have advised several of them to travel to Marburg for foreign
education.[26]

We can follow the rise in Kolbe's fortunes by following his increasingly proud
reports to his good friends Vieweg and Frankland. In winter semester 1862/63
there were eighteen *Praktikanten,* and in the following semester twenty. In summer semester 1864 thirteen of the eighteen *Praktikanten* came from outside

---

[24] These numbers are calculated from data given in Meinel, *Chemie an der Universität Marburg*
(cit. n. 8), p. 472.

[25] Kolbe to Vieweg, 31 Dec. 1860, letter 164, 311K, Vieweg archive. He reported the presence of
only one foreigner that semester, a Dane. The previous six semesters he had not had a single non-
German foreigner.

[26] S. N. Vinogradov, "Chemistry at Kazan University in the Nineteenth Century: A Case History
of Intellectual Lineage," *Isis,* 1965, *56*:168–173; and B. Menshutkin, "N. A. Menshutkin," *Ber.
Deutschen Chem. Gesell.,* 1907, *40*:5087–5098. The Russian names were gathered from the university's *Matrikel* (305a. II, Nr. 11, Hessisches Staatsarchiv), and then transformed from German into
standard Anglo-American transliterations.

Kurhessen. In the fall of 1864 the overall number jumped to twenty-nine, which, together with a few unmatriculated advanced workers, exceeded the capacity of the lab. Moreover, ever larger numbers of foreign Germans—Prussians, Saxons, Bavarians, and so on—were enrolling. Even non-German foreigners such as the nine Russians mentioned, three Englishmen, two Scotsmen, two Swiss, and two Americans enrolled during Kolbe's last two Marburg years. One of the Americans was Charles W. Eliot (1834–1926), who attended Kolbe's practicum in winter semester 1864/65; four years after that he became the president of Harvard University.[27] One of the Englishmen was E. T. Chapman, who later published some excellent research in organic chemistry before his untimely death in 1872. Most of the foreigners at the entire university, Kolbe bragged in one letter, were his students, and the university's matriculation registry bears out the boast.[28]

The names of most of Kolbe's *Praktikanten* during his fourteen years in Electoral Hesse are preserved in the Hessisches Staatsarchiv in Marburg; they number 216, but a few gaps in the records suggest that the total number was about 240. Few of these students, however, intended chemistry as a career, produced any respectable research, or materially assisted Kolbe in his work. How many can be considered members of Kolbe's Marburg research group? The widest definition would include the union set of (1) all who published at least one paper from the lab, whether or not they took a degree; (2) all who received a Ph.D. under Kolbe, whether or not they published; (3) all assistants, *Privatdozenten,* and postdoctoral guests, whether or not they published; and (4) all who were mentioned as having assisted in any published paper. According to these criteria, twenty-eight individuals can be counted as constituting Kolbe's Marburg research group, of whom eighteen actually received a doctoral degree from him. Many of these students have been mentioned above.

By the early 1860s Kolbe had earned a remarkable international reputation. A knowledgeable anonymous commentator writing in the *Westminster Review* in 1866 thought that "the Marburg laboratory has played a very considerable part in the chemical history of the last seven years," and referred to Kolbe as "one of the few chemists who have succeeded in forming a school." Kolbe's pupils—he named Lautemann, Griess, Guthrie, and Carl Ulrich—were, he thought, "distinguished for a certain kind of originality, and for great practical skill." Moreover, the writer regarded Kolbe as, next to Liebig, "the most successful chemical teacher in Germany."[29]

The one thing Kolbe still lacked was an adequate physical facility. In 1862 he was still working in essentially the same laboratory that he had inherited from Bunsen, who had had it constructed over twenty years earlier; Kolbe hated it, referring to it as a "junk box" (*Rumpelkasten*). He suffered regularly from breathing

[27] Henry James, *Charles W. Eliot: President of Harvard University,* 2 vols. (Boston: Houghton Mifflin, 1930), Vol. I, pp. 135–137, 145–147. I thank Dr. Jun Fudano for this reference; as far as I could determine, Eliot's name does not appear anywhere in the archives of Leipzig University.

[28] Kolbe to Vieweg, 9 Nov. 1863, 22 June, 6 Nov. 1864, letters 197, 206, 211, 311K, Vieweg archive; Kolbe to Edward Frankland, [ca. 27 Oct. 1864], 12 Nov. 1864, microfilm frames 01.04.84, 01.04.89, Edward Frankland papers, Milton Keynes; and 305a. II, Nr. 11, Hessisches Staatsarchiv.

[29] Untitled anonymous review of Kolbe, *Das chemische Laboratorium Marburg* (cit. n. 14), in *Westminster Review,* 1866, *29*:548–549.

the fumes—hydrogen cyanide was a common reagent—and considered the lack of ventilation to be positively dangerous, with good reason.[30]

But Kolbe's sudden success in research dramatically increased his local power and leverage, and in May 1863 his constant requests for a renovated lab were finally granted by the Hessian ministry.[31] The laboratory space was completed astonishingly quickly, by the beginning of the next term (11 November 1863). Kolbe was immoderately proud of his new lab. It was not just a good, it was an "elegantly outfitted laboratory," somewhat smaller but even better equipped than Bunsen's in Heidelberg, and very similar to that in Göttingen. He reported to Vieweg that the gas burners, both at the bench and overhead, allowed him and his students to work about twice as fast as was previously possible; to his administration he predicted a "new era" in the history of the chemical institute.

This new era, at least under Kolbe's aegis, was of short duration. Less than two years later he exchanged Marburg for Leipzig.

VI. THE LEIPZIG RESEARCH GROUP

Kolbe's tenure at Leipzig lasted roughly as long as that at Marburg, but began, as we saw in Section III, with considerably better support. There are other differences as well, not all of them expected. As we did for the Marburg period, let us begin our examination with some numerical measures of research productivity, using the standard unit of productivity—the published paper—and this time taking data across Kolbe's entire career (see Table 2).

Some patterns are apparent. In the early Marburg period—before acquisition of the "carbonic acid theory"—Kolbe's research productivity was low, as was that of his students. The high point of Kolbe's career came during the 1860s, when he was publishing around three good papers per year and his group around ten per year. This overall level of productivity roughly doubled after the great surge in enrollment in the early 1870s, so that he began to publish half a dozen or more solo papers per year, and his group around twenty per year. However, this late period was not as productive as might first appear. For one thing, he had far more students with which to work—five to ten times as many as in Marburg—so that in this light a doubling of total yield appears modest, even disappointing. Moreover, the great majority of his own publications (especially after 1875) were polemical critiques or short notes with no experimental results.

How does this overall productivity compare to that of Kolbe's contemporaries and near contemporaries? His numbers were meager compared to those of Liebig or Wöhler a half generation earlier, to Hofmann in his generation, or to Baeyer a half generation later, each of whom had several hundred personal and collaborative papers; Baeyer's research group at Munich alone is said to have published over 1,600 papers.[32] On the other hand, Kekulé himself, certainly the most

[30] Kolbe to Vieweg, 30 June, 9 Nov. 1863, letters 192, 197, 311K, Vieweg archive; and Kolbe, *Das chemische Laboratorium Marburg* (cit. n. 14), pp. 8–9.

[31] Information in this paragraph is based on Meinel, *Chemie an der Universität Marburg* (cit. n. 8), pp. 16–18, 30–31, 51–63, 98–112, 435–444; on Kolbe, *Das chemische Laboratorium Marburg* (cit. n. 14), pp. 1–17; and on Kolbe to Vieweg, 19 Oct., 9 Nov. 1863, 21 Feb. 1864, letters 196, 197, 199, 311K, Vieweg archive.

[32] Fruton, *Contrasts in Scientific Styles* (cit. n. 1), Ch. 4.

Table 2. Kolbe's Research Productivity

	Kolbe's papers			Student papers[a]	Total papers per year
	Solo	Solo per year	With coauthor		
Marburg					
1841–1850	9	1	2	—	1
1851–1858	4	0.5	1	10	2
1859–1865	22	3	9	37	10
Leipzig					
1865–1869	15	3	2	38	11
1870–1874	34	7	2	82	24
1875–1879	25	5	2	58	17
1880–1884	47	9	2	62	22
Totals	156		20	287	

NOTE: This table is divided chronologically not by uniform time increments, but by events in Kolbe's life; therefore an intensive measure (papers per year) is also given. Averages are rounded to nearest integers. A "paper" is any publication, including notes, comments, and polemical articles. Papers are dated by the publication date of the journal issue in which it appeared; papers from 1865 are divided according to where the work was performed.

[a] Represents papers describing research performed in Kolbe's laboratory, whether the author was a student in the strict sense or not; thus this category includes independent papers by assistants, *Privatdozenten,* and postdoctoral workers and even some student papers directed by assistants or *Privatdozenten.* It does not include papers for which Kolbe was a coauthor.

theoretically important chemist during the third quarter of the century, published only 131 papers, all but 18 of these during the years 1850–1873.[33] As has often been rightly remarked, numbers of publications do not necessarily correlate to quality or significance.

Of course, Kolbe's students and junior colleagues in Leipzig assisted in his research. Among the best known were Ernst von Meyer, Henry Armstrong, A. M. Zaitsev, V. V. Markovnikov, Constantin Fahlberg, Ernst Schmidt, Hermann Ost, Ernst Beckmann, Rudolf Leuckart, and Theodor Curtius. Unfortunately, documents that could illuminate details of practical instruction in the Leipzig laboratory do not seem to have survived. The semester enrollments suggest that Kolbe instructed on the order of sixteen hundred *Praktikanten* during his nineteen years in Leipzig. Records of promotions to the doctorate do survive and indicate that he served as doctoral advisor to sixty-eight chemists.[34] From three assistants in 1865 Kolbe worked his way up to four in 1870, then five by late 1872. Advanced *Praktikanten* numbered a dozen or so per semester early in Kolbe's Leipzig period, and more like thirty to fifty during the 1870s.[35] During the latter period Kolbe had three of his assistants carry out the primary supervision of the

[33] Richard Anschütz, *August Kekulé,* 2 vols. (Berlin: Verlag Chemie, 1929), Vol. II, pp. 953–960.

[34] The relevant records are Phil. Fac. 82, Phil. Fac. 83, Phil. Fac. B 128, Universitätsarchiv Leipzig.

[35] Carl Graebe, then *Privatdozent,* wrote Carl Liebermann that 36 of Kolbe's 130 *Praktikanten* were full-day workers. He added that his own lecture course on organic chemistry was drawing forty students: Graebe to Liebermann, 7 Nov. 1869, No. 1933/1, Sondersammlungen des Deutschen Museums, cited in Elisabeth Vaupel, "Carl Graebe (1841–1927): Leben, Werk und Wirken im Spiegel seines brieflichen Nachlasses" (Ph.D. diss., Univ. Munich, 1987), p. 189. Graebe had worked in Kolbe's Marburg lab in 1862. In another letter he remarked on his friendly relations with Kolbe, but "I

beginners on the ground floor, while a fourth helped him with the advanced workers upstairs; the fifth assistant was dedicated to the lecture experiments.

But Kolbe kept abreast of the progress of every *Praktikant,* no matter how inexperienced he might be, or how crowded the laboratory became.[36] Indeed, Kolbe
regarded such personal attention as a fundamental pedagogical principle. It led,
he averred, to a certain "patriarchal relationship" between him and his students,
which developed over the long term into a permanent esprit de corps that reinforced the positive qualities he was seeking to instill. His hierarchical bureaucratic organization thus had pedagogical justification, and moreover it seems to
have operated well, without the authoritarian tone that many expected.

Kolbe explicitly stated that his pedagogical philosophy and teaching methods
as developed in Marburg continued without essential change in Leipzig.[37] Those
methods were described above. Two firsthand reminiscences by Leipzig students,
Markovnikov in 1866–1867 and Armstrong in 1867–1870, were also cited; these
confirm the open, conscientious, and broad-minded attitudes that Kolbe claimed
for himself in his monograph on the Leipzig institute. Armstrong in particular repeatedly emphasized that Kolbe encouraged his research students to develop
their own ideas and follow them to their logical conclusions.[38] One more witness
may be introduced here, that of his student and eventual son-in-law Ernst von
Meyer (1847–1916).

Meyer, descended from an aristocratic Hessian family, was second cousin to
Kolbe's wife and knew her slightly from Marburg. He became intimate with the
entire family soon after his matriculation in November 1866. His reminiscences
of the laboratory routine dovetail with those of Markovnikov and Armstrong, as
well as with Kolbe's descriptions.

> A better school than Kolbe's I could not wish for. . . . With the help of able assistants
> (Finkelstein and Drechsel) he was able to devote himself to everyone, even the begin-
> ners; he would not tolerate any of the many reactions we observed to remain unclear
> to us. At that time there were still no printed short introductions to qualitative analy-
> sis, as are ordinarily in use today. Our handwritten observations were examined and
> reviewed by an assistant, also by Kolbe himself. This kind of instruction instilled in
> the beginner a firm foundation for further development.

Meyer earned the doctorate in 1872, whereupon he became one of Kolbe's assistants. In 1875 he became engaged to Kolbe's eighteen-year-old daughter Johanna,
and they married the following year.[39]

---

will not come with him into a closer relationship, as this is too little in his nature": Graebe to his par-
ents, 24 Nov. 1869, No. 1933-78/14, Deutsches Museum, also cited in Vaupel, p. 189.

[36] Kolbe, *Das chemische Laboratorium Leipzig* (cit. n. 14), pp. xl–xli. Exceptions to this generalization occurred during the three peak semesters 1872–1874, when forty students were entrusted completely to assistants, and during some isolated semesters in the late 1870s and early 1880s when Kolbe
was too ill to work in the lab regularly.

[37] *Ibid.,* pp. vii, xl.

[38] H. E. Armstrong, "Persönliche Erinnerungen und Gedanken," *Chemiker-Zeitung,* 1927, *51*:114–
116.

[39] Meyer, *Lebenserinnerungen* (cit. n. 14), *passim.* As assistant, Meyer lived in the same building as
the Kolbe family; he and Johanna had been playing chamber music together since shortly after their
first meeting in 1866. Meyer's relationship with "Vater Kolbe" was extraordinarily cordial and remained undisturbed by Kolbe's increasingly intemperate conduct toward his professional peers.

Table 3. Kolbe's Research Group

	Marburg, 1851–1865	Leipzig, 1865–1884
Total *Praktikanten*	ca. 240	ca. 1,600
Total research group	28	137
Avg. no. of Praktikanten	ca. 16	ca. 125
Avg. no. of advanced Praktikanten	ca. 4	ca. 40
Total recorded Ph.D.s	18	68

NOTE: The data derive from sources listed in notes 18 and 34, and the categories are discussed in the text.

Because class lists have not survived, a complete analysis of the Leipzig group by name or even by precise statistics is not possible. Many of the students were not chemistry majors and had no further contact with the science after their one brief exposure, and even some of the chemistry and pharmacy majors doubtless had virtually no impact on the institute. As we did for Marburg, we need to ask how many people can properly be considered members of Kolbe's research group in Leipzig. Using the same widest-sense definition as for Marburg, we find that the Leipzig group consists of 137 identifiable people, just half of whom (68) completed Ph.D. dissertations under Kolbe, and all but 12 of whom appeared as authors of papers. These numbers suggest that an average of something like 30 of them were present at any given time, so that (adding a few nonmembers of the group) his group of advanced *Praktikanten* may have averaged around 40. Collating these numbers with those from Marburg, we arrive at the summary found in Table 3.

Whereas Kolbe's Marburg group was, until his last few years there, almost exclusively composed of Hessian students, the group in Leipzig was far more cosmopolitan. About a fourth of the group was foreign, and of the Germans only about a third came from Saxony. In his entire career Kolbe could boast of having taught 21 Russian, 20 British, 10 American, 7 Swiss, and 3 Austrian students and a smattering from five other countries (but no French, Italian, or Spanish students). Of these, 5 Russian and 7 British students actually took their Ph.D. degrees with Kolbe.[40]

Indeed, it was with his foreign students that Kolbe had many of his greatest educational successes. Edward Frankland (as something of an unofficial Kolbean) and Henry Armstrong (1848–1937) were two of the most influential science educators in England of their day, and they were considered the deans of (respectively) late nineteenth- and early twentieth-century British chemistry. A. M. Zaitsev, N. A. Menshutkin, and V. V. Markovnikov (1838–1904), all world-class chemists, made a great impact in Kazan, St. Petersburg, and Moscow during and

---

Meyer was inducted into modern structural chemistry by Carl Graebe, who served for one semester (winter 1869/70) as *Privatdozent* in Leipzig.

[40] Namely, the Russians A. Bazarov (1868), H. Byk (1868), S. Byk (1879), C. Fahlberg (1873), and A. M. Zaitsev (1866), and the British H. Armstrong (1870), C. Bingley (1854), E. Cook (1865), F. Guthrie (1855), W. James (1882), H. Smith (1877), and F. Wrightson (1853).

after the life of their teacher Butlerov. After receiving his Leipzig Ph.D., the Russian Constantin Fahlberg (1850–1910) bounced around several positions before spending a year as an assistant to Ira Remsen at Johns Hopkins University in Baltimore, where he (systematically) discovered saccharin and (serendipitously) its sweetening properties; in 1886 he founded a factory near Magdeburg to manufacture the substance, with great success and profit.

As for the Americans, H. P. Armsby (1853–1921), who became a noted agricultural chemist at the University of Wisconsin and Pennsylvania State College, was a Leipzig *Praktikant* in 1875/76, as was the New York private analyst Gideon Moore (1842–1895). A last American *Praktikant* worth mention was Sidney A. Norton (1835–1918), who for twenty years was the head (and only member) of the chemistry department of Ohio State University.[41] Perhaps the most curious foreign career path was traveled by the Bavarian Oscar Loew (1844–1941), who had stints at the City College of New York, the United States Geological Survey and Department of Agriculture, and Tokyo University before returning to his homeland at the age of seventy as honorary professor at Berlin. He was the last significant Kolbe-*Schüler* to die.

The highest prestige that a German professor could wish for one of his students was that he become an *ordentlicher* professor himself at another German university. Here Kolbe had little success. Only three of his students ever gained a university *Ordinarius:* Ernst Beckmann (1853–1923) at Erlangen, Leipzig, and Berlin; Theodor Curtius (1857–1928) at Kiel, Bonn, and Heidelberg; and Ernst Schmidt (1845–1921) at Marburg. Schmidt, the only undistinguished chemist of the three, became the first to achieve this rank—ironically, at Kolbe's former university and in the very year of Kolbe's death (this was as Constantin Zwenger's successor as director of the pharmaceutical institute).[42] This poor record of spawning new full professors contrasts with that of Liebig a half generation earlier, and with Baeyer a half generation later, each of whom taught close to thirty future German university *Ordinarien*.[43]

This last enumeration counts only those who actually took the Ph.D. with Kolbe, not his entire research group; moreover, there were, of course, other educational institutions besides universities, other ranks besides the *Ordinarius,* and other countries besides Germany. Of the total group of 137 students, 31 (23%) pursued academic careers. Among Kolbe's Leipzig research workers who did not take their degrees with Kolbe were such future academics as Carl Graebe (who had spent a semester in Kolbe's lab in Marburg), Edmund Drechsel, Hermann Credner, and Gustav Hüfner, as well as many of the foreigners mentioned above. Among those who never made it to *Ordinarius* but nevertheless attained a reputa-

---

[41] A convenient source for Fahlberg, Moore, and Norton is Wyndham D. Miles, ed., *American Chemists and Chemical Engineers* (Washington, D.C.: American Chemical Society, 1976), s.vv. As a member of the Case Western Reserve faculty, I read with interest that Norton was a native Clevelander who attended Western Reserve College for one year (1852/53) and taught high school in Cleveland before spending a semester in Leipzig in 1870.

[42] One of Schmidt's doctoral students was Richard Fischer; Fischer taught Henry Schuette, who was Aaron Ihde's doctoral advisor. As I am an Ihde student, I can claim Kolbe as my *Doktor-Ur-Ur-Urgrossvater*—were I so inclined.

[43] Fruton, *Contrasts in Scientific Styles* (cit. n. 1), pp. 32, 141. The smallest number of German *Ordinarien* among scholarly progeny for any of the six chemists that Fruton studied (Liebig, Baeyer, Emil Fischer, Felix Hoppe-Seyler, Willy Kühne, and Franz Hofmeister) was sixteen for Kühne.

tion in chemistry were Conrad Laar (1853–1929), who coined the term *tautomerism*, Rudolf Leuckart (1854–1889), the developer of an eponymous synthetic reaction that yields complex aliphatic amines, and Friedrich Fittica (1850–1912) at Marburg.

A final group of academics comprises those who worked at the trade schools and *technische Hochschulen*, which were gradually raising their status during the latter part of the century. Kolbe's Marburg student Rudolf Schmitt had an excellent career at the Dresden Polytechnic, and when ill health forced him to retire his successor was Ernst von Meyer. Hermann Ost (1852–1931) was at the Hanover Technische Hochschule for nearly forty years, and in all about a dozen of our 137 Leipzig Kolbeans spent major portions of their careers at technical schools.

It was noted above that only 23 percent of Kolbe's Leipzig group—or, to put the matter more starkly, only 2 percent of his *Praktikanten*—achieved a subsequent academic career of any sort. The majority of Kolbe's *Praktikanten* were in fact future physicians, pharmacists, schoolteachers, businessmen, civil servants, and so on, no doubt even including a few law and theology students.[44] The future academics were in the minority even among the future professional chemists, for in the last third of the century a university education was becoming a common, even expected, preparation for a career in chemical industry. Unfortunately, biographical sources for industrial employees are poor by comparison to reference works for academics, and it is therefore difficult to identify Kolbe's budding industrialists even from an accurate list of names.

Some identifications, however, can clearly be made. Kolbe's Marburg student Wilhelm Kalle founded what would become an extremely successful dye firm two years after his Ph.D., in 1863. Ludwig Mond, the later ammonia-soda magnate, also studied in Marburg. Griess and Gerland were Marburg students who worked in chemical industry, as did Graebe for a few years. In Leipzig there was a larger (and, understandably, an increasing) percentage of technical students. The case of Fahlberg has already been mentioned, and this example is representative; some two dozen Leipzig students can be shown to have entered industry, but the true number is certainly very much higher. A rough estimation can be made that perhaps a quarter (ca. 400) of Kolbe's Leipzig *Praktikanten* became industrial chemists, contrasting with perhaps a tenth (ca. 20–25) of his Marburg students.[45]

Meyer, Ost, and other junior colleagues contributed far more to the liveliness and success of Kolbe's institute than has been appreciated. Both Meyer and Ost

[44] This statement cannot be quantified, as records that would allow one to sort Kolbe's students by field of study have not survived.

[45] I derived these estimates in the following fashion. Peter Borscheid has estimated that there were around 380 university-educated chemists working in German chemical industries in 1851, 900 in 1865, and 2,100 in 1884: see Borscheid, *Naturwissenschaft, Staat und Industrie in Baden (1848–1914)* (Stuttgart: Klett, 1976), pp. 84–87, 234. Taking 1,200 as an average round number for the period 1865–1884, one can presume that the requisite increment for such a work force might be something like 130 new chemists per year (65 representing the average 5.4 percent growth rate indicated by Borscheid, plus an equal number for replacement due to death, retirement, and so on). Since Leipzig had about 16 percent of total German university enrollment, Kolbe may have trained an average of around 21 industrial chemists per year. It is true that Kolbe was not the only chemist at Leipzig, but given Saxony's strength in chemical industry, such a number is not unreasonable. The total over nineteen years is thus something like 400 chemists, or around 25 percent of his *Praktikanten*. The figure I cite for Marburg was derived in a similar fashion. See also Lothar Burchardt, "Die Ausbildung des Chemikers im Kaiserreich," *Zeitschrift für Unternehmungsgeschichte*, 1978, *23*:31–53.

were assistants and *Privatdozenten* in the institute from the early 1870s until Kolbe's death in 1884, Meyer being promoted to *Extraordinarius* in 1878. They had capable colleagues in their fellow long-term assistants Anton Weddige (1843–ca. 1904) and Ernst Carstanjen (1836–1884), both of whom also became *Extraordinarien* at Leipzig, but neither of whom progressed further along the academic ladder.

Although all doctoral degrees in chemistry were officially granted with the Kolbe imprimatur, it appears that Ost and especially Meyer increasingly took charge of the day-to-day direction of the *Doktoranden*, especially after Meyer's promotion to *Extraordinarius*. Judging by acknowledgments in doctoral dissertations and by Meyer's later statements, it seems that the majority of the doctoral students after 1877 got most of their advice, and even many of their original topics, from junior colleagues in the institute. Meyer mentioned that his Ph.D. topic, selected in 1871, was of his own devising. Such a trend toward detachment from the director was especially clear after the mid 1870s, when Kolbe's health began to decline. The fact that the two most eminent Kolbe students, Ernst Beckmann and Theodor Curtius, were in this late group, speaks to the quality of Meyer's mentoring.[46]

During the first Leipzig decade, of course, Kolbe's role was stronger and more direct. There are many indications (from Kolbe's acknowledgments of specific students' assistance in some of his papers, from students' acknowledgments to Kolbe in their papers, and from retrospective accounts) that particularly during the Marburg and early Leipzig years Kolbe often used his students as extra "hands" to pursue his own concerns; examples include much of the organosulfur research, and his search for missing aromatic isomers predicted by his (and not by Kekulé's) benzene theory.

Indeed, Kolbe's Leipzig period might be viewed as exhibiting all the prerequisites for an ideal "research school." Taking J. B. Morrell's criteria for such an entity, we can affirm that Kolbe was a man of eminence and personal charm, perhaps even charisma; that his students formed a cohesive group with excellent esprit; that they were allowed to publish under their own names, and, after 1870, in Kolbe's own proprietary journal; that Kolbe had a distinctive theoretical research program to be elaborated, with a set of dependable and predictable techniques; and finally, that he had plenty of manpower, more than adequate physical facilities, and generous institutional and financial support.[47] Why, then, was the Leipzig research group not more successful at generating papers, scientific innovation, and future academic stars? The final section of this paper will attempt to

---

[46] In his *Lebenserinnerungen* (cit. n. 14) Meyer describes his growing independence and increasing share of direction of *Doktoranden*. "I could name many chemists here," Meyer concludes, "but I will confine myself to mentioning my especially famous students E. Beckmann, Th. Curtius and Hermann Ost" (p. 115). Other dissertations directed by Meyer include those of Paul Degener (1879), J. William James (1882), M. Wallach (1882), O. Henzold (1883), and G. McGowan (1884); those directed by Ost include A. Klinkhardt (1881) and E. Mennel (1882). Meyer's love and sincere regard for his boss and father-in-law is beyond question, and so it is unlikely that he was consciously distorting the facts with these claims; I am inclined to believe them. One of Fruton's conclusions in *Contrasts in Scientific Style*, after studying six research groups, was that junior colleagues made far greater contributions to the life of their institutes than has hitherto been appreciated. This pattern holds in Kolbe's case.

[47] Morrell, "Chemist Breeders" (cit. n. 1), pp. 3–7.

answer this question, and in the process offer some reflections on problems associated with the analysis of scientific research schools.

VII. CONCLUSION

The first point to emphasize is that the two principal denotations of the term *research school*—one defined by the *institutional* setting in which group research takes place, the other by a *cognitive* network of similarly minded workers which may be geographically dispersed—are distinguishable in a historical as well as a semantic sense. This distinction is mentioned by several of the writers in this volume, but it has not hitherto been sufficiently stressed; authors of previous studies have generally assumed that the two "school" phenomena must necessarily develop together. In this essay I have focused exclusively on the former denotation, hence have preferred the more empirically descriptive term *research group*.

In fact, the story of Kolbe's "school" illustrates how the first kind of group can have a lively existence over many years, without the least evidence developing of the second kind. The reason was that Kolbe's theoretical approach was so distinctive as to be characteristic virtually of him alone, because he did not convince even his advanced students and guest workers of the advantages of his approach to the study of chemical constitutions. Kolbe's ideas were hard to sell because they proved unproductive in comparison to those of his competitors at other universities; or, to speak more precisely and with only a touch of hyperbole, the ideas were powerful only to the extent that they happened to coincide with structuralist notions. The projects that emanated from Kolbe's conviction that a difference existed between carbon valences, or his denial of chain formation, or his unique ("trimethine-trimethane") benzene theory, or his belief in the characteristics of the "fundamental radical" all proved scientifically sterile.[48]

A second point that emerges from these considerations is that research groups are not always the cohesive and distinctive units they are usually thought to be. Historians are in the habit of assuming, in absence of explicit contrary evidence, that members of a research group are necessarily "in the camp" of the director, that they become so by influence from the top of the hierarchy, and that their work invariably derives directly or indirectly from the director's research program. Such assumptions are not always warranted. Difficulties inhere in the historical sources themselves, or rather in the usual absence of those of a crucial sort; indications of transmission of ideas from teacher to student may be inferred, but dependable statistical data can rarely if ever be constructed. In our particular case, for instance, we may ask, Exactly which themes were suggested by Kolbe, which by his research colleagues, which by the students themselves? Formal acknowledgments by students to the group leader were expected courtesies, not necessarily accurate historical indications of intellectual influence, and so do not really tell us very much. Even when we can determine that the project started as a definite assignment from the group leader, scientific research is such that few projects lead in a straight line from conception to conclusion, and the twists and

---

[48] Detailed substantiation of the assertions in this paragraph may be found in Rocke, *Quiet Revolution* (cit. n. 6), Chs. 12 and 13.

turns along the way are often the real points of interest. Who was doing the turning at each point?

If such analytical problems are difficult to resolve for *Praktikanten* and *Doktoranden,* they are even worse for guest workers with Ph.D.s, assistants, *Privatdozenten,* and *Extraordinarien.* The German university system was often fluid, junior colleagues frequently traveling from university to university; many of those in Kolbe's laboratory had not been his students originally. Nor was it just the junior colleagues, for even the *Doktoranden* were sometimes a peripatetic lot. Moreover, organic chemistry, at least, had developed a national scientific culture that was quite similar at the various German universities. Structural chemistry was in fact alive and well in Kolbe's institute, even while Kolbe was turning apoplectic over it. Many instances of the independence of students' themes from Kolbean concerns can be cited, a trend that can be discerned even in the Marburg and early Leipzig periods. This point is highlighted by the not infrequent disagreements between Kolbe and his students, use of explicit structural theories by members of his group, or refutations of Kolbe's own predictions generated from within the research group—usually published under explicit aegis of the Kolbe institute![49]

Such examples are surprising considering Kolbe's well-deserved reputation as a tyrannical polemicist and a cold and unfriendly man. There were two sides to his character, however. Vicious with opponents at other universities, Kolbe was warm and amiable in his inner circle; he gave his students as much independence as they could wish, urging them to think for themselves and to try out whatever ideas came to mind. In this sense Kolbe was much more like, for example, Justus Liebig, Franz Hofmeister, or Adolf Baeyer than Emil Fischer, Rudolf Fittig, or Frederic Clements.[50] This circumstance poses a difficulty in accounting for the poor record of the Kolbe research group overall, for most case studies correlating directorial style to a group's overall success have appeared to indicate that a loose, informal style by a charismatic director producing a strong esprit de corps in the group—which is what we have here—is a powerful recipe for success.

But the difficulties can be resolved by reviewing other—largely cognitive—factors that were even more important in the Kolbe case. Kolbe's group research was notably moribund until he acquired a powerful theory, largely equivalent to structure theory, which he then exploited with energy and mastery. He trans-

[49] E.g.: (1) Guthrie and Kolbe, "Über die Verbindungen des Valerals mit Säuren," *Annalen,* 1859, *109*:296–300, demonstrating, contra Kolbe's prediction, that glycol does not dehydrate to acetaldehyde; (2) Kolbe, "Muthmaassliche Existenz zweier Kohlenoxysulfide," *J. Prakt. Chemie,* 1871, *112*:381–382, a conjecture disproved by his student F. Salomon, "Über Kohlenoxysulfid," *ibid.,* 1872, *113*:476–480; (3) Constantin Fahlberg, "Über Oxyessigsäure (Glycolsäure)," *ibid.,* 1873, *115*:329–346, demonstrating contra Kolbe the identity of the two named acids; and (4) Kolbe "Über die chemische Natur der Salylsäure," *ibid.,* 1875, *120*:151–157, disproving the existence of salylic acid. Some of his assistants (Ernst Carstanjen, for example) habitually used Kekulé's benzene hexagon in published papers, which Kolbe was well known to loathe. H. E. Armstrong, always a staunch defender of Kolbe, recollected that Kolbe "held most peculiar views as to [benzene's] structure, which we [students] often disputed with him": H. E. Armstrong, "The Riddle of Benzene: August Kekulé," *Journal of the Society of Chemical Industry,* 1929, *48*:914–918, on p. 914. A contemporary letter from Armstrong to his father supports the account: H. E. Armstrong to Richard Armstrong, 6 Feb. 1870, quoted in J. Vargas Eyre, *Henry Edward Armstrong* (London: Butterworths, 1958), pp. 51–52.

[50] See Jeffrey Johnson, "Hierarchy and Creativity in Chemistry, 1871–1914," *Osiris,* 1989, *5*:214–240, on p. 225; Fruton, *Contrasts in Scientific Style* (cit. n. 1.), Chs. 2, 4, 5; and the essay by Joel Hagen in this volume. Note that Fruton's view of Liebig's style is more "dictatorial" than the usual one.

ferred to Leipzig in the middle of the period of his greatest productivity. As we have seen in the detailed discussion above, the sudden and dramatic improvements in institutional setting, personal power, financial and material resources, and numbers of students—nicely paralleling the maturation of the field of organic chemistry in Germany—made remarkably little difference to his success rate and general standing in the field, or even to the productivity of his group research if measured by a proper (intensive) yardstick. Productivity and standing only began to decline when Kolbe began to focus exclusively on those points of difference between his and the structuralists' theories, in an attempt to destroy his scientific enemies. Instead, it was Kolbe who was destroyed.

Here, finally, is the principal reason why the Leipzig research school was not more scientifically productive and influential. For Kolbe, at least, the focus should not be on distinctiveness as an advantage—especially not as a sine qua non for a successful school as some have viewed it—for we have seen that in his case distinctiveness could only hurt in the long run. Rather, attention needs to be directed to the power and empirical stature of the ideas driving the research. Kolbe's increasing concern—virtually an obsession—with precisely those details of his carbonic acid theory that proved most sterile ensured that his own research would be moribund. One consequence was that direction of the laboratory in more fruitful areas was left exclusively to junior associates, whose ideas may have been more powerful, but whose lower positions in the hierarchy meant that they were less able to lead and inspire. Another was that as Kolbe's stature in the field fell and he continued to make bitter enemies, his word meant less in recommendations for his students; this contributed to his nearly total failure to produce new German *Ordinarien.* The net result was that Kolbe's Leipzig "school" was gradually transformed from an exciting and productive example of a team conducting group research into a combination of a director following a quixotic personal research program, with a group carrying out mass research of a rather conventional character.

Vision Studies in Germany:
Helmholtz versus Hering

By R. Steven Turner*

MONG THE SCHOOL WARS that impelled German science and scholarship during the nineteenth century, none was more infamous than that
fought between the schools of Hermann von Helmholtz and Ewald Hering over
the nature of visual perception. The passionate exchanges between these groups
shed light on the relationship of scientific schools to scientific controversy; illustrate how school formations are affected by disciplinary specialization and
change; and demonstrate how emotional bonds, forged within the context of a scientific school, can affect the development of a research field.

I. THE ISSUES

The controversy between the two schools hinged on three sets of interrelated issues. The first was the physiological, neural, and psychological mechanisms that
mediate human color vision. In the second volume of his famous *Handbuch der
Physiologischen Optik* (1860), Helmholtz had joined James Clerk Maxwell as
cochampion of a theory of color vision advanced earlier by Thomas Young.[1]
Young's theory hypothesized that the retinal nerve endings consist of three dis-
crete types of receptors, which when stimulated produce respectively the sensations of red, green, and violet (blue, in some versions). All color sensations are
"psychological mixes" of these three fundamental hues. The theory interpreted
white as the simultaneous excitement of all three receptor types at the correct relative intensities, and black as the absence of retinal stimulation.[2]

Department of History, University of New Brunswick, Fredericton, New Brunswick, Canada E3B
5A3.
[1] Hermann L. F. von Helmholtz, *Handbuch der Physiologischen Optik*, 3 vols. (Leipzig: Voss, 1856,
1862, 1866; reissue 1867); 2nd. rev. ed., ed. Arthur König (Hamburg/Leipzig: Voss, 1896), issued in
17 parts, 1886–1896; 3rd ed. (based on the text of the first) with supplementary material, ed. A.
Gullstrand, J. von Kries, and W. Nagel (Hamburg/Leipzig: Voss, 1910); and *Helmholtz's Treatise on
Physiological Optics, Translated from the Third German Edition*, ed. James P. C. Southall, 3 vols. in 2
(New York: Optical Society of America, 1924–1925; rpt. New York: Dover, 1962). Unless otherwise
noted, all following citations of the *Handbuch* are given as *Optics* and refer to the Dover edition. On
Helmholtz's career see Leo Koenigsberger, *Hermann von Helmholtz*, 3 vols. (Brunswick: Vieweg,
1902–1903); and David Cahan, ed., *Hermann von Helmholtz and the Foundations of Nineteenth-
Century Science* (Berkeley/Los Angeles: Univ. California Press, forthcoming). On Helmholtz and
Maxwell on color vision see Richard L. Kremer, "Innovation through Synthesis: Helmholtz and Color
Research," forthcoming in *Helmholtz and the Foundations*, ed. Cahan.
[2] Paul D. Sherman, *Colour Vision in the Nineteenth Century: The Young-Helmholtz-Maxwell The-
ory* (Bristol: Hilger, 1981), *passim*; and Edwin G. Boring, *Sensation and Perception in the History of
Experimental Psychology* (New York: Irvington, 1942), *passim*.

© 1993 by The History of Science Society. All rights reserved. 0021-1753/93/8401-0005$01.00

OSIRIS 1993, 8 : 80–103   80

In 1874 Ewald Hering, then professor of physiology at the University of Prague, proposed an alternative theory, which postulated the existence of three sets of antagonistic color receptors corresponding to red-green, yellow-blue, and white-black. A particular receptor would respond with one hue or its antagonist depending upon its own momentary, internal state and upon the frequency and intensity of the stimulus light; the resulting net sensation would be a psychological mix of signals from all three receptor types. Hering's opponent-process theory obviously conceived black very differently from the Young-Helmholtz theory, as it did the process of adaptation and the notion of color saturation.[3] Both theories made largely similar predictions about normal color vision, but different ones about the perceptions of color-blind individuals; the vexed issue of color blindness therefore became the main focus of the subsequent disputes.[4]

The second area of controversy, often called the nativist-empiricist dispute, concerned the nature of the visual perception of space.[5] In the third volume of his *Handbuch* (1866), Helmholtz had analyzed our ability to discriminate objects visually by direction (two-dimensional localization) or by absolute or relative distance (depth localization or the perception of relief); these topics had already been the focus of several polemical exchanges with Hering between 1864 and 1866. Helmholtz argued there that these capacities are acquired by every individual during the early months of life through visual experimentation coordinated with the sense of touch. Hering retorted that while experience and learning certainly influence spatial perception, those perceptions rest on an organic, inborn capacity to perceive patterns of retinal stimulation as spatially distributed in particular ways. This controversy ramified into many other issues: the nature of infant visual experience; the coordination of eye movements; the variabilty in the so-called corresponding or identical points on the two retinas; the relationship of binocular disparity to the perception of the relief; the objective accuracy of visual localization; and the relative importance of the various empirical cues that govern depth perception.[6]

The third area of controversy embraced a number of visual phenomena and their interpretation: visual contrast, optical illusions, adaptation, and the color

[3] Ewald Hering, "Grundzüge einer Theorie des Farbensinnes," in his *Zur Lehre vom Lichtsinne: Sechs Mittheilungen an die kaiserl. Academie der Wissenschaften in Wien* (Vienna: Carol Gerold's Sohn, 1878), Pt. 6 (15 May 1874), pp. 107–141. On Hering see Vladislav Kruta, "Karl Ewald Konstantin Hering," *Dictionary of Scientific Biography*, 16 vols. (New York: Scribners, 1970–1980), Vol. VI, pp. 299–301; Leo M. Hurvich and Dorothea Jameson, introduction, in Ewald Hering, *Outlines of a Theory of the Light Sense*, ed. and trans. Hurvich and Jameson (Cambridge, Mass.: Harvard Univ., 1964), pp. i–xxv; and Leo M. Hurvich, "Hering and the Scientific Establishment," *American Psychologist*, 1969, *24*:497–514.

[4] R. Steven Turner, "Paradigms and Productivity: The Case of Physiological Optics, 1840–94," *Social Studies of Science*, 1987, *17*:35–68, esp. pp. 50–53.

[5] Gary Hatfield, *The Natural and the Normative: Theories of Spatial Perception from Kant to Helmholtz* (Cambridge, Mass.: MIT Press, 1990), *passim*; Boring, *Sensation and Perception in Psychology* (cit. n. 2), pp. 28–34, 233–238, and *passim*; Julian E. Hochberg, "Nativism and Empiricism in Perception," in *Psychology in the Making: Histories of Selected Research Problems*, ed. Leo Postman (New York: Knopf, 1962), pp. 255–330; and William Woodward, "From Association to Gestalt: The Fate of Hermann Lotze's Theory of Spatial Perception, 1846–1920," *Isis*, 1978, *69*:572–582.

[6] Timothy Lenoir, "The Eye as Mathematician: Clinical Practice, Instrumentation, and Helmholtz's Construction of an Empiricist Theory of Vision"; and R. Steven Turner, "Consensus and Controversy: Helmholtz on the Visual Perception of Space"; both forthcoming in *Helmholtz and the Foundations*, ed. Cahan (cit. n. 1).

constancy of objects.[7] Helmholtz attributed many of these phenomena to psychological factors, "unconscious inferences" occurring in the brain and heavily conditioned by prior perceptual experience and expectations. He believed that few if any raw visual sensations come to consciousness "uninterpreted" by higher-order psychological processes.[8] Hering, on the other hand, interpreted most of these effects as the automatic responses of innate organic mechanisms located in the retina itself. He defended the existence and importance of a broad range of primitive, uninterpreted sensory experience.[9]

Deeper methodological and philosophical issues also divided the two schools. Hering denounced Helmholtz's approach as too physicalist in orientation, too obsessed with physical models of end-organ function, and too prone to confound physical stimulus with subjective response or to postulate a simplistic isomorphism between them. The whole biophysical approach represented by Helmholtz and his school seemed to Hering to regard thc organism as an absurdly simple mechanism, responding passively to stimuli in predictable ways. Helmholtz, he insisted, took the position of the physicist, not the true physiologist.

But Hering objected to more than Helmholtz's reductionist approach. When biophysical explanation of any sensory response failed, Hering observed, Helmholtz was ready to banish the intractable phenomenon into the higher functions of psychology and attribute it to learning and experience. This produced ingenious but untestable psychological explanations and marked in Hering's view a premature abandonment of the search for legitimate physiological accounts. Thus while Helmholtz regarded the sensate organism as a simple mechanism, he also seemed to postulate a mysterious mind in it to account for spontaneity and perceptual function. In ironic attacks that surely rankled Helmholtz to the core, Hering denounced this philosophy of the organism as vitalistic and speculative.[10]

Hering, for his part, operated from a conception of the organism that stressed the constant activity of living tissue in maintaining a dynamic equilibrium of as-

[7] Boring, *Sensation and Perception in Psychology* (cit. n. 2), pp. 165–171 and *passim*; Kremer, "Innovation through Synthesis" (cit. n. 1); R. Steven Turner, "Fechner, Helmholtz, and Hering on the Interpretation of Simultaneous Contrast," in *G. T. Fechner and Psychology*, ed. Josef Brozek and Horst Gundlach (Passau: Passavia Universitätsverlag, 1987), pp. 137–150; and Armin Tschermak-Seysenegg, "Die Hell-Adaptation des Auges und die Funktion der Stäbchen und Zapfen," *Ergebnisse der Physiologie, Abt. II: Biophysik und Psychophysik*, 1902, *1*:695–800.

[8] Helmholtz's most important presentations of this position are "Concerning the Perceptions in General," *Optics*, Vol. III, pp. 1–36; and *Die Thatsachen in der Wahrnehmung, Rede gehalten . . . 1878* (Berlin: Hirschwald, 1879), the latter reprinted in Helmholtz, *Vorträge und Reden* (Brunswick: Vieweg, 1884) and subsequent editions. In the very large literature on Helmholtz's epistemology see esp. Hatfield, *Natural and Normative* (cit. n. 5), pp. 286–351; Richard M. Warren and Roslyn P. Warren, introduction to *Helmholtz on Perception: Its Physiology and Development* (New York: John Wiley & Sons, 1968), pp. 3–23; Carlos-Ulises Moulines, "Hermann von Helmholtz: A Physiological Approach to the Theory of Knowledge," in *Epistemological and Social Problems of the Sciences in the Early Nineteenth Century*, ed. H. Jahnke and M. Otte (Dordrecht: D. Reidel, 1981), pp. 65–73; and Herbert Hörz and Siegfried Wollgast, "Hermann von Helmholtz und du Bois-Reymond," in *Dokumente einer Freundschaft: Briefwechsel zwischen Hermann von Helmholtz und Emil du Bois-Reymond* (Berlin: Akademie-Verlag, 1986), pp. 11–66.

[9] See Ewald Hering, *Beiträge zur Physiologie*, 5 pts. (Leipzig: Wilhelm Engelmann, 1861–1864); and Hering, "Der Raumsinn und die Bewegungen des Auges," in *Handbuch der Physiologie des Menschen*, ed. Ludimar Hermann (Leipzig: Vogel, 1879–1880), Vol. III, Pt. 1, pp. 343–601.

[10] See esp. Hering, *Zur Lehre vom Lichtsinne* (cit. n. 3), Pt. 1 (1872), pp. 1–3; and Ewald Hering, "Ueber das Gedächtnis als eine allgemeine Funktion der organisierten Materie" (1870), in his *Fünf Reden*, ed. H. E. Hering (Leipzig: Engelmann, 1921), pp. 5–32.

similative and dissimilative processes. When outside stimuli disturb this equilibrium, the body responds in complex ways not to be correlated readily or simply with the external stimuli themselves.[11] Visual sensation is the psychophysical correlate of some of these complex responses. This philosophy led Hering to a strongly phenomenalistic approach to the analysis of perceptual experience, even though he was more than ready to speculate about hypothetical neural mechanisms. Hering admitted that experiential and psychological factors influence perception, but he instinctively distrusted explanations based upon such effects, and he preferred to equate experience to primitive organic response. Why, Hering demanded, is "up and to the right" not as primitive a visual response as "green"? On the basis of what possible visual experience, he inquired, is the Young-Helmholtz theory entitled to conclude that black is a different kind of color perception from white or blue?[12]

All this struck Helmholtz as obscure and vitalistic. He denounced Hering's approach as far too trusting of our ability to distinguish primitive from compounded sensations through introspection. He attacked Hering's readiness to explain visual effects by postulating hypothetical neural mechanisms as wholly speculative and at the mercy of Ockham's razor. Worse, he found Hering's approach over-inclined toward philosophical idealism in its readiness to assert the autonomy of the organism's subjective, perceptual responses from the patterns of objective, external stimuli that provoke them. Helmholtz clearly found no such dangers in his own philosophy of the organism. His belief that the ego actively (if unconsciously) shapes the nature of its perceptual awareness on the basis of its experience and its life needs seemed to strike deep chords in Helmholtz, as evidence of the rational mastery of self and nature that individuals can wield.[13]

Most exchanges between Helmholtz and Hering on these questions took place between 1864 and 1867; thereafter Helmholtz abandoned sensory physiology for physics. Although he continued to develop his epistemological views in popular lectures and returned to research on color vision in the years just before his death in 1894, his position in the controversy was defended mostly by others. Hering, by contrast, continued to take an active role in the controversy right down to his death in 1918, ably assisted by a small but formidable circle of scientific allies. In German-speaking Europe Helmholtz's position probably remained the scientifically orthodox one, as measured, for example, by elementary textbook presentations.[14] But Hering, as the accepted European authority on eye movements and the leader of an influential school, was too important to ignore. Ludimar Hermann (a Helmholtz sympathizer) recruited Hering to contribute the long section on the "spatial sense and the movements of the eye" to his multivolume *Handbuch der Physiologie* in 1879, and a Hering supporter, Oskar Zoth, was selected by Willibald Nagel (also ostensibly in the Helmholtz camp) to contribute

[11] See esp. Hering, "Antwortsrede" (1908) and "Zur Theorie der Vorgänge in der lebendigen Substanz" (1888), *Fünf Reden*, pp. 133–140, 53–104.

[12] Hering, "Raumsinn und die Bewegungen des Auges" (cit. n. 9), p. 556; and Hering, *Zur Lehre vom Lichtsinne* (cit. n. 3), Pt. 4 (1874), pp. 55–69.

[13] Helmholtz, "Critique of Theories," in *Optics*, Vol. III, pp. 531–559, esp. p. 558; and Helmholtz, *Handbuch der physiologischen Optik* (cit. n. 1), 2nd. ed., pp. 376–382.

[14] See, e.g., Ludimar Hermann, ed., *Grundriß der Physiologie des Menschen*, 4th ed. (Berlin, 1872); 7th ed. (Berlin, 1882); 10th ed. (Berlin, 1892); 13th ed. (Berlin, 1905). The title changes slightly between editions.

the comparable section to the *Handbuch der Physiologie* that Nagel edited in 1905. Hering's students also contributed several of the state-of-the-field discussions to the prestigious journal *Ergebnisse der Physiologie* between 1902 and 1910.[15] Moreover, Hering's views on most issues rapidly made ground after 1880 and received increasing textbook coverage.

II. THE SCHOOLS

Table 1 lists the names of twenty-nine "significant partisans" who contributed to the Helmholtz-Hering controversies between 1867 and 1918 in German-speaking Europe. It includes a few figures whose entire careers revolved about the controversy and others who contributed only a few pieces of original research or critical surveys. All those listed, however, were acknowledged by other participants to be significant to the controversy, and each explicitly espoused one side or wrote in such a manner that no informed contemporary could doubt his alignment or purpose. "Significant partisans" did not have to agree slavishly with Helmholtz or Hering. Both Ernst Mach and Georg Elias Müller, for example, defended theories of color vision somewhat different from Hering's own.[16] Johannes von Kries had modified Helmholtz's original position on many points by 1910.

Table 1 has several limitations as a prosopographical sample. It excludes important participants in the debate who refused to identify publicly with one side or the other, espoused definite intermediate positions, or defended quite distinct programs of their own; in this sense it differs from Harry Collins' notion of a "core-set."[17] The grouping also omits partisans who did not contribute to the technical literature of the controversy: authors of elementary textbooks, those whose loyalties were attested mainly in book reviews and commentaries, and the many academics who expounded one position at the expense of the other in their lecture halls and institutes. Even the list of contributors to the technical literature is incomplete. The issues of the controversy were so sweeping that it was hard to write on any aspect of visual perception without adopting the perspective of one school or the other: an informed reader can peruse the articles of the *Archiv für Ophthalmologie* or the *Zeitschrift für die Physiologie und Psychologie der Sinnesorgane* and frequently classify the theoretical perspective espoused, usually tacitly, by the authors. Nonetheless, Table 1 certainly includes all the major partisans in the controversy. Used in conjunction with other data, it suggests some interesting conclusions about the composition of the opposed camps.

Among the significant partisans on behalf of Ewald Hering, one factor especially stands out as significant in shaping the common theoretical commitment:

[15] Hering, "Raumsinn und die Bewegungen des Auges" (cit. n. 9); Oscar Zoth, "Augenbewegungen und Gesichtswahrnehmungen," in *Physiologie der Sinne*, Vol. III of *Handbuch der Physiologie des Menschen*, ed. W. Nagel (Brunswick: Vieweg, 1905), pp. 283–437; and articles in *Ergebnisse der Physiologie* (Wiesbaden), 1902–1910.

[16] On Mach and Hering see Richard L. Kremer, "From Psychophysics to Phenomenalism: Mach and Hering on Color Vision," in *The Invention of Physical Science*, ed. Mary Jo Nye, Joan Richards, and Roger Stuewer (Dordrecht: Kluwer, 1992), pp. 147–173.

[17] Harry M. Collins, "The Investigation of Frames of Meaning in Science: Complementarity and Compromise," *Sociological Review*, 1979, 27:703–718; and Collins, *Changing Order: Replication and Induction in Scientific Practice* (London: Sage, 1985), pp. 142–147. See also Martin J. Rudwick, *The Great Devonian Controversy: The Shaping of Scientific Knowledge among Gentlemanly Specialists* (Chicago: Univ. Chicago Press, 1985), pp. 418–429.

Table 1. Significant Partisans in the Helmholtz-Hering Controversies

Helmholtz supporters		Hering supporters	
Supporter	Field	Supporter	Field
Bezold, J. F. W. von (1837–1907)	Physics	Bielschowsky, Alfred* (1871–1940)	Ophth.
Brodhun, Eugen* (1860–1938)	Physics	Brücke, Ernst Theodor von* (1880–1941)	Physiol.
Brücke, Ernst (1819–1892)	Physiol.	Garten, Siegfried* (1871–1923)	Physiol.
Dieterici, Conrad* (1859–1929)	Physics	Hess, Carl von* (1863–1923)	Ophth.
Exner, Franz (1849–1926)	Physics	Hillebrand, Franz* (1863–1926)	Psych.
Exner, Sigmund* (1846–1926)	Physiol.	Hofmann, Franz* (1869–1926)	Physiol.
Fick, Adolf (1829–1901)	Physiol.	Mach, Ernst (1838–1916)	Physics, physiol.
Fleischl von Marxow, Ernst (1846–1891)	Physiol.	Müller, Georg Elias (1850–1934)	Psych.
Graefe, Alfred (1830–1899)	Ophth.	Sachs, Moriz* (1865–1930)	Ophth.
Holmgren, Frithiof (1831–1897)	Physiol.	Stilling, Jakob (1842–1915)	Ophth.
König, Arthur* (1856–1901)	Physics	Tschermak-Seysenegg, Armin* (1870–1952)	Physiol.
Kries, Johannes von* (1853–1928)	Physiol.	Zoth, Oskar (1864–1903)	Physiol.
Leber, Theodor* (1840–1917)	Ophth.		
Lummer, Otto* (1860–1925)	Physics		
Müller, J. J.* (1846–1875)	Physics, physiol.		
Nagel, Willibald (1870–1911)	Ophth.		
Raehlmann, Edward (1848–1917)	Ophth.		

* Student or laboratory assistant

personal connection with Hering himself. At least eight of the twelve individuals listed were former students of Hering and in most cases his institute assistants. Carl von Hess and Franz Hofmann were assistants to Hering at the University of Prague and followed him to Leipzig in 1895. Siegfried Garten had been introduced to physiology by Carl Ludwig, but turned to sensory studies under Hering after his arrival at Leipzig; Garten spent his career with Hering at Leipzig and followed him in the chair for physiology. The psychologist Franz Hillebrand studied with Hering at Prague; the ophthalmologist Alfred Bielschowsky and the physiologists Ernst Theodor von Brücke and Armin Tschermak-Seysenegg served as his assistants during the Leipzig period. Ernst Mach, although never a student of Hering, his contemporary, was his colleague at the University of Prague for twenty-five years. The ophthalmologist Jakob Stilling apparently never studied with Hering, but may have had contact with him in Vienna. The psychologist G. E. Müller and the physiologist Oskar Zoth had no institutional connection with Hering during their careers. Both, however, had strong Austro-Hungarian connections, like many of Hering's defenders. Müller taught briefly at Czernowitz and Zoth was a student of and successor to Alexander Rollet at Graz; both ended their careers at Göttingen.

Trying to characterize this alignment points up some of the terminological ambiguities in the notion of a school. Most of these partisans had strong personal and institutional ties to Hering, and many produced important contributions while working under Hering's immediate direction. These facts show that during much of his career Hering presided over a "research school" according to the strong criteria laid down by Gerald Geison and J. B. Morrell, or over what the twentieth century would call a "research group."[18] The fact that many of its members continued to develop and to defend Hering's program after leaving his laboratory suggests that the term *research school* (as distinct from *research group*) might usefully be applied to other than local groupings. This essay employs *research school* in this wider sense. Finally, Hering also trained many more advanced students who either did not specialize in sensory research or who did not contribute directly or significantly to the controversy. They, as well as others who had not studied under Hering, can be imagined to have espoused, taught, and defended his views. Contemporaries might legitimately have regarded them as members of Hering's "school," in the loose general sense of adhering to a particular intellectual alignment distinguished from other contemporary alignments.

The significant partisans of Helmholtz differ considerably from those of Hering. Only eight of the seventeen supporters listed in Table 1 were actually Helmholtz's students or assistants, although Ernst Brücke and Adolf Fick were fellow students of his at Berlin and J. F. W. von Bezold a colleague from 1885 to 1894. Among Helmholtz's students the most significant were Theodor Leber, who took a Ph.D. with Helmholtz at Heidelberg; J. J. Müller, who did the same and died prematurely at twenty-nine; the famous Johannes von Kries, who worked with Helmholtz in Berlin in 1877; and the physicist Arthur König, Helmholtz's protégé, who collaborated with him on color vision experiments in the decade before his death. Eugen Brodhun, Conrad Dieterici, and Otto Lummer were young physicists from Helmholtz's institute who collaborated with König on that same series of experiments.

This roster, however, still exaggerates the significance of personal connections with Helmholtz in determining partisanship. Kries, although he became the foremost advocate of Helmholtz's views, was primarily a student of Ludwig's and worked with Helmholtz scarcely a year; his own student and collaborator Willibald Nagel never worked with Helmholtz.[19] Brücke operated the physiology institute in Vienna as a Helmholtzian outpost in a region populated by sympathizers of Hering; Brücke first interested Ernst Fleischl von Marxow and Sigmund

[18] Gerald L. Geison, "Scientific Change, Emerging Specialties and Research Schools," *History of Science*, 1981, 9:20–40; and J. B. Morrell, "The Chemist Breeders: The Research Schools of Liebig and Thomas Thomson," *Ambix*, 1972, 9:1–46.
[19] "Johannes von Kries," *Die Medizin der Gegenwart in Selbstdarstellungen*, ed. L. R. Grote (Leipzig: Meiner, 1925), pp. 124–187, esp. pp. 129–130.

Exner in physiological optics, even though Exner later went to Berlin to study with Helmholtz. The primary influence on the ophthalmologists Theodor Leber and Alfred Graefe was the latter's uncle, Albrecht von Graefe. Arthur König managed a small but vigorous research group in Berlin between 1884 and 1896 that set new standards for precision colorimetry; it advanced Helmholtz's theory of color vision on many fronts. Helmholtz served as the group's patron, but it is unclear how closely he was involved in its actual work. Brodhun, Dieterici, and Lummer worked primarily with König and published joint papers with him. They seem to have had limited contact with Helmholtz himself, and after leaving the Berlin physics institute, they abandoned physiological optics entirely for physical optics. A "Helmholtzian school" existed in physiological optics as a clearly recognizable (and in some quarters, strongly defended) intellectual alignment, but except for the group around König, it did not constitute a research school by the strong criteria of Morrell and Geison.

In one sense this is not surprising. After 1871, when the controversy with Hering grew most intense, Helmholtz turned almost exclusively to physics; the physics institute he led concentrated naturally enough on the problems of electromagnetism and physical optics; and while the problems of vision fell readily within the disciplinary purview of physics at mid century, this became increasingly less the case as the century wore on. In a deeper sense, however, the nature of the alignments reflects important differences in scientific style and leadership between Helmholtz and his archrival.[20]

III. STYLES OF SCIENTIFIC LEADERSHIP

Ewald Hering was one of the most charismatic research directors of his era. He trained not only students, but disciples. To some of them he passed on his unparalleled talent as a polemicist, his consummate skills as an introspective observer and experimenter, and his militant perception of himself as being an oppressed outsider at war with the physiological establishment. What accounts for this unlikely charisma of Hering, a man whose writings reveal him as a vicious polemicist, an implacable opponent, and a master of sarcasm?

Part of Hering's charisma arose from the militancy of his scientific stance and from the profound reluctance of many of the most famous names in German science to cross him in print. His students must have feared him, too. Siegfried Garten recalled Hering as a modest and generous man, one who held himself under rigid self-control, yet could explode with primitive rage at a perceived offense and would rarely forgive thereafter.[21] Helmholtz, one of the few who ever bested Hering in a public exchange, gossiped to Emil du Bois-Reymond that Hering had been mentally disturbed.[22]

[20] See Joseph S. Fruton, "Contrasts in Scientific Style: Emil Fischer and Franz Hofmeister: Their Research Groups and Their Theory of Protein Structure," *Proceedings of the American Philosophical Society,* 1985, *129*:313–370; and Fruton, *Contrasts in Scientific Style: Research Groups in the Chemical and Biochemical Sciences* (Philadelphia: American Philosophical Society, 1990), *passim.*

[21] Siegfried Garten, "Ewald Hering zum Gedächtnis," *Pflüger's Archiv für die Gesammte Physiologie,* 1918, *170*:501–522, on p. 522.

[22] Helmholtz to du Bois-Reymond, *Briefwechsel* (cit. n. 8), No. 97, p. 215; cf. *Briefe von Ernst Wilhelm von Brücke an Emil du Bois-Reymond,* ed. Hans Brücke *et al.* (Graz: Akademische Verlagsanstalt, 1978), No. 173, p. 171.

Fear did not prevent Hering's students from loving him. His fiercely pro-German, anti-Czech political activity at Prague was said to have been crucial to the founding of the German university there in 1881. This story followed Hering and enhanced his stature among his students as a German nationalist and patriot. Those who left recollections of him agree that he lavished attention on his advanced students and regarded them as an extension of his scientific aspirations. They were able to include long lists of these students. The publications of the Leipzig Physiology Institute are said to contain 115 articles by his students, each carefully checked and revised by Hering himself. Hering instilled a sense of mission in his students. He convinced them, as Tschermak-Seysenegg wrote, that his ideas "belonged to the future."[23] Through the decade of the 1890s and after his students could undoubtedly sense that his ideas were in the scientific ascendancy.

The writings of Hering's students attest to the emotional tie that bound them to one another and to Hering's memory. In 1932 Tschermak-Seysenegg was still writing of the "close spiritual comradeship" among Hering's disciples, who had faithfully and systematically "pursued our way" without fear or favor toward anyone and unperturbed by the "ignorant and intemperate criticism" from all sides.[24] Dr. Franziska Hillebrand, the former student and widow of psychologist Franz Hillebrand, provided perhaps the surest proof of that emotional tie. She published her *Lehre von den Gesichtsempfindungen* in 1929 as a tribute to her late husband; it was to survey the field of visual perception and lay out her husband's life's work in its problems on the basis of his private papers and notes. The book, however, is a tribute less to Hillebrand than to Hering himself, who dominates its pages. Both scientifically and morally Hillebrand's young widow identifies him completely with Hering: the epitome of her praise for her late husband is that the virtues "which ought to be attributes of every researcher, and which had developed themselves in Hering to a rare perfection, may also be ascribed to Hillebrand to an extraordinary degree."[25] Ties of loyalty and love, as well as intellectual commitment, bound Hering's students to their menacing and unlikely master.

Hering contributed more to his research school than charismatic leadership and a sense of mission. He successfully placed his students in good university positions. Most of those placements came in Austria, eastern Europe, and South Germany; only two of his students listed in Table 1 saw their careers culminate in Prussian or North German universities, despite Hering's strong ties to Leipzig.[26] Hering also showed great skill in drawing recruits from a broader range of disci-

[23] Garten, "Hering zum Gedächtnis" (cit. n. 21), p. 522; Arnim Tschermak-Seysenegg, "Zu Ewald Herings 100. Geburtstag: Gedenkrede, gehalten an der Universität Köln von Prof. Tschermak-Seysenegg in Prag," *Münchener Medizinische Wochenschrift*, 1934, *81*:1230–1233, quoting from p. 1232; Ernst Theodor von Brücke, "Ewald Hering," *Deutsches Biographisches Jahrbuch*, Supplement II: *1917–1920* (Berlin: Deutsche Verlags-Anstalt, 1928), pp. 258–263; and Franz Hillebrand, *Ewald Hering: Ein Gedenkwort der Psychophysik* (Berlin: Springer, 1918).

[24] Armin Tschermak-Seysenegg, *Der exakte Subjektivismus in der neueren Sinnesphysiologie*, 2nd. ed. (Vienna: Emil Haim, 1932), p. 3 ("Vorrede zur zweiten Auflage").

[25] Franziska Hillebrand, "Vorwort," in Franz Hillebrand, *Lehre von den Gesichtsempfindungen auf Grund hinterlassener Aufzeichnungen*, ed. Franziska Hillebrand (Vienna: Springer, 1929), p. iv.

[26] They were Siegfried Garten, who followed Hering at Leipzig, and Franz Hofmann, who became *Ordinarius* in Berlin in 1923.

plines than physiology alone. Both at Prague and at Leipzig he was closely associated with the ophthalmologist Hubert Sattler. Hering and Sattler counted numerous ophthalmologists as well as physiologists among their students, including Hess, Hofmann, and Bielschowsky from Table 1. Similarly, Hering attracted experimental psychologists to his views, including Franz Hillebrand, who was his student, and G. E. Müller, who was not. Hering's pedagogical access to students of psychology weakened after he came to Leipzig in 1895, for psychology there was dominated by Wilhelm Wundt, an old enemy and past victim of Hering's polemical pen.

Helmholtz, too, exercised great charisma as the most versatile scientist in Europe and later as the acknowledged senior statesman of German science. His institutes, first in physiology at Heidelberg and then in physics at Berlin, produced a modest flow of student research on topics mostly related to his own interests and closely directed by him. In physiology, however, if not also in physics, Helmholtz trained surprisingly few disciples who seized upon and extended the central directions of his work in ways characteristic of the research schools of the period.[27] His personal bearing as an institute leader and research director did not forge the emotional bonds or the sense of mission among his students that Hering's did. Wundt, his assistant at Heidelberg from 1858 to 1863, complained that Helmholtz was so reticent as to be almost unapproachable; Kries made a similar charge in more muted tones after his brief sojourn with Helmholtz.[28] Eugen Goldstein, who had worked in Helmholtz's physics institute, recalled Helmholtz in more flattering terms as reserved and cool, sometimes vague, in his dealings with the laboratory *Praktikanten*, but at the same time generous, tolerant of contradiction, forgiving of student mistakes, and almost excessively modest. Contrary to the stories circulated about him, Goldstein insisted, Helmholtz spent nearly six hours daily in his institute consulting individually with his advanced students, and that despite his heavy administrative duties outside the institute. David Cahan's recent study also accords Helmholtz high marks as a research director in his role as first president of the Physikalisch-Technische Reichsanstalt, although Helmholtz emerges there as an Olympian administrator-statesman rather than as an inspirational master.[29]

Some of the apparent contradictions in the style of Helmholtz's scientific leadership are resolved by considering the character of his science. Much of his

[27] Karl E. Rothschuh, *History of Physiology*, ed. and trans. Guenter B. Risse (Huntington, N.Y.: Krieger, 1973), pp. 212–220, on 217; and Paul L. Cranefield, "Freud and the 'School of Helmholtz,'" *Gesnerus*, 1966, *23*:35–39. On Helmholtz's institutes see Christa Jungnickel and Russell McCormmach, *The Intellectual Mastery of Nature: Theoretical Physics from Ohm to Einstein*, 2 vols. (Chicago: Univ. Chicago Press, 1986), Vol. I, pp. 307–310 (Heidelberg), and Vol. II, pp. 18–32 (Berlin).

[28] Wilhelm Wundt, *Erlebtes und Erkanntes* (Stuttgart: Alfred Krönser, 1920), pp. 155–160; cf. Solomon Diamond, "Wundt before Leipzig," in *Wilhelm Wundt and the Making of a Scientific Psychology*, ed. R. W. Reiber (New York: Plenum Press, 1980), pp. 3–70, on pp. 28–31. Kries was disappointed that "the nature of my activity in the institute afforded little occasion for the deeper discussion of scientific questions": *Medizin in Selbstdarstellungen*, ed. Grote (cit. n. 19), p. 130.

[29] E. Goldstein, "Helmholtz: Erinnerungen eines Laboratoriumspraktikanten," *Naturwissenschaften*, 1921, *9*:708–711 (cf. Joseph F. Mulligan, "Hermann von Helmholtz and His Students," *American Journal of Physics*, 1989, *57*:68–74); and David Cahan, *An Institute for an Empire: The Physikalisch-Technische Reichsanstalt, 1871–1918* (Cambridge: Cambridge Univ. Press, 1989), esp. pp. 59–125.

achievement resulted from his broad powers of synthesis. His greatest work typically pulled disparate but already-existing strands of research and interpretation together to achieve a new degree of generalization and theoretical suggestiveness. His work could therefore dominate the fields to which he contributed and readily become an orthodoxy. The work's character and comprehensiveness, combined with the awe in which he was held, attracted mature and talented researchers to his ideas and his institute. That attraction, however, depended little on his personal magnetism, and many were prepared to build on his ideas who had never worked with the man himself. Among those who did work with him he inspired awe, respect, and sometimes affection, but rarely the sense of unity, mission, and personal devotion that marked Hering's school.

IV. SCHOOLS AS LINGUISTIC COMMUNITIES

How these elements of style and leadership affected the debates over physiological optics is more elusive. Most obviously the animosity between the two protagonists intensified and prolonged the disputes. From the beginning there was no shortage of observers who felt that the issues had been unnecessarily polarized by the principals and that effective compromises were ready to hand. As early as 1881, the great Dutch ophthalmologist Franz Donders suggested that color sensitivity in the retina might be mediated by the Young-Helmholtz mechanism, and neural output from this mechanism be reprocessed at some higher neural level by Hering-type processes. This "zone theory" compromise would preserve the advantages of both hypotheses and help make sense of the confused data on color blindness. Kries also became a champion of the zone theory compromise.[30]

As to the visual perception of space, many commentators opined that the theory of evolution undermined the whole basis of the nativist-empiricist controversy. In evolutionary terms the organic mechanisms that mediate spatial perception could be thought of as "learned" or "acquired" during the phylogenetic development of the species rather than during the early life of the individual, thus apparently satisfying the principal demands of both schools.[31] Some suspected that the range of agreement between the principals themselves had been broader than the polemics suggested. Hering had never denied the importance of empirical factors in spatial perceptions; Helmholtz himself at one point in the *Handbuch* had quietly made a significant concession to the nativists, that our ability to distinguish the relative contiguity of stimulated retinal points must be an inborn capacity.[32] By 1910 the neo-Kantian Kries was prepared to concede to nativists the innate and a priori nature of the spatial sense per se, so long as they would concede that the ability to localize objects within that a priori space

[30] F. C. Donders, "Ueber Farbensysteme," *Archiv für Ophthalmologie*, 1881, *26*:155–223; and Johannes von Kries, "Die Gesichtsempfindungen und ihre Analyse," *Archiv für Anatomie und Physiologie: Abteilung für Physiologie, Supplement-Band*, 1882, pp. 1–178, esp. p. 171.

[31] Emil du Bois-Reymond, "Leibnizische Gedanken in der neueren Naturwissenschaften" (1870), in his *Vorträge über Philosophie und Gesellschaft*, ed. Siegfried Wollgast (Berlin: Akademie Verlag, 1974), pp. 25–44; and Franz Cornelius Donders, "Ueber angeborene und erworbene Association," *Archiv Ophthal.*, 1872, *18*:153–164.

[32] Helmholtz, *Optics*, Vol. III, pp. 220, 226; and Hering, *Zur Lehre vom Lichtsinne* (cit. n. 3), Pt. 1 (1872), pp. 1–8.

was of largely empirical origin.[33] In the face of this extensive middle ground, many contemporaries dismissed the controversy as moot or open to compromise.

Supporters of both principals also tacitly abandoned some of the more extreme claims of Helmholtz and Hering. By 1890, for example, few if any specialists still agreed with Helmholtz that conjugate eye movements have no organic basis in the musculature or innate neural mechanisms. Perhaps none denied that some physiological mechanism of retinal induction underlay the phenomenon of simultaneous contrast, or maintained with Helmholtz that it arose wholly from errors of unconscious judgment in the instantaneous comparison of colored fields. Most of Hering's supporters, although not all, had quietly backed away from his hypothesis of innate retinal depth values; indeed, Hering himself seems also to have done so.

Each of these disputes has its own complex history, but in general it was Hering and his followers who refused the proffered compromises and who kept the pot boiling with attacks upon the mainline supporters of Helmholtz. Again their motives for this stance varied with the issues and always reflected a mixture of empirical and strategic considerations, pride, and resentment.

Most significantly, their refusal to compromise arose also out of a deep incommensurability between the views of the two schools. Hering's program rested upon a unique terminology of his own invention. He and his school insisted that terms such as *Sehraum, Sehding, Gegenfarben, Reinheit, Kernflache, Raumwert, Umstimmung*, and the like could not be translated conceptually or terminologically into the traditional usages of sensory physiology, which had been taken over by Helmholtz. Conversely, when the Helmholtzian orthodoxy spoke of *Projektion*, the *Ermüdung der Retina, rotfarbige Lichtwellen, Rot-* or *Grunblindheit*, or *Täuschungen der Empfindungen*, their very vocabulary, Hering charged, not only betrayed tacit theoretical assumptions underlying the usage, but also committed them to an understanding of perceptual processes which blurred physical and psychophysical components.[34]

Yet the compromises proffered to Hering's school, as they saw them, were always cast in the language of Helmholtz. They might represent significant theoretical concessions, but to Hering they also represented semantic and hence conceptual cooptation. He and his school steadfastly refused zone theory compromises, for example, because the usual terminology of their presentations tacitly preserved a color association, and hence a psychological significance, for the neural output of the trichromatic receptors. The suggestion that spatial awareness, but not necessarily our ability to visually localize objects in space, might be regarded as innate met the intense scorn of Hering's school. To them it perpetuated the Kantian semantic confusion that postulated spatial perception without spatial qualities. The *Sehraum* of perception is not a "receptacle," Hering and his

[33] Johannes von Kries, "Helmholtz als Physiolog," *Naturwissenschaften*, 1921, 9:673–693; and Kries, "Empirismus und Nativismus," "Ueber den Ursprung der Gesetze der Augenbewegung," and "Historisch-kritische Bemerkungen," supplementary material in *Handbuch*, 3rd ed. (1910), rpt. in *Optics*, Vol. III, pp. 607–661, esp. pp. 640–651.

[34] See, e.g., Hillebrand, *Ewald Hering* (cit. n. 23), pp. 24–36; Ewald Hering, "Ueber Newton's Gesetz der Farbenmischung," *Lotos: Jahrbuch für Naturwissenschaft, n.s.*, 1887, 7:177–268, esp. pp. 181–182; Hering, "Kritik einer Abhandlung von Donders 'Ueber Farbensysteme,' " *Lotos*, 1882, 2:69–101, esp. pp. 86–101; and Armin Tschermak-Seysenegg, *Einführung in die physiologische Optik* (Berlin: Springer, 1942), pp. 63–69, 123–126, and *passim*.

supporters insisted, and hence should not be described in the language of physical space.[35]

The Helmholtzians, enjoying the traditional and dominant position, were less sensitive to these elements of terminological incommensurability. To speak occasionally of "red light rays" or "the projection of a perception into external space" was to them merely a terminological shorthand understood by everyone. They resented as fussy and pedantic Hering's polemical tirades against such usages. Hering's own iconoclastic vocabulary invited the rival school to resort to quoting it with a sneer; its individual elements could not be operationalized or readily lifted out of the whole system for analysis and criticism. Some despaired over Hering's scheme for analyzing color sensations, with its notion of the "purity" and "nuancing" of colors. Attacking Hering on empirical grounds often required the Helmholtzians to translate their own concepts and empirical results laboriously into Hering's system of thought, only to be refuted with the charge that they had not really understood Hering's meaning.[36] Among its many other functions, Hering's unique semantics played the crucial rhetorical role of insulating the ideas of his school from corruption and cooptation from abroad.[37]

This element of semantic incommensurability must not be exaggerated. It did not prevent either side from mobilizing experimental results against the other, or prevent a mutual acceptance of certain empirical results, even when they told heavily for or against one side. Such a case occurred in 1889, when Franz Hillebrand measured the "specific brightness of colors" for a low-intensity spectrum and a dark-adapted eye; within months König and Hering independently confirmed that it matched the spectral-brightness curve of a subject who was totally color-blind.[38] Hering's theory explicitly predicted this match; Helmholtz's did not. The discovery sent shock waves through the Helmholtzian establishment, and the crisis was not really alleviated until Kries announced the duplicity theory of vision in 1894.

But semantic incommensurability was important in the controversy, and the fact points to a larger consideration of how school formations influence scientific debates. In order to survive, a language or a dialect requires a linguistic community, one large enough and cohesive enough that its members' speech acts are

[35] Hillebrand, *Lehre von den Gesichtsempfindungen* (cit. n. 25), pp. 169-201, 96; and Hering, "Ueber Newton's Gesetz der Farbenmischung," *Lotos*, 1887, *7*:177-268, esp. pp. 181-182.

[36] Ewald Hering, "Ueber den Begriff, 'Urteilstäuschung' in der physiologischen Optik und über die Wahrnehmung simultaner und successiver Helligkeitsunterschiede," *Pflüger's Archiv Ges. Physiol.*, 1887, *41*:91-106; Hering, "Ueber die von v. Kries wider die Theorie der Gegenfarben erhobenen Einwände, III: Ueber die sogenannten Ermüdungserscheinungen," *ibid.*, 1888, *43*:329-346.

[37] Cf. Mario Biagioli, "The Anthropology of Incommensurability," *Studies in History and Philosophy of Science*, 1990, *21*:183-209; John A. Schuster and Richard R. Yeo, introduction to *The Politics and Rhetoric of Scientific Method: Historical Studies*, ed. Schuster and Yeo (Dordrecht: D. Reidel, 1986), pp. xix-xxvii; Geoffrey Cantor, "The Rhetoric of Experiment," in *The Uses of Experiment*, ed. David Gooding, Trevor Pinch, and Simon Schaffer (Cambridge: Cambridge Univ. Press, 1989), pp. 159-180; and Rudwick, *Great Devonian Controversy* (cit. n. 17), pp. 445-450.

[38] Franz Hillebrand, "Ueber die spezifische Helligkeit der Farben," *Sitzungsberichte der Kaiserlichen Akademie der Wissenschaften in Wien, Mathematisch-naturwissenschaftiche Classe, Abt. III*, 1889, *98*:70-145; Hering, "Untersuchungen eines total Farbenblinden," *Pflüger's Archiv Ges. Physiol.*, 1891, *49*:563-608; and Arthur König, "Ueber den Helligkeitswerth der Spectralfarben bei verschiedener absoluter Intensität," in *Beiträge zur Psychologie und Physiologie der Sinnesorgane: Hermann von Helmholtz als Festgruß zu seinem siebzigsten Geburtstage dargebracht* (Berlin: Springer, 1891), pp. 309-388, esp. p. 186.

mutually reinforcing and insulated from outside corrupting influences.[39] The conditions of modern scientific communications, especially in an age of international journals, militate against the existence of such linguistic pockets. Whether from the perspective of exchange theory or from that of constructivism, science as an activity pushes toward linguistic uniformity. In that kind of communications environment, research schools—institutionally localized, inward-looking, internally reinforcing, militant toward external rivals—offer the only settings in which linguistic or dialect pockets can establish themselves even temporarily. Thomas S. Kuhn, who first insisted on incommensurability as a necessary correlate of all deep change in science, has increasingly emphasized the semantic and linguistic aspects of conceptual incommensurability.[40] On that Kuhnian position, research schools may be the only real nuclei of radical scientific change, because they are the only adequate loci of semantic innovation.

V. SCHOOLS AND THE MIDDLE TERM OF CONTROVERSY

Gerald Geison's classic essay, "Scientific Change, Emerging Specialties, and Research Schools," observed that "research schools scarcely existed before the so-called 'Second Scientific Revolution' of the nineteenth century, during which the natural sciences became widely and firmly institutionalized in the universities."[41] The revolution to which Geison refers, however, had cognitive and taxonomic dimensions as well as institutional ones. Rudolf Stichweh characterizes it as a transition in which the institutionalized structure of knowledge in universities (particularly in German universities) was made increasingly isomorphous with the accepted cognitive divisions of knowledge. That rapprochement proceeded from two sides at once. On the one hand, the natural cognitive divisions of knowledge were increasingly identified with disciplines, a taxonomic form which the eighteenth century had usually regarded as secondary or conventional or as based merely on tradition or practicality. On the other hand, the most fundamental institutional divisions of universities increasingly came to be identified with chairs, one to a discipline or subdiscipline, and each presided over by a full professor with an institute or seminar to help him propagate his kind. Older institutionalized structures, like the faculties, lost their former cognitive significance and with it their institutional primacy, or, like the fields of *Naturgeschichte, Kameralistik,* and *Weltweisheit,* they were wholly fragmented into disciplines. As Stichweh observed, the age-old problem of classifying knowledge ceased to be a problem in

---

[39] K. M. Petyt, *The Study of Dialect: An Introduction to Dialectology* (Boulder: Westview Press, 1980); Ronald Wardhaugh, *An Introduction to Sociolinguistics* (New York: Basil Blackwell, 1986); and Wardhaugh, *Languages in Competition: Dominance, Diversity, and Decline* (New York: Basil Blackwell, 1987).

[40] Thomas S. Kuhn, *The Structure of Scientific Revolutions* (Chicago/London: Univ. Chicago Press, 1962; 2nd. ed. 1970); Kuhn, "Second Thoughts on Paradigms," in *The Essential Tension: Selected Studies in Scientific Tradition and Change* (Chicago/London: Univ. Chicago Press, 1977), pp. 293–319; Kuhn, "Metaphor in Science," in *Metaphor and Thought,* ed. Andrew Ortony (Cambridge: Cambridge Univ. Press, 1979), pp. 409–419; Kuhn, "What are Scientific Revolutions?" (1981), rpt. in *The Probabilistic Revolution,* ed. L. Krüger, L. J. Daston, M. Heidelberger, Vol. I: *Ideas in History* (Cambridge, Mass.: MIT Press, 1987), pp. 7–23; Kuhn, "Commensurability, Comparability, Communicability," in *PSA,* 1982, *2:*669–688, 712–716; and Paul Hoyningen-Huene, "Kuhn's Conception of Incommensurability," *Stud. Hist. Phil. Sci.,* 1990, *21:*481–492.

[41] Geison, "Scientific Change" (cit. n. 18), p. 35.

the early nineteenth century: the classification was simply there, institutionally reified in the evolving system of chairs and institutes in the German university.[42]

Of research schools Geison also observed that "to 'succeed' or to produce recognized innovations, a school must engage in dialogue with outsiders. At some point, the activities of a research school take on meaning only when attention is shifted back to the level of the discipline as a whole."[43] For the research schools of the nineteenth century, "dialogue" usually meant "controversy." The science and scholarship of nineteenth-century Germany, where research schools most flourished, were notorious for the bitter wars of method that flared between competing schools. Contemporary scholars, including some who led the most combative schools of the period, associated them with scholarly and personal polemics and often denounced the so-called spirit of schools.[44] Combining Geison's two insights sheds light on how research schools altered the nature of scientific controversy in the nineteenth century.

Scientific and scholarly controversies are often about at least two kinds of things simultaneously. Most obviously they are about ostensible matters of truth and how it is reached: the efficacy of that method, the legitimacy of this historical testimony, the corroboration of that theory or this interpretation. At another level controversies often mirror deep structures of political beliefs and needs or religious commitment. The Helmholtz-Hering controversies can be analyzed on both levels. Timothy Lenoir suggests that the biophysical, experimental approach of the 1847 school of physiology, and by implication Helmholtz's empiricist approach to the problem of vision, may be correlated with a generational turn toward social and political realism and material interests in the wake of the political failures of the 1840s.[45] Similarly, it has been suggested that the resurgence of nativism after 1885 was part of that more general societal retreat from optimism, rationalism, and materialism often said to characterize German culture at the *fin de siècle*.[46]

In the nineteenth century the restructuring of knowledge along disciplinary lines introduced a new "middle term" of scientific controversy, a third thing that

[42] Rudolf Stichweh, *Zur Entstehung des modernen Systems wissenschaftlicher Disziplinen: Physik in Deutschland 1740–1890* (Frankfurt am Main: Suhrkamp, 1985), pp. 1–94, esp. pp. 10, 93. See also R. Steven Turner, "Towards a Disciplinary Order of Sciences," *Minerva*, 1986, *24*:495–502 (an essay review of Stichweh); and Martin Guntau and Hubert Laitko, "Entstehung und Wesen wissenschaftlicher Disziplinen," in *Der Ursprung der modernen Wissenschaften: Studien zur Entstehung wissenschaftlicher Disziplinen*, eds. Guntau and Laitko (Berlin: Akademie-Verlag, 1987), pp. 17–92.

[43] Geison, "Scientific Change" (cit. n. 18), p. 35.

[44] See the pervasive concern over schools found in the statutes of the Verein Deutscher Philologen und Schulmänner (1838), which took as one of its purposes "die Wissenschaft aus dem Streite der Schulen zu ziehen" and which pledged all its members to observe a fair and modest tone in scientific exchanges: *Verhandlungen der ersten Versammlung Deutscher Philologen und Schulmänner in Nürnberg 1838* (Nürnberg: Riegel & Wiessner, 1838), p. 1.

[45] Timothy Lenoir, "Social Interests and the Organic Physics of 1847," in *Science in Reflection: The Israel-Boston Colloquium: Studies in History, Philosophy, and Sociology of Science*, 1988, *3*:169–181; Lenoir, "Science for the Clinic: Science Policy and the Formation of Carl Ludwig's Institute in Leipzig," in *The Investigative Enterprise: Experimental Physiology in Nineteenth-Century Medicine*, ed. William Coleman and Frederic L. Holmes (Berkeley/Los Angeles: Univ. California Press, 1988), pp. 139–178; and Lenoir, "The Eye as Mathematician," in *Helmholtz and the Foundations*, ed. Cahan (cit. n. 1). Cf. Steven Shapin and Simon Schaffer, *Leviathan and the Air-Pump: Hobbes, Boyle, and the Experimental Life* (Princeton, N. J.: Princeton Univ. Press, 1985), pp. 283–344.

[46] Turner, "Consensus and Controversy," in *Helmholtz and the Foundations*, ed. Cahan (cit. n. 1).

scientific controversies could be said to be about. As cognitive and institutional structures grew increasingly isomorphous, they unleashed a quasi-Darwinian, selective process of scientific change. Disciplinary (now more likely sub-disciplinary) variants were continuously generated and subsequently selected or destroyed, in an ongoing struggle for scarce resources of money, prestige, and professional recruits within relatively fixed bureaucratic frameworks. Research schools, along with any unique methodology or focus that might have character-ized them, seem to have functioned like genetic variants in this process.[47] If suc-cessful, a school might become the nucleus of a new specialty or subdiscipline that could achieve institutional entrenchment; or it might, as Geison insisted, succeed by imposing its new direction on the entire existing field of which it was a part.[48]

Darwinian models of disciplinary change are open to various criticisms and de-serve to be treated warily. Stichweh, for example, cautions that Darwinian models cannot be applied to the early stages of disciplinary formation between 1770 and 1830, before the "disciplinary order of sciences" had been established.[49] Beyond doubt, however, the mechanism of disciplinary and subdisciplinary formation unexpectedly endowed academic controversies of the most esoteric nature with an unprecedented relevance to such matters as how resources would be allocated, how institutional structures would evolve, and which subdisciplinary variants would flourish and which face extinction. The new middle term of scientific con-troversy placed the material and social interests of participants at unprecedented risk. As never before, commitment to the method, outlook, or specialization that characterized a particular school came to constitute a personal investment on which hinged one's career, reputation, and sense of intellectual self-worth; invest-ments of that kind required fierce defense.

Early in the nineteenth century this middle term of controversy centered on the definition and legitimation of disciplines: adjudicating boundary disputes, expel-ling amateur practitioners, forging consensus about methods and research agen-das, and formulating a social apology for academic function. Concerns like these constitute a usually unarticulated but crucially important element in, for exam-ple, the academic disputes that racked classical philology in Germany between 1815 and 1850.[50]

Later the middle term centered on issues of autonomy and the budding off of subfields from a parent discipline. This concern underlay many of the scholarly controversies surrounding the institutional establishment of comparative linguis-tics, experimental psychology, and biochemistry and physical chemistry. In each form the middle term generated new, if often unarticulated, criteria for judging a

[47] See David L. Hull, *Science as a Process: An Evolutionary Account of the Social and Conceptual De-velopment of Science* (Chicago: Univ. Chicago Press, 1988), esp. pp. 9–18, 432–476; and the article by Joel B. Hagen in this volume.

[48] Stichweh, *Disziplinen* (cit. n. 42), pp. 94–99; Geison, "Scientific Change" (cit. n. 18), pp. 27–34; Robert E. Kohler, *From Medical Chemistry to Biochemistry* (Cambridge: Cambridge Univ. Press, 1982), pp. 1–10; and Gerard Lemaine et al., eds. *Perspectives on the Emergence of Scientific Disciplines* (The Hague: Mouton & Co., 1976), pp. 1–26.

[49] Stichweh, *Disziplinen* (cit. n. 42), pp. 48–51. Cf. Hull's discussion of some common objections to genetic models in *Science as a Process* (cit. n. 47), pp. 440–468.

[50] R. Steven Turner, "The Prussian Universities and the Concept of Research," *Internationales Archiv für Sozialgeschichte der deutschen Literatur*, 1980, 5:68–93, esp. pp. 86–93; and Turner, "The Great Transition and the Social Patterns of German Science," *Minerva*, 1987, 25:56–76, esp. pp. 67–72.

controversial issue: How did possible outcomes bear upon one's investment in research expertise? What were the implications of these outcomes for the autonomy
and legitimacy of one's discipline or subfield? Toward what research agenda did
the possible outcomes compel the specialty?

VI. DISCIPLINARY APPEAL AND THE CONTROVERSIES OVER VISION

The study of vision cut across several scientific disciplines, and the field never
pretended to subdisciplinary status or institutional autonomy. That very inter-
disciplinarity, however, illustrates how discipline-specific agendas could affect scientific debates as part of the new middle term of controversy. Disciplinary
allegiance increasingly determined the theoretical alignment of scientists in the
debates over vision. How did the respective positions of Helmholtz and Hering
appeal to the four major disciplines involved, and how was that appeal reflected
in the composition of the schools?

Helmholtz's orientation held a clear attraction for those trained as physicists;
seven of the seventeen partisans listed in Table 1 specialized in that discipline.
Physicists and mathematicians, including Maxwell, Charles Wheatstone, Hermann Grassmann, J. B. Listing, and Gustav Fechner, had been mainly responsible for the paradigmatic reformulation of vision studies that had occurred
around mid century. Helmholtz had borrowed heavily from them all, extended
their methods, and brilliantly applied mathematical-analytical techniques to the
problems of the field. Especially in color-vision studies, his approach invited sophisticated mathematical analysis (the "higher colormetrics," it has been called)
and reliance on experimental methods requiring a deep knowledge of physical optics and instrumentation.[51] In the 1850s, for example, Maxwell had laid down the
methods of mixing colors in order to generate metameric matches and color equations. Some of Maxwell's research had employed a primitive colorimeter, but
most of those who copied him relied primarily upon the simple rotating color
wheel with colored-paper sectors. By the 1890s, however, experimental data on
color mixing not obtained from technically sophisticated colorimeters, on which
brightness could be more readily controlled, were likely to be regarded with con-
descension and suspicion. Physicists who studied vision, even as they became
fewer by 1900, were attracted to Helmholtz's approach over that of his rivals,
partly in order to exploit their natural advantage in the mastery of these required
skills.

Helmholtz's approach appealed to physicists for a further pragmatic reason.
Not without some justification, Hering charged that Helmholtz consistently tried
to explain perceptual phenomena either through physicomechanical analysis of
end-organ function or by "banishing" the phenomena into the inaccessible cortex and seeking to understand them as quasi-rational, inferential processes.
Helmholtz did this by making radically simplifying assumptions about the neural
linkages that intervene between the end organs and the sensorium. Those assumptions had a strong, if tacit, methodological implication. They minimized the

---

[51] The claim that Helmholtz's theory appealed primarily to physicists is common; see Yves Le
Grand, *Light, Colour and Vision*, trans. R. W. G. Hunt *et al.*, 2nd. ed. (London: Chapman & Hall,
1968), p. 429; and Leo M. Hurvich and Dorothea Jameson, "Human Color Perception: An Essay Review," *American Scientist*, 1969, *57*:143–166, on pp. 153–154.

importance of investigative techniques involving microscopic anatomy, physiological chemistry, or animal models. Helmholtz's orientation to sensory studies therefore enhanced the methods of the physicist over those of the physiologist.

For ophthalmologists a choice between schools was less clear and less necessary. It was complicated, moreover, by their enshrinement of Helmholtz as a prestigious founding father in their drive to make ophthalmology a modern, institutionally entrenched medical specialty. Ophthalmology established its disciplinary autonomy in the German universities between 1852 and 1882, with most of the new chairs and institutes created between 1870 and 1880.[52] Ophthalmologists justified this new status by appeal to therapeutic breakthroughs (a series of surgical procedures developed around mid century, mostly in the school of Albrecht von Graefe), a new diagnostic efficacy (resulting largely from Helmholtz's invention of the ophthalmoscope in 1852), and a new, definitive understanding of the dioptrical functioning of the eye (capped by Helmholtz's work on accommodation in the early 1850s).[53] Although Helmholtz had never been an ophthalmologist himself or ever been much interested in medical problems, ophthalmologists readily appropriated him and the new science of vision he represented, both for their prestige and for their actual results.

Once ophthalmology was established as a specialty, however, neither Helmholtz's nor Hering's scientific approach offered a particular advantage in the field's practical, medical concerns. The scientific controversies that did touch ophthalmological practice—the role of the ciliary fibers, the physiology of accommodation, the nature of astigmatism—did not divide the schools of Helmholtz and Hering. In some areas, however, Hering's insistence that organic, physiological mechanisms, not psychological ones, underlie visual perception promised wider avenues and greater efficacy for ophthalmological intervention. Strabismus, or squint, was one such area. If, as Helmholtz's school insisted, those who suffer from squint can *sometimes* acquire empirically new patterns of corresponding retinal points to compensate for their defect, then surgical intervention to correct the condition may be unnecessary or even harmful. If, as Hering insisted, a full capacity for binocular vision is possible only through the "natural" and innate pattern of correspondence, then surgical intervention is strongly indicated for some strabismus sufferers.[54]

Considerations like these seem eventually to have won Hering the sympathy of

[52] Sabine Fahrenbach, "Zur Herausbildung der Ophthalmologie als eigenständige Wissenschaftsdisziplin in Preußen unter Berücksichtigung der Wechselwirkung zwischen Disziplinbildungsprozeß und der Tätigkeit der wissenschaftlichen Schuls A. v. Graefes" (Ph.D. diss., Wilhelm-Pieck-Universität Rostock, 1983); Avraham Zloczower, "Konjunktur in der Forschung," in *Innovation und Widerstände in der Wissenschaft*, ed. Frank Pfetsch and Zloczower (Düsseldorf: Bertelsmann, 1972), pp. 32–33; and Hans-Heinz Eulner, *Die Entwicklung der medizinischen Spezialfächer an den Universitäten des deutschen Sprachgebietes* (Stuttgart: Ferdinand Enke, 1970), p. 406.

[53] Arleen Tuchman, "Helmholtz and the German Medical Community," in *Helmholtz and the Foundations*, ed. Cahan (cit. n. 1); Sabine Fahrenbach, "Die Herausbildung der Ophthalmologie in Preussen und die wissenschaftliche Schule Albrecht von Graefes (1828–1870)," in *Ursprung der modernen Wissenschaften*, ed. Guntau and Laitko (cit. n. 42), pp. 315–327; Wolfgang Münchow, *Kurze Geschichte der Augenheilkunde* (Leipzig: Georg Thieme, 1966), *passim*; and Julius Hirschberg, *The History of Ophthalmology* (1911), 11 vols. (Bonn: J. P. Wayenborgh, 1985), esp. Vols. V–VIII.

[54] Helmholtz, *Optics*, Vol. III, pp. 405–407; Alfred Bielschowsky, *Lectures on Motor Anomalies* (Hanover, N.H.: Dartmouth College Publications, 1945); Franz Bruno Hofmann, "Die neueren Untersuchungen über das Sehen der Schielenden," in *Ergeb. der Physiol., II: Bioph. Psychoph.*, 1902, *1*:801–846; Kries, "On Changes of Localizations for Anomalous Adjustments of the Eyes," in *Optics*,

ophthalmologists. Certainly by the 1920s the observations of ophthalmologists on eye movements, strabismus, and binocularity were widely seen as supporting Hering's positions on space perception. Moriz Sachs in 1927 argued that the victory of nativism had been won "in the clinic." Hering cultivated ophthalmologists and made a significant contribution to the debate over strabismus in 1899.[55] Four of the twelve Hering supporters listed in Table 1 were ophthalmologists by profession, and the Hering-Sattler school included numerous others. Helmholtz had a roughly similar proportion of ophthalmologists among his supporters, but none were his own students.

Most of the names appearing in Table 1 are those of physiologists. When physiology made its successful push for disciplinary autonomy and institutionalization in the 1850s and 1860s, it did so on the intellectual basis of new approaches that distinguished it sharply from anatomy and morphology, the fields with which it had traditionally been combined. The most successful and prestigious of these was the experimental, biophysical approach represented by the 1847 school; the successes of this approach were greatest in sensory physiology.[56] Adherents to this approach included some of the most powerful and productive institute directors of the era, men like Brücke, du Bois-Reymond, and Ludwig. Even when they did not involve themselves directly in the Helmholtz-Hering controversies, their prominence in the field and their known association with Helmholtz enhanced the sense that Helmholtz's views on visual perception must represent disciplinary consensus and orthodoxy.

But Hering also appealed directly to the disciplinary loyalties of German physiologists. He insisted that the dignity of physiology should not rest on particular methodologies, but on a philosophy of the organism, on the unique, dynamic conception of life which he himself articulated and from which he argued that all physiological research should depart. Physiology must avoid subservience to biophysical materialism and in the study of the senses also avoid becoming "the stepdaughter of psychology"—both dangers simultaneously represented by the school of Helmholtz.[57]

Long-term changes in the focus of sensory studies reinforced Hering's program for physiology. Physiological studies of sensation and perception at the middle of

---

Vol. III, pp. 578–580; and Zoth, "Augenbewegungen und Gesichtswahrnehmungen" (cit. n. 15), p. 396.

[55] Ewald Hering, "Ueber die anomale Localisation der Netzhautbilder bei Strabismus alternans," *Deutsches Archiv für klinische Medizin*, 1899, *64*:15–32. Sachs is cited in Hillebrand, *Lehre von den Gesichtsempfindungen* (cit. n. 25), p. 198.

[56] Paul C. Cranefield, "The Organic Physics of 1847 and the Biophysics of Today," *Journal of the History of Medicine*, 1957, *12*:407–423; Richard L. Kremer, "Building Institutes for Physiology in Prussia, 1836–1846: Contexts, Interests, and Rhetoric," in *The Laboratory Revolution in Medicine*, ed. Perry Williams and Andrew Cunningham (Cambridge: Cambridge Univ. Press, 1992), pp. 72–109; Lenoir, "Ludwig's Institute in Leipzig" (cit. n. 45); Lynn K. Nyhart, "The Disciplinary Breakdown of German Morphology, 1870–1900," *Isis*, 1987, *78*:365–389; Nyhart, "Physiology and the Sciences of Animal Life in Germany, 1845–1870" (MS, 1991); Arleen M. Tuchman, "From the Lecture to the Laboratory: The Institutionalization of Scientific Medicine at the University of Heidelberg," in *Investigative Enterprise,* ed. Coleman and Holmes (cit. n. 45), pp. 65–99; and Tuchman, *Medicine, Physiology and the State: The Institutionalization of Scientific Medicine at the University of Heidelberg, 1830–1870* (New York: Oxford Univ. Press, in press).

[57] Hering, *Beiträge zur Physiologie* (cit. n. 9), Pt. 5 (1864), pp. iii–v; and Hering, "Zur Theorie der Nerventätigkeit" (1899), *Fünf Reden* (cit. n. 10), pp. 105–131, esp. 105–109.

the nineteenth century had been overwhelmingly psychophysical in approach. They consisted of presenting stimulus patterns to subjects, obtaining information about the sensory or perceptual response by inquiry or introspection, and then reasoning about the intervening processes and mechanisms that must mediate the observed pattern of responses.

Gradually, however, research that did not involve psychophysical methods became more and more important in vision studies. These techniques included studies of brain localization, comparative visual anatomy, the embryological development of visual systems, and the electrophysiology of the eye and the optic nerve, as well as chemical studies of retinal pigments and their photosensitivity. In 1845–1854 vision research *not* involving psychophysical approaches constituted about 15 percent of the literature; by 1885–1894 it constituted about 28 percent.[58] Psychophysical approaches became increasingly associated with psychology, while physiologists relied more on animal models and vivisection. In that changing methodological climate, Hering's approach to the problems of visual perception had a stronger appeal to physiologists, in light of their predispositions and methodological investments, than did Helmholtz's. Hering assigned a central role to organic structures and processes within the tissues, exalted physiology over psychology, took greater cognizance of phylogenetic relationships, and implicitly narrowed the gap between perceptual processes in humans and animals.

More than physiology itself, it was the new experimental psychology that inherited the dilemmas of the Helmholtz-Hering controversy. A marginal group numerically in 1860, by the 1880s the psychologists had begun to differentiate themselves from philosophers and to secure specialized chairs and institutes. Early German psychologists concentrated on the study of sensation; they modeled their field in part on sensory physiology and adopted many of the methods and agendas of the physiologists.[59]

The new psychologists were concerned to establish an autonomous scientific field, and neither Helmholtz's nor Hering's approach fitted that need particularly well. Hering's philosophy, with its reductionist overtones, threatened to dissolve psychology into physiology. Helmholtz's empiricism, despite its congenial emphasis on mind, learning, and experience, portrayed the mental processes that mediated perception as "inferential" in nature. If such mental processes were taken as inferential, explanations built on them harked dangerously back to the quasi-rationalistic tradition of philosphical psychology from which the experimentalists were trying to distance themselves. But if the processes were understood as simple associations, then they left too little room for will or volition and thus prevented a legitimate science of the mind from being built on them.[60]

---

[58] Turner, "Paradigms and Productivity" (cit. n. 4), pp. 47–49.

[59] "Zur Einführung," *Zeitschrift für Psychologie und Physiologie der Sinnesorgane*, 1890, *1*:1–4; Mitchell G. Ash, "The Emergence of Gestalt Theory: Experimental Psychology in Germany, 1890–1920" (Ph.D. diss., Harvard Univ., 1982); Ash, "Academic Politics in the History of Science: Experimental Psychology in Germany, 1879–1941," *Central European History*, 1980, *13*:255–286; Ash, *Holism and the Quest for Objectivity: Gestalt Psychology in German Culture* (New York: Oxford Univ. Press, in press); Joseph Ben-David and Randall Collins, "Social Factors in the Origin of a New Science: The Case of Psychology," *American Historical Review*, 1966, *31*:451–472 (with a critique by Dorothy Ross); and Turner, "Paradigms and Productivity" (cit. n. 4), pp. 45–50, 62–65.

[60] Carl Stumpf, "Hermann von Helmholtz and the New Psychology," *Psychophysical Review*, 1895,

What did appeal to the new psychologists in Hering's writings was the primacy he gave to phenomenological experience, his insistence (not always observed in his practice) that the primitive sensory capacities of the mind have to be studied as we find them and not "reduced" to rationalistic inferences or physicochemical mechanisms. By this methodological criterion, many psychologists agreed, Hering's insistence that there are four, not three, fundamental color sensations seemed undeniable. Like Hering, many of them found it impossible to believe that a sensation so apparently primitive as that of space could really be "emergent," a psychic synthesis of other sensory capacities. By 1900 many experimental psychologists like Carl Stumpf, Hermann Ebbinghaus, and Oswald Külpe were moving toward positions more compatible with Hering's than with Helmholtz's.[61] The list of Hering's most immediate defenders includes the psychologists Hillebrand and Müller. Hillebrand in particular revered Hering, and in the 1890s he mounted an impressive experimental defense of Hering's theory of retinal depth values and his concept of the core surface. Helmholtz had no comparable defenders among the new psychologists, although Theodor Lipps espoused a general empiricism on the origins of spatial perception. The views of Wilhelm Wundt had much in common with those of Helmholtz, but Wundt mostly emphasized the differences between them.[62]

By the early 1900s the conceptual theories of both Helmholtz and Hering were becoming increasingly irrelevant to the new psychology. The phenomenological movement owed a deep and often-acknowledged debt to Hering, but its promoters Ernst Jaensch and David Katz (both students of the Hering supporter Müller) largely abandoned the physiological aspects of Hering's program and its concern with punctiform models of retinal response. Jaensch wrote in 1921, shortly after the death of Hering, of the "metamorphosis of nativism" into a "new nativism," which was abandoning the traditional insistence on anatomical and physiological substrates in favor of "a system of [psychological] functions, which condition sensory experience and also make it possible."[63]

As for the partisans themselves, they realized that the new psychologists represented the crucial scientific public, the allegiance and support of which had to be captured. Hering in his later papers invoked the support of Ebbinghaus and Franz Brentano; Kries in 1923 embraced the views of Katz, Jaensch, and even Hillebrand as proof that the positions of Helmholtz and Hering were susceptible

2:1–12; and R. Steven Turner, "Helmholtz, Sensory Physiology, and the Disciplinary Development of German Psychology," in *The Problematic Science: Psychology in Nineteenth-Century Thought*, ed. William R. Woodward and Mitchell Ash (New York: Praeger, 1982), pp. 147–166.

[61] Carl Stumpf, *Ueber den psychologischen Ursprung der Raumvorstellung* (Leipzig: S. Hirzel, 1873), pp. 97–103 and *passim*; Hermann Ebbinghaus, *Grundzüge der Psychologie*, 4th ed. (Leipzig: Veit & Comp., 1919), pp. 490–494; and Oswald Külpe, *Grundriß der Psychologie* (Leipzig: Wilhelm Engelmann, 1893), pp. 385–387. See also Ash, *Emergence of Gestalt Theory* (cit. n. 59), pp. 85–135.

[62] For Hillebrand's publications see his *Lehre von den Geschichtsempfindungen* (cit. n. 25), p. 201; Theodor Lipps, *Psychologische Studien* (Leipzig: Dürr, 1885); and Lipps, "Die Raumanschauung und die Augenbewegung," *Z. Psych. Physiol. Sinnesorgane*, 1892, *3*:123–171. On Wundt see Diamond, "Wundt before Leipzig" (cit. n. 28); and Kurt Danziger, "Wundt and the Two Traditions of Psychology," in *Wilhelm Wundt*, ed. Reiber (cit. n. 28), pp. 73–88.

[63] Ernst R. Jaensch, "Ueber den Nativismus in der Lehre von der Raumwahrnehmung," *Zeitschrift für Sinnesphysiologie*, 1921, *52*:229–234, quoting from p. 233.

of synthesis.[64] Those efforts notwithstanding, the disciplinary goals of German psychology were by now no longer well served by either Helmholtz or Hering.

As this analysis suggests, the disciplinary fragmentation of vision studies tended more and more to override the fragmentation represented by the competing perspectives of Helmholtz and Hering. The American psychologist Leonard Thompson Troland complained in 1922 that the 180 articles on vision published in 1920 had been scattered in fifty-eight different periodicals and reflected eleven separate disciplines or fields. Even the literature reviews were discipline-specific, so that none captured more than a small portion of the total literature. "The diffuseness of the literature," Troland went on, "is reflected by the methods and conceptions employed by investigators publishing in the several fields, each showing a lack of acquaintance with the problems and results with which others are concerned."[65] Disciplinary fragmentation had introduced an institutional incommensurability on top of the existing semantic and conceptual ones.

This fact suggests an irony about the schools of Helmholtz and Hering. Research schools are often considered the primary vehicles of scientific change and specialization. In this case the schools played the opposite role. While they flourished as transdisciplinary constellations, they helped to insulate vision studies on the continent *against* disciplinary fragmentation and specialization.

VII. CONCLUSION: THE CONTROVERSY IN THE TWENTIETH CENTURY

The issues that divided the schools of Helmholtz and Hering have persisted, still fundamental and most unresolved, into twentieth-century studies of vision. Modern approaches to visual perception, such as the Gestalt approach or the information-processing theories of cognitive psychology, are occasionally still categorized as "nativist" or "empiricist" in orientation.[66] Twentieth-century studies of perception, however, have been able to draw upon a new sort of evidence—microelectrode studies that record the response characteristics of individual cells in the optical tract of animals. The impact of that evidence has been strongly nativist, although it has scarcely settled the issue definitively.[67] Other approaches to perception, like the so-called direct theories pioneered by James J. Gibson, claim to have transcended the terms of the nativist-empiricist dichotomy altogether.[68]

[64] Ewald Hering, "Beitrag zur Lehre vom Simultankontrast," *Z. Psych. Physiol. Sinnesorgane*, 1890, *1*:18–28, on p. 1; Hering, "Ueber den Einfluss der *Macula lutea* auf spectrale Farbengleichungen," *Pflüger's Archiv Ges. Physiol.*, 1894, *54*:277–312, on p. 1; and Johannes von Kries, *Allgemeine Sinnesphysiologie* (Leipzig: Vogel, 1923), pp. 218–220, 284.

[65] Leonard Thompson Troland, *The Present Status of Visual Science*, special issue of *Bulletin of the National Research Council of the National Academy of Sciences*, 1922, *5.2* (27):10.

[66] P. C. Dodwell, "Contemporary Theoretical Problems in Seeing," in *Seeing*, Vol. V of *Handbook of Perception*, ed. Edward C. Carterette and Morton P. Friedman, (New York: Academic Press, 1975), pp. 57–77; Hochberg, "Nativism and Empiricism in Perception" (cit. n. 5), pp. 255–330; and Julian E. Hochberg, "Visual Perception," in *Stevens' Handbook of Experimental Psychology*, 2 vols., 2nd. ed., ed. Richard C. Atkinson *et al.* (New York: Wiley, 1988), Vol. I, pp. 195–276.

[67] See Hochberg, "Visual Perception," pp. 26–28; Dodwell, "Theoretical Problems," p. 65; and, e.g., David H. Hubel and Torston Wiesel, "Receptive Fields of Cells in Striate Cortex of Very Young, Visually Inexperienced Kittens," *Journal of Neurophysiology*, 1963, *26*:994–1002.

[68] James J. Gibson, *The Perception of the Visual World* (Boston: Houghton Mifflin, 1950); Edward S. Reed, *James J. Gibson and the Psychology of Perception* (New Haven: Yale Univ. Press, 1988); and Hochberg, "Visual Perception," pp. 240–248.

Only in the field of color vision has a definitive compromise between the positions of Helmholtz and Hering been reached. Between 1955 and 1965 various direct techniques established the existence of three photopigments in the retinal cones. These were shown to provide neural inputs to cells higher in the visual tract, which in turn display chromatic opponency in a manner very similar to that predicted by the original Hering theory. The American psychologists Leo M. Hurvich and Dorothea Jameson emerged as leading proponents of the resulting zone theory of vision. They placed it on a firm basis of sensory experimentation, quantified it, and interpreted it as a resounding victory for Hering. Single-cell response studies also detected center-surround configurations in the receptive field of cells, which were thought to provide an innate mechanism for contour enhancement and simultaneous contrast, again largely as Hering had predicted.[69]

The history of these post-1950 developments, however, is not the history of the Helmholtz-Hering controversy; they possess only a tenuous linkage, conceptually or historically, to the original nineteenth-century dispute. That dispute underwent a basic change in the 1920s, for it lost the characteristics of a true school controversy. The issues persisted, but arguments about them were neither as pointed nor as intensely polarized as earlier. The antagonistic positions were no longer defended by individuals who had staked their careers upon them, and the few remaining partisans, like Tschermak-Seysenegg, were shunted to the scientific periphery.

Against that background, the trichromatic theory of vision persisted into the 1950s as a vague orthodoxy that sometimes represented itself as theoretical agnosticism. Hering's theory of color vision was also widely represented internationally in textbooks, although it usually received more sympathetic treatment from psychologists than from physiologists or physicists. Nevertheless, between 1930 and 1950 it seems to have had few aggressive champions, especially outside Germany. Theorists writing on perception in general and spatial perception in particular usually disclaimed the nativist and empiricist labels with great disdain. Textbooks and quasi-historical treatments held up the original nativist-empiricist dispute to students as a cautionary example of theoretical obscurantism in science.

During the early twentieth century various factors undermined the former, intense polarization of the dispute into competing schools. As suggested before, disciplinary fragmentation and the incommensurability of disciplinary perspectives and agendas tended to override the old fragmentation by schools. Another factor was the internationalization of vision studies. Helmholtz's positions were always widely known and followed internationally; in the 1920s the third German edition of the *Handbuch* was translated into English, with sympathetic commentaries by Kries and other German luminaries. Hering's writings, in contrast,

---

[69] See C. L. Hardin, *Color for Philosophers: Unweaving the Rainbow* (Indianapolis: Hacket, 1986), pp. 1–45; R. L. De Valois and K. K. De Valois, "Neural Coding of Color," in *Seeing*, ed. Carterette and Friedman (cit. n. 66), pp. 117–166; Leo M. Hurvich and Dorothea Jameson, "An Opponent-Process Theory of Color Vision," *Psychological Review*, 1957, *64*(6):384–404; "Leo M. Hurvich and Dorothea Jameson," in *A History of Psychology in Autobiography*, Vol. VIII, ed. Gardner Lindzey (Stanford, Calif.: Stanford Univ. Press, 1989), pp. 156–206, esp. pp. 184–187; and Dorothea Jameson, "Color Vision Theory in 1948: Issues and Origins," (MS prepared for a symposium in honor of Leo M. Hurvich, March 1981). I am very grateful to Professor Jameson for a copy of her unpublished manuscript.

were less well known outside central Europe and were rarely translated.[70] As Germany's former dominance of vision studies declined after 1900, Hering's views therefore lost relative ground on the international scene.

Death also undermined the respective schools. Hering's own indomitable personality had sustained the controversy for almost two scientific generations, and his school did not long survive him. As Table 1 shows, most of his militant supporters were nearing the end of their effective careers in the 1920s. Death, and especially the untimely loss of Arthur König and Willibald Nagel, disrupted the amorphous Helmholtz school as well, but the survival of Helmholtz's program had never depended upon personal discipleship to the extent that Hering's had.

The loss of that continuity which Hering's vigorous school had provided left his theories particularly vulnerable. The discussion above stressed that Hering's approach to visual perception was embedded in an alternate semantics unique to him and his school. Age and institutional dispersal of the school rendered it increasingly unable to preserve those semantic and conceptual structures against corrupting influences. The secondary accounts of Hering's ideas that were circulated and debated between 1925 and 1955, whether hostile or friendly, usually were produced by outsiders to the school, and they described those ideas in ways and in a terminology that did not capture their full coherence.[71] English accounts, in particular, stressed the four-color characteristic over that of opponency, and they rarely dealt with Hering's intricate theory of brightness or adequately represented the important roles of contrast and adaptation in his theory of vision. The comparable accounts of spatial perception analyzed Hering's specific claims about localization, but rarely within the philosophical context in which Hering and his students had embedded them. Although in the 1950s new supporters and new methods were to lead to a partial vindication of his approach, the period 1925–1955 marked the nadir of Hering's influence on the international study of vision.

---

[70] See Turner, "Paradigms and Productivity" (cit. n. 4), pp. 36–45. Helmholtz's *Handbuch* appeared in English translation in 1924–1925; a number of his papers and his very important popular lectures were available in English as early as 1873: *Popular Lectures on Scientific Subjects*, 2 vols., trans. E. Atkinson (New York: Appleton, 1873). The first major work of Hering's to appear in English translation seems to have been his *Spatial Sense and Movements of the Eye*, trans. Carl A. Radde (Baltimore: American Academy of Optometry, 1942); his work on color vision seems to have appeared first in English in his *Outlines of a Theory of the Light Sense*, ed. and trans. Leo M. Hurvich and Dorothea Jameson (Cambridge, Mass.: Harvard Univ. Press, 1964).

[71] See, e.g., John Herbert Parsons, *An Introduction to the Study of Colour-Vision*, 2nd. ed. (Cambridge: Cambridge Univ. Press, 1924); Wilhelm Trendelenburg, *Die Gesichtssinn: Grundzüge der physiologischen Optik* (Berlin: Springer), 1st. ed. (1943), 2nd. ed. (1961); Dean B. Judd, "Basic Correlates of the Visual Stimulus," in *Handbook of Experimental Psychology*, ed. S. S. Stevens (New York: Wiley, 1951), pp. 811–887; and Le Grand, *Light, Colour and Vision* (cit. n. 51.).

W. H. Perkin, Jr.,
at Manchester and Oxford:
From Irwell to Isis

By Jack Morrell*

W HILE THE CAREER of Sir William Henry Perkin (1838–1907), the discoverer of the first synthetic dye, mauve, continues to attract justifiable attention, that of his son of the same name (1860–1929) has been curiously neglected. He is not even mentioned in two recent excellent surveys of the history of chemistry.[1] Yet after his death he received a rare accolade from the Chemical Society of London in the form of an obituary published as a special number of its journal; and his chemical colleagues, who regarded him as the leading organic chemist of his generation in Britain, lamented that he was not awarded a Nobel Prize.[2] The purpose of this essay is to show why such judgments were made, by examining Perkin's attitude to "original work" and "original investigations," his favorite synonyms for research. My main focus will be his career as Waynflete Professor of Chemistry at the University of Oxford, an ancient and conservative arts-oriented institution into which he introduced Germanic notions and practices of research. This Indian summer on the banks of the Isis from January 1913 to June 1929 cannot be understood in isolation from Perkin's golden age, as he styled it, as professor of organic chemistry at Owens College, Manchester, on the banks of the Irwell from 1892 to September 1913. His Mancunian period drew on

* Department of European Studies, University of Bradford, Bradford, West Yorkshire, BD7 1DP, England.

Research for this article was facilitated by a grant from the Leverhulme Trust, a supernumary fellowship at Brasenose College, Oxford, and a study leave from the University of Bradford. For permission to cite manuscripts in their care I thank the archivists of the University of Manchester, University of Oxford, and Magdalen College, Oxford, and the librarian of the Museum of History of Science, Oxford.

[1] Colin A. Russell, ed., *Recent Developments in the History of Chemistry* (London: Royal Society of Chemistry, 1985); and Robert Bud and Gerrylynn K. Roberts, *Science versus Practice: Chemistry in Victorian Britain* (Manchester: Manchester Univ. Press, 1984). For the father see most recently Herbert T. Pratt, "Sir William Henry Perkin Visits America," *Textile Chemist and Colorist*, 1988, *20*(11):25–32; and Anthony S. Travis, "Perkin's Mauve: Ancestor of the Organic Chemical Industry," *Technology and Culture*, 1990, *31*:51–82. See also Sidney Edelstein, "William Henry Perkin," *Dictionary of Scientific Biography*, ed. Charles C. Gillespie, Vol. X (New York: Scribners, 1975), pp. 515–517.

[2] John Greenaway, Jocelyn Field Thorpe, and Robert Robinson, *The Life and Work of Professor William Henry Perkin* (London: Chemical Society of London, 1932); H. E. Armstrong, "Obituary of Perkin," *Nature*, 1929, *124*:623–627; and Robinson, "William Henry Perkin, Jr.," *Journal of the Society of Chemical Industry*, 1929, *48*:1008–1012. For personal recollections of Perkin I am indebted to Professor Wilson Baker, Dr. H. J. Stern, and Dr. F. W. Stoyle.

debts incurred as a young researcher to his two German teachers: Johannes Wislicenus, under whom he studied at Würzburg, 1880–1882; and Adolf von Baeyer, with whom he worked in Munich, 1882–1886. I shall discuss in turn Perkin's German, Mancunian, and Oxonian periods, with particular reference to research atmosphere and practice.

I. AN EDUCATION FOR RESEARCH

Although Perkin grew up in a very chemical household and unconsciously imbibed from his father the idea of research as a supreme good, his father did not give him systematic instruction but sent him to the Royal College of Chemistry, London, where he studied under Edward Frankland and under W. R. E. Hodgkinson, head of the laboratories, who had worked under Wislicenus. Perkin then went to Würzburg to study for his Ph.D. under Wislicenus, a master of organic syntheses based on the reactions of ethyl acetoacetate and diethyl malonate. Not surprisingly, Perkin learned about the use of these compounds in syntheses, which he subsequently developed in his early research on the formation of compounds made up of closed carbon rings. He also saw in action a particular model of a successful leader of laboratory research. Perkin was impressed by Wislicenus's splendid character: he was kind, genial, direct, and (though not fifty years old) even venerable. His paternalism was associated with an undictatorial and generous attitude to his research pupils: he was as much concerned with developing their own initiative and pride as with solving his own research problems. By example he imbued his students with his own persistence in difficult research, so that abandoning it became unthinkable.[3]

Having taken his doctorate, Perkin spent four years at Munich with Baeyer as a privatdozent and personal research assistant. For Perkin, Baeyer soon became a scientific hero who remained an object of lifelong intellectual devotion. Perkin modeled himself on the qualities he most admired in his revered teacher. He was amazed by the way Baeyer had designed laboratory buildings, first occupied in 1877, on a grand scale way ahead of the apparent needs of the 1870s: here was a model of excellent laboratory design and of planning for posterity which Perkin never forgot. Perkin also found in Baeyer his ideal of what a professor and research chemist should be. Supported by a wide knowledge of current literature and endowed with a strong chemical instinct, Baeyer showed what could be achieved by steadfastness of research purpose focused on the laboratory: he refused to waste time and energy on general university politics, which he regarded as diversionary. His research productivity, extraordinary in quality, quantity, and regularity, was achieved with simple and small-scale apparatus. Primarily an experimenter at the bench, he was not greatly interested in theory except in the field of structural formulae, where his strain theory correlated the stability of cyclic compounds with the ring angles.[4]

Baeyer was so devoted to structural organic chemistry that he was indifferent to

[3] W. H. Perkin, Jr., "Wislicenus Memorial Lecture" (1905), in *Memorial Lectures Delivered before the Chemical Society, 1901–1913* (London: Chemical Society, 1914), pp. 59–92.

[4] Colin A. Russell, *The History of Valency* (Leicester: Leicester Univ. Press, 1971), pp. 235–239; and Aaron J. Ihde, "The Development of Strain Theory" in *Kekulé Centennial*, ed. O. Theodore Benfey (Washington, D.C.: American Chemical Society, 1966), pp. 140–162.

the then-new physical chemistry, an attitude that Perkin also maintained throughout his career. Baeyer was a positivist who used experiments not to test his views but to discover how substances behave under a variety of conditions. Above all, he created by example an atmosphere in which research was the only thing that mattered. As Perkin recalled, "There was a feeling in the laboratory that no one was of any account who did not research, and, moreover, the position of each researcher and the esteem in which he was held depended solely on the quality of the work he was engaged in."[5] Perkin saw that not only did this research ethos attract talented researchers such as Otto Fischer, Eugen Bamberger, and Hans von Pechmann, who were his contemporaries at Munich; it also made the laboratory a frequent port of call for visitors such as Victor Meyer and Emil Fischer, two of Baeyer's most distinguished former pupils.

Baeyer's research group at Munich was distinguished by its size, its productivity, and its endurance. Although some of his privatdozenten also supervised research, Baeyer himself was the driving force. Over a period of forty years, from 1875 to 1915, at least 560 people were members of the group, which generated about 1,200 papers on organic chemistry. Of these 560, no fewer than 395 took a Ph.D. under Baeyer or one of his many lieutenants, so that on average ten doctorates a year were gained. As one of those lieutenants, Perkin appreciated the importance of size, productivity, and endurability in a successful research school. He also saw that over half of Baeyer's researchers went into industry or commerce, one of his contemporaries at Munich being Carl Duisberg, who was head of IG Farben from 1925. In all these ways Baeyer provided for Perkin an example to be followed or modified; but in one respect they diverged. Baeyer was so relentlessly single-minded that he had no time for the theater or for music; in contrast Perkin came from a highly musical family and was an accomplished pianist. At Munich he luxuriated in the operas of Wagner and Mozart, whereas Baeyer (as Perkin sadly recalled) regarded *Gotterdämmerung* as the ultimate bore.[6]

It was at Munich that Perkin began a stint of eleven years devoted to synthesizing compounds containing rings composed of three, four, and five atoms of carbon; he not only confounded the experts of the day but also made an important contribution to confirming Baeyer's strain theory. When Perkin left Munich in 1886, his reputation was such that Harold Baily Dixon invited him to occupy a vacant laboratory in the chemistry department at Owens College in Manchester. He soon attracted students to it. In 1887 Perkin was elected the first professor of chemistry at Heriot-Watt College, Edinburgh, where he continued his work on closed rings and initiated his research on alkaloids. On the death in 1892 of Carl Schorlemmer, the first professor of organic chemistry at Owens College, Perkin accepted an invitation to succeed him.[7]

[5] William H. Perkin, Jr., "Baeyer Memorial Lecture" (1923), in *Memorial Lectures Delivered before the Chemical Society, 1914–1932* (London: Chemical Society, 1933), pp. 47–73, on p. 72.

[6] Jeffrey A. Johnson, "Hierarchy and Creativity in Chemistry, 1871–1914," *Osiris*, 1989, 5:214–240, on p. 225; Joseph S. Fruton, *Contrasts in Scientific Style: Research Groups in the Chemical and Biochemical Sciences* (Philadelphia: American Philosophical Society, 1990), pp. 118–162, 327–374; and Perkin, "Baeyer" (cit. n. 5), p. 69.

[7] On Perkin's research see William H. Perkin, Jr., "The Early History of the Synthesis of Closed Carbon Chains," *Journal of the Chemical Society*, 1929, pp. 1347–1363. In 1886 H. B. Dixon (1852–1930) had just succeeded Roscoe as professor of chemistry at Owens and was concerned to augment the considerable reputation of its chemistry department. For a useful overview see G. N. Burkhardt,

II. PERKIN AT MANCHESTER: BUILDING A SCHOOL

When Perkin joined the professoriate at Owens College, he followed a chemist who had deserted the laboratory bench in order to pursue literary work. When Schorlemmer became professor of organic chemistry at Owens in 1874, he in fact occupied the first chair of its kind in Britain. But though he was a good laboratory teacher, he devoted the last fifteen years of his life continuously and almost exclusively to authorship, especially of textbooks and the history of various aspects of chemistry. To the chagrin of ambitious undergraduates such as Julius Cohen, Schorlemmer gave nothing but lectures, neither demonstrating preparations nor allowing students to make them. It was Cohen, who studied under Baeyer in 1882–1884 for his Ph.D., who on his return to Manchester in 1885 as a demonstrator initiated the teaching of practical organic chemistry at Owens and codified his practice in a textbook on practical organic chemistry of 1887, the first of its kind in Britain. As befitted a pupil of Baeyer, Cohen was very much a laboratory bench man, an unflagging publishing researcher, and he might well have developed practical organic chemistry at Owens had he not moved in 1890 to the Yorkshire College of Science, Leeds, at the invitation of Arthur Smithells—yet another student of Baeyer's—to build up organic chemistry there. In his Mancunian period Cohen guided one research pupil, Arthur Harden, who became a Nobel Prize winner in 1929; in his practical teaching he regarded the careful preparation of organic compounds as a prelude to "original work," and he stressed that the original sources given before the details of each preparation were essential and not ornamental.[8]

Although Cohen had left Owens, Perkin was not isolated there in his commitment to research. History, represented by A. W. Ward and T. F. Tout, shone brightly. In the natural sciences Manchester could boast of Dixon, Horace Lamb, Arthur Schuster, Osborne Reynolds, Boyd Dawkins, and F. E. Weiss. Later professorial colleagues included Ernest Rutherford and H. C. H. Carpenter. Perkin's particular contribution was to create in Manchester what Baeyer had built in Munich, namely, an internationally renowned school of organic chemistry that Emil Fischer regarded as equal to his own in Berlin. In an otherwise gloomy survey of British chemical research, Raphael Meldola reported in 1907 that with the exception of Manchester no university had called into existence "an active centre of research—a school in the continental sense of the term."[9] He alluded here not only to Perkin but also to Dixon, the founder at Manchester of a school of combustion research, who like Perkin stressed that research ought to be not an

"Schools of Chemistry in Great Britain and Ireland, XIII: The University of Manchester (Faculty of Science)," *Journal of the Royal Institute of Chemistry*, 1954, *78*:448–460. On Owens College see Robert H. Kargon, *Science in Victorian Manchester: Enterprise and Expertise* (Baltimore/London: Johns Hopkins Univ. Press, 1977), pp. 153–234, on pp. 175–183, 190–212.

[8] See Arthur Harden, "Carl Schorlemmer (1834–1892)", *J. Chem. Soc.*, 1893, *63*:756–763; Arthur Smithells, introduction to Carl Schorlemmer, *The Rise and Development of Organic Chemistry* (London: Macmillan, 1894) pp. xi–xxiv; H. S. Raper, "Julius Berend Cohen (1859–1935)," *Obituary Notices of Fellows of the Royal Society*, 1935, *1*:503–513; and Julius Cohen, *The Owens College Course of Practical Organic Chemistry* (London: Macmillan, 1887).

[9] Raphael Meldola, "The Position and Prospects of Chemical Research in Great Britain," *J. Chem. Soc.*, 1907, *91*:626–658, on p. 637.

ornamental luxury but an ingrained habit. In 1908 the university recognized Perkin's contribution to its chemistry department by raising his salary to £1,000 per annum and by making him director of the organic laboratories, previously directed by Dixon.[10]

Though Perkin was a gifted lecturer, his forte was working at the laboratory bench, where he was noted for his speed, accuracy, fruitful instinctiveness, and rare ability to induce reactions to take place. Like Baeyer he saw the laboratory bench as the *fons et origo* of all discovery. Again like Baeyer, in the pursuit of research he had little patience for nonresearchers. According to H. E. Armstrong, Perkin was "as mad as several *Mad Hatters*" in his devotion to research, presumably an allusion to the way in which he began his day's stint at one end of a bench full of clean apparatus and worked his way along it, leaving a trail of dirty apparatus to be dealt with by a washing-up boy.[11] Perkin believed that laboratory workers should use every available moment in carrying out "original investigations," and he maintained an "atmosphere of research" so that for his students research became a natural and even necessary part of scientific existence as they worked under him and with their fellows. He wished to promote postgraduate research degrees, fellowships, and studentships; and he yearned to make the completion of a research project indispensable for the award of a B.Sc. degree. Again like Baeyer, he believed that technical organic chemistry depended on the work of research chemists who undertook it for purely scientific reasons, a telling example for him being the research done in Baeyer's Berlin laboratory by Carl Graebe and Carl Liebermann on the structure and synthesis of alizarin. Perkin was quite certain that the days of the untrained works chemist were numbered: research chemists were necessary—not optional—in industry to improve processes and invent new products, a point that Perkin thought was well appreciated in German firms such as Friedrich Bayer and Badische Anilin but neglected by British manufacturers until circa 1890. For Perkin research in organic chemistry was both luciferous and prospectively fructiferous: like Baeyer he was happy for his research pupils to become leaders in both academe and industry.[12]

Perkin's success as a designer and planner of impressive new laboratories for research and his enviable knack of being associated with munificent external endowments were also quickly apparent. His first success was the Schorlemmer Memorial Laboratory, the first British university laboratory exclusively for organic chemistry, opened in May 1895. On Schorlemmer's death a memorial fund of £2,500 was raised in England and Germany to erect a laboratory for organic chemistry to be named after him. The Council of Owens matched this pound for pound in order to erect a new laboratory for elementary instruction alongside the Schorlemmer Laboratory. The architect was Alfred Waterhouse, who was helped by Perkin in planning and fitting the new laboratories. At the opening ceremony

[10] Professors and Lecturers Appointments, 12 Feb. 1908, RA/29/1, Manchester University Archives.

[11] Armstrong, "Perkin" (cit. n. 2), p. 625.

[12] William H. Perkin, Jr., *The Progress of Organic Chemistry: An Address Delivered in the Owens College at the Opening of the Department of Arts, Science, and Law, Session 1893–94* (Manchester: Cornish, 1893), p. 13. Perkin was chairman of a committee set up by the British Association for the Advancement of Science to inquire into the training of chemists employed in the British chemical industry. It discovered that in a sample of 502 only 59 were British graduates: *Report of the British Association for the Advancement of Science Held in 1902* (London: Murray, 1903), pp. 97–98.

the two main speakers were Ludwig Mond, the industrialist who had headed the memorial fund, and Henry Roscoe, the chemist largely responsible for the college's rise to scientific eminence. As befitted an industrialist who had researched under Hermann Kolbe and Robert Bunsen at Marburg and Heidelberg, Mond expressed his belief that apprenticeship and even technical courses in special laboratories were outmoded as means of producing successful industrial chemists: the future of the chemical industry depended on laboratory discoveries made by chemists trained in research. Roscoe took a different line: he looked to Perkin to do in Manchester what Justus Liebig had achieved at the University of Giessen in the 1830s and 1840s. Roscoe even hoped that "as Giessen was, under Liebig, the means of raising the standard of chemical education throughout the fatherland, so the chemical department of Owens College might . . . be . . . the institution in England which had done the same for this great empire." These aims were to be achieved in the Schorlemmer Laboratory, which in some respects was arranged like Baeyer's Munich laboratories: witness the lead-lined gutter of each bench, the drains, and the abundant draught cupboards enclosing the lower portion of each large window. A second adjunct to the Schorlemmer Laboratory, a laboratory for advanced technical organic chemistry supported financially by the Manchester dye-stuffs manufacturer Ivan Levinstein, was opened under Perkin's direction in session 1895/6. Its aim was not to instruct dyers and printers but to train graduates for leading positions in industry, especially dyeworks, via technical organic research, especially the synthesis of new dyes in quantities sufficient for industrial purposes.[13]

In 1904 Perkin became the major beneficiary of the bequest made in 1899 by Edward Schunck, a Manchester chemist and industrialist who had devoted his whole career to research in the then-neglected field of natural-products chemistry. In 1895 Schunck had donated £20,300 to Owens College to promote chemical research. Subsequently in his will he left his laboratory and library to the chemistry department at Owens, exclusively for pure research. His laboratory was removed brick by brick from his home and reerected at Owens. It was connected to the Schorlemmer Laboratory by a new building that contained the Dalton and Perkin laboratories, all three being opened by the elder Perkin in 1904. Appropriately, Perkin moved into the laboratory named after his father, and his research workers migrated to the Schunck Laboratory.[14]

The increase in the number of research students (twenty-nine in all in session 1908/9) led again to problems of accommodation. These were solved in October 1909, when Roscoe opened the John Morley Laboratories, named after the university's Chancellor and paid for mainly by Andrew Carnegie, who in summer 1909 had offered £10,000—his first benefaction of a laboratory as opposed to his previous endowments of libraries. The architect was Paul Waterhouse, a son of

[13] P. J. Hartog, *The Owens College, Manchester: A Brief History of the College and Description of its Various Departments* (Manchester: Cornish, 1900), pp. 64–68; "The Schorlemmer Laboratory," *J. Soc. Chem. Ind.*, 1895, *14*:525; "The Opening of the Schorlemmer Organic Laboratory in the Owens College," *ibid.*, pp. 552–554; and Owens College, Manchester, *Calendar for the Session 1895–6* (Manchester: Cornish, 1895), p. 110.

[14] Greenaway, Thorpe, and Robinson, *Life and Work of Perkin* (cit. n. 2), p. 24; W. V. Farrar, "Edward Schunck, F.R.S.: A Pioneer of Natural-Product Chemistry," *Notes and Records of the Royal Society of London*, 1977, *31*:273–296; and *Manchester Guardian*, 2 July 1904.

Alfred Waterhouse; the detailed designing and equipping of these laboratories, in which organic chemistry was given pride of place, were again supervised by Perkin (see Figure 1). The biggest room had large windows and skylights, open timber work of pitch pine, no plaster, little exposed ironwork, elaborate floor channels for drains, and walls totally faced with glazed bricks. The Morley Laboratories suite completed what was known as the chemical quadrangle. Bounded by the Schorlemmer, Dalton, Perkin, Schunck, and Morley laboratories, it was devoted mainly to organic chemistry and in 1912/13 housed no fewer than thirty-six graduate researchers. In this now greatly increased accommodation Perkin launched an innovation in the technical organic research he had nurtured since 1895. In addition to his own graduates, research chemists employed by local firms studied technical research methods, the preparation of intermediate and final products made in local dyeworks, and the conditions under which substances could be made on a large scale.[15]

These laboratories were the home of what Robinson called the Perkin family of organic chemists. Some became prominent in industry not only as product and process chemists but also, after 1899, as research chemists.[16] The best known was C. J. T. Cronshaw of Imperial Chemical Industries, who ended his career as one of ICI's directors.[17] But Perkin's specialty lay in producing creative academic organic chemists, often from Manchester graduates. He had a particularly good run between 1902 and 1908, when the following chemists graduated: Frank Lee Pyman (1902); John Lionel Simonsen (1904); Robert Robinson (1905); W. N. Haworth (1906); and Edward Hope (1908). Pyman, who chose Manchester because under Perkin it was the center of organic chemistry in Britain, became professor of technological chemistry at Manchester in 1918 and then director of research for Boots Pure Drug Company in 1927. Simonsen, who as an undergraduate was impressed by Perkin's clarity as a lecturer, spent four years with him as a postgraduate, derived his lifelong interest in terpenes from him, and like his mentor was a superb bench experimentalist relatively uninterested in theory. Simonsen ended his career as professor at University College of North Wales, Bangor—one of his pupils there being E. R. H. Jones, the next successor but one to Perkin in the Waynflete Chair at Oxford. Haworth spent a total of four years working with Perkin on terpenes before moving first to Imperial College, London, and then to St. Andrews University, where he relinquished this Perkinian field and expanded his work on the structure of sugars. He ended his career as Mason

[15] "Chemical Research at the University of Manchester," *Nature,* 1908/9, *74*:233; *Manchester Guardian,* 5 Oct. 1909; Greenaway, Thorpe, and Robinson, *Life and Work of Perkin* (cit. n. 2), p. 25; Victoria University of Manchester, *Calendar 1909–1910* (Manchester: Manchester Univ. Press, 1909), pp. 249–250; Victoria University of Manchester, *Calendar 1910–1911* (1910), p. 274; and University of Manchester, *Description of the New Chemical Laboratories Opened by Sir Henry Roscoe, on October 4th, 1909* (Manchester: Manchester Courier, 1909).

[16] Robert Robinson, "The Perkin Family of Organic Chemists," *Endeavour,* 1956, *15*:92–102; and Owens College, Manchester, *Report of the Council to the Court of Governors, 5th October 1899* (Manchester: Gill, 1899), p. 124. James Donnelly, "Industrial Recruitment of Chemistry Students from English Universities," *British Journal for the History of Science,* 1991, *24*:3–20, shows that industrial recruitment was important and widespread in the late nineteenth century and not mere spin-off from the supply of teachers, and that the more specialized students tended to go into industry, the generalists going into schools.

[17] On Cronshaw see, e.g., W. J. Reader, *Imperial Chemical Industries: A History,* Vol. II, *The First Quarter Century, 1926–1952* (London: Oxford Univ. Press, 1976), p. 504.

Figure 1. The John Morley Laboratories: the gable on the West Quadrangle. From University of Manchester, Description of the New Chemical Laboratories *(Manchester: Manchester Courier, 1909). Courtesy of the Director and University Librarian, The John Rylands University Library of Manchester.*

Professor of Chemistry at the University of Birmingham, where he led an internationally renowned school of carbohydrates research. In 1937 he became the first British organic chemist to be awarded a Nobel Prize. Edward Hope, unlike most of the others mentioned here, was never knighted and never became a professor; but, after a promising start at Manchester under both Perkin and Robinson, he eventually achieved in 1919 a most unusual distinction: though not an Oxford graduate, he was elected a tutorial fellow of Magdalen College.[18]

Robinson's career was closely connected with Perkin's. His attendance at Perkin's lectures decided him to become an organic chemist in the Perkin mold. Having spent no fewer than seven postgraduate years in Perkin's department, where they began their long collaboration, Robinson embarked on an academic odyssey that took him to chairs at Sydney, Liverpool, St. Andrews, Manchester, and University College, London, before he settled in Oxford in 1930 as Perkin's

[18] Harold King, "Frank Lee Pyman (1882–1944)," *Obit. Not. Fellows Roy. Soc.,* 1944, *4*:681–697; Robert Robinson, "John Lionel Simonsen (1884–1957)," *Biog. Mem. Fellows Roy. Soc.,* 1959, *5*:237–252; E. L. Hirst, "Walter Norman Haworth (1883–1950)," *Obit. Not. Fellows Roy. Soc.* 1951, 7:373–404; and S. G. P. Plant, "Edward Hope (1886–1953)," *J. Chem. Soc.,* 1953, pp. 3730–3732.

successor in the Waynflete chair. In 1947 Robinson was awarded the Nobel Prize
for his work on plant products, especially alkaloids, a topic that he first attacked
with Perkin in Manchester. Robinson's debt to Perkin may be gauged from his
publications: of his first thirty papers twenty-four were written with Perkin; all
told they published sixty-four joint papers.[19]

Of non-Mancunian graduates, the best-known pupil of Perkin turned out to be
J. F. Thorpe, who spent fourteen years with him as research fellow, demonstrator,
and lecturer in organic chemistry, collaborating first on the terpenes work and
then on the synthesis of the degradation products of camphor such as camphoronic and camphoric acids. Whereas Perkin was concerned to determine the
structure of natural products via degradation, to recognize the fragments, and
then to synthesize them, Thorpe was concerned with synthesis and not analysis.
He ended his career as professor of organic chemistry at Imperial College, London, with two other postgraduate pupils of Perkin—H. C. H. Carpenter and
William Bone. Carpenter, who spent three postdoctoral years with Perkin and
was professor of metallurgy at Manchester from 1906 to 1913, came to Imperial
College in 1914. Bone, who found his time with Perkin useful for his later
Dixonian work on the combustion of organic compounds, was professor of chemical technology at Imperial from 1912 to 1936. These three formed a powerful tri-
umvirate by the outbreak of World War I.[20]

Of the foreigners attracted to Perkin's Manchester laboratories, the one des-
tined for international fame was Chaim Weizmann, a Russian Jew who came to
Manchester in 1904 from the University of Geneva and became lecturer and then
senior lecturer in organic chemistry, assistant director of the organic laboratories
and lecturer in biochemistry in 1909, then reader in biochemistry for 1913–
1916—and eventually the first president of Israel in 1949. Weizmann chose
Manchester because he thought Perkin the most outstanding professor of chemistry in England; he soon became part of the circle of Perkin, whom he called by his
nickname of "Pa." From 1906 he supervised teaching and research in the
Schorlemmer and then the Morley laboratories, introduced research projects in
the final year of the undergraduate course, and guided a small colony of researchers that included Maurice Copisarow, Henry Stephen, and Gertrude Walsh—who
in 1912 married Robinson.[21]

Launching a distinguished research school did not prevent Perkin from undertaking industrial research and consultancies—despite his public disclaimers
about the impropriety of doing commercial work in his university laboratories,

[19] A. R. Todd and J. W. Cornforth, "Robert Robinson (1886–1975)," *Biog. Mem. Fellows Roy. Soc.*,
1976, *22*:415–527; Robert Robinson, *Memoirs of a Minor Prophet: Seventy Years of Organic Chemistry*, Vol. I (Amsterdam/London: Elsevier, 1976); and Trevor I. Williams, *Robert Robinson: Chemist
Extraordinary* (Oxford: Oxford Univ. Press, 1990).

[20] C. K. Ingold, "Jocelyn Field Thorpe (1872–1940)," *Obit. Not. Fellows Roy. Soc.*, 1941, *3*:531–
544; C. A. Edwards, "Henry Cort Harold Carpenter (1875–1940)," *ibid.*, pp. 611–625; and G. I. Finch
and A. C. Egerton, "William Arthur Bone (1871–1938)," *ibid.*, 1939, *2*:587–611.

[21] Chaim Weizmann, *Trial and Error: The Autobiography of Chaim Weizmann* (New York: Harper,
1949), pp. 95–102, 134–135; Todd and Cornforth, "Robinson" (cit. n. 19), pp. 417–420; Jehuda
Reinharz, *Chaim Weizmann: The Making of a Zionist Leader* (New York: Oxford Univ. Press, 1985),
pp. 233–260; and Norman A. Rose, *Chaim Weizmann: A Biography* (London: Weidenfeld &
Nicolson, 1987), pp. 88–96. See also *The Letters and Papers of Chaim Weizmann, Series A*, Vol. III:
September 1903–December 1904 (1972); Vol. IV, *January 1905–December 1906* (1973); Vol. V, *January 1907–February 1913* (1974) (London: Oxford Univ. Press; Jerusalem: Israel Universities Press).

and despite the view expressed by the university in 1908 that in any consultancy work its staff should not give services and results exclusively to one firm.[22] With Thorpe he researched for Whipp and Todd Ltd., Manchester, on nonflammable fabrics in 1902. More important was the work he carried out on synthetic rubbers with Weizmann (no stranger to consultancy and patent work) for Strange and Graham Ltd., London, beginning in 1910. Perkin was engaged by E. H. Strange, formerly a research assistant to Dixon at Manchester, at £1,000 per annum plus royalties as a consultant; he quickly appointed Weizmann as his research assistant at £250 per annum, plus a third of the profits. The work soon involved the cooption by Strange through Weizmann of Auguste Fernbach, a leading biochemist at the Pasteur Institute in Paris and director of its fermentation laboratory from 1900 to 1935. The aim was to develop commercial processes for making synthetic rubber, using discoveries already made in 1910 by Fernbach and by F. E. Matthews, chief chemist to Strange and Graham. Fernbach had produced acetone and fusel oil (containing isoamyl alcohol) by fermenting starch; Matthews, artificial rubber from isoprene using sodium as the polymerizing agent. The Anglo-French syndicate worked on three ways of producing butadiene or isoprene (two of which involved fermentation) from isoamyl alcohol, butyl alcohol, and aldol. Weizmann worked in collaboration with Fernbach on these fermentation problems. Strange then decided to float a company to exploit all these discoveries and wanted Perkin to speak favorably about their commercial viability at a meeting of the Society of Chemical Industry in mid June 1912.

Suspecting that in this lecture Perkin would ignore his assistant's role in the research on fermentation, the impulsive and paranoiac Weizmann tried to make a private financial deal with Fernbach. Perkin duly gave the lecture, in which he minimized his own contribution, praised Fernbach, referred to Weizmann and others as coworkers, and was cautious about the viable commercial synthesis of synthetic rubber. Weizmann then attacked Perkin openly and demanded to be free of his professor's control, while retaining his percentage of Perkin's annual consultancy fee, or he would consider himself a free agent to use his knowledge of fermentation processes as he wished. Outraged at his assistant's effrontery and duplicity, Perkin dismissed Weizmann from the synthetic rubber team in late June 1912. For Weizmann, "Pa" Perkin was suddenly transformed from a hero into a "well-bred cat" who saw to it that his unadvertised Manchester chair in organic chemistry was filled in May 1913 by his brother-in-law Arthur Lapworth, who at that time was not renowned as an organic specialist, while Weizmann was promoted to a new readership in biochemistry.[23]

[22] For the changing university attitude to consultancy work see Council Minutes, 6 Nov., 4 Dec. 1912, 5 Feb. 1913, RA/3/1; and Council Committees, 12 Feb. 1908, RA/3/3; all Manchester University Archives.

[23] The murky and convoluted Strange affair and its consequences are best covered by Reinharz, *Weizmann* (cit. n. 21), pp. 351–367, 374. He perpetrates such gaffes as calling organic chemistry neglected at the University of Manchester in 1904, and he does not cite W. H. Perkin, Jr., "The Production and Polymerisation of Butadiene, Isoprene and Their Homologues," *J. Soc. Chem. Ind.*, 1912, *31*:616–624 (15 July issue). Fernbach brought unsuccessful action against Weizmann in 1926 for alleged infringement of his process for making acetone. Weizmann discovered a process for making acetone and butyl alcohol bacterially from sugar and starchy materials in 1912, as part of the search for making isoamyl alcohol, from which it was hoped to make artificial rubber. Weizmann's process was widely used industrially in Britain in World War I.

The unhappy fracas with Weizmann, formerly his protégé and copatentee but now seen as an aggressive, brash, and threatening schemer, may well have induced Perkin, who had previously refused offers from institutions such as University College, London, to contemplate leaving Manchester and to show interest in the Oxford chair. The chair was offered to him on 23 November 1912, and he accepted it formally on 10 December, when he was 52 years old. Furthermore, Perkin knew that in early November 1912 the university had begun to extend to heads of departments its regulations about work done for outside bodies in university laboratories. From February 1913 on the fees received for such work were to be credited to the department and not to the individual, the whole cost of materials was to be charged to the client, and consultancy work for business or legal purposes which involved absence from the university was forbidden. Thus the opportunity previously enjoyed by Perkin for lucrative consultancy work was being curtailed just when he received the Oxford offer, which, with college perks, gave him about the same emolument as his Manchester chair. Perhaps Perkin also felt somewhat bereft intellectually as a result of the departure to Australia in autumn 1912 of Robinson, his favorite collaborator.

III. PERKIN IN OXFORD

At Oxford Perkin once again replaced a literary chemist, in this case William Odling, who had retired from the Waynflete chair in 1912 at age 83, after occupying it for forty years. A cultivated Nestor of chemistry, Odling was a connoisseur of engravings but not interested in the patient pursuit of detail via experiments done at the laboratory bench. Preferring the philosophical and speculative aspects of chemistry, Odling was not the slave of his laboratory, which he thought it a breach of etiquette for the professor to enter. His last research papers had been published in 1876, and so it was not surprising that he founded no school. One of his obituarists was reduced to claiming on his behalf that "it was not that Odling *discouraged* research." A man who did not answer letters, Odling was not one to pursue the exacting career of a successful discipline builder.[24]

Oxford was organized differently from Manchester, where professors ruled monolithic departments. In England's oldest university, the tutorial fellows of the various colleges were responsible for teaching undergraduates and could act independently of the professor, who carried far less power than at Manchester. When Perkin arrived, five of the colleges (Magdalen, Queen's, Christ Church, Jesus, and Balliol and Trinity in collaboration) even had their own laboratories not only for teaching but also for research. Their very existence implied that there were deficiencies in the regime of Odling and in the university chemical laboratory, which was modeled on the medieval Abbot's Kitchen at Glastonbury. Indeed, in 1909 the university had sought and received advice, not always harmonious, on how to organize a subject in which besides the one university laboratory there were five run by colleges—of which only one was devoted to organic chemistry. Some advisers were trenchant about Oxford's poor reputation in chemical research: Dixon advocated the Manchester model of two professors, a centralized

[24] J. E. Marsh, "William Odling (1829–1921)," *J. Chem Soc.,* 1921, *119*:553–564; and H. B. Dixon, "William Odling (1829–1921)," *Proceedings of the Royal Society*, 1922, *100*:i–vii, on p. iii.

department, and the aim of "advanced research"; while Armstrong denounced as a disgrace Oxford's failure to count as "a school of chemical research." Stung by such criticisms, the university had found £15,000 and a site for a new chemistry laboratory by 19 November 1912.[25]

It would be misleading to suggest that, when Perkin assumed his Oxford chair in 1913, organic chemistry there was negligible. He inherited several demonstrators, whose job was to lecture to undergraduates and to run the laboratory classes for them. Three of these demonstrators were competent organic chemists, namely, James Ernest Marsh, Frederick Chattaway, and Nevil Sidgwick, all of whom had enjoyed postgraduate experience in Germany. In the 1890s Marsh, a pupil of Kekulé's at Bonn, had worked on camphor and the related group of terpenes; he produced a structural formula for camphene which soon suffered eclipse, though he continued to advocate it. Most chemists supported the formula for camphor advanced in 1893 by Julius Bredt, whose views were soon confirmed by the research of Perkin and Thorpe on camphoronic and camphoric acids. Thus when Perkin arrived in Oxford, Marsh was eclipsed as the expert on terpenes, and in order to save his credibility he soon moved from laboratory demonstration to teaching the medical and historical aspects of chemistry.[26] Chattaway had an impeccable pedigree, having studied with Bamberger under Baeyer at Munich, where he obtained his Ph.D., and with Georg Bredig at Heidelberg. An exact contemporary of both Perkin and Marsh, Chattaway was head of the Queen's College laboratory, where he specialized in organic preparations and purification. Though he was an active publisher, Chattaway did not work on natural products and never led a research school; but he had research collaborators and produced a small cohort of pupils who were indebted to him for experimental ingenuity and revered him as "The Poisoner."[27] Sidgwick, a fellow of Lincoln College who had studied under Bredig in Ostwald's laboratory at Leipzig and then in von Pechmann's laboratory at Tübingen, preferred interpreting other people's results to experimenting at the bench on a single group of organic compounds such as terpenes or sugars—the kind of procedure that could provide a basis for a research school. He was neither an ardent experimenter nor a gifted adviser about research topics and methods. His forte, apart from biting people verbally, was weaving the threads of others' discoveries into an ordered and harmonious pattern, his first major effort in this genre being his *Organic Chemistry of Nitrogen* (1910), which created an accessible and interesting subject out of what had previously been a jumble. Indeed, Sidgwick deprecated Perkin's style of organic

[25] Harold Hartley, "Schools of Chemistry in Great Britain and Ireland; XVI: The University of Oxford," *J. Roy. Inst. Chem.*, 1955, 79:116–127, 176–184; Hartley, "The Contribution of the College Laboratories to the Oxford School of Chemistry," in Hartley, *Studies in the History of Chemistry* (Oxford: Clarendon Press, 1971), pp. 223–232; Keith J. Laidler, "Chemical Kinetics and the Oxford College Laboratories," *Archive for History of Exact Sciences*, 1988, 38:197–283; and Chemistry and Lee's professorships, MR/7/2/7, Oxford University Archives. (The Abbot's Kitchen is one of three buildings standing of a former monastery in Glastonbury.) For comparison see, on the organization of chemistry at Cambridge, Gerrylynn K. Roberts, "The Liberally Educated Chemist: Chemistry in the Cambridge Natural Science Tripos, 1851–1914," *Historical Studies in the Physical Sciences*, 1980, 11:157–183.

[26] Frederick Soddy, "James Ernest Marsh (1860–1938)," *Obit. Not. Fellows Roy. Soc.*, 1939, 2:549–556; and Greenaway, Thorpe, and Robinson, *Life and Work of Perkin* (cit. n. 2), pp. 48–62.

[27] G. R. Clemo, "Frederick Daniel Chattaway (1860–1944)," *Obit. Not. Fellows Roy. Soc.*, 1944, 4:713–716.

chemistry as limited, narrow, and old-fashioned, while Perkin thought that
Sidgwick's physical approach to organic chemistry was bogus.[28] Thus, as J. C.
Smith stressed, when Perkin arrived in Oxford in 1913, its organic chemistry was
elegant and intelligent but not dominating—and quite unlike its counterpart in
Manchester under Perkin.[29]

Research as the Thing

Perkin accepted the Oxford chair, which he occupied until his death, on the understanding that his research time would not be interrupted by low-level teaching
or shredded in other ways, his aim being to build up a school of research as rapidly as possible. For Perkin research, not teaching, was the basis of the reputation
of any university school of science. Unlike Odling, he set a grand personal example, appearing and working in the laboratory six or seven hours a day and maintaining a flow of important publications. In 1916 his famous paper on the
alkaloids cryptopine and protopine, which ran to 214 pages, took up a whole
number of the *Journal of the Chemical Society*. Even his undergraduate lectures
were research-orientated, with their stress on original sources, and intended
mainly for research students; but his top priorities remained research at the laboratory bench and building up a research school. Well aware of the danger of a
British university professor becoming "an academic fossil and unproductive," he
emphasized the centrality of "output of research," and soon Oxford's publications in organic chemistry began to surge at Manchester's expense.[30]

Perkin's research orientation was not always happily received at Oxford. In
1921 his chemical colleagues defeated his and Hope's proposal that there be no
lectures between 10:00 and 11:00 A.M. in order to give three hours of uninter-
rupted laboratory work in the morning; and Oxford's tradition of using the time
between lunch and tea for various forms of muscular recreation on river and pitch
meant that he never implemented for undergraduates a Baeyer regime of ten continuous laboratory hours from 8:00 A.M. to 6:00 P.M. But in other ways he was successful in pursuing his vision of research as "the thing."[31] He had long believed

[28] H. T. Tizard, "Nevil Vincent Sidgwick (1873–1952)," *Obit. Not. Fellows Roy. Soc.*, 1954, *9*:237–
258; and L. E. Sutton, "Sidgwick," *Proceedings of the Chemical Society*, 1958, pp. 310–319. In *The Organic Chemistry of Nitrogen* (Oxford: Clarendon Press, 1910) Sidgwick assumed, contra Perkin, that
organic chemistry could not be adequately treated without reference to those aspects of physical
chemistry which it involves.

[29] J. C. Smith, "The Development of Organic Chemistry at Oxford," typescript, 2 pts., no date, Pt. I,
p. 14. Copies of this valuable work are available in the Dyson Perrins Laboratory, Oxford, and in the
Royal Society of Chemistry, London.

[30] Greenaway, Thorpe, and Robinson, *Life and Work of Perkin* (cit. n. 2), p. 28; Perkin's evidence to
the Asquith Commission on the University of Oxford, 28 Sept. 1920, MS Top. Oxon.b.109, Bodleian
Library; Perkin, "Cryptopine and Protopine," *J. Chem. Soc.*, 1916, *109*:815–1028; and Perkin, "The
Position of the Organic Chemical Industry," presidential address, March 1915, *ibid.*, 1915, *107*:557–
578, on p. 561. On the publications see W. P. Wynne, "Universities as Centres of Research," *ibid.*,
1925, *127*:936–954, on p. 939, which used the following major categories: Oxford; Cambridge;
Manchester; Imperial College, London; provincial universities other than Manchester; and university
colleges. On Perkin's lectures see Kenneth Hutchison, *High Speed Gas: An Autobiography* (London:
Duckworth, 1987), p. 28.

[31] Perkin, "Organic Chemical Industry" (cit. n. 30), p. 569; and Chemistry Sub-faculty Minute Book
1910–1927, 14 Nov. 1921, MS Museum 136, Museum of History of Science, Oxford. Wilson Baker re-
calls that Perkin, when writing him in 1926 to offer a demonstratorship at Oxford, added, "Research is
the thing" (personal communication, 15 Jan. 1987).

that the normal three-years B.Sc. in British universities was stereotyped and deficient in that it involved no requirement to do research; and his early experience in Oxford quickly convinced him that in order to master organic chemistry students needed to spend more time in the laboratory.

The outbreak of war in 1914 and the government's scheme of 1915 for the organization of scientific and industrial research provided Perkin with his opportunity to lead a campaign to add a fourth year of research (Part 2) to the existing three-year degree course (Part 1) in chemistry. He convinced his colleagues that research training was essential even if employers of graduate chemists in industry and schools were indifferent to it; that research experience was necessary for all honors students and not a luxury restricted to first-class ones; and that the rapid changes taking place in the chemical industry would lead in the near future to a demand for research chemists. At a time of national emergency, the new examination regulations in chemistry, which required each candidate to present "records of experimental investigations," were quickly approved without opposition by the university in May 1916—even though there was no compulsory research year in any other degree course in science.[32] As one who believed that the German emphasis on research was worth copying at both the bachelor and doctoral levels, Perkin was influential in connection with the introduction in May 1917 of the D.Phil. degree and the associated creation of the category of advanced student. Thus by summer 1917 Perkin had available *in potentia* a route and rewards for aspiring young Oxford organic chemists: they would do a year's research for the award of a bachelor's degree and, if promising, continue with research for two to three years for a D.Phil. It was characteristic of Perkin, whose marriage was childless, that in his will he made provision for the bulk of his estate (£43,000 gross) to revert after his wife's death to Magdalen College, to which his chair was attached, for research studentships to promote postgraduate research in organic chemistry at Oxford by male graduates from commonwealth universities and to enable Oxford graduates to visit commonwealth universities.[33]

Industrial Research

The war also enabled Perkin to introduce into Oxford industrial research, an activity that some of his chemical colleagues regarded as a temporary necessity but one he had long advocated and practiced. His views were clearly set out in March 1915 in his second presidential address to the Chemical Society. He attacked the decadence of the British organic chemical industry for its rule-of-thumb methods, its assumption that the dyestuffs industry was like the large-scale heavy alkali industry, its neglect of the importance of research in organic chemistry, and its obsession with short-term commercial interests. At a time of national emergency the answer was to establish contact and cooperation on the German model

[32] Greenaway, Thorpe, and Robinson, *Life and Work of Perkin* (cit. n. 2), p. 32; Perkin, "Organic Chemical Industry," pp. 561, 569; Report of the Sub-faculty of Chemistry, [1915], Natural Sciences Faculty Board Reports, NS/R/1/2, Oxford University Archives; Natural Sciences Faculty Board Minutes, 1 June 1915, 8 Feb. 1916, NS/M/1/3, *ibid.;* and *Oxford University Gazette*, 1915/16, *46*:328, 341–342, 350–351, 423–424, 448–450, 458–460, quoting from p. 458.
[33] *Nature*, 1916/17, *98*:441–442; *Ox. Univ. Gaz.*, 1916/17, *47*:251, 303–304, 352, 428–431, 448–450, 466; and Smith, "Development of Organic Chemistry" (cit. n. 29), Pt. I, p. 43.

between industry and universities, to mutual advantage—distasteful though that might be to some British academics.[34]

During the war Perkin did "war work" for the Department of Explosives Supplies on making acetone from alcohol, for the Air Board on noninflammable rubber coating for air ships, and on mustard gas; but his chief contribution was to encourage in his laboratory industrial research done by chemists employed by fine-chemical firms, especially the government-backed British Dyes. British Dyes (from 1919 to 1926 the British Dyestuffs Corporation) was formed in 1915 to strengthen and rationalize the industry. By early 1916 Perkin was chairman of British Dyes' advisory council and supervised its research department, which was composed of colonies of organic chemists in several universities, including Oxford. Not surprisingly, British Dyes carried out industrial research at Oxford far longer—from 1916 to 1925 (ten years)—than Boake, Roberts and Company (eight years) or W. J. Bush and Company (six years). When the Oxford colony began to run down in 1922, Perkin maintained his industrial research interests by being made in 1923 adviser to the research staff of the British Dyestuffs Corporation at Blackley, Manchester, which he visited almost weekly for two years.[35] In a university notoriously suspicious of manufacturing, Perkin had shown that academic work and industrial research could occur side by side to mutual advantage. Yet the success of British Dyes' Oxford colony relied far more on young chemists recruited from outside Oxford than on Oxford graduates. Of the leading or enduring members of the colony, only F. A. Mason was an Oxonian. William Kermack came from Aberdeen University; George Clemo from a Cornish school; Joseph Kenyon from Blackburn Technical College; and Hope, of course, from Manchester University. Only Hope found permanent employment at Oxford, the remainder becoming heads of department and professors elsewhere.[36]

A New Laboratory

As soon as Perkin appeared in Oxford in January 1913, he attended to the question of the promised new laboratory, which was to be devoted entirely to organic chemistry. He convinced the university that the architect should be Paul Waterhouse, the trusted designer of the Morley Laboratories at Manchester: he would be cheaper than anyone else because the various measurements made for

[34] Perkin, "Organic Chemical Industry" (cit. n. 30), p. 563. For the first use of "industrial research" in a published Oxford document see Perkin, "Report of the Waynflete Professor of Chemistry, 1916," *Ox. Univ. Gaz.*, 1916/17, *47*:556–557.

[35] Greenway, Thorpe, and Robinson, *Life and Work of Perkin* (cit. n. 2), pp. 32–33; *Nature*, 1915/16, *96*:542, 1917, *99*:499; Reader, *ICI* (cit. n. 17), Vol. I, *The Forerunners, 1870–1926* (1970), pp. 266–275; and annual reports of the Waynflete Professor of Chemistry, published in *Ox. Univ. Gaz.*

[36] Kermack ended his career as professor of biochemistry at the University of Aberdeen: J. N. Davidson and F. Yates, "William Ogilvy Kermack (1898–1970)," *Biog. Mem. Fellows Roy. Soc.*, 1971, *17*:399–430. Kenyon ended as head of chemistry at Battersea Polytechnic, London: E. E. Turner, "Joseph Kenyon (1885–1961)," *ibid.*, 1962, *8*:49–66. Clemo ended as professor of organic chemistry and head of department at Armstrong College, Newcastle upon Tyne, now the university: B. Lythgoe and G. A. Swan, "George Roger Clemo (1889–1983)," *ibid.*, 1985, *31*:65–86. Frederick Alfred Mason (1888–1947) took a first at Oxford in 1909; gained a Munich doctorate in 1912 under Dimroth in Baeyer's department; worked for British Dyestuffs Corporation, 1916–1926; lectured at Manchester College of Technology, 1926–1931; and ended his career as one of His Majesty's Inspectors of schools and technical colleges apropos chemistry and its industrial applications. (I thank the archivist of St. John's College, Oxford, for supplying information on Mason.)

the Morley Laboratories could be used in Oxford. Perkin even invited Oxonians to Manchester in February 1913 to gain a "pretty accurate idea of what the suggested accommodation really amounts to." As before, Perkin collaborated with his architect on the design. The new Oxford laboratory copied the Morley Laboratories in several respects: in height, in the professorial eyrie on the top floor from which Perkin could look down into the main teaching laboratories, and in the public-lavatory style of walls, lined with hard-glazed brown and cream bricks—which Perkin regarded as a necessity, not a luxury.[37]

As at Manchester, Perkin was able to attract external funding for the new building. By summer 1915 he had secured from C. W. Dyson Perrins, after whom the Oxford laboratory was named, a total of £30,000 to supplement the £15,000 available from the university. Dyson Perrins provided £5,000 for the building, £5,000 for equipment, and a permanent endowment of £20,000, the interest on which was to be used for promoting research under the direction of the Waynflete Professor only for as long as organic chemistry remained the chief subject of his chair. The Dyson Perrins Trust, used to cover maintenance costs, was of great value to Perkin because it made his laboratory less dependent for income on the university and on laboratory fees. Dyson Perrins, an Oxford graduate in law and partner in the famous Lea and Perrins Worcester Sauce firm, was a very wealthy philanthropist who was presumably impressed by Perkin's general approach and in particular by his research on the alkaloid berberine, of which Dyson Perrins' father had established the empirical formula in 1862.[38]

The Dyson Perrins Laboratory was built in two stages, the first ending with the completion of the central block and western wing in 1916, which enabled Perkin and his coworkers to move from the old Abbot's Kitchen laboratory. The second stage was completed in 1922 at a final cost almost twice that of the first, which had required £20,000 for the building and £5,000 for apparatus. Perkin had gained the confidence of the university to such an extent that much of the total cost of the second stage (£45,600) was met by the university, the rest (£7,500) being secured by Perkin as gifts (mainly £5,000 from the British Dyestuffs Corporation and £1,000 from Barclays Bank). The university resorted to two financial devices. First, in a remarkable act of financial obfuscation it borrowed the capital of £20,000 from the Dyson Perrins' Trust with his permission and undertook to replace it with annual installments of £1,000 payable for twenty years, without affecting at all the interest payable to the laboratory! This loan doubled, at one stroke, the university's total borrowing. Second, it borrowed £19,000 from the Special Reserve Fund. Thus by 1922 Perkin had secured a palace of chemistry that solved the intolerable congestion produced by the postwar increase in research students.[39]

---

[37] Chemistry and Lee's Professorships, Oxford University Archives, MR/7/2/7; W. H. Perkin to E. B. Poulton, 23 Feb. 1913, New Chemistry Laboratory Papers, UM/F/4/15, *ibid.*; Smith, "Development of Organic Chemistry" (cit. n. 29), Pt. I, pp. 15–22; *Nature*, 1915, *95*:527; and *Ox. Univ. Gaz.*, 1914/5, *45*:781, 804–805.

[38] "Charles William Dyson Perrins (1864–1958)," *Berrow's Worcester Journal*, 31 Jan. 1958.

[39] "Statement of the Financial Arrangements for the Completion of the Organic Chemistry Laboratory," *Hebdomadal Council Papers*, 1921, *118*:61–63; and "Report of the Committee on the Finance of the Departments of Chemistry," *ibid.*, 1922, *121*:87–93.

A Research School at Oxford

Not until World War I had ended did vacancies arise or new posts appear in college fellowships in chemistry. Perkin had one early success in securing the election of a Perkinian organic chemist to a college fellowship. Though Queen's College predictably rewarded the loyal Chattaway with a fellowship in 1919, Magdalen College elected Edward Hope to a tutorial fellowship the same year, thus breaking the monopoly of physical and inorganic Oxonian chemists. Perkin used his own position as a professorial fellow of Magdalen in favor of Hope, one of his Manchester graduates and a member of the British Dyes team. Subsequently Perkin had no success in placing his protégés in these fellowships, which continued to go to physical chemists (e.g., Alexander Russell, Christ Church, 1920; Cyril Hinshelwood, Trinity, 1921; Edmund Bowen, University College, 1922) or physical organic chemists (e.g., Thomas Taylor, Brasenose, 1920; D. L. Hammick, Oriel, 1921)—most of whom went on to lead distinguished careers. Moreover, the physical organic chemists worked in the Dyson Perrins Laboratory and as college fellows occupied independent fiefdoms even in the laboratory for which Perkin was responsible overall. Perkin did not like physical chemistry but tolerated it if applied to organic compounds. Not surprisingly, the physical chemists tried to disguise their work by making it smell like classical organic chemistry: Hammick, for example, a demonstrator in the Dyson Perrins Laboratory, used to let "the Old Man" have a nauseous whiff of pyridine from his bench in order to deceive him into thinking that proper organic research was being done. It is significant that Sidgwick, a long-serving demonstrator, relinquished this post in 1923; he regarded Perkin's exclusive concern with the analysis and synthesis of natural products as narrow and passé.[40]

Another disappointment for Perkin was that the introduction of Part 2 into the undergraduate degree course increased the grip of the college tutors on their more ambitious charges, whom they usually steered into physical chemical topics for their research year. The scheme, on which Perkin laid such store, thus backfired: it did not produce a large crop of graduate organic chemists agog to take D.Phil.s in organic chemistry as Perkin protégés. After the war Perkin found only two of his organic demonstrators and researchers from among recent Oxford graduates, namely, Sydney Plant and Harry Ing. Plant had graduated under wartime conditions in 1918 from St. John's College and Magdalen. In 1919 he became a demonstrator while working for his D.Phil. under Hope (also appointed a demonstrator that year) and Perkin; after Hope was taken ill in 1925, he became the general factotum in the Dyson Perrins Laboratory, though never a college fellow. In 1921 Ing began a five-year stint of demonstrating while an undergraduate. He took his D.Phil. under Perkin, left to be a research fellow at Manchester under Robinson, and eventually finished back at Oxford as reader in chemical pharmacology.[41]

The majority of demonstrators in organic chemistry came from outside Oxford

[40] E. J. Bowen, "Dalziel Llewellyn Hammick (1887–1966)," *Biog. Mem. Fellows Roy. Soc.,* 1967, *13*:107–124; and Smith, "Development of Organic Chemistry" (cit. n. 29), Pt. II, p. 2.

[41] M. Tomlinson, "Sydney Glenn Preston Plant (1896–1955)," *J. Chem. Soc.,* 1956, p. 1920; and H. O. Schild and F. L. Rose, "Harry Raymond Ing (1899–1974)," *Biog. Mem. Fellows Roy. Soc.,* 1976, *22*:239–255.

and often had a connection with Robinson or Manchester—John Gulland, R. D. Haworth, and Wilson Baker being cases in point. Gulland, a demonstrator in Dyson Perrins Laboratory from 1924 to 1931, was an Edinburgh graduate who did research on alkaloids under Robinson at St. Andrews and then at Manchester (1921–1924). Haworth studied with Lapworth, Perkin's brother-in-law, at Manchester, where he took his B.Sc. in 1919 and his Ph.D. in 1922. Baker, a Manchester B.Sc. (1921) and Ph.D. (1924), had collaborated with Lapworth and Robinson there before coming to Oxford as a demonstrator in 1927—the result of Robinson's having a word with Perkin over dinner. The arrival of Haworth in 1921 as an 1851 Exhibition Research Scholar permitted Perkin to initiate at last, in 1922, a loose and intermittent lieutenant system in which some of his colleagues gave detailed supervision of research. Perkin suggested the main, though flexible, lines of projects, often as a small part of a large project synthesizing a substance such as morphine. Of his four subalterns—Hope, Clemo, Plant, and Haworth—only Plant was entirely an Oxford product. Clemo was never a demonstrator but part of the British Dyestuffs Corporation team, while Haworth's five years at Oxford were supported mainly by research studentships. Haworth and Clemo found it expedient to leave Oxford in the mid 1920s, being followed by Gulland in 1931; as distinguished professors of organic chemistry at Sheffield, Newcastle, and Nottingham, respectively, they spread the Perkin gospel. Of the imported demonstrators only Hope and Baker secured college fellowships, and Baker did not replace Chattaway as fellow in chemistry at Queen's College until 1936, after Perkin's death.[42]

The college structure, the dominance of the physical chemical college fellows, and their control of their pupils' research through the Part 2 examination ensured that in the 1920s relatively few Oxford graduates embarked upon research for a D.Phil. in organic chemistry. There was no equivalent in Perkin's Oxford period to the way in which he had nurtured the research careers of promising young undergraduates at Manchester, such as Robinson and W. N. Haworth. Consequently, as with his British Dyes team, his demonstrators, and his research lieutenants, Perkin recruited many of his graduate students from outside Oxford. Among the subsequently well-known migrants were Thomas Stevens from Glasgow, who eventually followed Haworth as professor at Sheffield; William Davies from Manchester, who as professor of organic chemistry developed laboratory research at Melbourne; Osman Achmatowicz from Poland, who became a professor at Lodz Polytechnic and eventually an official in the Polish ministry of higher education; Louis Fieser from the United States, who later became a professor at Harvard; and V. M. Trikojus, who became professor of biochemistry at Melbourne. Other graduate students came from as far as Sweden, India, and Japan.[43]

[42] R. D. Haworth, "John Masson Gulland (1898–1947)," *Obit. Not. Fellows Roy. Soc.*, 1948, 6:67–82; and E. R. H. Jones, "Robert Downs Haworth (1898–1990)," *Biog. Mem. Fellows Roy. Soc.*, 1991, 37:265–276.

[43] On the migrants see the sources listed s.vv. in Joseph S. Fruton, *A Bio-Bibliography for the History of the Biochemical Sciences since 1800* (Philadelphia: American Philosophical Society, 1982), and the supplement (1985).

An Indian Summer

Oxford was a collegiate university devoted to arts subjects, teaching, and connoisseurship; science was seen as peripheral, specialist publication suspected as narrow, and from the colleges' enclave, research seen as an ungentlemanly, boorish, and even foolish German idea. Thus Oxford's structures and interests were inimical to Perkin's cherished aims. In some college common rooms his notions of output of research and industrial research, not to mention his view that research was more important than teaching, would have been viewed as incomprehensible or outrageous. His Oxford period could have been a lamentable failure; but it turned out to be an Indian summer after his golden age at Manchester because his administrative prowess and character, in conjunction with his proven record at Manchester, enabled him to implement some of his major aims. He secured a splendid new laboratory and endowment for it. He played a leading role in persuading the university to establish research degrees. He showed by personal example and through his school the overriding importance of research. Exploiting the dire contingency of war, he introduced into Oxford the notion and practice of industrial research. Though he failed to persuade many Oxford graduates to do research with him, his reputation drew researchers, demonstrators, and research supervisors from elsewhere.

Perkin was a persuasive and efficient administrator who ruled his laboratory without putting pen to paper. In his dealings with the university he showed straightforwardness, worldly wisdom, good humor, and considerable charm. His colleague Frederick Soddy, appointed in 1919 to the new Lee's Chair of Chemistry, tried to subjugate the college tutorial fellows and to centralize teaching and research in physical chemistry. Averse to compromise, he was soon at furious loggerheads with most of them; and, though he won the Nobel Prize for chemistry in 1921, he patently failed to build up at Oxford the expected school of radiochemistry: instead he worked on economics.[44] In contrast Perkin accepted with good grace the peculiarities of the Oxford system, which gave a professor charge of a university laboratory but which in part staffed it with college fellows who were statutarily independent of him and had as great a say as he had in the subfaculty of chemistry and in the natural sciences faculty board. Accepting the clear limitations of these arrangements, Perkin persuaded the university and Dyson Perrins to provide for him a laboratory that was the first major step towards the creation of the science area at Oxford.

The secret of Perkin's persuasiveness was noted by one of his Magdalen contacts: Perkin "often gave the impression of being only imperfectly acclimatized and of maintaining a good natured suspicion of those who professed to be bound by statutes or regulations. . . . He could not have fitted better into an Oxford college with its widely different associations if he had been a member of such a body for the whole of his life."[45] Perkin's adaptability was based partly on his character,

[44] Smith, "Development of Organic Chemistry" (cit. n. 29), Pt. I, p. 35; Hartley, "Schools of Chemistry; XVI: Oxford" (cit. n. 25), pp. 176–177; and A. D. Cruickshank, "Soddy at Oxford," in *Frederick Soddy (1877–1956)*, spec. issue of *Brit. J. Hist. Sci.*, 1979, *12*:277–288.

[45] P. V. M. Benecke, "Laurie Magnus: 'Herbert Warren of Magdalen,'" Magdalen College MS 407, p. 67. I owe this reference to Dr. Brian Harrison. Perkin's affability has been stressed by Dr. H. J. Stern and Dr. F. W. Stoyle, who worked with Perkin in the early 1920s (personal communications).

*Figure 2. An Indian summer:
W. H. Perkin, Jr. (right), in
the old laboratory at Oxford,
modeled on the Abbot's
Kitchen, in 1926. Courtesy
of the Librarian, Museum
of the History of Science,
University of Oxford.*

which was amiable and endearing, and partly on his wide interests in music, hor-
ticulture, hospitality, and travel—all of which mollified the suspicion that his
Germanic emphasis on research engendered in some quarters. At Manchester he
was such an accomplished pianist that he played duets with the violinist Adolf
Brodsky, the leader of the Hallé Orchestra in 1895/6 and principal of the Royal
Manchester College of Music during 1895–1929, who gave the first performance
of Tschaikovsky's violin concerto. At his Oxford home Perkin soon removed a
partition wall in order to create a long room for chamber music performances. To
the end of his life he practiced at his piano every day before breakfast. He believed that like organic chemistry, a Beethoven sonata needed to be worked at. For
diversion on a train journey he used to read the score of a string quartet. In his
horticultural work he also attained as a devotee a high professional standard, specializing in flowering plants, of which many were donated to the University Parks.
He kept a good cellar and was extremely hospitable, especially at Magdalen,
where he gave many lunch and dinner parties. In the long vacation he and his wife
regularly visited the Swiss and Italian lakes.[46] These wide interests, allied to his

---

[46] Greenaway, Thorpe, and Robinson, *Life and Work of Perkin* (cit. n. 2), pp. 29, 34–36; Smith, "Development of Organic Chemistry" (cit. n. 29), Pt. I, pp. 38–39; Robinson, "Perkin" (cit. n. 2), p. 1021;
Armstrong, "Perkin" (cit. n. 2), p. 627; and Robinson, *Memoirs* (cit. n. 19), p. 26.

pleasant, polite, and considerate character, helped to make Perkin acceptable and liked in Oxford; he was the ideal man to introduce Germanic research practices into Oxford.

IV. PERKIN AND "THE CHEMIST BREEDERS"

In 1972 I published an article on chemist breeding which, to the great surprise of my father's son, has been hailed recently for capturing the excitement of the new social history of science in the 1970s and for securing a reputation as one of the most influential publications in history of science in the last twenty years. Readers of a volume about laboratory-based research schools may justifiably wonder whether my account of Perkin fits the so-called model that I posited almost twenty years ago, and whether my views have changed. In answering the second question, I now think that occasionally the language used in 1972 was too prescriptive: for instance, I claimed to have drawn attention "to the most propitious conditions under which a laboratory-based research school could flourish in the first half of the nineteenth century."[47] In such passages, fortunately few, I took my cue from Liebig's success and offered unwittingly a substantive and normative model that purported to comprehend the chief elements responsible for all the species of a given historical enterprise. That exaggerated claim was made because I was determined to stress that matters such as careers of students, institutional power, physical plant, and financial support, which at that time were scoffingly categorized as external or background, were often constitutive elements that historians should consider when analyzing laboratory-based research enterprises. I objected then, as I still do, to the way in which some historians prejudged that some factors were important and that others could be dismissed; I was trying to suggest that in an analysis of research schools, institutional and financial matters could be as important and crucial as intellectual and technical ones.

Despite the occasional historiographical flourish, much of the 1972 article presented nothing more than a heuristic model of a research school, that is, it suggested and considered the various types of factor which might have been responsible for a given historical situation. In the particular case of research schools of chemistry, it proposed that questions be asked not just about research programs and the laboratory techniques used but also about the recruitment, training, and careers of workers in the school, their publication opportunities, the director's institutional power, his style of direction, the nature of his laboratory accommodation, and—last but certainly not least—the money for salaries, capital expenditure, and running expenses. As a heuristic model it induced one to cast a wider net in one's research than was usual at that time in the history of chemistry; it also suggested a way in which social history of science could be written which did not downgrade science as cognition, which bypassed the sterile dichotomy between internal and external history of science, and which avoided any form of naive reductionism. By today's standards it was sketchy: particular aspects of Liebig's research school have been fruitfully explored in great detail in recent articles by Joseph Fruton and Frederic L. Holmes; and in a comprehensive

[47] Jeffrey L. Sturchio, "Reviews of Journals: *Ambix,*" *Isis*, 1990, *81*:300–302, on p. 302; and J. B. Morrell, "The Chemist Breeders: The Research Schools of Liebig and Thomas Thomson," *Ambix*, 1972, *19*:1–46, on p. 3.

survey Gerrylynn Roberts has shown how much the social history of chemical education and institutions has changed in the last twenty years.[48]

Though "The Chemist Breeders" has been overhauled on particular points, such as the analysis of the careers of Liebig's students, it had the merit of trying to give a rounded account of the research schools of Liebig and Thomson that would be comprehensible to general historians interested in one of the most important social practices of modern science. We forget at our peril that in *la longue durée* science has become successful and powerful in modern Europe. That happened in part because the nineteenth-century laboratory-based research school provided for science the equivalent of the Renaissance artist's studio, in that each was a locus for apprenticeship, the transmission of craft skills, and cultural production. Such matters remain interesting to historians concerned with the changing public face and position of science in Europe. It was therefore not accidental that the 1972 article grew out of a lecture given to undergraduate historians who were studying nineteenth-century cultural history.

Provided the model of 1972 is used heuristically and not prescriptively, it still has its moments. If applied to Perkin, it highlights certain features of his career and reveals that there was no single golden road to success as director of a research school. Unlike Liebig and others, Perkin did not endure frustrations as a young man: capitalizing on his legacy from a famous father, he was inspired by Wislicenus's paternal approach and by Baeyer's success as a discipline builder. His field of research was not new or wide: he worked on the determination of the structure of naturally occurring organic substances, using the established procedures of degradation and synthesis. No reagent, reaction, or piece of apparatus was named after him, though in his time his "triangle" was useful in collecting fractions during distillation under reduced pressure. His speciality, it seems, was the rapid exploitation of new reactions and reagents discovered by others such as Arthur Michael (1887) and Victor Grignard (1900) to synthesize a naturally occurring substance by a series of controlled reactions whose course was indisputable, synthesis being for him the goal of structural organic chemistry. Synthesis in his view offered wide scope for supplementing what was known about the chemical compounds produced by the degradation of naturally occurring substances. His Mancunian pupils dominated British university organic chemistry as long as it was concerned with structure, not mechanism, and as long as physical methods of investigation were not widely employed. Perkin could operate in this way because at Manchester he headed a monolithic department, enjoyed power in a science-based university, and in the laboratory inspired his pupils by his personal example as a bench man who adored the laboratory and its ineffable art.[49] At Oxford his power *qua* professor in the university was much less than at Manchester, and the physical chemists held the upper hand, so that he could not recruit researchers as effectively from the undergraduate body as he had done before. On

[48] Joseph S. Fruton, "The Leibig Research Group: A Reappraisal," *Proceedings of the American Philosophical Society,* 1988, *132*:1–66; Fruton, *Contrasts in Scientific Style* (cit. n. 6), p. 16–71; Frederic L. Holmes, "The Complementarity of Teaching and Research in Liebig's Laboratory," *Osiris,* 1989, *5*:121–164; and G. K. Roberts, "Chemical Education and Chemical Institutions," in Russell, *Recent Developments in History of Chemistry* (cit. n. 1), pp. 24–48.

[49] Colin A. Russell, "The Changing Role of Synthesis in Organic Chemistry," *Ambix,* 1987, *34*:169–180.

the other hand, his affable personality and his wide interests enabled him to introduce Germanic and Mancunian research practices into Oxford in a more disturbed and difficult period of his career. Perhaps above all, he had a happy knack
of being associated with several munificent endowments of laboratories for organic chemistry at Manchester, and at Oxford of persuading Dyson Perrins to
contribute substantially to a new laboratory for organic chemistry. Unlike
Schorlemmer and Odling, his predecessors at Manchester and Oxford, he was not
just a chemist who trod the *via dolorosa* of literary composition but a discipline
builder whose reputation was based on his triumphs at the laboratory bench.
With his large hands and spatulate fingers, using nothing more than simple glass-
ware, he was a renowned manual experimentalist. In the opinion of his pupils he
had a sixth sense, which he exercised unconsciously in overcoming practical
bench problems. Using a test tube, a glass rod, and various solvents, he had a rare
ability to help his students by making their intractable gums crystallize. Unlike
Liebig, who did not replicate at Munich the chemist breeding he had launched at
the University of Giessen, Perkin tried to repeat at Oxford what he had done at
Manchester as a researcher, a research school director, a designer of new laboratories, and a securer of external funding. The different results he achieved were not
just the result of his becoming older; they were also determined by the different
institutional opportunities and constraints he experienced at Manchester, the
pioneer red-brick provincial university, and Oxford, England's most ancient one.

Spain's First School of Physics: Blas Cabrera's Laboratorio de Investigaciones Físicas

By José M. Sánchez-Ron* and Antoni Roca-Rosell**

IT HAS LONG BEEN RECOGNIZED that "science does not flourish every-where,"[1] not at least to the same degree. National scientific productivity can be strongly influenced by population, economic power, social, political, and cultural history, geographical location, and perhaps even climate among other factors, now as in the past. We know a great deal about the specific effects of several of these factors, but mainly in the case of the big nations that contributed significantly to the development of science. Such standard sources as Joseph Ben-David's classic *The Scientist's Role in Society* seldom go beyond Germany, Great Britain, France, or the United States.[2] Few case studies are devoted to smaller countries that made significant contributions to science (e.g., Holland or Italy), and the body of secondary literature declines, geometrically or even exponentially, for small nations with a less-celebrated scientific history.

In this essay we investigate the first research physics laboratory of any significance founded in Spain, the Laboratorio de Investigaciones Físicas, created in Madrid in 1910 by the Junta para Ampliación de Estudios e Investigaciones Científicas (Board for the Promotion of Studies and Scientific Research).[3] This state-supported institution was not attached to any university, although most of its senior researchers were university professors. Nothing resembling a "research group" or "research school" of physics existed in Spain before that laboratory went into operation. Indeed, the great merit of the Laboratorio was that it succeeded in establishing what Gerald Geison has denominated a "research school"; that is, "a small group of mature scientists pursuing a reasonably coherent

* Departamento de Física Teórica, Universidad Autónoma de Madrid, Cantoblanco, 28049 Madrid, Spain.

** Grup de Treball d'Història de la Ciència, Institut d'Estudis Catalans, c/. Carme 47, 08001 Barcelona, Spain.

We are grateful to Gerald Geison and Lewis Pyenson, who read the first draft of the paper and gave valuable comments and advice, and to Frances Coulborn Kohler for her careful editing of the manuscript.

[1] Thomas Schott, "Scientific Productivity and International Integration of Small Countries: Mathematics in Denmark and Israel," *Minerva,* 1987, *25*:3–20.

[2] Joseph Ben-David, *The Scientist's Role in Society* (Englewood Cliffs, N.J.: Prentice-Hall, 1971; 2nd ed., Chicago: Univ. Chicago Press, 1984).

[3] Chemistry (mostly physical chemistry) was also covered in the Laboratorio, but we will not examine this discipline in detail here.

programme of research side-by-side with advanced students in the same institutional context and engaging in direct, continuous social and intellectual interaction."[4]

To get a proper perspective on the foundation and fate of the Laboratorio we need first to consider the more general situation of Spanish science at the turn of the century. The Laboratorio appeared in an institutional and cultural context so different from the contexts discussed (or assumed) elsewhere in this volume, and so unfamiliar to most historians of science, that we have devoted almost half of this essay to this background. Only then will we be able to understand the reasons for the creation of the Laboratorio, some of the difficulties it faced during its existence, and why it was effectively dismantled in 1939, less than thirty years after its founding.

As becomes clear in Section III, the Laboratorio was a creation of the Spanish state, established in 1910 and funded for two decades thereafter by a new governmental organization, the Junta. The dependence of the Laboratorio on the state—and thus on the shifting national political situation—worked sometimes to its benefit and sometimes to its detriment, disastrously so with the rise of a fascist Spanish regime under Franco in the late 1930s.

During its first three decades, as we show in Sections IV and V, the Laboratorio produced some solid experimental work in physics and physical chemistry under the leadership of Blas Cabrera, a specialist in the measurement of magnetic units, and his collaborator Miguel Catalán, a spectroscopist best known for his discovery in 1922 of multiplets in the spectra of manganese. In Sections V and VI we address several issues that find a place in most of the other contributions to this volume—funding, personnel, research programs, and laboratory buildings and equipment. The research carried out by the staff of the Laboratorio never attained a high level of theoretical originality, and its leading research programs were imported by Laboratorio scientists who spent time abroad on fellowships from the Junta. Yet the experimental contributions of the Laboratorio won respectful international attention, enough so as to attract the interest of the Rockefeller Foundation's International Education Board, which ultimately provided the funds for the construction of a large and splendidly equipped new laboratory building, the Instituto Nacional de Física y Química, completed in 1931.

By then, however, the research programs of "the school of Cabrera" had stagnated, and within a decade the Instituto found itself under effective attack by scientists loyal to Franco. Unlike Enrico Fermi's group in Fascist Italy, the Instituto no longer had a political patron who could secure the protection and resources it

---

[4] Gerald L. Geison, "Scientific Change, Emerging Specialties, and Research Schools," *History of Science,* 1981, *19*:20–40; on p. 23. The term *research group,* which Joseph S. Fruton favors, could also be applied to the Laboratorio in that it was a community of scientists (*group*) located at a single institution, and that all the physicists who left it for other institutions in Spain stopped doing research (though mostly because physics was so poorly institutionalized in Spain). See Fruton, *Contrasts in Scientific Style: Research Groups in the Chemical and Biochemical Sciences* (Philadelphia: American Philosophical Society, 1990), Ch. 1, note 1. Yet one can also speak of a school because the influence of the Laboratorio persisted long after its closing in the Spanish Civil War (1936–1939): scattered throughout universities and a few other centers, some of the Laboratorio's young physicists and chemists continued research on topics and with approaches similar to those they learned at the Junta laboratory.

needed to pursue its research programs. In any case, Cabrera had never been a physicist of the stature of Fermi, and in the end his research school must be considered a relative failure, certainly by comparison with Fermi's group of nuclear physicists in Rome as well as most of the schools discussed elsewhere in this volume.

I. A NATION SCIENTIFICALLY UNDERDEVELOPED

In 1898 Spain lost its war against the United States and was forced to abandon its last colonies, Cuba and the Philippine Islands. At the time many Spaniards thought that the cause of the defeat was the scientific and technological inferiority of their country. At the Cortes (Spanish parliament), the deputy Eduardo Vincenti exclaimed on 23 June 1899:

> I will not stop saying, putting aside false patriotism, that we must follow the example that the United States has given to us. This country defeated us not only because it is stronger, but because it has a higher level of education than we have; in no way because they were braver. No Yankee has come up against our navy or army, but rather a machine invented by some electrician or machinist. There has been no fight. We have been defeated in the laboratory and in the offices, not at sea or on the mainland.[5]

The 1898 defeat helped advance science in Spain, but other factors also contributed. Although Spain did not become an industrialized nation until the middle of this century, a bourgeois revolution (called La Gloriosa) began as early as 1868. Among the liberal causes that this revolution promoted was the Free Education Act, which abolished censorship, introduced modern science courses into university programs, and established new departments (e.g., those of physiology and histology at the University of Madrid).

In the climate of intellectual freedom introduced by La Gloriosa, the independence of science from religion became an openly debated issue. For centuries the Catholic credo and curia had reigned supreme in Spain. Suddenly, it appeared to liberals and freethinkers that the old chains had finally been broken. Thus in 1869, in the wake of the revolution, the physician Francisco Sunyer Capdevila felt confident enough to proclaim at the Cortes: "Man is Science, God is Ignorance; Man is the Truth, God is an Error."[6]

Darwinism, of course, fitted extremely well into this new *Zeitgeist*. Before 1868 Darwin's ideas had made few inroads in Spain, but La Gloriosa changed the situation completely. Indeed, evolutionism became the leitmotif of the scientific literature of the day, the scientific theory par excellence, although more because of the philosophical possibilities it offered to the left than because

[5] Eduardo Vincenti y Reguerra, *Política pedagógica: Treinta años de vida parlamentaria* (Madrid: Imp. Hijos de Hernández, 1916); quoted in Yvonne Turin, *L'éducation et l'école en Espagne de 1874 a 1902: Liberálisme et tradition* (Paris: Presses Universitaires, 1959), p. 375. One of the more outspoken commentators on the scientific dimension of the defeat was the biological chemistry professor at the University of Madrid, José Rodríguez Carracido. On Carracido see Antonio Moreno González, ed., *José Rodríguez Carracido* (Madrid: Fundación Banco Exterior, 1991).

[6] See Guillermo Sánchez Martínez, *Guerra a Dios, a la tisis y a los reyes: Francisco Suñer y Capdevila, una propuesta materialista para la segunda mitad del siglo XIX español* (Madrid: Ediciones de la Universidad Autónoma de Madrid, 1987), p. 215.

of the revolutionaries' understanding of the needs and situation of contemporary science or the details of Darwinian theory. Not surprisingly, the orthodox right did not accept the new theory at all; when the Restoration reestablished "official science" in 1874, reintroducing religion into the university curriculum and bringing back censorship as well, Darwinism lost its official standing and became the touchstone of a fierce polemic between the "two Spains"—liberal and conservative, modern and traditional.[7] The ideological character of the debate precluded the existence of any "civil discourse"—to use Thomas Glick's expression[8]—on both sides, and the level of scientific discourse was abysmally low. It was not science, but politics, religion, or philosophy that was at stake, and the opportunity to make Darwinism the occasion for promoting and institutionalizing science was lost. When a sort of agreement, or, better, normalization, was attained, well into the first decade of the new century, evolutionism could no longer be considered the *scientific* theory par excellence, and it ceased to be a symbol for those who defended the importance of science for the future of the country.

The return of the old political structures with the Restoration of 1874 did not mean, however, that science fell back to the level of the first half of the century. By the 1870s and 1880s scientific knowledge underpinned so many contemporary needs and devices that even in underdeveloped Spain science could not stagnate completely. The biomedical disciplines underwent a notable development. In some instances, support for scientific research was a consequence of the growth of industrial cities. Thus in 1886 the Municipality of Barcelona founded the first microbiological laboratory in Spain devoted to the production of the Pasteurian rabies vaccine; its director was Jaume Ferran, who in 1884 had developed a cholera vaccine, the first one applied to humans.[9]

If we exclude the biomedical sciences, where a rudimentary network of institutions existed in which professionals could be sheltered (hospitals, university chairs, laboratories), the typical situation in Spain all through the nineteenth century was the isolated scientist. By the end of the eighteenth century, as part of the diffusion of the Enlightenment and thanks to some extent to the efforts of King Carlos III, scientific organizations had been founded in Seville, Valencia, Vergara, Barcelona, and Madrid; physics, as well as technology (not always clearly distinguished from physics), figured among the topics cultivated in those institutions. But war against France (1808–1814), which had invaded and dominated Spanish soil, and then the reign of the far-from-liberal Fernando VII once the Napoleonic forces had been defeated, meant the end—whether by physical destruction, lack of support, or explicit interdiction—of most of the existing institutions. Only in the second half of the century did the situation begin to improve.

---

[7] Several leading Darwinians lost their chairs, for example. On Darwinism in Spain see Thomas F. Glick, "Spain," in *The Comparative Reception of Darwinism,* ed. Glick, 2nd ed. (Chicago: Univ. Chicago Press, 1988), pp. 307–345.

[8] Thomas F. Glick, *Einstein in Spain* (Princeton: Princeton Univ. Press, 1988). This division was a general trend, not a universal rule: among others, Josep Joaquim Lánderer, a Catholic paleontologist, accepted some tenets of the Darwinian hypothesis.

[9] Antoni Roca Rosell, *Història del Laboratori Municipal de Barcelona: De Ferran a Turró* (Barcelona: Ajuntament de Barcelona, 1988). Ferran's vaccine, like many others, was controversial.

II. THE PHYSICAL SCIENCES IN SPAIN DURING THE
NINETEENTH CENTURY

As far as research is concerned, the Spanish universities played no role in physics in Spain during the nineteenth century. Not until 1857 was a law passed creating faculties of science; until then such studies were pursued in the faculty of philosophy. This situation was not unique to Spain. Physics, mathematics, and some of the natural sciences and humanities were lodged in philosophy faculties in Germany also; only at the end of the nineteenth century did a few German universities create special sections or faculties for the natural sciences.[10] In Spain physics, mathematics, chemistry, and natural sciences initially constituted the sections of the faculty of science in the state system, but in fact the science of Newton had a very slim presence.[11] Until 1913 Madrid and Barcelona were the only universities where science students could specialize in physics; and the doctorate could be awarded, in the sciences as in all disciplines, only by the University of Madrid.[12] There, training in the physical sciences was more complete; one could learn advanced astronomy and mathematical physics, for instance. Even at Madrid, however, doctoral dissertations were not expected to be original contributions to the discipline, and so research was neglected there as well. Other countries followed similar paths, but not for as long as Spain. In the early nineteenth century French *doctorats-ès-sciences,* particularly in physics and chemistry, were not expected to constitute original pieces of work; candidates only had to summarize the literature and reflect on it. Originality and quality steadily became the touchstone of the doctoral program, however: between 1847 and 1881 about fifty-seven theses were rejected as unsuitable or too low in quality for the doctorate in the Faculty of Sciences in Paris.[13] Another difference is that in France all the universities could grant doctoral degrees.

That university faculties in Spain lacked research incentives and facilities began to disturb some professors by the turn of the century. One significant episode followed the reception of Wilhelm Röntgen's discovery of X rays in 1895. Professors of physics in the Faculty of Sciences at Barcelona replicated the generation of X rays and presented their promising results at a public lecture on 10 February 1896—quite an early date. But when they tried soon after to perform some experiments with the new and mysterious rays (they thought that they could detect deflection of X rays), they found, to their dismay, that the few

[10] Christa Jungnickel and Russell McCormmach, *The Intellectual Mastery of Nature: Theoretical Physics from Ohm to Einstein,* Vol. I: *The Torch of Mathematics, 1800–1870* (Chicago: Univ. Chicago Press, 1986), Ch. 1.

[11] The number of sections varied during the period under consideration; sometimes physics and mathematics formed one section, at other times physics and chemistry. For a detailed study of physics at Spanish universities during the nineteenth century see Antonio Moreno González, *Una ciencia en cuarentena: La física académica en España (1750–1900)* (Madrid: Consejo Superior de Investigaciones Científicas [CSIC], 1988).

[12] The regulation allowing only the University of Madrid to grant doctorates was not rescinded until the 1950s.

[13] Terry Shinn, "The French Science Faculty System, 1808–1914: Institutional Change and Research Potential in Mathematics and the Physical Sciences," *Historical Studies in the Physical Sciences (HSPS),* 1979, *10*:271–332; and Harry W. Paul, *From Knowledge to Power: The Rise of the Science Empire in France, 1860–1939* (Cambridge: Cambridge Univ. Press, 1985), pp. 54–55.

old experimental devices available to them made it impossible to carry out the experiments.[14]

In Spain, only in astronomy and meteorology was research of any significance carried out towards the end of the century. The observational character of experiments carried out in these fields allowed them to be conducted by individuals, mostly amateurs. Such observers could still contribute, even with modest equipment, to knowledge about the surface of Mars or the satellites of Jupiter, for instance. Meteorological measurements (e.g., telluric currents) and some geophysical research could also be done by individuals, whether attached to an academic institution or outside.[15] Various posts were also available in these fields. By 1860 the Spanish government had organized a network of meteorological stations, most of them attached to state schools and science faculties. In 1888 the government founded the Instituto Central Meteorológico, directed by Augusto T. Arcimís, to provide weather forecasting, a service that many modern, or would-be modern, states had already established by that time. Even before 1800 two official astronomical and meteorological observatories existed in Spain; a civil one in Madrid, established in 1790, and a naval one in Cádiz, founded in 1753 and moved in 1798 to the nearby village of San Fernando.[16] Although these centers carried out important routine work, most late-nineteenth-century scientists felt that they did not produce advanced research, and San Fernando, located in the South of Spain, was too far away from the main university and cultural centers to have much impact on the development of academic science.

Some late-nineteenth-century Spanish scientists nevertheless saw observatories as a possible route to institutionalizing physical sciences as a research-oriented discipline. In Barcelona the leading scientists of the Academia de Ciencias y Artes attempted to found an observatory in the city from 1883 onwards. They achieved partial success in 1902, when a textile industrialist gave a large sum of money to establish it. The Barcelona Observatory began functioning in 1904, but its funding was so meager that it could not conduct major scientific projects. The Spanish Jesuits also focused on observatories as a way of institutionalizing scientific research: by the 1860s they had founded meteorological and astronomical stations in Cuba and the Philippine Islands.[17] Once Spain lost these colonies, the Jesuits brought their experience back to the Iberian Peninsula, founding two geophysical observatories in 1904, in Granada and Roquetes.[18]

[14] See Antoni Roca Rosell, "La física en la Cataluña finisecular: El joven Fontserè y su época" (Ph.D. diss., Universidad Autónoma de Madrid, 1990), Ch. 5.

[15] The most representative scientists working in these fields were Josep Joaquim Lánderer, Eduard Fontserè, and Josep Comas Solà: see Roca, La física en la Cataluña (cit. n. 14), Chs. 1, 2. The issue of working within these constraints was discussed by Fontserè in "Sobre les ciències d'observatió a Catalunya," Nova Ibèrica, 1937, 2, rpt. in Ciència, 1982, 2:284–285.

[16] J. Tinoco, Apuntes para la historia del Observatorio de Madrid (Madrid: Talleres del Instituto Geográfico y Catastral, 1951); and Antonio Lafuente and Manuel Sellés, El Observatorio de Cádiz (1753–1831) (Madrid: Ministerio de Defensa, 1988).

[17] Metereological and astronomical studies were the most appropriate for a colonial setting: see Lewis Pyenson, Cultural Imperialism and Exact Sciences: German Expansion Overseas, 1900–1930 (New York/Berne: Peter Lang, 1985), and Pyenson, Empire of Reason: Exact Sciences in Indonesia, 1840–1940 (Leiden: E. J. Brill, 1989).

[18] See P. de Bvregille, "Les observatoires de la Compagnie de Jésus au début du XXe siècle," Revue des Questions Scientifiques, 1906, 3rd ser., 9:10–72, 493–579.

In the late nineteenth century a special circumstance increased the popularity of astronomy in Spain. From 1860 through 1912 a series of total eclipses of the sun could be observed from the Iberian peninsula. As a consequence, several foreign astronomical expeditions visited Spain; the spectacular nature of the phenomenon had a great impact on public opinion, and hitherto-isolated Spanish astronomers could interact with their more sophisticated counterparts from abroad.

Highly important to physics in nineteenth-century Spain were the engineering schools. These schools, founded or reorganized around 1850, enjoyed much higher prestige than university faculties; they were conceived on the French model, so that physics and especially mathematics were important components of their programs. As in France, physics was "sold" mostly for its role in the training of engineers. It is not surprising, therefore, that engineers played a leading role in introducing new mathematical and physical ideas and theories into Spain. Gumersindo de Vicuña and José Echegaray, professors at the prestigious Escuela de Caminos (Civil Engineering School) of Madrid, were prominent exponents of thermodynamics and Maxwellian electrodynamics in the last quarter of the nineteenth century.[19] A measure of engineers' significance in Spanish science is found in the composition of the Real Academia de Ciencias Exactas, Físicas y Naturales, founded in 1847 in Madrid and considered the most prestigious scientific institution in Spain. By 1865, when Echegaray was elected a member of the Academia, of the thirty-six *académicos,* eleven were engineers, seven high-ranking military officers, five physicians, three pharmacists, two astronomers, two physicists, and the remainder were a miscellaneous group. The contributions (mainly textbooks, or series of general articles) of these engineers were almost never original, but they fostered the modernization of the teaching and knowledge of mathematical physics in particular. The weakness of mathematical and physical training at the science faculties, where physics was studied for its own sake, and the lack of opportunities for science graduates and scientists maintained the influence of these engineers until the first decades of the twentieth century, and even that late many physicists and mathematicians had studied at engineering schools.[20]

III. A NEW INSTITUTION FOR A NEW CENTURY:
THE JUNTA PARA AMPLIACIÓN DE ESTUDIOS E INVESTIGACIONES CIENTÍFICAS

In the end the social crisis that resulted from losing the war against the United States in 1898 had beneficial consequences for Spanish culture and science. We have already pointed out that lack of education was identified as one of the causes of the defeat. Although many reforms had been implemented, or at least

[19] On Echegaray and mathematical physics in Spain see José M. Sánchez Ron, "José Echegaray: Matemático y físico-matemático," in *José Echegaray,* ed. Sánchez Ron (Madrid: Fundación Banco Exterior, 1990), pp. 13–132; and Sánchez Ron, "La física matemática en España: De Echegaray a Rey Pastor," *Arbor,* 1990, No. 532, pp. 9–59. Echegaray, a versatile character, won the Nobel Prize for literature in 1904. In France also a good many contributors to physics were graduates of the Ecole Polytechnique or the Ecole Naval: see Terry Shinn, *Savoir scientifique et pouvoir social: L'Ecole Polytechnique, 1794–1914* (Paris: Presses de la Fondation Nationale des Sciences Politiques, 1980).
[20] Sánchez Ron, "La física matemática" (cit. n. 19). The military and naval authorities hired many highly trained engineers and allowed them the leisure to publish theoretical treatises in many areas.

promoted, in the Spanish educational system during the second half of the nineteenth century (e.g., the creation of *institutos* on the model of French *lycées*), no specific Ministry of Education existed as the century reached its end.[21] In 1900, however, the Ministerio de Instrucción Pública y Bellas Artes (Ministry of Public Instruction and Fine Arts) was established.

It would be difficult, if not impossible, to link that ministry with any clear-cut political line, if only because it persisted through a rapid succession of governments of different ideological orientations, all of which took some measures to improve education. That improvement, however, was centered mainly on the elementary level (the *primaria* and *secundaria* schools), as was in fact appropriate in a country in which 71.5 percent of the population was illiterate as late as 1900. (By 1930 the percentage had lowered to a still high 44.5 percent.) At the university level new reforms were introduced, but they applied only to the organization of studies, that is, to teaching, which was essentially "theoretical" (i.e., little attention was paid in the curriculum to practical applications). As for the faculties of sciences, all contemporary accounts agree that by 1900 the few rooms in which experiments were performed could hardly be called laboratories. In 1917, referring to his budget for 1887 through 1901, José Rodríguez Carracido, professor of biological chemistry in Madrid (a chair with teaching duties at the faculties of medicine, pharmacy, and sciences), complained as follows: "During fourteen years, biological chemistry was taught as if it were metaphysics, all the ministers opposing unanimously (here there were no differences among the different parties) the request for the elements indispensable to establishing a most necessary laboratory." Finally, in 1901 the Cortes approved a budget of 6,000 pesetas annually for scientific material for the five faculties of the University of Madrid; but that still meant a ridiculously low amount per chair: 38.25 pesetas quarterly, for example, to each of the chemistry chairs.[22]

Against that background, a new and, by Spanish standards, revolutionary institution was created by the Ministerio de Instrucción Pública in January 1907, when the liberals were in power: the Junta para Ampliación de Estudios e Investigaciones Científicas. It was a revolutionary institution not only from the standpoint of Spain's past history, but in the international context: no other institution, public or private, of any country tried at that time to cover as much ground. Despite its official origin, this Junta proved autonomous and independent throughout its existence, though at times, especially under conservative governments, it encountered serious difficulties.

The Junta was created thanks to the efforts and influence of a small group of intellectuals related to the Institución Libre de Enseñanza, a private and progressive educational institution founded in 1876 by a few professors who had been expelled from their universities in 1867–1868 (before the revolution of Septem-

---

[21] The establishment of these *institutos* was important to the development of science, as graduates in physics could find jobs at them. Several leading twentieth-century Spanish physicists and mathematicians (e.g., José María Plans, Miguel A. Catalán, Pedro Puig Adam) taught at these centers, some for their entire career.

[22] José Rodríguez Carracido, *Estudios histórico-críticos de la ciencia española* (Madrid: Imprenta de "Alrededor del Mundo," 1917; rpt. Barcelona: Alta Fulla/Mundo Científico, 1988), quoting from p. 389. The situation in Carracido's laboratory improved greatly after the Junta was created. The Junta bore a portion of the laboratory's expenses for upkeep and instruction in exchange for desk space and use of the laboratory for the special courses it offered in chemistry.

ber 1868), owing to their liberal ideas.[23] The Junta's first president was Santiago Ramón y Cajal, the great histologist who won the 1906 Nobel Prize for medicine and physiology. Cajal, who had to learn anatomy by digging up corpses from the graveyards with the help of his father, a country doctor, knew full well the difficulties faced by scientists and young students of science in Spain. He held the post of president of the Junta until his death in 1934. The moving spirit of the Junta was, however, its secretary, José Castillejo, professor of Roman law and a disciple of the *institucionista* Francisco Giner de los Ríos.[24] Castillejo's initiatives and ideas were approved more often than not by the permanent board of twenty-one members who composed the Junta.

The aim of the Junta was to help renew and improve the Spanish educational system at all levels, by promoting and developing not only the exact and natural sciences, but disciplines like history, philology, law, art, and philosophy. Believing that one of the main problems in Spain was the lack of knowledge of what was going on in more developed countries, the Junta made it a basic policy to send graduate students, as well as school and university professors, abroad. The decree creating the Junta in 1907 was explicit on this point: "The country that lives in isolation holds up progress and becomes a decadent one. Because of this, all the civilized nations take part in that movement of international scientific relationship [that we are witnessing at present], including not only the small European countries, but also nations that seem far away from modern life, such as China and even Turkey, whose colony of students in Germany is four times the Spanish one; that is, [we are] last but two among all the Europeans."[25]

During its existence (1907–1938) the Junta received approximately 9,000 requests for grants, of which more than 2,000 were granted (22%). As to the countries chosen, 29% of the holders of the scholarships went to France, 22% to Germany, 14% to Switzerland, 12% to Belgium, 8% to Italy, 6% to Great Britain, 4% to Austria, and 3% to the United States. Of the 560 university professors who applied for a grant, 73 (13%) taught at faculties of sciences, 216 (38.7%) at faculties of medicine, 53 (9.4%) at faculties of philosophy, and 150 (26.7%) at faculties of law. The percentages for each discipline (not all are listed here) are significant: pedagogy, 18.5%; medicine, 18.6%; art, 10.6%; law, 9.7%; chemistry, 6%; history, 5.7%; natural sciences, 5%; philology and literature, 4%; engineering, 3.6%; physics, 2.4%; mathematics, 2%; and philosophy, 1%.[26] These percentages might seem

[23] Vicente Cacho Viu, *La Institución Libre de Enseñanza* (Madrid: Rialp, 1962); Antonio Jiménez-Landi, *La Institución Libre de Enseñanza y su ambiente: Los orígenes* (Madrid: Taurus, 1973); and Jiménez-Landi, *La Institución Libre de Enseñanza*, Vol. II: *Periodo parauniversitario*, 2 vols. (Madrid: Taurus, 1987).

[24] On Castillejo see Luis Palacios Bañuelos, *José Castillejo, última etapa de la Institución Libre de Enseñanza* (Madrid: Narcea, 1979); Carmela Gamero Merino, *Un movimiento europeo de renovación pedagógica: José Castillejo* (Madrid: CSIC, 1988); and Irene Claremont de Castillejo, "I Married a Stranger: Life with One of Spain's Enigmatic Men," MS (April 1967). We are grateful to Prof. Leonardo Castillejo, University College, London, for providing a copy of this last document.

[25] "Preámbulo del Real Decreto de 11 de Enero de 1907, creando la Junta para Ampliación de Estudios e Investigaciones Científicas," in *Legislación* (Madrid: Junta para Ampliación de Estudios, 1910), pp. 6–7.

[26] These numbers are drawn from the *Memorias* that the Junta published biannually. On the Junta see also Francisco Laporta, Alfonso Ruiz Miguel, Virgilio Zapatero, and Javier Solana, "Los orígenes culturales de la Junta para Ampliación de Estudios," *Arbor*, Jan. 1987, No. 493, pp. 17–87; July/

to indicate that physics was not particularly favored by the Junta, but what they reveal instead is that physics was not a major discipline in Spain. The Junta's commitment to the discipline is clear from a letter it sent the Rockefeller International Educational Board:

> Physics and chemistry have been considered by the Junta fundamental studies for scientific progress. Between 1907 and 1924, the Junta granted scholarships in physics and chemistry to 66 professors and graduates for laboratory work, for one or two and in some cases for three years in different countries, viz.: in Germany 25 scholars; in Switzerland 17; in France 15; in the United States 10; in England 5; in Holland 2; in Belgium 1; in Russia 1; in Monaco 1.[27]

The Junta was also convinced that improving the country's scientific standing required more than sending individuals abroad. For what would happen when those individuals returned to Spain? In the opinion of those who created the Junta, the universities had no way of profiting from so many trained scientists; on the contrary, they would spoil their scientific potential. Consequently, one of the Junta's aims from the very beginning was to create centers of its own in which advanced research could be done. In 1910 it established two such centers, the Centro de Estudios Históricos and the Instituto Nacional de Ciencias Físico-Naturales, designed to control the laboratories and departments the Junta might support or create. The Laboratorio de Investigaciones Físicas was founded that same year. But before turning to it, we must still consider other general aspects of the Junta.

To carry out the program the Junta was planning required no small amount of money. Past experience had shown that on research matters the Spanish treasury was far from generous. Nevertheless, and contrary to all expectations, the Junta was able to secure a budget that, although meager, was far superior to that received by any other Spanish institution or center at the time, including the universities. It is hard to specify the reason for this unprecedented generosity, though a detailed study of the Junta's history would reveal the great ability and perseverance of Castillejo especially, but also of Cajal, in dealing with ministers of different political stripes; in fact, the Junta survived under regimes as different as the monarchy, the dictatorship of General Primo de Rivera (1923–1930), and the Spanish Republic (1931–1936/9). To some extent Castillejo played the same role in relation to the Junta in general and to the Laboratorio de Investigaciones Físicas in particular that Orso Mario Corbino played on behalf of Fermi's physics laboratory in Fascist Rome. Corbino, a senator of the Kingdom of Italy as well as a professor of experimental physics (he was also minister of public instruction in 1921) had enough political influence to be able to secure funds for Fermi and his group.[28] It was also as a result of Corbino's efforts that, despite the basically rigid

August 1987, No. 499/500, pp. 9–137; and the various articles in José M. Sánchez Ron, ed., *La Junta para Ampliación de Estudios e Investigaciones Científicas 80 años después, 1907–1987,* 2 vols. (Madrid: CSIC, 1988).

[27] José Castillejo to Wickliffe Rose, 21 July 1924, International Educational Board (IEB), 1.2, 41.577, Rockefeller Archive Center, Pocantico Hills, Tarrytown, New York.

[28] Gerald Holton, "Fermi's Group and the Recapture of Italy's Place in Physics," in his *The Scientific Imagination: Case Studies* (Cambridge: Cambridge Univ. Press, 1978), pp. 155–198.

structure of the Italian university, a chair in theoretical physics was created at the University of Rome, and in such a way that it could be filled only by Fermi. It thus seems that in countries with the social, political, economic, and cultural characteristics of Italy and Spain between 1910 and 1940 an adequate political shelter was necessary for maintaining a stable research group. Neither Italy nor Spain had yet reached the stage of social, economic, and educational development that made overtly political patronage unnecessary; not surprisingly, only a few research groups then existed in either country.

The first budget of the Junta was 328,000 pesetas, the greater part of which (150,000) went that initial year to scholarships abroad; 24,000 pesetas was spent on scientific material of different kinds. The budget increased steadily, with some variance in allocation that reflect changing political circumstances. Thus in 1912 the Laboratorio de Investigaciones Físicas received 29,876 pesetas from the Junta for apparatus, and 16,013 pesetas in 1913, but when in 1914 the state authorized 789,655 pesetas for the Junta, only 6,495 went to the Laboratorio. The following year, with the same budget, the Laboratorio received 23,440 pesetas. During the 1920s the budget increased considerably; in 1923 it reached 1,609,693 pesetas, with 38,953 for the physics laboratory. In 1933, when a new Instituto Nacional de Física y Química replaced the old Laboratorio, the Junta's budget rose to 3,649,721 pesetas, of which the Instituto received more than 300,000.[29] By then the Junta's budget was meeting one of Geison's conditions for the sustained success of a research school—namely, that it "must have or must quickly acquire sufficient power in the local and national institutional setting to secure adequate financial support and an institutionalized commitment to [the] enterprise."[30]

But even as the Junta obtained increasing amounts of money from the treasury, the laboratories at the universities, engineering schools, and other institutions had limited success in securing new funds. Some laboratories were created—especially in Madrid; Barcelona had fewer and Saragossa fewer still. In 1903, to cite only examples in the capital, a Laboratorio de Radioactividad was installed under the direction of the chemist José Muñoz del Castillo, and in 1907 a Laboratorio de Mecánica Aplicada directed by Leonardo Torres Quevedo. However, the physics laboratories (general physics, thermodynamics, electricity and magnetism, and acoustics and optics) of the Faculty of Sciences at Madrid were still in a poor condition.[31] When in 1925 August Trowbridge, formerly a physics professor at Princeton and then director for Europe of the Physical and Biological Sciences Section of the International Educational Board, visited Madrid (for reasons discussed in Section VI), he stated that the "regular laboratories of the

[29] Figures obtained from the *Memorias* published by the Junta, e.g., *Memoria correspondiente a los años 1912 y 1913* (Madrid: Junta para Ampliación de Estudios, 1914); and from the Libros de Actas (notebooks) kept at the Junta Archives, Residencia de Estudiantes, Consejo Superior de Investigaciones Científicas (CSIC), Madrid.

[30] Geison, "Scientific Change, Emerging Specialties, and Research Schools" (cit. n. 4), p. 26.

[31] For Madrid circa 1913 see *Reseña de los principales establecimientos científicos y laboratorios de investigación de Madrid* (Madrid: Asociación Española para el Progreso de las Ciencias, 1913), pp. 155–163, esp. "Laboratorios y cátedra de física de la Facultad de Ciencias." For some information on Barcelona and Saragossa see Roca Rosell, *La física en la Cataluña* (cit. n. 14); Antoni Roca Rosell and José M. Sánchez Ron, *Esteban Terradas: Ciencia y técnica en la España contemporánea* (Barcelona: INTA/El Serbal, 1990); and Mariano Tomeo Lacrué, *Biografía científica de la Universidad de Zaragoza* (Zaragoza, 1962).

University" in which instruction or research in physics or chemistry was carried out were "in my opinion not worth considering—physics is a little better than chemistry in equipment (chemistry has about none whatever) and possibly the lecture courses in elementary science have some value, but taken as a whole, I have never seen anywhere worse conditions in University laboratories."[32]

Not surprisingly, voices were raised in the university against what was considered a most unjust situation. At the Congress of the Asociación Española para el Progreso de las Ciencias (Spanish Association for the Advancement of Science) held in Seville in 1917, for example, José González Martí, professor of general physics at Madrid, declared in one of the main lectures at the meeting that he could neither understand nor accept that the Junta was offered resources denied to the university. Since the directors, and even the majority of the scientists working at the Junta laboratories, were university personnel, the effect of the state support of the Junta was, insisted González Martí, "to divide the professors into two categories," with those remaining exclusively at the university unable to carry out original research because of lack of resources.[33] He, as well as others, argued that the Junta was making the necessary decentralization of research efforts impossible, and that its laboratories would remain in the end the only real scientific centers throughout Spain.

In fact, five years before the Seville congress González Martí had already tried to give force to his critique of the Junta with the help of two right-wing professors of the Madrid Faculty of Sciences, José Muñoz del Castillo, also a member of the Cortes, and Bartolomé Feliú, a member of the Senado. On 13 July 1912 the physicist Jerónimo Vecino, then working at the Laboratorio de Investigaciones Físicas, warned Blas Cabrera, its director, that González Martí (who had been one of Cabrera's teachers at the university) planned "to abolish the Junta and the Laboratorio, and to use the money that these centers spend to give salaries to the assistants who help with experiments at universities and institutes. Arguments for such abolition: that the Laboratorio is useless as a center because the role of the university is to train professors and not researchers."[34] On that occasion Cabrera, Castillejo, and Cajal reacted quickly and energetically, obtaining the support of a large number of Spanish university professors. Yet the wide support may not have been completely sincere in all instances, for less than thirty years later some who

[32] August Trowbridge to Wickliffe Rose, 4 May 1925, IEB 1.2, 41.577, Rockefeller Archive Center. Trowbridge also mentioned the chemical laboratories of the Faculty of Pharmacy ("on the whole these are good . . . [although] not large enough to take care of all applicants and the greater number of the university students are forced to work under intolerable conditions"); the laboratories of the Department of Public Health ("no instruction in the parts devoted to physics and chemistry. These laboratories are testing labs pure and simple"); and the laboratories connected with the Ordnance and the Engineer Corps of the Spanish Army ("Here the equipment in physics and chemistry is good, some instruction is given to younger officers who volunteer for training in these lines. There is a semi-permanent staff connected with these laboratories, though as the scientists must be members of the military establishment, they are not likely to be men of any scientific training in research"). See also the discussion of Trowbridge's visit to Madrid in Thomas F. Glick, "La Fundació Rockefeller i Espanya: La crisi dels laboratoris," in Història de la física, ed. Luis Navarro Veguillas (Barcelona: CIRIT, 1988), pp. 367–371.

[33] José González Martí, "Estado de la enseñanza de la física en las universidades de España," Actas Sexto Congreso de la Asociación Española para el Progreso de las Ciencias, 1917, 1:35–57.

[34] Jerónimo Vecino to Blas Cabrera, 13 July 1912, Junta Archives, CSIC. The complete history of this episode will be documented in José M. Sánchez Ron, "El mundo de Blas Cabrera" (book in preparation).

in 1912 sided with the Junta appeared as ferocious critics of it.[35] On the other hand, in 1912 it would not have been easy to answer a personal letter from the imposing and vehement Cajal in the negative.

As to González Martí's arguments in 1917, it is difficult to say whether a uniform and more equitable distribution of resources would have allowed the university professors to become more creative scientists. The tactic chosen by the Junta, and indirectly and most probably unwittingly by the politicians, in fact yielded splendid fruits, especially, though not only, in the case of physics. The centralization of scientific research in the Laboratorio de Investigaciones Físicas and its isolation from other centers in Spain meant that it was easy, in fact almost unavoidable, to establish a "school of physics" there. Isolation, continuity, lack of satisfactory professional opportunities elsewhere, scientific competence, and a minimum level of success are elements that seldom fail to produce what can be called a *school*, even when several branches of physics were being cultivated simultaneously, as was the case with our Laboratorio.

IV. BLAS CABRERA'S RESEARCH PROGRAM

Blas Cabrera (1878–1945), the director of the Laboratorio de Investigaciones Físicas, was Spain's foremost physicist in the first half of the twentieth century; indeed, he was the first physicist of any international stature in the history of Spanish science.[36] Born in Arrecife, Lanzarote, in the Canary Islands, he traveled to Madrid in 1894 with the aim of studying law, but soon moved to the Faculty of Sciences, obtaining his degree (*licenciado*) in 1900. To qualify for the doctoral examination in the physicomathematical section, in addition to submitting a dissertation, it was necessary to follow three courses: theoretical and experimental astronomy, mathematical physics, and meteorology. Cabrera's thesis, submitted in October 1901, dealt with a topic in meteorology, the diurnal variations of the wind, and did not involve any experimental work. As far as we know he had no supervisor, something frequent (indeed, almost the rule) at the time.[37] Soon after obtaining his doctorate, Cabrera revealed himself as a prolific researcher, publishing eight papers between 1903 and 1904 on topics dealing with electrolytes and with elementary questions of electromagnetism.

In January 1903, just at the time that Cabrera was launching his career in research, a professional society of physicists and chemists, the Sociedad Española de Física y Química, was created. Perhaps the time was ripe for the institutionalization of physics and chemistry in Spain. One purpose of the new society was to publish a journal, the *Anales de la Sociedad Española de Física y Química*. Its first issue, a modest booklet of forty pages, appeared in March 1903; Cabrera

[35] E.g., the physician Enrique Suñer, who attacked the Junta pitilessly in his *Los intelectuales y la tragedia española* (Burgos: Editorial Española, 1937).

[36] A few aspects of Cabrera's life and career are considered in *En el centenario de Blas Cabrera* (Las Palmas: Universidad Internacional "Pérez Galdos," [ca. 1978]). For a full study see Sánchez Ron, "El mundo de Blas Cabrera" (cit. n. 34).

[37] Blas Cabrera, *Variación diurna del viento* (Santa Cruz de Tenerife: Imprenta de A. J. Benítez, 1902). The lack of a supervisor again parallels the case in France, where technically there were no thesis directors, only *présidents* of the examining jury—although in practice the president was a professor who worked with the student in organizing the dissertation.

contributed two papers to that issue, something that no one else did.[38] In fact, although the Laboratorio had its own publication, the *Trabajos del Laboratorio de Investigaciones Físicas,* the *Anales* constituted the main instrument for the publication of the results of the researches performed at the Laboratorio and its successor, the Instituto. Although the scientists of the Laboratorio did not control the *Anales* completely, they clearly never had any difficulty publishing their papers in it. In this respect, the Laboratorio fulfilled one of Geison's characteristics of a successful "research school."

Initially, the members of the new Sociedad Española de Física y Química numbered 249, among whom the largest group (39) was pharmacists, who would presumably have been more interested in chemistry than physics. The next largest group was formed by professors in the faculties of sciences (38); then came the engineers (36), always present in the history of Spanish physicomathematical sciences. There followed 34 nonuniversity teachers, 29 *licenciados* and Ph.Ds, 14 assistant professors at the faculties of sciences, 9 astronomers, 7 clearly identified as chemists, 7 military men, 2 priests, and a miscellaneous group of 30 other persons.[39]

In March 1905 Cabrera was appointed Professor of Electricity and Magnetism at the Madrid Faculty of Sciences. Up to then most of his works had dealt with magnetism and electricity. When in 1909 he was elected a member of the Real Academia de Ciencias Exactas, Físicas y Naturales, he chose as the subject for his inaugural address (delivered in 1910), "The Ether and Its Relationship with Matter at Rest." He did not mention Einstein, some of whose works he already knew, although apparently he did not completely understand them at the time (in particular, he did not perceive how different Einstein's standpoint was from Lorentz's).[40] Soon, however, Cabrera understood the meaning of Einstein's contribution and became the main interpreter of his ideas in Spain.[41]

By 1910 Cabrera was at the summit of his profession; at the Academy, for example, he and González Martí—much older than Cabrera—were the only true physicists. Consequently, it is not surprising that when the Junta para Ampliación de Estudios started looking for a director for the physics laboratory it

[38] Cabrera published 68 papers in the *Anales* throughout his career; only two chemists, Enrique Moles and José Muñoz del Castillo, published more (111 and 76, respectively). For a bibliometrical analysis of the papers published in the *Anales,* see Manuel Valera and Pedro Marset, "Aspectos bibliométricos e institucionales de la Real Sociedad Española de Física y Química para el periodo 1903–1937," in *El científico español ante su historia: La ciencia en España entre 1750 y 1850,* ed. Santiago Garma (Madrid: Diputación Provincial de Madrid, 1980), pp. 391–432.

[39] For the list see *Anales de la Sociedad Española de Física y Química,* June 1904, No. 14, pp. 255–264. Thomas Glick had similar results when he analyzed the Sociedad in 1920, when there were 346 members: see *Einstein in Spain* (cit. n. 8). For the numerical evolution of the membership to the Sociedad see Valera and Marset, "Aspectos bibliométricos" (cit. n. 38), p. 413.

[40] Blas Cabrera, *El éter y sus relaciones con la materia en reposo* (Madrid: Real Academia de Ciencias, 1910). At the first meeting of the Asociación Española para el Progreso de las Ciencias, held in Saragossa in 1908, Cabrera presented a paper on the theory of electrons that explained Maxwellian and Hertzian electromagnetic concepts of light. He mentioned Einstein's theory only as a refinement of Lorentz's electron theory. On the introduction of relativity to Spain see Glick, *Einstein in Spain* (cit. n. 8); and Thomas F. Glick, "Relativity in Spain," in *The Comparative Reception of Relativity,* ed. Glick (Boston: Reidel, 1987), pp. 231–263.

[41] See, e.g., Blas Cabrera, *Principio de relatividad* (Madrid: Publicaciones de la Residencia de Estudiantes, 1923; 2nd. ed., Barcelona: Altafulla/Mundo Científico, 1986), where see also the introduction, José M. Sánchez Ron, "Blas Cabrera y el principio de relatividad," pp. v–xxi.

wanted to create, it fixed its eyes on the young professor of electricity and magnetism. And since Cabrera was essentially an experimentalist, interested especially in the magnetic properties of matter, as well as in some aspects of physical chemistry, he was an appropriate candidate to lead an experimental center covering physics and some branches of chemistry (especially, physical chemistry). Even the "theoretical" papers he published were never intended as original contributions, but rather as reviews, if not popularizations, of the new theories of other physicists.

This lack of original theoretical talent was one of Cabrera's main weaknesses as a physicist. Indeed, all the scientists, whether physicists or chemists, who gathered at the Laboratorio and Instituto throughout their existence shared the same exclusively experimental approach to physics and chemistry. No significant theoretical paper ever came out of either incarnation of the institute. The reason is difficult to specify. Perhaps at the beginning of the century, when theoretical physics was not yet well established in Spain, the focus on experiment was unavoidable for a group of physicists and chemists starting to do research in a country without a tradition of original scientific investigation. It was then easier to manipulate apparatus than to elaborate theories, especially since the mathematicians of the country were also trying to consolidate themselves as modern professionals, paying attention mostly to pure mathematics at the expense of applied mathematics.[42] Indeed, it is striking how the situation in Spain resembled that in a country as different as the United States, where, as John Servos has shown, mathematics was making great strides, but mainly in areas remote from the needs of experimental scientists.[43]

Soon after assuming the directorship of the Laboratorio, Cabrera asked for one of the scholarships granted by the Junta. No doubt he realized that it was one thing to be a successful physicist in Spain, publishing there easily and often, and quite another to be a competitive international physicist. On 12 April 1912 the Junta granted him the scholarship, "for five months, with 400 pesetas monthly, plus 600 for travel, and 500 for material, to visit physics laboratories and to work on magnetism in France, Switzerland, and Germany."[44]

Cabrera spent the greater part of his grant period at the Zurich Polytechnikum, working in the laboratory of the French physicist Pierre Weiss, who was by then a scientist with an established reputation in the European scientific community, especially in the field of magnetism. Cabrera's projected stay almost came to nothing: The Spanish physics professor and *académico* arrived in Zurich early in May 1912, together with his wife and son, without either knowing Weiss or having informed him of his forthcoming visit. It was only with difficulty, although rather quickly, that he and the chemist Enrique Moles (head of the chemistry section of

---

[42] On this point see Sánchez Ron, "La física matemática en España" (cit. n. 19). One exception was the attention paid to tensor calculus in the 1920s and 1930s, owing to the popularity of Einstein's theory of general relativity in Spain. However, Spanish physicists (or mathematicians) did not make original contributions to this theory during this period.

[43] John W. Servos, "Mathematics and the Physical Sciences in America, 1880–1930," *Isis*, 1986, 77:611–629. Most Spanish physicists and chemists who went abroad did so to perfect their skills in the laboratory. The main difference is that in Spain the trend lasted till the Civil War (1936), while in the United States it began to change significantly around 1914.

[44] Libros de Actas, Junta para Ampliación de Estudios, Junta Archives, CSIC.

the Laboratorio, who accompanied him to Zurich) attracted Weiss's interest and confidence.[45]

The months spent in Zurich were crucial in Cabrera's scientific career, not only because most of his research thereafter dealt with the study of weakly magnetic substances, but also because he would join forces with Weiss in trying to prove the existence of the "Weiss magneton," which was, according to the French professor, the natural unit of molecular magnetism.[46] Throughout his career, Cabrera accumulated a wealth of carefully selected experimental measurements that he thought proved the existence of this magnetic unit, which was nevertheless eventually displaced as the fundamental unit of magnetic moment by the "Bohr magneton," approximately five times bigger than the Weiss unit. Indeed, one of the conclusions to be drawn from the history of Spanish physics from 1907, when the Junta was created, until 1936, the year when the Spanish Civil War began, is that physicists seldom abandoned their first interests, especially those they acquired while studying or working abroad. Cabrera's case certainly confirms the rule.[47]

Because the Weiss magneton was meaningful only in a non-quantum context, whereas the Bohr magneton, which was deduced from the quantification of the electron orbits, was a proper quantum construct, Cabrera's commitment to Weiss's view often placed him in a difficult position, especially after about 1930. For example, at the 1930 Solvay Conference, which was devoted to magnetism, Cabrera could only concede that

> if one considers all the phenomena so far known in the physics of the atom, then the success of the quantum theory is remarkable in dealing with atoms or with molecules which can be considered as polynuclear atoms. . . . All cases of paramagnetism in gas belong to this group and may be interpreted with a high degree of exactitude by this theory.

In particular, the Weiss magneton appeared clearly only in the more complex chemical structures,

> where the quantum theory cannot be accurately developed, because the atom's surface is heavily deformed. . . . [T]he persistence with which the Weiss magneton appears in these cases as the natural unit of atomic moments cannot be attributed to pure chance. In the case of rare earths, the theory has given quantitative results so near to the empirical observations that it is certainly difficult not to ascribe to that agreement the value of a proof of its exactitude; hence the verification of the Weiss

[45] Moles, a prolific and competent chemist, had much more international experience than Cabrera; from 1908 till 1910 he worked in the Ostwald Institute of Leipzig, under Carl Drucker.

[46] Weiss introduced the magneton in 1911: Pierre Weiss, "Sur la rationalité des rapports des moments magnétiques moléculaires et le magnéton," *Journal de Physique,* 1911, *1*:900–912, 965–988. For a study of the Weiss magneton see Pierre Quédec, "Weiss's Magneton: The Sin of Pride or a Venial Mistake?" *HSPS,* 1988, *18*:349–375. Referring to Weiss and Cabrera, Quédec states (p. 360): "Their joint combat on behalf of the magneton would last nearly thirty years."

[47] For another instance of the profound influence of the lessons and models learned by a young or inexperienced scientist when studying abroad, see the article on William H. Perkin, Jr., by Jack Morrell in this volume. Perkin, as Morrell points out, never forgot Adolf von Baeyer's ideology of research. The case of the Madrid Laboratorio is peculiar only in the intensity of the phenomenon; as there were no models available in the country, Junta scientists had to import them from abroad.

magneton is still more certain. *In our opinion it is evident that the mechanics of electronic systems is not yet completely established* [emphasis added].

In other words, Cabrera was led to the conclusion that the problems in understanding the Weiss magneton in terms of the new quantum theory, far from discrediting that unit, meant that a new theoretical formulation was needed:

> If one takes into account the way in which the new mechanics, on one side, and the idea of the Weiss magneton, on the other, represent the experimental results, then one is led to consider them as successive approximations in the interpretation of reality.[48]

To some extent, this suggestion was an agreeable way of eluding the problem, because it allowed Cabrera to keep believing in the Weiss magneton, while at the same time accepting quantum mechanics as a satisfactory theory for the time being, though clearly not a final one. Indeed, Cabrera himself promoted the introduction of quantum theory in Spain through books, articles, and lectures, and contributed, alone or with some of his collaborators in the Laboratorio and Instituto, to its development.[49] Thus, when John Van Vleck reviewed the literature of measurements on the magnetic susceptibilities of rare earth salts for inclusion in *The Theory of Electric and Magnetic Susceptibilities,* he found that many of those measurements had been made by Cabrera, whose name thus appeared in the book more frequently than any other experimenter's.[50] Other significant contributions by Cabrera included his modification of the Curie-Weiss law for the rare earths, and the derivation of an equation for the atomic magnetic moment that included the temperature effect.[51]

[48] Blas Cabrera, "L'étude expérimentale du paramagnétisme: Le magnéton," in *Le magnétisme: Rapports et discussions du sixième Conseil de Physique, tenu à Bruxelles du 20 au 25 Octobre 1930* (Paris: Gauthier-Villars, 1932), pp. 81–159, quoting from pp. 149–150. John Van Vleck said later of the congress that "by and large [it] was composed of people of very great distinction, but oftentimes without much background in magnetism, some of whom did not understand or sympathize with quantum mechanics. Weiss was a hold-out for his Weiss magneton, which is now recognized to be completely spurious, but which took a great deal of the time at that Congress." Van Vleck, interview with Charles Weiner, 28 Feb. 1966, p. 13, Center for History of Physics, American Institute of Physics, New York. Nine years before the congress Van Vleck himself thought otherwise. In a Harvard paper he wrote: "The Weiss magneton is probably connected in some way with the quantum theory, for it occurs too regularly to be explained in a satisfactory way by the theory of probability and pure chance, but no quantitative explanation according to the quantum theory has yet been given." Quoted in Frederick H. Fellows, "J. H. Van Vleck: The Early Life of a Mathematical Physicist" (Ph.D. diss., Univ. Minnesota, 1985).

[49] See, e.g., Blas Cabrera, "La estructura de los átomos y moléculas desde el punto de vista físico," *An. Soc. Españ. Fís. Quím.,* 1925, *23*:101–122, 211–222, 239–249; Cabrera, *El átomo y sus propiedades electromagnéticas* (Madrid: Editorial Paez, 1927); and Cabrera, "Ideas actuales sobre la materia," *Las Ciencias,* 1934, *1*:53–63. On the early stages of the introduction of the quantum ideas in Spain see Antoni Roca Rosell, "L'impacte de la hipòtesi quàntica a Catalunya," in *El científico español ante su historia,* ed. Garma (cit. n. 38), pp. 383–387; and José M. Sánchez Ron, "La ciencia española se internacionaliza: La introducción de la teoría cuántica en España (1908–1919)," in *Cinquanta anys de ciència i tècnica a Catalunya* (Barcelona: Institut d'Estudis Catalans, 1987), pp. 71–88.

[50] John Van Vleck, "Cabrera's Experiments and the Early Theory of Paramagnetism," in *En el centenario de Blas Cabrera* (cit. n. 36), pp. 21–30. Van Vleck's book was a pillar of the quantum theory of magnetism: *The Theory of Electric and Magnetic Susceptibilities* (Oxford: Oxford Univ. Press, 1932).

[51] Some of Cabrera's works are summarized in Blas Cabrera, *Dia- et paramagnétisme et structure de la matière* (Paris: Hermann, 1937); and Cabrera, *El magnetismo de la materia* (Buenos Aires: Institución Cultural Española, 1944).

A perceptive, though by no means complete, view of Cabrera's approach to research was expressed by the physicist Charles Mendenhall when he visited Madrid in March 1926 on behalf of the Rockefeller International Education Board. In his report to the IEB he stated:

> Prof. Cabrera is largely, if not exclusively, interested in the study of magnetism, particularly in its bearing upon the theories of Langevin and Weiss. He impressed me as experimentally ingenious, but perhaps somewhat too much interested in working out nice arrangements of apparatus which could be used with the maximum of convenience by the experimenter during a long series of observations. He showed me a number of very beautifully constructed instruments which had been made in the shop of the laboratory but I saw little or nothing which indicated much interest in improving apparatus or in trying out new ideas.[52]

In 1928, thanks to the quality of his work, and probably also to his position as a representative of a marginal scientific community, Cabrera was elected a member of the Commission Scientifique Internationale of the Institute International de Physique Solvay. In 1930 he was also made a member of the Comité International des Poids et Mésures in Paris, of which he became secretary in 1933. In Spain, though he was never so public figure as Cajal, Cabrera got all the honors he could reasonably expect, being named rector of the University of Madrid and president of the Academy of Sciences and of the Sociedad Española de Física y Química. When the Spanish Civil War began in 1936, Cabrera soon went with his family to Paris, receiving a small salary from the Bureau des Poids et Mésures. Although he planned to return once the war was over, the new political regime let him know clearly that he would not be welcome, no doubt because of his past relation with the Junta, an institution that Franco's regime saw as a dangerous and leftist organization that contributed to the degeneration of many Spanish intellectuals. Confronted with such a situation, Cabrera, like so many Spanish intellectuals, went in 1941 to Mexico City, in whose Faculty of Sciences he taught until his death in 1945.

V. THE LABORATORIO DE INVESTIGACIONES FÍSICAS

The Laboratorio de Investigaciones Físicas was established by the Junta in 1910. It was housed in the so-called Palacio de la Industria y de las Artes, a large building that also accommodated the Museum of Natural Sciences, Torres Quevedo's Laboratory of Applied Mechanics, the School of Industrial Engineers, and the Royal Society of Natural History. Initially, the Laboratorio had four sections: metrology, electricity, spectroscopy, and physical chemistry; it had nine rooms (two for each group, plus one for library and seminars).[53] Though there were obvious shortcomings, such as the impossibility of keeping the temperature constant in

[52] Charles Mendenhall, "Report of Visit ... in Madrid," 24 March 1926, pp. 1–2, IEB 1.2, 41.579, Rockefeller Archive Center. Mendenhall's statement agrees with our earlier comment that Spanish physicists found it very difficult to abandon their first interests.

[53] Some documents indicate that the Laboratorio began operating in a provisional manner in 1909; see Leonardo Torres Quevedo, "Proyecto de creación de un centro técnico para el fomento de la investigación científica," 2 Jan. 1909, Junta Archives, CSIC. For a description of the laboratory see "Laboratorio de Investigaciones Físicas," in *Reseña de los principales establecimientos* (cit. n. 31), pp. 167–173.

the rooms, or the mechanical instability of the floors, it was adequate for the intended work, which, by the way, was not restricted only to research; it was also the Laboratorio's duty to offer experimental courses for advanced students. These courses usually covered basic techniques related to the research subjects dealt with at the Laboratorio, thus supporting Kathryn Olesko's seemingly obvious but often disregarded point: a school could neither form nor continue to exist without some mechanism for instructing advanced students. The provision for instruction also fulfills one of Geison's criteria for a successful research school—"a readily available pool of talented potential recruits."[54] Moreover, almost all the senior scientists of the Laboratorio were professors at the University of Madrid and thus able to recruit research students easily, as the Laboratorio was practically the only place in town where a *licenciado* could expect to do serious research.

The surviving documents do not allow us to know exactly who worked at the Laboratorio during 1910 and 1911, but it seems almost certain that Cabrera and Enrique Moles did most of the preliminary planning and research. Moles, for instance, designed the section of physical chemistry following the model of the Ostwald Institute in Leipzig, where he had studied.[55] By 1912, however, there was already a senior staff: the physicists Cabrera, Jerónimo Vecino, and Manuel Martínez Risco, and the chemists Moles, Angel del Campo, Julio Guzmán, Santiago Piña de Rubíes, and León Gómez—nearly all of them full or assistant professors at the Madrid Faculty of Sciences, which meant that they had to divide their time between the two institutions. To judge from the authorship of the twenty-one papers published during 1912–1913 and the eight in progress then, eighteen persons worked at the Laboratorio at that time.[56]

By 1914 the structure of the laboratory was almost complete. There were five central groups: physics, directed by Cabrera, and dedicated mainly to such rather general and miscellaneous topics as the physical properties of metals in electric and magnetic fields, and optics; physical chemistry (Moles); magneto-chemistry (Cabrera); electrochemistry and electroanalysis (Guzmán); and spectroscopy (del Campo). At least until the 1920s these were the main topics pursued at the Laboratorio. The scheme was very simple: the groups were centered on a leader, and the emphasis was upon physics, especially magnetism, and physical chemistry—the fields of Cabrera and Moles. Such a limited and interconnected field of interests had some advantages; in particular, the groups collaborated to a high degree during the first years, when Cabrera coauthored papers with Moles, Guzmán, and Piña de Rubíes. In this sense, too, one can speak of a "research school," although in at least one aspect it differs from the "ideal" research school with a "charismatic" director posited by Jack Morrell.[57] Although he was a competent scientist and administrator, Cabrera was far from possessing the scientific stature or charisma of a Liebig, an Ostwald, a Sommerfeld, or a Fermi.

[54] See Kathryn M. Olesko's article in this volume, as well as Olesko, *Physics as a Calling: Discipline and Practice in the Königsberg Seminar for Physics* (Ithaca, N.Y./London: Cornell Univ. Press, 1991); and Geison, "Scientific Change" (cit. n. 4), p. 26.

[55] Moles described his activities at Ostwald's laboratory in "Un curso teórico y práctico de Química-Física," *Anales de la Junta para Ampliación de Estudios e Investigaciones Científicas,* 1911, 4:69–87.

[56] *Memoria correspondiente a los años 1912 y 1913* (cit. n. 29).

[57] Jack B. Morrell, "The Chemist Breeders: The Research Schools of Liebig and Thomas Thomson," *Ambix,* 1972, 9:1–46.

During these early years the Laboratorio reached out to the international scientific community in several ways and acquired some international standing in the process. At the simplest level, it was a policy of the Junta and the Laboratorio to invite foreign scientists to lecture in Madrid; although not very many came, they were distinguished: Albert Einstein, Arnold Sommerfeld, Hermann Weyl, Pierre Weiss, Erwin Schrödinger, Otto Hönigschmidt, and Paul Scherrer, for example. Even more important was the Junta's policy of sending the Laboratorio researchers abroad, as we saw in the case of Cabrera and Moles, who went to Zurich on Junta scholarships in 1912. Almost all the physicists and chemists who became senior researchers in the Instituto, whether permanently or temporarily, received grants to study and work abroad. Thus in 1909 Angel del Campo went to Paris to work with Georges Urbain; in 1909–1910, Manuel Martínez Risco visited Amsterdam, where he collaborated with Peter Zeeman, carrying out the research for his doctoral dissertation.[58] In 1912–1913 Julio Guzmán went to Leipzig to work with Carl Drucker; Santiago Piña de Rubíes spent six months in Geneva and Russia; and Jerónimo Vecino spent three months in Paris, studying metrology at the Bureau International des Poids et Mésures. In 1916–1918 Julio Palacios, who would become the leader of the X-ray diffraction group of the Laboratorio, went to Leyden to work with Heike Kammerlingh Onnes on low temperatures. In 1921 Juan Cabrera, Blas's younger brother, went to Paris, where he worked with Maurice de Broglie in his Laboratoire de Recherches Physiques. In 1929 and 1932 Arturo Duperier, Cabrera's collaborator, who while in exile in England in the late 1930s won fame for his research on cosmic rays, went successively to Strasbourg, where he worked with Pierre Weiss, and to Paris, where he worked with Charles Maurin. In the light of Spain's past scientific history, these scientific voyagers constitute a rather impressive group, with well-chosen objectives.

Besides exposing the recipients of the grants to work at the center, these international visits brought Spain to the international attention of the wider scientific community. Cabrera's stay in Zurich may have led Jakob Laub, Einstein's first coauthor, to arrange to spend a few months (December 1915–March 1916) in Madrid. Laub, who had occupied the chair of geophysics at the National University of La Plata in Argentina since 1911, spent part of an Argentine summer with Pierre Weiss in Zurich before World War I. While in Madrid, Laub published two pieces of work, one written alone and one with Cabrera.[59]

The most striking example of the way in which scholarships abroad could pay off was that of Miguel Catalán. Catalán, a chemist in the spectroscopy group since 1915, spent 1920–1921 at Alfred Fowler's laboratory at the Imperial College of Science and Technology in London. When he first joined the Laboratorio, the work done by the spectroscopy group under the directorship of Angel del Campo, a chemistry professor at the University of Madrid, consisted primarily of

[58] Manuel Martínez Risco, *La asimetría de los tripletes de Zeeman*, rpt. in Martínez Risco, *Oeuvres scientifiques* (Paris: Presses Universitaires de France, 1976).

[59] Jakob Laub, "Sobre una especie de radiación difractada producida iluminando los bordes de los cuerpos con rayos Röntgen," *An. Soc. Españ. Fís. Quím.*, 1916, *14*:52–61; and Laub and Blas Cabrera, "Acerca de la acción de los bordes de los orificios en los rayos gamma," *ibid*, 1917, *15*:51–54. On Laub see Pyenson, *Cultural Imperialism and Exact Sciences* (cit. n. 17), pp. 163–202, 227–228; and Lewis Pyenson, "Silver Horizon: A Note on the Later Years of the Physicist-Diplomat Jakob Laub," *Jahrbuch für Geschichte von Staat, Wirtschaft und Gesellschaft Lateinamerikas*, 1988, *25*:757–766.

"spectrum analysis of minerals."[60] When Catalán returned to Spain, the nature of the spectroscopical works carried out at the Laboratorio changed dramatically. While studying the spectra of manganese in London, he discovered multiplets.[61] The discovery brought sudden fame to the Laboratorio and placed it at the forefront of the research then being done in quantum physics. Indeed, from that time onwards one of Cabrera's arguments, when asking for more resources as director of the Laboratorio, was that the Spanish group (i.e., Catalán and a few collaborators) should not lose the prestigious position they had achieved in the world of physics.

It is well known that Catalán's discovery rapidly received a theoretical interpretation from Arnold Sommerfeld in Munich. (This episode also reveals the good effect of the Junta's policy of bringing in foreign lecturers.) In the spring of 1922 Sommerfeld visited Barcelona and Madrid under the auspices of the Junta, lecturing on several aspects of quantum theory.[62] In Madrid he met Catalán, already back from London. As a result of that visit, a collaboration began between Madrid and Munich. On 20 June 1924 Sommerfeld approached the International Educational Board asking it to grant a scholarship to Catalán so that the latter could spend a year at the Munich Institute, "as he is married and has to provide for his living himself." (Catalán was in fact a high school teacher and obtained a university professorship—a special one, sponsored by the Academy of Sciences—in 1932.) Referring to Catalán's "fundamental work on the spectrum of mangan," and the "exchange of thoughts on scientific questions" that the two had had "continuously" since their meeting in Spain, Sommerfeld went on:

> His work on the mangan-spectrum . . . fitted admirably in with the aspect of the quantum theory which I developed in 1920 in the "Annalen der Physik" Vol. 63. I myself have interpreted on a theoretical basis in the "Annalen der Physik" Vol. 70, Mr. Catalan's results. Mr. Catalan has since used my method in a series of further important treatises (published in "Anales de Sociedad Española") on the spectrum of Sc, Mo, Cr. He also got very good results on the spectrum of iron, a study that goes together with his work in Washington and Munich.[63]

With Sommerfeld's support, Catalán got the grant. Appropriately, the next year (1925–1926), another grant from the IEB sent Karl Bechert, with whom Catalán had collaborated in Munich, to Madrid.[64]

The very strength of the Laboratorio as the central institution in Spain maintaining contacts abroad had a corresponding drawback: only those who remained in the Laboratorio upon their return from scholarships abroad kept doing research. Thus Martínez Risco conducted none during his tenure in Saragossa

[60] For a description of works in progress in 1914–1915 see *Memoria correspondiente a los años 1914 y 1915* (Madrid: Junta para Ampliación de Estudios, 1916), on pp. 199–200.

[61] Miguel A. Catalán, "Series and Other Regularities in the Spectrum of Manganese," *Philosophical Transactions of the Royal Society of London*, 1922, *223A*:127–173.

[62] See "El profesor Arnold Sommerfeld," *Revista Matemática Hispano-Americana*, 1922, *4*:81–86; and *Ibérica*, 1922, *17*:341. See also José M. Sánchez-Ron, "Documentos para una historia de la física moderna en España: Arnold Sommerfeld, Miguel A. Catalán, Angel del Campo y Blas Cabrera," *Llull*, 1983, *5*:97–109.

[63] Arnold Sommerfeld to Wickliffe Rose, 20 June 1924, IEB 1.2, Rockefeller Archive Center.

[64] See Trowbridge to Rose, 16 April 1925, IEB 1.2, 41.577, Rockefeller Archive Center.

(1914–1919) as professor of acoustics and optics. When he returned to Madrid and the Laboratorio, in 1919, his work met with little success. Vecino got a chair in Santiago de Compostela in 1914 and one in Saragossa the following year; thereafter he did no scientific work of significance until his premature death in 1929. The same can be said of Juan Cabrera, who in 1920 obtained a chair in Saragossa and spent the rest of his career there. If we assume that these physicists were not very different from those who remained in Madrid and continued doing research, then we must conclude that it was the lack of resources or of a congenial scientific atmosphere that brought their research to a stop. And when we consider that Saragossa was probably the third university in importance in scientific studies after Madrid and Barcelona, we are further led to appreciate the special position held by the Laboratorio de Investigaciones Físicas.

VI. THE INSTITUTO NACIONAL DE FÍSICA Y QUÍMICA

Despite the relative success of the Laboratorio in the 1920s, it became clear that the resources available to the Junta were not enough to cope with the dynamics of the development of the researches being conducted or projected there. Because, as mentioned, Catalán's investigations were internationally known, Cabrera frequently wrote Castillejo for special funds on his behalf, as on 18 July 1923, to allow Catalán and his coworkers "to confirm his researches on the constituents of spectra, which have attracted so much attention from the specialists."[65]

Faced with such requests and limited resources, Castillejo turned to the newly organized International Educational Board of the Rockefeller Foundation. Castillejo had earlier contacted the Rockefeller Foundation for help in improving the sanitary situation in Spain, during a visit to the United States in August 1919. Wickliffe Rose, now director of the IEB, visited Madrid in March 1922 on behalf of the Rockefeller Foundation. He was impressed on that occasion and wrote the foundation's president that Castillejo's group was "the most hopeful force" for progress in Spain: "[they] are giving themselves . . . with a very enlightened enthusiasm to the promotion of contacts with foreign countries, to education of a group of teachers and scientific men, and to the providing of facilities for scientific research in connection with the University. They are a tremendous leaven and one cannot talk with them without being convinced that in the end they are going to win." Rose again visited Spain in January 1924, and Castillejo took him to visit the main laboratories of physics, chemistry, natural sciences, and agriculture at Madrid, then sounded him out as to whether the IEB would make a donation for a new physics and chemistry laboratory.[66]

Seven months later Castillejo wrote a memorandum to the IEB in which he noted that the Junta owned (and thus supported completely) Cabrera's Laboratorio and supported in part Carracido's laboratory of organic and biological chemistry at the Faculty of Pharmacy and José Casares's laboratory of analytical chemistry at the Faculty of Sciences. He then made a plea for

[65] Blas Cabrera to José Castillejo, 18 July 1923, Junta Archives, CSIC.

[66] See *Memoria correspondiente a los cursos 1922-3 y 1923-4* (Madrid: Junta para Ampliación de Estudios, 1925), on pp. 128–136; and Wickliffe Rose to George Vincent, 2 March 1922, RF 1. 62.885, Rockefeller Archive Center, quoted in Robert E. Kohler, "Science and Philanthropy: Wickliffe Rose and the International Education Board," *Minerva,* 1985, *23*:75–95; on pp. 82–83.

Figure 1. *The Instituto Nacional de Física y Química after its completion, in 1932. Courtesy of the Consejo Superior de Investigaciones Científicas (CSIC).*

support, emphasizing the professional caliber of the laboratories and the meager funds available to them:

> All these laboratories have published contributions and monographs, some of them in periodicals, others in special series edited by the Junta. . . . [They] offer opportunities to prepare young men for going abroad, and are scientific homes for them on their return.
>
> But . . . the Junta had to give its attention and money to many other branches of science and education. . . . The total amount granted by the Junta in the last year . . . 91,000 pesetas for equipment, material, and salaries . . . is so small that the laboratories lack adequate supply of material, and the salaries, ranging from 150 to 500 pesetas a month do not allow full time work.
>
> There are already in Spain enough trained scientists to start an institute of physics and chemistry for graduate research work, destined to promote the future progress of medicine, natural sciences, engineering and agriculture.

The Junta hoped that the Spanish government for its part would provide

> a) Resources to secure full time work for the most important members of the Institute and scholarships for others to cover living expenses; b) enough money for material; c) opportunities for the professors and graduates of the universities and engineering schools to attend the Institute so as to make of it a seminar for the training of teachers in the highest levels of physics and chemistry; d) means of assistance to invite foreign professors to direct special researches or to teach new methods.[67]

Castillejo also mentioned earlier plans for either remodeling the building in which the Laboratorio was housed or purchasing or renting an ordinary building—plans since abandoned. Thus "the chemists [who most strongly insisted on the need for a new building], the Junta and the Spanish Government agree" that the IEB might "either provid[e] buildings and equipment for an Institute of Physics and Chemistry which Spain shall maintain . . . or giv[e] a contribution for equipment which could be immediately available for the current laboratories in their temporary quarters, postponing until the future the project of a new Institute."

---

[67] Castillejo, memorandum to the IEB, 21 July 1924, IEB 1.2, 44.577, Rockefeller Archive Center.

Just in case the Board decided to help only with equipment, Cabrera prepared a list, appended to the memorandum, of the materials most urgently needed in the Laboratorio. The list gives a good idea of the problems that the Laboratorio was then facing:

1. MAGNETIC CHEMISTRY. In this department there is enough apparatus for the determination of the magnetic constants (some of the results obtained have already been published, others are in preparation). But for a complete study of the iron group the installation of X-ray apparatus is essential. This would require the spenditure of 20 to 25,000 pesetas, a sum beyond the means of the Laboratory.

Furthermore for the prosecution of the study of the magnetic constants of the "rare earths," apparatus for liquefaction of gases and for obtaining low temperature, at least to that of liquid air, is indispensable.

2. ATOMIC WEIGHTS BY MEANS OF PHYSICAL-CHEMISTRY METHODS. For this work the apparatus for the production of low temperatures is also absolutely indispensable, in as much as there is in Madrid not even the possibility of obtaining liquid air at any moment.

3. SPECTRUM ANALYSIS. The well known studies of Dr. Catalán have reached the limit of our laboratory equipment. To continue them it is necessary to acquire two or three "spectrographs" of greater power of resolution and range. For this study the above mentioned X-ray apparatus will be useful. The scope of the proposed investigation must depend on the equipment. To start it on a solid basis a sum of about 50,000 pesetas for the two above mentioned pieces of apparatus will be required.[68]

The International Education Board took the Junta's proposal seriously and sent Trowbridge to Madrid. He reported that in the Laboratorio the "space for physics is adequate for present needs; that for physical chemistry is inadequate— for neither [project] is it all well adapted to needs. The equipment is well chosen for the work which is being done, evidently care has been had to buy only what was immediately needed." After this general statement, he specified the chief immediate needs of the laboratory, pointing out that "Cabrera is very anxious to start a line of investigation in X-ray spectra of those elements with which he has been working on the side of magnetism; he has the man to do the work; he has the materials on which he has carried out the magnetic work, but he lacks a part of the auxiliary apparatus." As to a new institute, Trowbridge doubted whether the Government would really support the project: "I gathered by visits to the Minister of Education and to the Acting Dictator [Primo de Rivera] nothing but vague assurances that the Government was ready to do what was necessary, etc. and the definite assurance that the written answer to the Junta demand would be given soon." Nonetheless, Trowbridge concluded,

I am convinced, as a result of my visit to Madrid, that the Junta is the agency through which to work, if the I.E.B. proposes to attempt anything in that country in the pure sciences. A good deal may be done with fellowships, but for nearly twenty years the Junta itself has been administering a fellowship plan not very different from that of the Board, and in my opinion they have as a result a sufficient nucleus of foreign trained men in physics and chemistry to make it safe, *provided there are adequate government guarantees for support,* to invest a considerable sum in a model Institute for

[68] *Ibid.* The English is Cabrera's.

Research in Physics and Chemistry. There is no doubt but that Spain could properly support such an Institute and that it could do good service to science generally.[69]

Less than a year later, another representative from the Rockefeller board, Charles E. Mendenhall, physics professor at Wisconsin, corroborated Trowbridge's opinions:

> The general situation in Madrid as regards physics and chemistry should, I think, be very encouraging to the I.E.B., both from the standpoint of the attitude of those whom it proposes to benefit and from the extreme need of such assistance as the Board proposes to give. That is to say, I found a small group of enthusiastic and rather surprisingly active workers housed in an utterly inadequate manner and carrying on their work with, as far as I could see, no local encouragement except that which comes from the Junta. . . . I know of no institution at home at which comparable work is under way which is housed in such primitive and inefficient quarters.[70]

As the rather complex negotiations between the IEB, the Junta, and the Spanish government have recently been analyzed elsewhere,[71] we need not discuss the matter here, except to point out that the executive committee of the IEB decided on 1 March 1926 "to give to the Junta a building for an Institute of Physics and Chemistry in Madrid . . . to be completely finished and equipped, provided the sum which the International Education Board shall be called upon to pay under this resolution shall not exceed four hundred twenty thousand Dollars." For its part, the Spanish government was expected to donate the land and provide maintenance. After a visit to Madrid in 1931, I. Marcovich of the IEB office in Paris reported that the Spanish government "has lived up to our expectations."[72] In 1929 it gave the Instituto 100,000 pesetas and in 1930 200,000 pesetas.

Early in 1931, the year when the monarchy was abolished (a republic was established on 14 April), the institute was near completion and already in partial operation. In September the building was completed, and the brand new Instituto Nacional de Física y Química was handed over officially by the Junta to the government on 6 February 1932. Pierre Weiss, Arnold Sommerfeld, Richard Willstätter, Paul Scherrer, and Otto Hönigschmidt, all connected with scientists of the old Laboratorio, were present at the ceremony.

Soon after the official opening of the Instituto, in April 1932, Lauder W. Jones of the IEB's Paris office, visited the new center. He reported to New York:

> The entrance is large, and it is a full two stories high. It is finished with a bronzed brick, on the walls and ceiling there are heavy girders covered with a very reddish copper, and the wood work is in rich mahogany. The lecture room, seating several hundred, is absolutely echo-proofed with celotex, the front table extending all the way across the room, is of mahogany and ebony, with every possible contrivance for electricity, water, gas, compressed air and vacuum. The many research rooms are amply large, and equipped with the most modern equipment in great profusion.

[69] Trowbridge to Rose, 4 May 1925 (cit. n. 32). (Emphasis in original.)

[70] Mendenhall, "Report of Visit . . . in Madrid" (cit. n. 52).

[71] Thomas F. Glick, "La Fundación Rockefeller en España: Augustus Trowbridge y las negociaciones para el Instituto Nacional de Física y Química, 1923–1927," in *La Junta 80 años después,* ed. Sanchez Ron (cit. n. 26), Vol. II, pp. 281–300.

[72] I. Marcovich to IEB, 5 Oct. 1931, IEB 1.2, Rockefeller Archive Center.

The mechanicians shop has all of the latest drill presses, lathes and other equipment conceivable. It is more modern and more luxuriously equipped than any laboratory machine shop I have seen.

The ventilation and air conditioning equipment for the Institute is installed in the basement for general ventilation, and in each room used for chemicals, a hood with a fan has been installed. In the halls, all pipes and conduits are placed in a double wall, the outer of which, of corregated steel painted with aluminium, is readily demountable.[73]

Jones also looked into the research in progress. He saw Cabrera's laboratory, "where he is conducting his researches on magnetism, especially he is concerned with the theories of Weiss of Strasbourg." To Jones, Cabrera appeared to be working alone, because he "neither saw nor heard of any assistants working with him." Jones was somewhat mistaken. Cabrera was not entirely alone in his researches, but was by then not very energetic as a group leader. Moles, on the contrary, had "four to five rooms in which he has his students working on problems of atomic weight determination in mercury, for example; problems in molecular volumes and adsorption"; he seemed to the IEB delegate "a very vigorous and active individual." Catalán, who was working then on problems related to the spectra of manganese, molybdenum, silicon and boron, the Raman spectra, and the Zeeman effect, had five rooms, "all equipped with the latest and most up to date spectroscopic equipment I have seen. He has at least four Hilger spectrometers, vacuum, glass, quartz and liquid. I saw only two or three students." There were also groups in electrochemistry (Guzmán, with four rooms) working on problems of determinations of pH, electrical refining of metals, and electroanalysis in general; X-ray analysis (Julio Palacios),[74] concerned with crystal and molecular studies, as well as diffraction of electrons; and organic chemistry (Antonio Madinaveitia). This last group was the one originally at the Faculty of Pharmacy, which the Junta had been supporting since the times of Carracido. The new building allowed its removal to the Instituto.

The years from 1931 to 1936 were increasingly difficult in Spain, and the hectic social and political climate pervading daily life was not favorable to the needs of intellectual work. However, despite more mundane worries, the government of the Republic kept most of the promises made to the IEB by Primo de Rivera.[75] "An excellent proof of how well disposed the government is towards us," wrote Cabrera to Paris, "is the increase from 200,000 to 300,000 pesetas which at my request was included by the Ministry of Public Instruction in the draft of the budget for the year 1932. It is true that the budget must come before the Constituent House (Parliament) to be approved, but I am authorized to tell you that the government will do everything possible so that the mentioned figure will not be modified."[76]

[73] Lauder W. Jones, "Institute of Physics and Chemistry. 7th, 8th, 9th April, 1932" (diary entry), IEB 1.2, 41.580, Rockefeller Archive Center.

[74] Jones wrongly thought that the director of this section was T. Batuecas.

[75] Several of the authorities of the Republic had been associated with either the Junta or with the Institución Libre de Enseñanza, e.g., Fernando de los Ríos, minister of education when the Instituto was inaugurated.

[76] Blas Cabrera to Wilbur E. Tisdale, 26 Nov. 1931, IEB 1.2, Rockefeller Archive Center; see also "Resumen de cuentas," *Memoria correspondiente a los cursos 1933 y 1934* (Madrid: Junta para Ampliación de Estudios, 1935). This was the last *Memoria* published.

Figure 2. *Official inauguration of the Instituto Nacional de Física y Química, 6 February 1932. Blas Cabrera and the Spanish Minister of Education, F. de los Ríos, stand in the center. Courtesy of the CSIC.*

It is not our purpose here to analyze the history of the last years of the Instituto Nacional de Física y Química under Cabrera, but it seems clear that although a great deal had been achieved, the future was uncertain from the point of view of science. True, there was now a splendid laboratory, but perhaps it was too good for the research it housed, as Jones somewhat ironically pointed out in 1931, when he indicated that the "electrical equipment which has been installed by the German firm Siemens looked . . . to be complete, perhaps on the whole more complete than necessary for the work which is to be undertaken in the new Institute."[77] By then the budget of the Instituto allowed its six senior professors (Cabrera, Moles, Catalán, Palacios, Guzmán, and Madinaveitia) to dedicate more time to work at the center, and the new space allowed the number of researchers and students to increase. In 1933/34, for example, apart from these six professors there were nine senior researchers, twenty-one scholarship holders, and sixty-three assistants (unpaid students), but there was a danger that the ideas, the lines of research, might become old-fashioned. In physics, this was certainly the case with the aged Cabrera, but the great moment of Catalán had probably also gone. Mendenhall saw the potential problem when, in 1926, he wrote: "[Catalán] is interested in more modern points of view, and though he is considered by his colleagues as an experimentalist, he has had a very narrow training and seems reluctant to undertake experimental work involving equipment with which he is not already familiar."[78]

---

[77] Lauder Jones, "Log of professor L. W. Jones' trip to Spain, Portugal and Algeria" (diary entry), 31 March, 1 April 1931, IEB 1.2, 41.580, Rockefeller Archive Center.
[78] Mendenhall, "Report of Visit . . . in Madrid" (cit. n. 52).

Indeed, if we examine the number of papers on physics published in the *Anales de la Sociedad Española de Física y Química,* the official journal of Spanish physicists and chemists, then we find that during the years 1931–1936 most papers were on X-ray diffraction and determination of crystal structures: 46.5 percent of the total. In 1916–1930 spectroscopy, with 30 percent of the papers, had been the subject of greatest activity, while in 1903–1915 it had been electricity and magnetism, with 40 percent.[79] Since scientists working in the Junta's physics laboratories produced 72 percent of the physics papers published in the *Anales* during 1910–1936, a figure that shows the Junta's importance for Spanish science,[80] one is led to conclude that Cabrera left the lead to Catalán by the 1920s, and Catalán to Palacios by 1930.

VII. CONCLUSIONS

We have referred to the danger that the research performed in the Instituto was about to become old-fashioned; what did happen during 1931–1936 was that a new center began functioning, with more personnel and more resources than ever. But since this research center was not starting from scratch, its previous history affected its character, and consequently not all the groups had the same potential. The Rockefeller's funding of the Instituto meant that physics and physical chemistry became institutionalized in the Junta center, where an established group of researchers with access to good experimental facilities was already in place. Whether new scientists of merit would come out of the Instituto was a different issue, to be answered only in the future. One can say at least that competent new physicists were being trained there, since new *licenciados* then beginning to work in the Instituto became university professors in due course, after the Spanish Civil War.

The problem was that, in a sense, there was no future. The Civil War was not only cruel, it was also primitive, and it left no place for scientists. Cabrera (and Castillejo) went into exile; Moles, who was in jail for a time after the war, took over the directorship of the Instituto, but it was simply impossible for those who remained to do any real scientific work: the monarchist Palacios, for example, had serious problems in the Republican capital and could not enter the Instituto. And when the war was over, the new regime turned the Instituto, now part of the newly created Consejo Superior de Investigaciones Científicas (1939), over to scientists who included many fierce enemies of the Junta. For several years the Consejo was virtually the only place in Spain where any research could be performed, and the attitude of the new masters of Spanish science towards the school of Cabrera is shown in a document, undated and unsigned, but obviously prepared in 1939 by José María Albareda, who became the first General Secretary of

---

[79] Manuel Valera, "La física en España durante el primer tercio del siglo XX," *Llull,* 1983, 5:149–173, on pp. 154, 161–168. The production in physics was about one third of that in chemistry: between 1903 and 1937, 426 physics papers were published in the *Anales,* against 1,320 chemistry papers: see Valera and Marset, "Aspectos bibliométricos e institucionales de la Real Sociedad Española de Física y Química para el período 1903–1937" (cit. n. 38).

[80] After the Junta laboratories (219 papers), the laboratories of the University of Madrid produced 11.5 percent (49), and then the Madrid Astronomical Observatory 9 percent (38). See Valera and Marset, "La física en España durante el primer tercio del siglo XX" (cit. n. 79), pp. 161–162.

the new institution. Referring to the Rockefeller Institute, as it was often called, the unidentified author wrote:

> It is necessary to think carefully about [its] situation. The physicists of the school of Cabrera believe that today physics in Spain is a private property [*coto cerrado*], in which, once the group is established, nobody will be able to enter. They say that it is even impossible to pass a doctoral dissertation, as there is only one *catedrático* [full professor], Palacios. From this, they deduce that the return of Cabrera is essential, and the transfer to Madrid of some of his students.

The document asserts that, on the contrary, the physics cultivated by those *rojos* (reds) was of no interest:

> The rays of Catalán's spectroscope have become exhausted, and he has not been able ... to perform work on the most modern subject: the Raman effect. Cabrera's magnetism has become exhausted too. Of little interest [*van muy trilladas*] are Palacios's crystalline lattices ... We cannot remain condemned to having no more physics research than that which produces the technique that our physicists learnt when they were young. It is necessary to bring a foreign physicist here, something cheaper, simpler, and more effective than to begin sending people abroad.[81]

Not all of these criticisms were unfounded, as we have already pointed out, but any continuity with "the past" was made impossible by the fierce enmity that lay behind these arguments, put forward by scientists clearly inferior to those they were criticizing—indeed, no such continuity was desired. And we must not forget that continuity is an essential element of a research school. At the Laboratorio thirty years had passed since 1910—not quite in vain, but with a disappointing outcome nonetheless. The division produced by the Civil War was a major factor in this break with the scientific past, but it was not the only one. The Spanish state's decision to favor only one laboratory had been, as already pointed out, a risky one. Throughout the almost thirty years of its existence, the Junta's preferred laboratory of physics and chemistry had been isolated; it had been a *rara avis* in Spanish academia. Indeed, with the new, lavishly provided Instituto there was an obvious problem: where would the new physicists and chemists formed there go? This problem went beyond the scientists of the Instituto or the Junta authorities, and it raises more general questions about the inability of Spain to take advantage of the scientific manpower so generated. In the end, it seems evident that a "research shool" associated with a single center can hardly survive in a country lacking other such centers.

[81] José María Albareda, untitled MS, Junta Archives, CSIC.

CASE STUDIES:
BEYOND THE LABORATORY

Figure 1. John Henry Comstock's students worked both in the laboratory and in the field. Above: His lab at Cornell. Courtesy of Cornell University, Department of Manuscripts and University Archives, Anna Botsford and John Henry Comstock Papers. Below: Comstock with his wife, Anna Botsford Comstock, about 1928. Courtesy of Smithsonian Archives, Charles P. Alexander Papers.

The Comstock Research School in Evolutionary Entomology

By Pamela M. Henson*

THE LAST QUARTER of the nineteenth century was a period of growth and professionalization in institutions of higher education and science in the United States. It was also a period of conceptual change in biology, as the implications of Darwin's seminal work were explored. In this dynamic environment, a cohesive research group in evolutionary entomology emerged at Cornell University: that of John Henry Comstock (1849–1931). The interrelations between these researchers, new and emerging institutions, and conceptual innovations provide an interesting case study of the formation of a research school.

Comstock entered the new Cornell University to study medicine in 1869. Entranced by the insect world, he soon resolved to devote his life instead to the study of entomology. Indeed, by his junior year he had acquired so much knowledge about insects that he was asked to teach the first entomology course at Cornell to his fellow students. Comstock was equally fascinated by Darwin's new theory of evolution by natural selection and made it his own "theory to work by."[1]

After graduating in 1878, Comstock devoted his career to research and teaching in taxonomic entomology. He served as the first professor of entomology and invertebrate zoology at Cornell from 1874 to 1914 and remained affiliated with his alma mater until his death in 1931. Comstock also established the department of entomology at the new Stanford University in the 1890s. He held positions at both schools simultaneously for several years, teaching at Stanford in the winter and Cornell in the summer and fall. On these two campuses he brought together a group of researchers working on the evolutionary history of insects.[2]

Comstock was highly influential at other schools as well. His students secured teaching positions at many of the new state universities mandated by the Morrill Act of 1862. His basic textbook on entomology was in press from 1888 to 1988

---

* Smithsonian Institution Archives, MRC 414, Washington, D.C. 20560.

I wish to thank Lindley Darden, Joseph A. Cain, Donald T. Fitzgerald, Joel B. Hagen, and Lynn M. Wojcik for comments on this essay.

[1] Anna Botsford Comstock, *The Comstocks of Cornell: John Henry Comstock and Anna Botsford Comstock* (Ithaca, N.Y.: Comstock Publishing Company, 1953), pp. 34–46; and Waterman Thomas Hewett, *Cornell University: A History* (New York: World Publishing Society, 1905), Vol. I, pp. 392–399. For more detail on the material covered in this article see Pamela M. Henson, "Evolution and Taxonomy: John Henry Comstock's Research School in Evolutionary Entomology at Cornell University, 1874–1930" (Ph.D. diss., Univ. Maryland, 1990).

[2] James G. Needham, "The Lengthened Shadow of a Man and his Wife," Pts. I, II, *Scientific Monthly*, 1946, *62*:145–150, 221–222; and Edward H. Smith, "The Comstocks and Cornell: In the People's Service," *Annual Review of Entomology*, 1976, *21*:8–17.

and was used in classrooms all over the country. He was noted for requiring field and laboratory studies, in addition to traditional observations of museum specimens. His innovative teaching methods were copied by colleagues and former students.[3]

Comstock was also an important figure outside of the classroom. He was the founding president of the Entomological Society of America and served on the editorial boards of such journals as *The American Naturalist* and the *Annals of the Entomological Society of America*. He wielded a great deal of influence within the emerging field of economic entomology, placing students at the U.S. Department of Agriculture and state agricultural experiment stations—and earning a star in the first edition of *American Men of Science* as a leader in his field. In 1893 he established his own publishing house, Comstock Publishing Associates, which served as an outlet for the monographs and textbooks produced by his group of evolutionary systematists.[4]

Comstock was known for a distinctive intellectual position and research program. In the 1890s he developed a new method of analysis for taxonomy that utilized Darwin's concepts of evolution, natural selection, and undirected variation. His method was adopted by his students and promulgated through his popular textbooks and laboratory manuals. His students pursued the research questions he posed and incorporated his evolutionary classifications into their own work. In this way Comstock established a group of scholars in evolutionary entomology who proselytized his method and extended his work on the evolution of insects. In turn, Comstock's particular research questions and methods—which offered guidance but rewarded independence—had strong effects on the social structure of that research school.

Gerald L. Geison defines a research school as a small group "of mature scientists pursuing a reasonably coherent programme of research side-by-side with advanced students in the same institutional context and engaging in direct, continuous social and intellectual interaction." Such research schools are often headed by an individual who exerts a great deal of control over its members. Geison argues that the success of the research school may depend on characteristics and resources of this "mentor"—characteristics that range from personal style, such as charisma and the ability to inspire loyalty; through access to the means to build supporting institutions, such as having adequate financial support or controlling publication outlets; to conceptual issues relating to the research program, such as developing simple and rapidly exploitable experimental techniques and invading a new field of research. These traits are revealing criteria when used to analyze the structure of Comstock's research school (see Section III). Joseph Fruton also demonstrates the importance of the mentor's personality in shaping the research school in his study of laboratory leaders in Germany. He describes several different leadership styles, ranging from autocratic and self-promoting to liberal and supportive, a scale on which Comstock's personal style

---

[3] John Henry Comstock, *An Introduction to Entomology* (Ithaca, N.Y., 1888) (9th ed., Ithaca, N.Y.: Comstock Publishing Company of Cornell Univ. Press, 1988); and Laurence R. Veysey, *The Emergence of the American University* (Chicago: Univ. Chicago Press, 1965), pp. 57–86.

[4] *American Men of Science* (1906), s.v. "Comstock, John Henry"; and Simon H. Gage, "A Half Century of the Comstock Publishing Company," MS, 1944, pp. 4–12, Division of Manuscripts and University Archives, Cornell University.

as a mentor can also be placed. This study, then, will address the relationships between conceptual issues, personal style, and institutional support in the formation of a cohesive group of scholars. Because it focuses on a group in natural history, rather than the physical and laboratory sciences, the study will present interesting contrasts to Fruton's and Geison's work.[5]

I. DEVISING AN EVOLUTIONARY METHOD FOR TAXONOMY

Comstock had intellectual and institutional motives for creating a cohesive research school. He needed a group of scholars to carry out his research program in evolutionary entomology. By "research program" I mean the distinctive set of research questions and the theories, concepts, methods, and vocabularies to answer those questions that organizes the work of an individual or small group.[6]

As students, Comstock and his comrades in the department of zoology at Cornell became ardent Darwinians. The group house that several of his fellow students shared was even dubbed by one of them, David Starr Jordan, "The Struggle for Existence." This allegiance might seem surprising, because the faculty of the Cornell department had been picked by an opponent of Darwin's theory. Cornell's first president, Andrew D. White, turned to Louis Agassiz of Harvard, the leading figure in American biology in the 1860s, to establish the zoology program. But the former student Agassiz selected to staff the new department, Burt Green Wilder, did not accept Agassiz's views on the fixity of species. While in Cambridge, Wilder had observed the debates between Agassiz and the botanist Asa Gray over Darwin's theory. He was soon converted to evolutionary theory and brought these new and exciting ideas to his students at Cornell.[7]

As Comstock began his career in taxonomy, he believed that the "natural system of classification" was a product of evolution. Organisms showed affinities and could be grouped into species, genera, families, and so on, because they shared an evolutionary history and had descended from common ancestors. Taxonomic classification should, he believed, reflect that evolutionary history. Once he adopted this approach, Comstock remained a Darwinian for the rest of his life. Unlike many of his colleagues, he did not abandon this strong Darwinian position in favor of neo-Lamarckism as the nineteenth century drew to a close. Shared ancestry, undirected change, and natural selection continued to serve as important concepts in his research method.[8]

But when Comstock began his research project to uncover the evolutionary history of insects and produce evolutionary classifications, he found the taxonomic methods then in use inadequate to the task. Although many taxonomists paid lip

[5] Gerald L. Geison, "Scientific Change, Emerging Specialties, and Research Schools," *History of Science,* 1981, *19*:20–40; and Joseph S. Fruton, *Contrasts in Scientific Style: Research Groups in the Chemical and Biochemical Sciences* (Philadelphia: American Philosophical Society, 1990).

[6] See Lindley Darden and Nancy Maull, "Interfield Theories," *Philosophy of Science,* 1977, *44*:44.

[7] Anna Comstock, *Comstocks of Cornell* (cit. n. 1), pp. 34–46, 79; John Henry Comstock, "Burt Green Wilder," *Science,* 1925, *61*:533; Simon H. Gage, "Retirement of Professor Burt Green Wilder," *Anatomical Record,* 1911, *5*:360; and Hewett, *Cornell: A History* (cit. n. 1), Vol. I, pp. 392–399. Comstock himself did not live in the group house but in the bell tower, to earn his way through Cornell as chimes master.

[8] Comstock, *Introduction to Entomology* (1888) (cit. n. 3), pp. 44–48, 59, 125; Comstock, "Wilder," p. 533; and Gage, "Retirement of Wilder," p. 360.

service to Darwin, few had actually thought through the implications of evolutionary theory for taxonomy. In the traditional Linnaean method, a few characters were selected to "define" the "essence" of a group, such as the number of
stamens for classes of plants. Comstock abandoned the use of Linnaeus's essential characters because he did not believe organisms had unchanging essences.
But he had no new criteria for deciding which characters to study, nor a method
for analyzing how characters had changed over time. He complained that there
was a great deal of confusion over the concepts of "generalized" and "primitive"
characters, which were often conflated. Many taxonomists assumed that very generalized characters were primitive; Comstock demonstrated that in some cases,
such as parasitic insects, a simple and generalized form could be the end product
of a long evolutionary history. Indeed, he observed that his fellow taxonomists
seemed to conflate the most basic concepts of phylogeny and classification, using
the terms interchangeably. Comstock quickly realized that the phylogeny, or evolutionary tree, was fundamentally different from the classifications derived from
that phylogeny. In general, he did not find earlier attempts to apply evolutionary
theory very helpful. Alpheus Spring Packard, for example, had formulated "evolutionary" methods and classifications, but he relied on the neo-Lamarckian
principle of directed progress. Comstock believed this approach caused more
problems than it solved. The frustrated young scholar concluded he would have to
devise a new method for evolutionary taxonomy.[9]

Comstock read widely and even traveled to Germany in the late 1880s in his
search for clues to an evolutionary method. Already skilled at detailed mor-
phological studies of adult characters, he added microscopic and embryological
studies. He worked with the invertebrate zoologist Rudolf Leuckart at Leipzig,
learning the new microscopic techniques used in Leuckart's lab and studying development because he believed that immature characters could play an important
role in evolutionary taxonomy.[10] His final step was to utilize Darwin's concepts of
natural selection, undirected variation, and historical change to devise new methods of analysis of adult and immature taxonomic characters. In the early 1890s
Comstock synthesized his ideas, and in 1893 he presented a seminal paper setting
out his research questions and methods and an evolutionary classification.

In the essay, titled "Evolution and Taxonomy," Comstock asserted that the goal
of the evolutionary systematist was to uncover phylogeny and prepare classifications that reflected that phylogeny. He then outlined a method for systematic research based on Darwin's theory of evolution by natural selection. He called on
his colleagues to adopt this method to determine the evolutionary history of all

[9] John Henry Comstock, "Evolution and Taxonomy: An Essay on the Application of the Theory of
Natural Selection to the Classification of Animals and Plants, Illustrated by a Study of the Evolution
of the Wings of Insects, and by a Contribution to the Classification of the Lepidoptera," in *The Wilder
Quarter Century Book* (Ithaca, N.Y.: Comstock Publishing Associates, 1893), p. 49 (hereafter
Comstock, "Evolution and Taxonomy"); Comstock, *Introduction to Entomology* (1888), pp. 14–15;
and Comstock, *The Wings of Insects: An Exposition of the Uniform Terminology of the Wing-Veins of
Insects and a Discussion of the More General Characteristics of the Wings of the Several Orders of In-
sects* (1899) (Ithaca, N.Y.: Comstock Publishing Company, 1918), pp. vii, 1–3. See also James L.
Larson, *Reason and Experience: The Representation of Natural Order in the Work of Carl von Linné*
(Berkeley/Los Angeles: Univ. California Press, 1971), p. 55; and Alpheus Spring Packard, *Guide to the
Study of Insects, and a Treatise on Those Injurious and Beneficial to Crops* (Salem, Mass., 1869, 1884).
[10] Anna Comstock, *Comstocks of Cornell* (cit. n. 1), pp. 163–165.

insects and to formulate a taxonomic classification that would be compatible with insect phylogeny. Systematics—the study of the systems governing life—should replace taxonomy—the mere naming, describing, and cataloguing of organisms. To illustrate his method he presented a revised classification of the order Lepidoptera (butterflies and moths) based on an analysis of the evolution of their wing veins (see Figure 2). Comstock chose to study these structures, which provide strength to the wing, because they had undergone a great deal of change as the insects evolved.

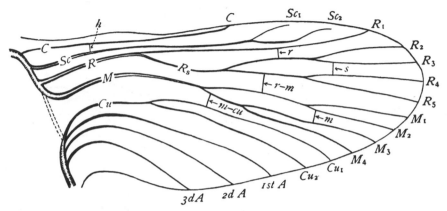

Figure 2. *Wing of the hypothetical primitive ancestor, with veins designated by letter and number. The letters stand for costa (C), subcosta (Sc), radius (R), media (M), cubitus (Cu), and anal (A). From John Henry Comstock,* The Wings of Insects *(Ithaca, N.Y.: Comstock Publishing Co., 1918), p. 19.*

Comstock was especially interested in higher classification at the family and order level, where the major trends in the evolution of insects could be seen. To facilitate this higher classification he developed a method of historical analysis of character changes. He not only rejected the notion of "essential" characters but argued that the characters that would prove of most value would in fact vary from group to group. Thus the evolutionary systematist must focus on those characters which had undergone significant change in the evolution of a particular group, as a result of the action of natural selection. The evolutionary systematist must study many characters, not just one or a few. Comstock advocated using immature as well as adult characters and incorporating information about paleontological forms, geographic distribution, and behaviors such as nesting, host plants, and mode of eating.[11]

Once appropriate characters had been chosen for study, Comstock advocated constructing sequences of character changes in a group, rather than merely counting or measuring characters. To assist in these historical analyses, he demonstrated how to distinguish ancestral from highly developed forms by studying embryological and paleontological forms. Comstock also noted that the same character could be lost more than once; thus its absence did not provide evidence

[11] Comstock, "Evolution and Taxonomy," pp. 44–45.

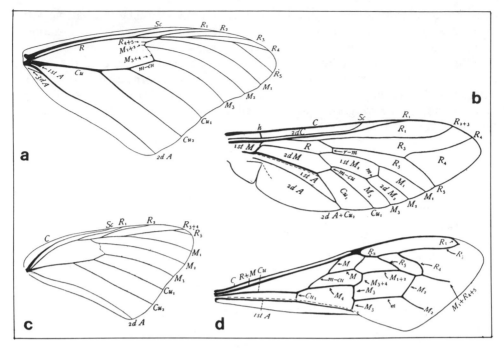

Figure 3. *Terminology for reduced veins:* a, *wing with 2dA but no 1stA due to atrophy* (Anosia); b, *coalescence from outer margin of 2dA+Cu₂* (Tabanus); c, *coalescence from base outward of* R_{3+4} (Pontia); d, *anastomization of radial and median veins from outer margin* (Apis). *From Comstock,* Wings of Insects *(1918), pp. 68, 333, 337, 375.*

of shared history. He demanded that the evolutionary systematist demonstrate that similar characters shared an evolutionary history.[12]

Further, Comstock suggested that after the evolutionary relationships between characters had been established, a uniform terminology should be used for body parts that shared the same evolutionary history. Workers on different orders of insects were then using different names for the wing veins. Comstock conjectured that the earliest winged insects had six principal groups of veins and demonstrated that all the orders of winged insects shared these six groups. He renamed the wing veins for all orders of insects, assigning a name to each principal group and a number to each vein in the group (see Figure 2). This system of terminology for wing venation thus incorporated evolutionary relationships into basic taxonomic work. Comstock believed that using terminology that reflected shared evolutionary history in this way would facilitate evolutionary studies and embed evolutionary thinking into taxonomic work. Many specialized modern forms had lost or gained wing veins, and the names assigned to the remaining or new veins had to reflect their relationship to the ancestral form. Thus if the first anal vein had been lost, the name 2dA and not 1stA would be assigned to the first anal vein left in this group (see Figure 3a). If two veins had coalesced, this would be re-

[12] *Ibid.,* pp. 44–48.

flected in their combined vein's name, such as R_{2+3} and $2dA+Cu_2$ (see Figure 3b). Comstock's system eventually came into wide use in entomology.[13]

Comstock provided examples of how to distinguish different paths of specialization to the same character state. In some modern insects, only four radial wing veins remain, but Comstock argued that counting "four radial veins" as a character was useless because the changes that natural selection works on are not directed, and therefore a decrease in the number of radial veins could have come about in several different ways. He demanded that the systematist determine which of the radial veins had been lost and how the loss had come about. In one group (Figure 3b), R_2 coalesced with R_3: the resulting vein should be called R_{2+3}. In another group (Figure 3c), R_3 coalesced with R_4, leaving vein R_{3+4}. In still others (Figure 3d), the radial veins had not coalesced at all, but rather had been anastomized. Comstock challenged the evolutionary systematist to demonstrate not only what the new character state was but how it had originated. The character "four radial veins" was not informative unless it could be demonstrated that the groups with four radial veins were a product of the same sequence of changes from the ancestral form. Comstock concluded that if one group had four radial veins as a result of the coalescence of R_{2+3} and another group had four radial veins as a result of the coalescence of R_{3+4}, this was evidence that the group was not closely related.[14]

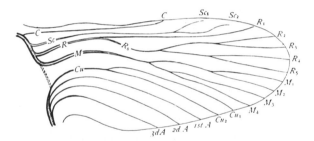

Figure 4. *Hypothetical primitive nymphal wing tracheation applying the Comstock-Needham system for adult wing veins to immature tracheae. From* Comstock, Wings of Insects *(1918), p. 16.*

In later papers Comstock began to use embryological information to clarify many of these changes. He noted that in some cases the immature form had not changed significantly from the immature form of the ancestor. Observations of developmental sequences might show just how a character had changed. This proved to be the case with the wing tracheae, which function in respiration in larvae but are replaced by wing veins in adults. Comstock demonstrated which trachea was correlated with which adult vein, as the nomenclature in Figure 4 illustrates. Even if the adult forms had specialized wing veins, the immature tracheae often retained the configuration of six principal groups of veins that characterized primitive winged insects. By rearing larvae and observing the transition from immature tracheae to adult veins, Comstock and one of his students, James G. Needham, could observe the processes of vein fusion and anastomization. They used evidence from immature forms to establish exactly which vein was R_1 or R_5, for example, if other veins had been lost, or which two veins had fused.

[13] *Ibid.,* pp. 52–79.
[14] *Ibid.,* pp. 62–64.

Such comparative study of adult, immature, and paleontological forms was required in order to uncover evolutionary history, Comstock argued.[15]

Comstock also incorporated the concept of natural selection into his analysis. He insisted on functional analyses of the characters he presumed to have undergone important changes in the evolution of the group in order to determine how they conferred a selective advantage on the organism. Once he formulated hypotheses of how and why a character had evolved, he derived new classifications from them, as in the new classification he offered of the Lepidoptera based on the steps he traced in the evolution of the wings of modern insects from those of a primitive ancestor.

Comstock, then, emphasized the importance of comparative study of a wide range of characters from adult, immature, and paleontological forms. Comstock was certain that evolutionary history could be uncovered if a series of historical analyses of taxonomic characters were carried out and compared. He asserted: "For in Nature's court, the testimony of different witnesses, if rightly understood, will agree. If any of these conclusions should prove to be incorrect, that fault will be found to lie with the translator and not with the record." If the conclusions from two or more independent lines of research coincide or are congruent, then a *consilience of inductions* has occurred that demonstrates that the conclusions are well supported. Darwin had advocated the use of William Whewell's concept of a consilience of inductions as the proper scientific method for evolutionary research. Indeed, his *On the Origin of Species* is an extended consilience argument. This use of a consilience of lines of evidence had important consequences for the structure of Comstock's research school.[16]

The research program Comstock pursued throughout his career reflected this emphasis on consilience of lines of evidence. In his seminal 1893 essay, "Evolution and Taxonomy," Comstock based his first hypotheses concerning the phylogeny and classification of Lepidoptera on evidence from the wing veins of adult butterflies and moths. In a series of essays published in 1898–1899, "The Wings of Insects," he compared that evidence with evidence from the wing tracheae of immature Lepidoptera. Finally, in his 1918 volume *The Wings of Insects,* he incorporated paleontological evidence concerning the wing veins of ancestral insects. With each comparison Comstock was able to refine his conclusions and corroborate or alter his earlier hypotheses. When additional evidence agreed with an earlier hypothesis, Comstock believed that hypothesis was demonstrably well supported.[17]

Comstock also used a consilience of lines of evidence from different taxonomic groups. His 1893 essay focused on the Lepidoptera, and the hypotheses he presented concerning the wing structure of the earliest of all winged insects were

[15] Comstock, *Wings of Insects* (1918) (cit. n. 9), pp. 85–90, 99–102; and John Henry Comstock and James G. Needham, "The Wings of Insects," *American Naturalist,* 1898, *32*:43–48, 81–89, 231–257, 335–340, 413–424, 561–565, 769–777, 903–911; 1899, *33*:117–126, 573–582, 845–860.

[16] Comstock, "Evolution and Taxonomy," p. 96, see also p. 93; and Charles Darwin, *On the Origin of Species by Means of Natural Selection; or, The Preservation of Favoured Races in the Struggle for Life* (1859), ed. J. W. Burrow (New York: Penguin Books, 1968, 1979), pp. 402–403, 408–409. See also Larry Laudan, "William Whewell on the Consilience of Inductions," *Monist,* 1971, *55*:368–370, 379–381.

[17] Comstock, "Evolution and Taxonomy," pp. 93, 96; Comstock, *Wings of Insects* (1918), pp. vii–ix, 8–11, 109; and Comstock and Needham, "Wings of Insects" (cit. n. 15), pp. 43–48, 84–86.

based on studies of that order. In his 1895 *Manual for the Study of Insects* he extended his research to other orders of insects and found his initial hypotheses corroborated by additional evidence. In each case Comstock compared the new line of evidence with his earlier work and made any necessary adjustments to his classifications and hypotheses concerning phylogeny. His ability to apply his method successfully to all the orders of insects Comstock regarded as further support for his evolutionary approach as well as for his specific conclusions about phylogeny and classification.[18]

Comstock's goal as an evolutionary systematist was not to focus on description and comparison of a few "essential" characters in a single order, as the traditional taxonomist did. His conviction that the evolutionary systematist must include many characters and study their various alterations under the pressure of natural selection meant that he could not hope to complete the ambitious research program he had laid out in a single lifetime. Therefore he encouraged his students to pursue this research program with him, in several ways. Some students chose a different character suite, such as the mouthparts or wing scales, and compared it with Comstock's hypotheses based on wing veins for a single taxonomic group. Others extended his research on adult wing veins of Lepidoptera to the study of adult wing veins in other taxonomic groups. Needham and a few others focused on immature characters and development. Both professor and students were pursuing the same research program: to formulate hypotheses about phylogeny and to construct a classification of insects that reflects their evolutionary history, using Comstock's method of character analysis on different characters and taxonomic groups.[19]

A hallmark of that method was its modularity, based on the notion of a consilience of independent lines of evidence. Comstock's students could define their own research projects, publish under their own names, and establish themselves as journeyman taxonomists in their own right. At the same time, they would not jeopardize their membership in their mentor's research school, even if their work challenged his classifications and evolutionary hypotheses. Comstock fully expected that the addition of new evidence would require modifications of his initial hypotheses. Students could, then, establish themselves within the field and remain part of Comstock's research school in evolutionary entomology, as long as they continued to use his method and work on his research questions.

II. COMSTOCK'S RESEARCH SCHOOL

Comstock's program thus not only required recruiting and nurturing a group of younger scholars to carry on his work, but facilitated it. Fruton argues that the success of a research school must be measured by the work of both mentor and students: the mentor alone often cannot be judged a success but deserves to be

---

[18] Comstock, "Evolution and Taxonomy," pp. 39–59, 96–113; and John Henry Comstock and Anna Botsford Comstock, *Manual for the Study of Insects* (Ithaca, N.Y.: Comstock Publishing Company, 1895), pp. 1–4, 76–77.

[19] For a detailed discussion of the work of Comstock's students see Henson, "Evolution and Taxonomy" (cit. n. 1), pp. 363–393.

evaluated in terms of the research produced by the students as well.[20] With his research group, Comstock extended his thesis to other taxonomic groups and characters and reached a far larger audience of taxonomists. Through his students Comstock's research method and evolutionary classifications became an integral part of the fabric of evolutionary entomology. The array of students he trained and introduced into the profession of entomology is impressive; indeed, some achieved greater prominence in the field than their professor.

Comstock established research groups at both Cornell and Stanford. He entered academia in general and entomology in particular during a period of growth and professionalization. As founder of the departments of entomology at Cornell and Stanford, he had freedom to shape them as he saw fit. As Comstock's departments grew, they were staffed solely by his own students. During his tenure all eleven faculty members of the Cornell department of entomology had studied under him. The early Stanford entomologists were Comstock students as well. The pool of potential applicants was limited in the last quarter of the nineteenth century, but there is no evidence that Comstock ever considered hiring a junior faculty member who had not studied under him. Indeed, in 1898 Comstock actively resisted the efforts of Charles P. Davenport, a noted embryologist, to join the Cornell faculty. Comstock hired instead his student and research assistant James Needham, with whom he was conducting the major study of immature wing tracheae described above.[21]

These junior faculty members coauthored research papers, monographs, textbooks, and laboratory manuals with Comstock. They also published papers under their own names, although many of these papers were clearly influenced by Comstock's research program. Ties between Cornell and Stanford were close, with students and faculty moving from one campus to the other for different phases of their careers. Although Comstock spent only part of the year at each school, that seems to have been sufficient to keep each group on track. The cohesive Cornell research school expanded to a second campus and, therefore, did go beyond the spatial limits set by Geison. Indeed, several students secured teaching positions at other universities but returned each summer to work with Comstock in the field and in the lab. These students continued to work on Comstock's research problems, use his evolutionary method, and, occasionally, coauthor works with him. They can, I therefore argue, be regarded as members of the research school as well.[22]

Comstock secured funding at both schools for modern laboratory facilities where students and faculty worked together closely. These labs were built according to his specifications and afforded sufficient space for students and mentor to work in comfortable proximity (see Figure 1). Comstock also built an "insectary"

---

[20] Fruton, *Contrasts in Scientific Style* (cit. n. 5), pp. 3, 9–11. See Joel Hagen's essay in this volume for the effects of a very different professorial style.

[21] Needham, "Lengthened Shadow" (cit. n. 2), p. 228. See also Charles P. Davenport to John Henry Comstock, 9, 22 Oct., 10 Nov. 1898, and Comstock to Davenport, 15 Oct., 3 Nov., 10 Dec. 1898, in the John Henry Comstock Papers, Division of Manuscripts and University Archives, Cornell University. At Cornell, Comstock hired his students James Chester Bradley, Cyrus Richard Crosby, William T. M. Forbes, Glenn W. Herrick, Oskar A. Johannsen, John T. Lloyd, Alexander Dyer MacGillivray, Robert Matheson, James G. Needham, William A. Riley, and Mark V. Slingerland. At Stanford he appointed his students Willis Grant Johnson and Vernon Lyman Kellogg.

[22] Henson, "Evolution and Taxonomy" (cit. n. 1), pp. 331–334, 363–380.

at Cornell, a building where insects were reared on their host plants so that the relations between insects and plants could be observed. His method required a great deal of laboratory work: microscopic observations, physiological studies, and observations of insect-plant relations. Indeed, Davenport wrote to Comstock that he wanted to join the Cornell department because of its "extensive grounds and spirit of experiment" in the study of evolution.[23]

Comstock also required a great deal of fieldwork for collecting and observing specimens. As a Darwinian, he believed that organisms must be observed in their natural environment in order to understand why characters had evolved in certain ways. Students of insect life needed to observe the interrelations of the organism with its physical surroundings and associated plants and animals. All stages in the life history had to be observed and understood. Long treks through the woods near Ithaca and Palo Alto to observe and collect with "the professor," as Comstock was called, fostered a spirit of camaraderie among the young entomologists. Comstock regarded fieldwork as so essential that in 1885 he offered it in one of the first summer courses ever given at Cornell. The summer group usually consisted of Comstock, postgraduates returning to work with their mentor, current Cornell undergraduate and graduate students, and special students interested in learning Comstock's method. Students were expected to begin their own reference collection of insects and to document the life histories of the organisms they were studying in the field, lab, museum, and classroom. Although Comstock suggested the topics, he expected his advanced students to complete at least one piece of independent research to establish themselves as scientists.[24]

With one short-lived exception, the Cornell and Stanford entomology departments enjoyed strong support from university administrators. Comstock and his wife, Anna Botsford Comstock (1854–1930), were close friends of Cornell's president Andrew D. White and were able to call on him personally for support. The Comstocks also maintained close personal ties with White's successors, Charles Kendall Adams, Jacob Gould Schurman, and Livingston Farrand. Stanford's president, David Starr Jordan, had been a student at Cornell with the Comstocks and invited his old friends to direct the course of entomology at his new school. Comstock was therefore able to secure the buildings, equipment, and financial support he needed to build strong departments. Only during Adams's tenure at Cornell did support falter, but when Comstock threatened to resign, Adams acceded to his demands. By the turn of the century Cornell had the largest department of entomology in the nation, and Stanford was noted for its strong program in entomology.[25]

Because he had struggled to fund his own education, Comstock knew the importance of financial support for students. He secured graduate assistantships funded by both universities and by the provisions for agricultural experiment work under the Hatch Act. If assistantships were not available, he often hired students out of his own pocket to work in the insectary, lab, or even around his home.

[23] Davenport to Comstock, 9 Oct. 1898, Comstock Papers. See also Anna Comstock, *Comstocks of Cornell* (cit. n. 1), pp. 139–141, 160–161.

[24] Anna Comstock, *Comstocks of Cornell*, pp. 148–151, 155.

[25] *Ibid.,* pp. 46–47, 51, 102–103, 144–145, 151–152, 158, 172–177, 192; and David Starr Jordan to John Henry Comstock, 26 Mar. 1891, and Charles Kendall Adams to Comstock, 19 Dec. 1885, Comstock Papers.

After they graduated, he worked hard to locate positions for them in the new state colleges and agricultural experiment stations.[26]

Letters and memoirs by his students reveal a genuine fondness for "the professor" and his wife, who took such good care of them. Comstock not only taught and hired his students, he created a close-knit community of scholars in his department at Cornell. The Comstocks' home was located on the Cornell campus with the insectary right behind it, and their cottage was the social center of the biology department. Several biology faculty members and many students actually lived there. At Stanford, evening coffee was always available for students and faculty in the Comstocks' rooms in Encina Hall.[27]

Comstock was a shy and retiring man but was complemented by his warm and outgoing wife (see Figure 1). Anna played an important role in her husband's research school. They met when she was a student in his invertebrate zoology class and married in 1878. For her bachelor of science degree Anna completed a thesis in systematic entomology. She assisted her husband in the laboratory and insectary and maintained her own office in the entomology department. She took up engraving to illustrate Comstock's textbooks, and she wrote one textbook and several popular books on insects with her husband. She does not seem to have contributed to his intellectual program, and she did no independent research after her thesis. She played a central role in the research school, however, through her friendships with university administrators, her writing and illustration of books, and her creation of a home where all the Cornell biology students were welcome. The Comstocks had no children of their own, and their research school seems to have become their extended family.[28]

The Comstocks' textbooks and popular works point to another institution that Comstock used to disseminate his research program and evolutionary method. In 1893 Comstock established his own publishing house, Comstock Publishing Associates, to ensure the quality, frequency, and low price he wanted for his books and to guarantee that volumes written by members of his research school were printed promptly and distributed widely. Textbooks, manuals, and monographs by the Comstocks and his students appeared under the Comstock imprint. The company was quite successful: the textbooks and manuals enjoyed long press runs and were adopted by schools across the nation, in part because the Comstocks controlled production and distribution. The Comstocks willed the company to the university, where it became the nucleus for Cornell University Press.[29]

Comstock and his students were also active in the profession of entomology. Indeed, the Entomological Society of America was founded at Cornell in 1907, and Comstock served as its first president. Comstock wanted a scientific society that would focus on basic systematic and evolutionary research, in contrast to the agri-

[26] Anna Comstock, *Comstocks of Cornell*, pp. 161, 166, 177.

[27] *Ibid.*, pp. 104–105, 147, 175, 177, 228; John Henry Comstock, "Reminiscences," *Journal of Economic Entomology*, 1922, *15*:31–34; Needham, "Lengthened Shadow" (cit. n. 2), p. 227; and Albert Hazen Wright, oral history interview, Division of Manuscripts and University Archives, Cornell University. See also correspondence with students such as Nathan Banks, Vernon L. Kellogg, and John Moore Stedman in the Comstock Papers, for close personal relationships with Comstock.

[28] Anna Comstock, *Comstocks of Cornell*, pp. 85–88, 102–103, 130, 137, 143–150, 158, 166–167. Hagen discusses the very different role played by Edith Clements in her husband's career.

[29] *Ibid.*, pp. 188–189, 248–249; and Gage, "Comstock Publishing" (cit. n. 4), pp. 10–14, 21–24, 30, 34–41.

cultural topics that dominated the American Association of Economic Entomologists. His new society grew rapidly and became a forum for members of his research school. Comstock and students of his were on the editorial board for the *Annals of the Entomological Society of America* from its inception until his death. Comstock also used his position on the editorial board of *The American Naturalist* and other journals to bring the work of his research school to national attention. In these journals members of Comstock's research school wrote positive reviews of each others' monographs and textbooks and attacked competing methods and classifications. They missed few opportunities to assail the work of neo-Lamarckians, such as Alpheus Spring Packard, and to remind readers of Comstock's Darwinian method and classification. Capitalizing on the outlets available to reach the larger professional community brought Comstock's views on evolution and taxonomy before a broad audience of American naturalists.[30]

Comstock's students and junior faculty members were, then, an important part of his research program. How important became clearer as the problem of an evolutionary classification for insects based on their phylogeny proved more complex than Comstock had originally anticipated. Anna Comstock recalled, "Mr. Comstock was nearing seventy and was working steadily eight or ten hours each day, trying to unravel the tangled skein of the evolutionary relations of insects, as shown by their wing venation. As soon as he worked one thread free, at one turn of the reel it would tangle again."[31] Comstock depended on his students to achieve a goal he could never reach alone.

Comstock's students followed a variety of career paths, institutionally and conceptually. James Chester Bradley (1884–1975) studied under Comstock and taught at Cornell from 1905 to 1952. He continued Comstock's research program in his monographs on the Hymenoptera (bees, ants, and wasps) and incorporated Comstock's method in his *Laboratory Guide to the Evolution of the Wings of Insects* of 1931, as the title clearly reflects. But Bradley also offered critiques of some of Comstock's hypotheses about wing veins and proposed revised classifications.[32] Comstock accepted Bradley's critiques and used the revised classification in his subsequent writings.[33] Perhaps more than any other Comstock student, Bradley continued to work in the Comstock research program for his entire career. Although he offered critiques of specific conclusions, he did not substantially revise Comstock's method or overall research goals. He remained in close proximity to Comstock both spatially and intellectually.

While studying for his Ph.D. at Cornell, James G. Needham (1868–1957) conducted research with Comstock on immature wings for their jointly published essays on the wings of insects of 1898–1899. When they revised Comstock's system

[30] "Introductory," *Annals of the Entomological Society of America*, 1908, *1*:1–5, 21–37; and Theodore J. Spilman, "Vignettes of the Presidents of the Entomological Society of America (1889–1989)," *Bulletin of the Entomological Society of America*, 1989, *35*:33–34. See, e.g., the following pieces in *The American Naturalist:* John Henry Comstock, "Ears of Insects," 1887, *21*:579; Comstock, "Entomological News," 1887, *21*:484; Vernon Lyman Kellogg, review of *Outdoor Studies: A Reading Book of Nature Study*, by James G. Needham, 1898, *32*:786; and Needham, review of *Elements of Insect Anatomy*, by John Henry Comstock, 1902, *36*:500–501.

[31] Anna Comstock, *Comstocks of Cornell*, p. 250.

[32] James Chester Bradley, *A Laboratory Guide to the Study of the Evolution of the Wings of Insects* (Ithaca, N.Y.: Daw, Illston, 1931, 1939); and Smith, "Comstocks and Cornell" (cit. n. 2), p. 15.

[33] Comstock, *Wings of Insects* (cit. n. 9), pp. viii, 70.

of nomenclature for wing veins, the professor shared credit with the student, and their terminology became known as the Comstock-Needham system of wing venation nomenclature. After he joined the Cornell faculty in 1907, Needham extended Comstock's work to other taxonomic groups, in papers with titles such as "A Genealogic Study of Dragon-fly Wing Venation."[34] Needham developed expertise in the study of immature forms, and Comstock came to rely on him for this work. Although he made major contributions to Comstock's research school, Needham did not devote his entire life to the Comstock research program but instead took his interest in Darwin's theory into the new fields of limnology and ecology. Needham chaired the Cornell department after Comstock's retirement and maintained the research school during his tenure, but he also developed programs in other emerging fields of biology.[35]

Other students left the Cornell campus but took Comstock's methods with them. Comstock's first Ph.D. graduate was Leland Ossian Howard (1857–1950). In his youth Howard had begun tramping through the woods near Ithaca with Comstock, and the two men remained close friends throughout Comstock's life. Once Howard received his degree, Comstock secured him a position at the USDA Bureau of Entomology, as an assistant to the bureau chief, Charles Valentine Riley. Although Comstock and Riley were often at odds, Riley still turned to Comstock when he had a vacancy to fill. Howard remained in the bureau for his entire career, rising to chief in 1894, and he in turn hired many of Comstock's students for pest control work in economic entomology.[36]

Howard was known as the leading figure in economic entomology in the nation, but he also played an important role in insect taxonomy. He was the Honorary Curator of Insects for the United States National Museum, and Smithsonian officials relied on his judgment when selecting new curators as the national collection of insects expanded. Howard appointed many of Comstock's students. His choice of Harrison Gray Dyar, who was not a Comstock product, as custodian of the Lepidoptera might seem to be an exception. But Dyar shared an interest in Darwinian theory, and he was an early convert to Comstock's method and a strong advocate for his revised classifications. Howard's appointments thus expanded the range of Comstock's influence to the National Museum and the Department of Agriculture.[37]

Perhaps the best known of Comstock's students was Vernon L. Kellogg (1867–1937). Comstock brought Kellogg from Cornell to teach at the new Stanford department of entomology. When Comstock could no longer continue teaching at

[34] James G. Needham, "A Genealogic Study of Dragon-fly Wing Venation," *Proceedings of the United States National Museum,* 1903, *26*:703–763.

[35] Needham, "Lengthened Shadow" (cit. n. 2), p. 226; James G. Needham and John Thomas Lloyd, *The Life of Inland Waters* (Ithaca, N.Y.: Comstock Publishing Company, 1916); and Arnold Mallis, *American Entomologists* (New Brunswick, N.J.: Rutgers Univ. Press, 1971), pp. 138, 174–178.

[36] Leland Ossian Howard, *Fighting the Insects: The Story of an Entomologist* (rpt. New York: Arno Press, 1980), pp. 13–14, 32–33, 52; and Mallis, *American Entomologists,* pp. 79–86.

[37] Harrison Gray Dyar, review of "Evolution and Taxonomy," by John Henry Comstock, *Canadian Entomologist,* 1894, *26*:53–54; Dyar, "A Classification of Lepidopterous Larvae," *Annals of the New York Academy of Sciences,* 1894, *8*:194–232; Dyar, "A Combination of Two Classifications of Lepidoptera," *Journal of the New York Entomological Society,* 1895, *3*:17–26; Marc E. Epstein and Pamela M. Henson, "Digging for Dyar: The Man Behind the Myth," *American Entomologist,* 1992, *38*:150–151, 154; and Mallis, *American Entomologists,* pp. 75, 79–86, 100–102, 180–183, 240–241, 372–373, 398, 487–488.

both schools, he turned the Stanford department over to Kellogg. The two men worked together closely for many years and especially enjoyed long field trips together. In 1895 they coauthored a popular laboratory manual, *The Elements of Insect Anatomy,* which utilized Comstock's method of laboratory research and taxonomic analysis. Kellogg applied Comstock's research method to other insect characters, such as the mouthparts, sclerites, and wing scales, and to other taxonomic groups, such as the Ephemeridae (mayflies) and Mallophaga (bird lice). Kellogg retained a lifelong interest in Darwinian theory, writing a survey of the state of the theory, *Darwinism To-day,* in 1907 and *Evolution: The Way of Man* in 1924. Stanford's president Jordan also encouraged him in this theoretical interest. Kellogg and Jordan together produced several volumes on the topic in which they focused on more general questions about the mechanisms of evolution. Kellogg eventually became a better-known scientist than Comstock, through his popular writings on evolution and his position as secretary of the National Research Council.[38]

Some of Comstock's students, such as Bradley, focused narrowly on the Comstock research program. Others took the Darwinian approach they learned from Comstock into new areas of research, such as ecology, and extended its influence far beyond the Cornell campus. Kellogg and Howard, in particular, became national figures in science. The considerable power they wielded allowed Comstock to continue to secure good jobs for his students. Their lifelong respect and real affection for the professor ensured his stature in the entomological community. Both scientists eventually moved beyond Comstock's research program, but both retained the interest in Darwinian theory inculcated by their mentor.

Other Comstock students secured teaching positions at colleges and universities throughout the nation. They were represented at most of the land grant colleges established across the United States in the last quarter of the nineteenth century. These young professors used Comstock's texts and lab manuals in their courses and required the same types of museum, field, and laboratory observations that their mentor had. They wrote to Comstock frequently, asking for advice on teaching and on problems they encountered in their own classifications. Many returned to Cornell in the summers to participate in the field course. These students, though less prominent than Kellogg or Howard, also disseminated the Comstock method for evolutionary systematics far beyond the Cornell and Stanford campuses.[39]

Even the students of Comstock's students continued in this tradition. Needham's student Anna Haven Morgan wrote papers such as "Homologies of

[38] Vernon L. Kellogg, *Darwinism To-day* (New York: Henry Holt, 1907); Kellogg, *Evolution: The Way of Man* (New York: Appleton, 1924); Kellogg, "The Development and Homologies of the Mouth Parts of Insects," *American Naturalist,* 1902, *36*:683–706; Kellogg, "The Ephemeridae and Venation Nomenclature," *Psyche,* 1895, *7*:311–315; Kellogg, "Mallophaga," *Genera Insectorum,* 1908, *66*; Kellogg, "The Sclerites of the Head of *Danais archippus* Fab.," *Kansas University Quarterly,* 1893, *2*:51–57; Kellogg, "The Taxonomic Value of Scales," *ibid.,* 1894, *3*:45–89; John Henry Comstock and Kellogg, *The Elements of Insect Anatomy* (Ithaca, N.Y.: Comstock Publishing Company, 1895); and David Starr Jordan and Kellogg, *Evolution and Animal Life* (New York: Appleton, 1907). See also C. E. McClung, "Biographical Memoir of Vernon Lyman Kellogg, 1867–1937," *Biographical Memoirs of the National Academy of Sciences,* 1939, *20*:245–257.

[39] For a detailed discussion of students such as George Francis Atkinson, Guy Chester Crampton, William Atwood Hilton, Philip Alexander Munz, Edith Marion Patch, and Mason B. Thomas, see Henson, "Evolution and Taxonomy" (cit. n. 1), pp. 385–390.

the Wing-Veins of May-flies," a straightforward continuation of Comstock's research program. Robert Evans Snodgrass, a USDA morphologist who studied under Kellogg at Stanford, went on to write such papers as "The Evolution of the Insect Head and the Organs of Feeding." There are literally dozens of papers with similar titles written by this group. At a time when, some historians claim, taxonomists were ignoring Darwin's theory, evolution by natural selection was a crucial component of the work of an ever-expanding group of entomologists.[40]

Anna Morgan's work raises the issue of gender in Comstock's research school. Women could not fully participate in this cohesive group by teaching and working in the Cornell labs. There were no female professors at Cornell until a professor of home economics was appointed in 1911. Anna Comstock was appointed the first woman professor at Cornell in 1898, but the Board of Trustees promptly reduced her title to instructor. She did not regain her professorship until 1913. Comstock accepted females as undergraduate and graduate students, but after commencement these women had to leave Cornell to hold professional positions. Morgan, for example, was a zoological assistant and instructor at Cornell before she left to become a professor at Mount Holyoke. If, as Geison argues, proximity within a spatially enclosed group is important to members of a research school, female scientists were denied full membership. Stanford had no such prohibitions, and Ruby Green Smith did continue as a faculty member there.[41]

The Comstock research school in evolutionary entomology was a powerful force in American entomology from the 1890s to 1930. Its success was due to the combination of intellectual, institutional, and personal factors detailed above. But the research school did not last long after Comstock's death in 1931. In 1920 Kellogg left Stanford and active research to become secretary of the National Research Council. Smith and others continued to work on evolutionary entomology, but the department no longer had the cohesive focus of the early decades of the century. After Comstock's retirement in 1914, his student Needham chaired the Cornell department and continued the evolutionary research program. However, many of the entomology courses were transferred to the School of Agriculture during his tenure and became economic in focus. After Needham retired in 1935, the department of entomology was merged with the department of zoology. Its chairman, Herbert J. Webber, was given a mandate to develop a strong program in Mendelian genetics. Bradley and some of his colleagues continued the Comstock research program, but entomology no longer enjoyed a premier position in the Cornell department of zoology. Comstock's research school, then, fell not to a competing school within the field of systematic entomology but rather to competing fields in biology, as Mendelian genetics began to dominate American biology classrooms and laboratories and as economic research assumed increasing importance in entomology. In addition, Comstock's personal style seems to

[40] Anna Haven Morgan, "Homologies of the Wing-Veins of May-flies," *Annals of the Entomological Society of America,* 1912, *5*:89–106; and Robert Evans Snodgrass, "Evolution of the Insect Head and Organs of Feeding," *Annual Report of the Smithsonian Institution, 1931* (Washington, D.C.: 1932), pp. 443–489.

[41] Anna Comstock, *Comstocks of Cornell* (cit. n. 1), pp. 85, 143–150, 190–198, 209–220, 244, 252–259; Charlotte Williams Conable, *Women at Cornell: The Myth of Equal Education* (Ithaca, N.Y.: Cornell Univ. Press, 1977), pp. 26–27, 48–51, 74–75, 84–87, 126–127; and Margaret W. Rossiter, *Women Scientists in America: Struggles and Strategies to 1940* (Baltimore: Johns Hopkins Univ. Press, 1982), pp. 9–11, 32, 35–37, 62–65, 282.

have been a crucial factor in holding the group together. His tight focus on a single research program and charismatic personality produced a cohesiveness that none of his students could maintain. Once the centripetal force of his personality was gone, the group dispersed.[42]

All of Comstock's work was not lost, however. His research program continued to play a central role in the work of many of his students and his students' students. These evolutionary entomologists saw themselves as reconstructing the history of life, not merely describing and cataloguing dead specimens. Comstock's research method and system of nomenclature became standard practice in systematic entomology. And many of his proposed reclassifications of insects, based on an analysis of their evolutionary history, were accepted by the entomological community and are retained in modern classifications.

III. CONCLUSION

John Henry Comstock had both the personal and intellectual characteristics needed to create a school to carry out his research program. He was not seeking to solve one small problem or exploit a single piece of equipment or lab technique: his goal was to reform the practices and conclusions of all of entomological taxonomy to conform with Darwin's theory of evolution. After solving his initial problems in classification by devising a new method, Comstock nurtured a group of scholars to complete his Darwinian research program. The program's modularity, based on a consilience of lines of evidence, facilitated the formation and longevity of a cohesive research school, one in which students sought answers to Comstock's central research questions through their own independent research projects.

Comstock created two departments of entomology, staffed by his students, where professor, junior faculty, and students worked in close proximity—even as he allowed his protégés to conduct and publish independent research. His research school in evolutionary entomology was not a laboratory group exactly like those Fruton and Geison describe for the physical sciences. Each group did, however, work together in the field, museum, and insectary as well as the lab, creating an analogous cohesiveness. It is true that the two groups were a continent apart and thus did not enjoy the continuous day-to-day contact that Geison includes in his definition of a research school.[43] But they maintained cohesiveness through correspondence and through summer study and fieldwork at Cornell—strategies that worked well for the students who left the original two campuses as well. And above all they focused on a single research program and a specific method.

Many of Comstock's students—especially the women—left the Cornell and Stanford campuses, but they took the Comstock research program with them to schools and museums nationwide. Comstock also expanded the reach of his

[42] Wright, interview (cit. n. 27); Gould P. Colman, *Education and Agriculture: A History of the New York State College of Agriculture at Cornell University* (Ithaca, N.Y.: Cornell Univ. Press, 1963), pp. 578–581; Simon H. Gage, "Retirement of Professor John Henry Comstock," *Cornell Countryman,* April 1914, p. 229; James G. Needham, "John Henry Comstock," *Science,* 1931, *73*:409–410; and Ruby Green Smith, *The People's Colleges: A History of the New York State Extension Service in Cornell University and the State, 1876–1948* (Ithaca, N.Y.: Cornell Univ. Press, 1949), pp. 452–453.
[43] Geison, "Scientific Change" (cit. n. 5), pp. 23, 32–33.

**Table 1. Geison's Characteristics of a Successful Research School
Applied to Comstock's School**

Trait	Comstock's school
1. Charismatic leader	+
2. Leader with research reputation	+
3. Informal setting and leadership style	+
4. Leader with institutional power	+
5. Social cohesion, loyalty, esprit de corps, discipleship	+
6. Focused research program	+
7. Simple and rapidly exploitable experimental techniques	−
8. Invasion of new field of research	+
9. Pool of potential recruits (graduate students)	+
10. Access to or control of publication outlets	+
11. Students publishing early under their own names	+
12. Significant number of students produced and placed	+
13. Institutionalization in university setting	+
14. Adequate financial support	+
Total of "+"s	13

+ Feature appears to be present
− Feature appears to be absent
NOTE: Based on Chart II, Gerald L. Geison, "Scientific Change, Emerging Specialties, and Research Schools," *History of Science,* 1981, *19*:24.

program and method through textbooks, laboratory manuals, research papers, monographs, and reviews of opponents' work—using his publishing company and professional journals to advance the work of his students as well as to disseminate his ideas. Eventually, however, the broad scope of his changes for taxonomic methods and the widespread adoption of his ideas made it difficult to distinguish a distinctive research school.

Its fate is similar to that of the Kohlrausch school as Kathryn Olesko describes it elsewhere in this volume. Comstock's students dominated the field of entomology, on college campuses and in museums. His textbooks and lab manuals were widely used. Many of his proposals for revising the classification of insects were accepted by the entomological community. His hypotheses concerning the earliest insects and general pattern of evolution in insects became textbook knowledge. His insistence on using the same terms for homologous parts in different orders became standard practice. In short, as Comstock's methods and conclusions became standard in the field, their success paradoxically blurred the distinctiveness of his research school.

Comstock embodies the characteristics Geison delineated for the mentor of a successful research school (see Table 1). He was a leader in his field with a research reputation, who had an informal style that fostered loyalty among his students. Although he was shy and retiring, his students regarded him with fondness and respect. He formulated a focused research program in the expanding field of entomology. He did not have a simple and rapidly exploitable experimental technique, but rather a modular approach to a broad research program that allowed his students to establish themselves independently within the field. Indeed the size and complexity of his research program forced him to turn to colleagues and protégés for assistance. He worked in a university setting with good financial support and a pool of potential recruits. He controlled publication outlets, encouraged his students to publish, and secured jobs for them in systematic and economic entomology. Although his students were dispersed, his personality and focused research program compensated for the lack of spatial proximity.

Comstock exhibits Fruton's liberal leadership style for mentors.[44] He shared credit for research by joint authorship and even by the joint naming of the Comstock-Needham system. He allowed his students a great deal of latitude in their research and encouraged them to publish under their own names and establish independent reputations. He cited their works himself and created publication outlets for them. Rather than being autocratic, his personal style inspired loyalty and esprit de corps among his students. The number of students who remained at Cornell and Stanford for many years demonstrates how supportive but open an environment he created. Some, like Bradley, may not have had the creativity to strike off on their own. But Kellogg and Needham made important contributions to the field while remaining within the school.

Thus the modular nature of Comstock's research program and his personal characteristics as a liberal mentor combined to produce a cohesive research school that exerted great influence on the field of systematic entomology. Conceptual aspects of his research program further facilitated the establishment and continuation of a cohesive group of scholars working together in a distinctive school.

[44] Fruton, *Contrasts in Scientific Style* (cit. n. 5), esp. the discussions of Adolf von Baeyer and Franz Hofmeister, pp. 118–229.

Clementsian Ecologists: The Internal Dynamics of a Research School

By Joel B. Hagen*

W HY ARE SOME RESEARCH SCHOOLS more successful than others? In his suggestive article "Scientific Change, Emerging Specialties, and Research Schools," Gerald Geison presented a set of factors that may account for these differences. More important, he used the presence or absence of these factors to compare various research schools, comparisons that he organized in a table. Geison was quick to acknowledge the obvious limitations of this type of analysis, and he was loath to claim that his table represented a model in any deep sense of the term.[1] Nonetheless, if not a model, the table is certainly more than a mere catalogue of factors.

Unfortunately, Geison ignored what was most intriguing about the table and emphasized what was least important. In his discussion, he drew attention to the correlation (albeit imprecise) between the total number of features possessed by a research school and the success of that school. More striking, however, is the strong positive correlation between certain factors and the success of a school; other factors appear to be only weakly correlated with success. Therefore, it would seem desirable to weight the various factors in Geison's table. Even more intriguing, some of the correlations in the table seem counterintuitive. For example, in the cases considered by Geison it appears that the success or failure of a research group cannot be accounted for by its institutional setting, the institutional power of its leader, his reputation, or his control over means of disseminating information. Successful and unsuccessful groups alike share common institutional features. Yet a group's success may depend quite heavily upon the personality and leadership style of its director. These observations may not count as predictions in a rigorous scientific sense, but they do suggest a point of departure for analyzing other research groups.

If one assumes that success depends heavily on the internal dynamics of a research group, the scope of Geison's analysis must be expanded. His is "top-down" history, focusing almost entirely on the group leader's characteristics. But characteristics of students or subordinate scientists in the group are also important. In the abstract an ideal student must be sufficiently independent to nurture and develop the leader's nascent ideas. By doing so the student expands the scope of the research program, perhaps extending it into areas that the leader never imagined

* Biology Department, Radford University, Radford, Virginia 24142.

[1] Gerald L. Geison, "Scientific Change, Emerging Specialties, and Research Schools," *History of Science,* 1981, *19*:20–40, on pp. 24 (table), 26–27.

178

at the outset. Yet this ideal student must be sufficiently loyal to the leader that the coherence and integrity of the research program can be maintained. Such a balance of intellectual qualities is not often found, and a group leader may have only limited control over selecting subordinates: the right person may not be available, attractive candidates may choose alternative occupations, the personalities of leader and subordinate may clash, or there may be social or institutional constraints that limit the leader's choice of coworkers. Not surprisingly, research groups are often ephemeral, and even a successful group may be the site of conflict.[2]

The objective of this article is to describe the internal dynamics of a research group, considering both the leader and a number of different subordinates. The historical case under consideration is the group organized by the ecologist Frederic Clements at the Carnegie Institution of Washington during the period from 1917 to 1941. The Carnegie supported the ecological research that Clements carried out, primarily at his small alpine laboratory near Pikes Peak, Colorado, for a quarter of a century. A few scientists spent virtually their entire careers working under Clements's supervision. A larger number of scientists worked in his group for periods of a decade or more. Although some members of this interacting group of biologists have vanished from the historical record, sufficient information exists to reconstruct the professional and intellectual relationships within it.

I. FREDERIC CLEMENTS AND THE CARNEGIE INSTITUTION

When Frederic Clements was appointed research associate at the Carnegie Institution in 1917, he was at the height of his career. The publication of two influential books had brought him international recognition. *Research Methods in Ecology* (1905), written when he was a young faculty member at the University of Nebraska, outlined a bold program for the fledgling discipline of ecology. *Plant Succession* (1916), published a decade later, presented a far more detailed discussion of many of the topics covered in the earlier book.[3] By 1920 Clements was one of the most important ecologists in the United States.

Clements's research program worked on a number of different levels. *Research Methods in Ecology* was more than a technical manual, but one of its objectives was to present ecologists with a set of rigorous, easily reproducible methods. The book is filled with descriptions of instruments and measuring techniques that could be used in the field. One notable technique that Clements perfected was the *quadrat*.[4] By counting the individuals of every species within measured areas (usually one square meter), the ecologist could quantify differences in vegetation among various geographical areas. The technique could also be used

---

[2] A good example would be the *Drosophila* group at Columbia led by the geneticist T. H. Morgan. The antagonism between Morgan and his student H. J. Muller is described in Garland E. Allen, *Thomas Hunt Morgan: The Man and His Science* (Princeton, N.J.: Princeton Univ. Press, 1978), pp. 188–208.

[3] Frederic Edward Clements, *Research Methods in Ecology* (Lincoln, Nebr.: University Publishing, 1905); and Clements, *Plant Succession: An Analysis of the Development of Vegetation* (Washington, D.C.: Carnegie Institution of Washington, 1916).

[4] Ronald C. Tobey, *Saving the Prairies: The Life Cycle of the Founding School of American Plant Ecology, 1895–1955* (Berkeley/Los Angeles: Univ. California Press, 1981), Ch. 3.

experimentally. After removing all of the vegetation from a quadrat, the ecologist could study the subsequent invasion and establishment of new plants, or sow a measured number of seeds of two different species in the same barren quadrat and study competition.

These new techniques were presented within a broader conceptual framework. For Clements, ecology was to be a "rational field physiology."[5] The ecologist would bring into the field exact quantitative techniques and experimental methods as rigorous as those used in the physiology laboratory. Like the physiologist, the ecologist studied problems involving the complex interplay between structure and function in the organism. Clements believed that organisms existed at more than one level of complexity. The plant community, made up of thousands of simple organisms, was itself a "complex organism." Like individual organisms, the community possessed distinctive structures and functions influenced by physical factors in the environment. Thus the community had its own physiology. It also had a form of ontogeny. Succession, the changes in the composition of a plant community over time, represented the life cycle of the complex organism.

Clements's *Plant Succession* did much to establish this developmental process as the central problem in pre–World War II ecology. His massive book quickly became the definitive work on the topic; indeed, it remains a point of departure for many discussions of succession today. Even critics hailed the book as an important contribution to the field.[6] It provided the first synthesis of the growing body of field studies on succession. As the life cycle of the community, succession was an orderly developmental process ending in the establishment of a climax community. The exact structure of this mature community depended upon climate; each region had its own distinct climatic climax. Like an organism, the climax community maintained a state of dynamic equilibrium with its surrounding environment. By identifying, measuring, and manipulating various environmental factors, the ecologist could investigate the structure and function of both the organism and the organismal community.

Not everyone was impressed with Clements's physiological perspective or his organicism. Critics sometimes ridiculed his ideas as "fantasies," "laughable absurdities," and "flights of fancy."[7] Burton Livingston, a physiological ecologist and one of his rivals at the Carnegie Institution, dismissed his first book, *Research Methods,* as "that *awful* book."[8] Such vituperative attacks highlighted the importance of Clements's first two books. Whether guiding his supporters' research or providing highly visible targets for his opponents' criticism,

[5] Clements, *Research Methods* (cit. n. 3), p. 10. See also Joel B. Hagen, "Organism and Environment: Frederic Clements's Vision of a Unified Physiological Ecology," in *The American Development of Biology,* ed. Ronald Rainger, Keith R. Benson, and Jane Maienschein (Philadelphia: Univ. Pennsylvania Press, 1988).

[6] Henry Allan Gleason, "The Structure and Development of the Plant Association," *Bulletin of the Torrey Botanical Club,* 1917, 44:463–481.

[7] Quoted in A. G. Tansley, "The Classification of Vegetation and the Concept of Development," *Journal of Ecology,* 1920, 8:118–144. See also J. Braun-Blanquet, *Plant Sociology: The Study of Plant Communities,* trans. George D. Fuller and Henry S. Conard (New York: McGraw Hill, 1932), p. 315.

[8] Janice Emily Bowers, *A Sense of Place: The Life and Work of Forrest Shreve* (Tucson: Univ. Arizona Press, 1988), p. 59.

Clements's ideas could not be ignored. He had identified a set of important research problems, described a methodology for studying them, and suggested a unified conceptual framework for explaining ecological phenomena.

Clements had been supported by small grants from the Carnegie Institution while he was writing *Plant Succession,* and the institution was enthusiastic about the work. Robert S. Woodward, president of the institution, praised it as "remarkable" and "profoundly instructive," a book that would do much to establish ecology as a legitimate science.[9] While writing the book, Clements had been the chairman of the botany department at the University of Minnesota, a position that he had held for a decade. Not always well-liked by his colleagues, Clements nonetheless had begun to build a small, but respectable, research program within the department. During the five-year period between 1914 and 1919 the department produced ten Ph.D.s, half of them Clements's students.[10]

Both professionally and intellectually Clements seemed to possess characteristics attractive to the administration of the Carnegie Institution. Under Woodward's leadership the funding policy of the institution was moving away from small grants-in-aid in favor of long-term funding of a few "exceptional men." In his letter of appointment Woodward hailed Clements as an exemplary scientist, a man the institution could use to demonstrate its commitment to research.[11] If he was attractive to the Carnegie Institution, the institution was equally attractive to him: an "escaped professor" was how the ecologist described himself when he learned of his appointment.[12] Clements enjoyed teaching and considered himself to be an innovative educator, but research was his passion, and the Carnegie provided him with resources to pursue ecology without interruption. Indeed, it gave him the best of both worlds: he did not have to teach, but graduate students from the University of Nebraska and elsewhere received academic credit for doing research at his laboratory in the Colorado Rockies.[13] He could devote all of his energies to research, and assemble a research group. Compared to the departments of genetics and embryology, the big biological programs at the Carnegie Institution, Clements's budget was quite modest. Nonetheless, he had the money to hire four or five scientists full-time and a number of assistants part-time. The Carnegie also provided Clements with a prestigious forum for promoting his ideas. Most of the books that Clements and his coworkers published, lavishly illustrated with photographs and drawings, appeared in the institution's extensive monograph series.

[9] Robert S. Woodward, "Report of the President, 1916," *Carnegie Institution of Washington Yearbook,* 1916, *15*:3–36, on pp. 9–10.

[10] See register of Ph.D. degrees, *The Bulletin of the University of Minnesota,* 1939, *42*:60–62.

[11] Letter of appointment of Frederic Clements, 17 March 1917, File "Ecology: Director: Personnel," Carnegie Institution of Washington Archives (hereafter **CIW**). On Carnegie policy see Nathan Reingold, "National Science Policy in a Private Foundation: The Carnegie Institution of Washington," in *The Organization of Knowledge in Modern America, 1860–1920,* ed. Alexandra Oleson and John Voss (Baltimore: Johns Hopkins Univ. Press, 1979).

[12] Edith S. Clements, *Adventures in Ecology: Half a Million Miles . . . from Mud to Macadam* (New York: Pageant Press, 1960), p. 102.

[13] This informal arrangement apparently created some tensions between Clements and the botanists at the University of Nebraska, but some graduate students were allowed to do their research under his direction. See the correspondence between Clements and Glenn Goldsmith, Box 62, and between Clements and William Penfound, Box 64, Edith S. and Frederic E. Clements Collection, University of Wyoming (hereafter **Clements coll.**).

By many of Geison's criteria, the research group that Frederic Clements organized at the Carnegie Institution was successful. Its longevity compares favorably with other programs that Geison characterized as enjoying "sustained success." The group was also remarkably productive throughout the decade of the 1920s: during it Clements and his coworkers published numerous articles and at least ten monographs. Although less productive later, the Clementsian research group did spawn at least one influential "descendant" in the early 1930s: a group that continues to work in much altered form at the Carnegie Institution laboratory at Stanford University. Despite these signs of success, the group's historical significance is ambiguous. Clements's ideas were tremendously controversial even during his lifetime. Although today he is universally recognized as an important intellectual pioneer, many ecologists use him as a scapegoat for supposedly discredited ecological concepts.[14] Further, during the 1930s and 1940s the younger members of the research group failed to elaborate Clements's early physiological and organicist perspective on ecology, and it fell to biologists unaffiliated with the Carnegie Institution to develop the perspective later. How can Clements's ambiguous legacy be explained? I believe that the answer lies primarily in the internal dynamics of the research group that he constructed: Clements's research program held considerable intellectual promise, but his research group was unable to build successfully on its leader's early ideas.

II. THE INTERNAL DYNAMICS OF THE CLEMENTSIAN GROUP

Photographs of Clements invariably show an intensely serious individual. By almost all accounts he was aloof, a bit arrogant, and inflexible in his scientific views. So obsessed was he with his research that as a young scientist he would forget to eat or sleep, a practice that sometimes led to hallucinations. Puritanical in personal habits, he abstained from tobacco and alcohol, and was distressed by colleagues who did not. As Roscoe Pound, the noted jurist and a fellow student at the University of Nebraska, commented wryly, "Clements has no redeeming vices." Even in Edith Clements's light-hearted memoir, *Adventures in Ecology,* her husband comes off as a prig.[15]

Given his controversial ideas, his dogmatism, and his prudishness, it is not surprising that Clements made professional enemies during his life. But apparently he was also an inspiring teacher who attracted a devoted coterie of students. Younger ecologists, even some who disagreed sharply with his ideas, were often deeply impressed by him.[16] During the twenty-four years that Clements was affiliated with the Carnegie, many biologists visited or worked briefly at his alpine laboratory in Colorado. A smaller group of scientists can be identified as making up a "Clementsian research group." These scientists worked with Clements for extended periods of time, often for a decade or more. A few members of the smaller group held university positions and worked with Clements only during the summers, but most were employed by Clements to work full-time on his research

[14] See, e.g., Robert P. McIntosh, *The Background of Ecology: Concept and Theory* (Cambridge: Cambridge Univ. Press, 1985), p. 80.

[15] E. Clements, *Adventures in Ecology* (cit. n. 12), p. 226 (hallucinations); and Edith Clements, "Biography of Frederic E. Clements," MS, p. 2 (quoting Pound), Box 109, Clements coll.

[16] Stanley A. Cain, *Foundations of Plant Geography* (New York: Harper & Brothers, 1944), p. xiv.

projects. Members of this group had typically been trained by Clements at the Universities of Nebraska and Minnesota. Intellectually, they usually continued to work within the narrow confines of Clements's research interests: once in the group they apparently had little opportunity or encouragement to expand their research outside the program outlined by their leader. In most cases publications were coauthored, Clements almost invariably being the senior author. The members of the group were not only intellectually subordinate to the Clementsian research program, but also dependent professionally and often financially upon Clements. In most cases these "investigators" had no independent status within the Carnegie Institution. Presumably if Clements had left the institution, the positions of his coworkers would have been terminated. This insecurity had important ramifications for the Clementsians. As we shall see, some members of the group became pawns in the power struggles that engulfed Clements at the Carnegie Institution.

This composite portrait highlights important characteristics shared by members of the Clementsian research group, but it also obscures an equally important stratification within the group. Being associated with Frederic Clements offered different opportunities and posed different problems for the various members of the group. The members possessed different resources for exploiting these opportunities and coping with the problems. In my analysis I divide the Clementsians into three groups, based upon how dependent they were on their leader.

The Inner Clementsians

Several scientists—Edith Clements, Frances Long, Glenn Goldsmith, Gorm Loftfield, and Emmett Martin—spent much of their careers working under Frederic Clements. With the exception of Martin, all of these individuals studied under Clements as either undergraduates or graduate students. Although they all published articles and monographs, their research was so closely related to that of Clements that he must have been directly involved in planning and supervising theirs as well. Little biographical information exists on some of these obscure scientists.[17] My discussion of this inner circle of Clementsians is based primarily on the experiences of the two women in the group: Edith Schwartz Clements and Frances Louise Long.

Edith Clements's status as Frederic's wife makes it easier to find biographical information on her, although it means that her case is by its nature not precisely like those of the other subordinate scientists working with him. Her undergraduate major was German, and she apparently had little interest in the natural sciences before meeting Frederic in her senior year at the University of Nebraska. "However, after marriage," she later wrote, "I immediately turned my attention to this subject under my husband's stimulation and enthusiasm, with the result that I received my Doctor's degree in 1907, with Ecology as my major, Philology and Geology as minors, and have since then worked continuously side by side

[17] Entries for Goldsmith and Martin can be found in *American Men of Science,* 6th and 8th eds. I have been unable to locate detailed biographical information about Loftfield, who was an undergraduate assistant in the botany department at the University of Minnesota when Clements was chairman, and who worked with the Carnegie group throughout the 1920s.

with him."[18] Edith Clements's doctoral research on the microscopic anatomy of leaves was published, and her husband used it in *Research Methods in Ecology* to illustrate the effects of environmental factors on the structure and function of plants.[19] However, although she wrote and illustrated a number of popular field manuals, Edith Clements did very little, if any, independent scientific research after completing her Ph.D.

Frederic and Edith Clements were inseparable (see Figure 1); during forty-six years of marriage they were continually together except for one three-day period shortly after their wedding. Professionally, the two formed a team, but although Frederic was an avowed feminist, the partnership was not egalitarian. As Edith recalled later,

> He furnished the brains and I the manual dexterity. His dislike of using his hands and extraordinary mental gifts and training led to a division of labor in which an early course in business college and experience as secretary to an uncle, enabled me to take over the typing of letters and manuscripts, and as the years passed, of sitting on the running-board of the current automobile and taking his dictation of field notes. . . . Of course all these outside pursuits were additional to my running the house, entertaining the faculty and friends, sewing, marketing, etc. etc.[20]

Edith Clements was a woman of considerable intelligence and creativity. But because she did no scientific research before meeting her husband, was drawn to graduate research in ecology by his "stimulation and enthusiasm," and later published scholarly works only with him as the coauthor, it is probably impossible to determine her intellectual contribution to their partnership. Even if her independent scientific contributions were minor, she did play an important subordinate role in the Clementsian research group. By her own account Edith "humanized" her husband, providing for the day-to-day needs of a man obsessed with his science.[21] Serving as his field assistant, driver, mechanic, secretary, photographer, and illustrator, she also contributed directly to the success of the research program. When Frederic became embroiled in political struggles within the Carnegie Institution, Edith rallied to his support, writing letters on his behalf to institution officials. Such intervention on her part did little to gain institutional support for the Clementsian research group, but it does indicate the degree to which she was involved in her husband's professional life.

Frances Louise Long provides interesting comparisons and contrasts with

---

[18] E. Clements, "Biography of F. E. Clements" (cit. n. 15), p. 2; and E. Clements, *Adventures in Ecology* (cit. n. 12), Ch. 1.

[19] Edith Schwartz Clements, "The Relation of Leaf Structure to Physical Factors," *Transactions of the American Microscopical Society,* 1905, *25*:19–102; and F. E. Clements, *Research Methods* (cit. n. 3), Ch. 3.

[20] E. Clements, "Biography of F. E. Clements" (cit. n. 15), pp. 2–3 (quotation). Such marital partnerships have not been unusual in the history of science; see, e.g., Nancy G. Slack, "Nineteenth-Century American Women Botanists: Wives, Widows, and Work," and Marilyn Bailey Ogilvie, "Marital Collaboration: An Approach to Science," both in *Uneasy Careers and Intimate Lives: Women in Science 1789–1979,* ed. Pnina G. Abir-Am and Dorinda Outram (New Brunswick, N.J.: Rutgers Univ. Press, 1987). I am also indebted to Nancy Slack for providing me with a copy of Slack, "Contrasting Sex Roles in American Botanical Couples," presented at the 1989 meeting of the History of Science Society in Gainesville, Florida.

[21] E. Clements, *Adventures in Ecology* (cit. n. 12), p. 226; and Tobey, *Saving the Prairies* (cit. n. 4), p. 76.

Figure 1. Frederic and Edith Clements in the field near La Jolla, California, in 1921.
Courtesy of the American Heritage Center, University of Wyoming.

Edith Clements. Long spent virtually her entire adult life working closely with
Frederic Clements.[22] She entered the University of Nebraska when Clements was
a young botany professor, receiving her B.A. in 1906. She followed her teacher to
the University of Minnesota, earning both an M.A. (1914) and a Ph.D. (1917)
under his direction. During her graduate studies she served as an instructor in the
department of botany, a position also held by Edith Clements during this period.
When Clements was appointed research associate with the Carnegie Institution
in 1917, Long became his assistant, a position that she held until Clements retired
in 1941. After 1941 she continued to work with Clements in a small laboratory at
his home in Santa Barbara. She died in 1946, less than one year after her mentor.

To a much greater extent than Edith Clements, Frances Long was a scientist in
her own right. Her research interests complemented those of Frederic Clements,
but she possessed skills that he lacked. Despite his physiological rhetoric and his
insistence that ecology become an experimental science, Clements was not a
skilled experimental biologist. Long, on the other hand, had a genuine interest in
physiological problems and the ability to work with laboratory instruments. Her
dissertation, "The Quantitative Determination of Photosynthate in Relation to
Light in Various Species," reflected her teacher's interest in relating plant functions to physical factors, but it also involved the type of instrumental analysis that
Clements probably would have been unable to do on his own.[23] Long was not a

---

[22] "Frances Louise Long," *Plant Physiology,* 1946, *21*:371–372.
[23] Register of Ph.D. degrees (cit. n. 10). Long's dissertation was later published as "The Quantitative
Determination of Photosynthetic Activity in Plants," *Physiological Researches,* 1919, *2*:277–300.

prolific researcher, but during the next twenty-five years she authored or coauthored at least seven articles and three monographs. Although none of these appear to have been very influential, some are intriguing, at least in retrospect. For example, in 1934 Long published a paper on the use of the bomb calorimeter in ecological research.[24] This article seems to have been largely ignored by her contemporaries, but it foreshadowed the widespread use of this instrument after World War II by biologists interested in ecological energetics.

The most striking feature of Long's publications is their diversity. Her books and articles covered a wide range of topics, including calorimetric techniques, histological techniques, measurement of photosynthesis, measurement of latex content in plants, pollination ecology, and inheritance of acquired traits. The brevity of her bibliography combined with this diversity gives the impression of a scientist who never found an intellectual niche to exploit; moving from one problem to another, she never left a lasting mark on any area of research.

Why was Frances Long not a more productive or influential scientist? One can suggest several plausible reasons. Part of the explanation lies in the relationship between Frederic Clements and his coworkers. None of the scientists who worked with him found it easy to establish an independent professional or intellectual identity. Working in the research group, in most cases, meant subordinating one's ideas to the Clementsian research program. Despite his programmatic statements about the close relationship between physiology and ecology, there is little indication that Clements ever encouraged Long to develop her dissertation work on photosynthesis into an independent line of physiological research. Instead, she apparently assisted him on whatever research project interested him at the moment. During the last decade of her life Long became almost totally preoccupied with Clements's quixotic attempts to demonstrate the inheritance of acquired traits.

Even with active encouragement from her mentor, Long might never have developed into an independent scientist. H. A. Spoehr, chairman of the Division of Plant Biology at the Carnegie, charged that she had limited scientific abilities, that she was incapable of truly creative research, and that even as a technician she required constant, minute supervision.[25] But while Spoehr had the opportunity to observe Long's work, he was not a disinterested critic. He and Clements were professional rivals, and they were embroiled in a bitter struggle over control of botanical research within the Carnegie Institution. Furthermore, Spoehr's specialty was plant physiology, specifically the study of photosynthesis. An ambitious scientist, jockeying for influence within the Carnegie Institution, he may have been unsympathetic toward Long's research in this area, particularly because she was working so closely with Clements.

Long's experience at the Carnegie Institution was perhaps made more difficult by the fact that she was a woman. The tone of Spoehr's criticism suggests a sexist attitude. For example, he questioned whether Long was capable of meeting the rigors of scientific life with its requirements for intellectual independence, ab-

[24] Frances Louise Long, "Application of Calorimetric Methods to Ecological Research," *Plant Physiology,* 1934, *9*:323–337. For Long's publications see "Frances Louise Long" (cit. n. 22).

[25] H. A. Spoehr to J. C. Merriam, 23 Sept. 1929, and Spoehr to F. E. Clements, 1 July 1929, Director's File "Laboratory for Plant Physiology," CIW.

stract thinking, and creativity. Spoehr suggested that she pursue a career in a more traditional feminine field, such as human relations. But if Long was the victim of sexual discrimination, it must be noted that many of her male colleagues also suffered under Spoehr's dictatorial leadership. By cutting Clements's budget, Spoehr was able to eliminate scientists whom he considered inferior. Long was able to keep her position in 1929, but Glenn W. Goldsmith, another member of the Clementsian research group, was forced to resign. And when Clements retired in 1941, his coworker Emmett V. Martin was also forced to do the same.[26] Even though both Goldsmith and Martin held doctoral degrees, published articles and books, and worked with Clements for many years, the Carnegie Institution considered them to be temporary assistants to whom the institution owed nothing more than a paycheck. When Long finally retired after twenty-four years of work, she at least received a pension from the Carnegie.

Clements clearly benefited from having a devoted group of assistants to carry out the fieldwork that he apparently found so distasteful. But what rewards did the research group provide for the inner group of Clementsians? The men and women who surround Clements were marginal scientists. Given their modest talents it seems unlikely that they would have been able to achieve independent careers in research. For such individuals the Clementsian research group offered a number of attractions. It provided an environment within which they could continue to work as scientists, under the auspices of a prestigious research institution, and under the direction of a prominent senior scientist they admired. Edith Clements acknowledged that marrying Frederic allowed her to share his "adventures in ecology."[27] There is reason to believe that other members of the research group felt much the same way. Glenn Goldsmith left a career in college teaching to work with Clements, and there is little indication that he relished a return to the classroom when he was forced to resign from the Carnegie Institution ten years later. Given the limited career opportunities for women in science, working with Clements might have been particularly attractive to Frances Long. Long probably could have found a position teaching at a small college or perhaps even at a university, but the Carnegie Institution provided her with the opportunity to pursue a career in research. Although Clements paid her several hundred dollars less than her male counterparts, her salary was higher than that of many women teaching in the Midwest.[28]

[26] See the correspondence concerning Goldsmith exchanged by Clements, Spoehr, and J. C. Merriam, July and Aug. 1929, File "Plant Biology: Investigations of Dr. Clements, 1927–1929," CIW. For Martin's situation at the Carnegie see G. W. Gilbert to H. A. Spoehr, 10 Aug. 1940, File "Plant Biology: Clements, Frederic E., 1940–1941," CIW. Clements's research group was not the only target of Spoehr's budget cuts: he eliminated even well-established programs such as the Carnegie's desert laboratory in Tucson; see Bowers, *Sense of Place* (cit. n. 8), Chs. 13, 17.

[27] E. Clements, *Adventures in Ecology* (cit. n. 12), p. 222; and Slack, "Women Botanists" (cit. n. 20).

[28] In 1920, three years after completing her Ph.D., Long was paid $1,800. At that time the average salary of female associate professors at the University of Nebraska was $1,830; assistant professors earned an average salary of $1,333. Average salaries paid to women at other schools in Nebraska ranged from $1,090 (Doane College) to $1,677 (three state normal schools). See "Opportunities and Salaries of Women in the Teaching Profession in Nebraska," *Journal of the Association of Collegiate Alumnae,* March–April, 1920, *13*:10–13. An excellent general discussion of the position of women in academia during the 1920s can be found in Margaret W. Rossiter, *Women Scientists in America: Struggles and Strategies to 1940* (Baltimore: Johns Hopkins Univ. Press, 1982), Chs. 6–7.

Semi-Independent Clementsians

Edith Clements may have found working with her husband to be an adventure, but more independent scientists chafed under his domineering personality. Although working with Clements provided significant advantages, these scientists found it necessary to distance themselves from the master intellectually, professionally, and geographically. Just how difficult this could be is illustrated by the career of John Weaver.

Weaver was one of five students of Clements to receive the Ph.D. from the University of Minnesota, completing his dissertation on the vegetation of eastern Washington State and Idaho in 1917.[29] He had already been teaching at the University of Nebraska as a graduate student, was promoted to full professor, and throughout the 1920s he spent his summers working as a member of Clements's research group. During a long and productive career as a botanist at the University of Nebraska, he was elected president of the Ecological Society of America in 1930. At the time of his death in 1966 he was recognized as the foremost authority on the ecology of North American grasslands.

Unlike those who worked full-time for Clements, Weaver pursued independent research, and he continued to do so long after he formally severed his ties with the Carnegie Institution in 1930. This research nonetheless fell within the broad conceptual framework of Clementsian ecology. As a grasslands ecologist Weaver continued to work in an area that Clements had pioneered at the turn of the century. During the 1920s and 1930s he coauthored a number of important books with his mentor. Although late in his career he apparently abandoned Clementsian organicism, his discussion of vegetational change on the North American prairies remained strongly influenced by his teacher's views on succession.[30]

Despite his professional independence, Weaver had difficulty severing the student-teacher relationship with Clements. Throughout his correspondence with his mentor, including letters written two decades after finishing his Ph.D., Weaver always opened his letters with a respectful "Dear Dr. Clements." Clements, on the other hand, used the less formal salutation "Dear Weaver." This seemingly trivial stylistic difference reflected the subordinate role that Weaver continued to play in the Clementsian research group throughout the 1920s. From Clements's perspective, Weaver was simply part of the larger "organic whole" of the Clementsian program.[31] Clements outlined the theoretical scope of the research, and Weaver carried out the actual fieldwork. Although he apparently never questioned this division of labor, Weaver occasionally became annoyed at Clements's tendency to dictate overly ambitious research projects. In the case of their joint research project on plant competition, for example, Weaver was faced with the arduous task of excavating the roots of numerous species of prairie plants, some of which extended many feet into the soil. Commenting on his

[29] Register of Ph.D. Degrees (cit. n. 10); and Edward E. Dale, Jr., "Resolution of Respect: John Ernst Weaver 1884–1966," *Bulletin of the Ecological Society of America,* 1967, *48*:107–109.

[30] J. E. Weaver, *North American Prairie* (Lincoln, Nebr.: Johnsen Publishing Co., 1954), pp. 314–325. Ronald Tobey emphasizes Weaver's disillusionment with important elements of Clementsian ecology after the great drought of the 1930s; see *Saving the Prairies* (cit. n. 4), Ch. 7.

[31] F. E. Clements to R. S. Woodward, 25 April 1918, and Clements to J. E. Weaver, 19 March 1918, Box 62, Clements coll.

mentor's plans for this project, Weaver wrote, "Now in regard to the root outline [for their book *Plant Competition*] let me say that it does not take much outline to involve an enormous amount of work."[32]

Clements not only dictated the direction and scope of Weaver's early research but also meddled in the younger scientist's professional life. Before he joined the Clementsian research group, Weaver had prepared a manuscript dealing with his research on the roots of prairie plants. He submitted the manuscript to the *Botanical Gazette,* edited by John Merle Coulter at the University of Chicago. The paper was accepted and was scheduled for publication, but under pressure from Clements, Weaver retracted the manuscript so that it could be published by the Carnegie Institution.[33] Clements made no attempt to hide his motivations in this matter: he was in the process of building a research group, and he believed that having Weaver's work appear in a Carnegie publication would enhance the status of the Clementsian program within the institution. This was not an isolated incident. Less than a year later Clements again pressured Weaver to withdraw a manuscript from the *Botanical Gazette.* This time Weaver held his ground, for he realized that his professional reputation was being threatened. He did not want to antagonize Coulter, nor did he want to have all of his work appear in Carnegie publications.[34]

Clements originally planned to have Weaver join his research group as a full-time worker.[35] But although Weaver preferred research to teaching, he ultimately refused Clements's offer. He based his decision on a number of factors, including the access to graduate students and equipment that his university position provided. Financial security was also a consideration. He was a tenured professor, and the position that Clements was offering came without comparable institutional status. Combining his salary from the University of Nebraska with the stipend that Clements paid for part-time research during the summer, Weaver could earn more than the $2,500 that Clements offered him as a full-time Carnegie investigator. This was not an unimportant consideration for Weaver, who was supporting a wife and four children. Another factor, though one that Weaver did not articulate, may have been his need to free himself from Clements's domineering personality. By remaining at the University of Nebraska, Weaver could continue to work during the summers with his mentor, but he could also maintain a degree of professional independence impossible for those working with Clements on a day-to-day basis.

Working at the Periphery of the Group

Besides his former students, Clements collaborated on major projects with a number of well-established scientists, notably the taxonomist Harvey Monroe Hall, the ecologist Victor Shelford, and the paleontologist Ralph Chaney. Some of these professional associations lasted for a considerable time: for example, Shelford and Clements spent over ten years writing *Bio-Ecology,* one of the first

---

[32] Weaver to Clements, 22 May 1918, *ibid.*
[33] See the correspondence between Clements and Weaver, Feb. and March 1918, *ibid.*
[34] Clements to Weaver, 17 Oct., 12 Nov. 1918, and Weaver to Clements, 30 Oct. 1918, *ibid.*
[35] Clements to Weaver, 23 Dec. 1918, 7 Jan. 1919, and Weaver to Clements, 2 Jan. 1919, *ibid.*

attempts to unite plant and animal ecology.[36] Although neither Shelford nor Chaney became a member of the Clementsian research group, Hall was hired by Clements and worked under him for nearly a decade.

Hall's case provides a striking contrast with those of John Weaver and Clements's other workers. Unlike most members of the Clementsian research group, Hall was an outsider with no ties to the University of Minnesota or Nebraska. He was trained as a plant taxonomist at the University of California at Berkeley, receiving his Ph.D. in 1906.[37] Hall and Clements were the same age, and by the time Hall joined the Carnegie Institution in 1919, he had already established his reputation as a talented taxonomist. He was therefore Clements's coequal to a much greater extent than any other scientist in the group. Significantly, he was the only member of the team to appear as senior author on a major Carnegie Institution publication written with Clements.

Before joining the Clementsian research group, Hall was a professor of botany at the University of California and a botanist at the state agricultural experiment station. During his seventeen years on the faculty Hall made major contributions toward building the department into an important research center, adding 200,000 specimens to the herbarium and actively lobbying for a botanical garden. He formally resigned his position in 1919 only after protracted negotiations, and he maintained close ties with the university during the period that he was associated with the Carnegie Institution. Like Weaver, he was concerned about exchanging the financial security of a faculty position at a major university for the uncertainties of working for Clements. In the end, a compromise was reached; he formally resigned his faculty position but was appointed "honorary curator" of the herbarium and allowed to maintain an office on the Berkeley campus.[38] Presumably if the arrangement with Clements turned sour, Hall would have been welcomed back by his former employer.

Hall's reluctance to leave the University of California was undoubtedly largely due to economic concerns, but it was also partly intellectual. By the time he joined Clements's research group, both men had established themselves professionally, and Hall realized that the two approached research in very different ways. "You are naturally radical and ready to take chances," Hall wrote Clements in 1918; "I am naturally conservative and want to carry the public with us. You are so anxious to get our results into immediate use that the early issuance of popular manuals is an important part of your program; I also want to serve in this manner but anticipate more keenly the intensive and detailed systematic studies in herbarium, garden, and field."[39] Hall's later experience would bear out these concerns; being allied with a scientific "radical" like Clements could be a risky business. Clements had many vociferous critics, and, as we shall see, Hall occasionally found himself caught up in the ecologist's scientific controversies.

Hall maintained a high degree of scientific independence, in contrast to Weaver

[36] Frederic E. Clements and Victor E. Shelford, *Bio-Ecology* (New York: John Wiley & Sons, 1939).

[37] For Hall's career at Berkeley see Ernest Brown Babcock, "Harvey Monroe Hall," *University of California Publications in Botany,* 1934, *17*:355–368; and Lincoln Constance, *Botany at Berkeley: The First Hundred Years* (privately printed, 1978).

[38] H. M. Hall to F. E. Clements, 17 Jan., 19 Jan. 1919, 25 Feb. 1919, Box 62, Clements coll.; and Babcock, "Harvey Monroe Hall" (cit. n. 37), p. 358.

[39] Hall to Clements, 18 Dec. 1918, Box 62, Clements coll.

and other members of Clements's research group. Although he and Clements did some fieldwork together, Hall continued to do most of his botanical research near Berkeley. While the rest of the Clementsians collaborated primarily with one another, Hall worked with biologists outside the group. He began a research project with his best friend, the University of California geneticist E. B. Babcock, just when Clements's relationship with Carnegie geneticists was deteriorating. He also established close ties with European botanists during his travels abroad.[40]

Clements brought Hall to the Carnegie Institution to help him develop his program in "experimental taxonomy." As Clements envisioned it, experimental taxonomy was to be a hybrid of ecology and traditional taxonomy. He hoped to demonstrate the evolutionary relationships among closely allied species, primarily through the use of transplant experiments. Building on the earlier experiments of Gaston Bonnier in the French Alps, Clements believed that by transplanting a species into a new environment one could, in some cases, transform it into a different, though closely related, species.[41] Hall never embraced Clements's neo-Lamarckian interpretations of these experiments, and, as we shall see, he was indirectly involved with their refutation. But during the early 1920s he shared Clements's enthusiasm for applying experimental methods to taxonomic research. The result of their collaboration was a provocative monograph, *The Phylogenetic Method in Taxonomy*. Although Hall and Clements reported the results of few actual experiments, their work caused a stir because it lumped many small species into a few large ones. Hall was forced to defend the monograph against criticism by Per Axel Rydberg at the International Congress of Plant Sciences held at Cornell University shortly after the work was published. Rydberg's vituperative attack on Hall and Clements apparently alienated many members of the audience. At least, Hall believed that he and Clements had carried the day. Not only did the audience accept their taxonomic revisions, but many apparently were also sympathetic to the idea of an experimental taxonomy.[42]

Hall relished Rydberg's defeat at Ithaca, but by nature he was not a confrontational individual. The events at the International Congress undoubtedly impressed upon him the dangers of being too closely associated with Clements's controversial ideas. And by 1926 Hall was becoming restless under the other's domineering leadership. Hall wanted to expand the scope of experimental taxonomy, particularly to incorporate methods from cytology and genetics. He had already published one joint paper with Babcock, and he wanted to cultivate cooperation with other geneticists, both in the Carnegie Institution and elsewhere. Clements was opposed to these plans, encouraging Hall to restrict his research to transplant experiments.[43]

[40] Babcock, "Harvey Monroe Hall" (cit. n. 37).

[41] Joel B. Hagen, "Experimentalists and Naturalists in Twentieth-Century Botany: Experimental Taxonomy, 1920–1950," *Journal of the History of Biology*, 1984, *17*:249–270.

[42] See Harvey Monroe Hall and Frederic E. Clements, *The Phylogenetic Method in Taxonomy* (Washington, D.C.: Carnegie Institution of Washington, 1923). For Hall's version of the imbroglio at Cornell see H. M. Hall to Carlotta Case Hall, 21 Aug. 1926, H. M. Hall papers, Bancroft Library, University of California, Berkeley; and Hall to J. C. Merriam, 25 Aug. 1926, File "Hall, Harvey M," CIW. Rydberg's attack on Hall and Clements was published as "Scylla and Charybdis," *Proceedings of the International Congress of Plant Sciences*, 1926, pp. 1539–1551.

[43] Hall to Merriam, 25 Aug. 1926; and H. M. Hall, "Contacts Between Experimental Taxonomy and Genetics," unpublished memo, File "Hall, Harvey M," CIW. For Hall's ideas on experimental

Hall and Clements remained on friendly terms, but during the late 1920s their relationship underwent a significant change. During this period the Carnegie Institution was reorganizing its program in botanical research. Against Clements's opposition, a new botanical laboratory was built on the campus of Stanford University. This facility was to be the headquarters for all botanical research, and it was headed by Clements's nemesis, H. A. Spoehr. These institutional changes worked to Hall's advantage. He had advocated closer ties between geneticists, ecologists, and taxonomists, and before the reorganization he cultivated a cordial relationship with Carnegie geneticists such as A. F. Blakeslee. Unlike Clements, who continued to work in relative isolation in Colorado and in Santa Barbara, Hall easily moved his base of operations from Berkeley to Stanford. While the antagonism between Clements and Spoehr was growing, Hall apparently got along well with the Carnegie administrator. He served with Spoehr and Blakeslee on the committee responsible for reorganizing botanical research at the Carnegie Institution. In the course of the reorganization administrative control over experimental taxonomy gradually shifted to Hall, and he was able to organize his own independent research team.

Hall's ascendancy within the Carnegie Institution was accompanied by Clements's decline. During the 1930s the latter's prestige within the Carnegie Institution continued to erode, and his research program was reduced to little more than an increasingly anachronistic attempt to demonstrate the inheritance of acquired traits. Ironically, it was the "experimental taxonomists" that Hall had hired who were most responsible for repudiating Clements's neo-Lamarckian claims. By the late 1930s they were providing a convincing Darwinian explanation for the results of Clements's transplant experiments.[44]

Hall did not live to see his own program in experimental taxonomy develop fully, but after his untimely death in 1932, his team—Jens Clausen, David Keck, and William Hiesey—perpetuated and greatly expanded his ideas. While the original Clementsian idea of experimental taxonomy was merely a hybrid of ecology and taxonomy, Hall had a much more ambitious interdisciplinary agenda. His close personal and professional relationship with E. B. Babcock convinced him of the important roles that cytology and genetics could play in evolutionary studies. With the hiring of Clausen, a respected Danish cytogeneticist, Hall brought a new dimension to the Carnegie Institution's programs in experimental taxonomy. Transplant experiments remained an important tool for Clausen, Keck, and Hiesey, but cytogenetics provided both a convincing theoretical explanation for evolutionary relationships among species and a new set of techniques for determining these relationships. Clements's program, with its emphasis upon inheritance of acquired traits, became an embarrassment to the Carnegie Institution. But by combining cytogenetics with taxonomy and ecology, Clausen, Keck,

---

taxonomy see Hall, "Heredity and Environment—As Illustrated by Transplant Experiments," *Scientific Monthly,* 1932, *35*:289–302; and Ernest Brown Babcock and Harvey Monroe Hall, "*Hemizonia congesta*: A Genetic, Ecologic, and Taxonomic Study of Hayfield Tarweeds," *University of California Publications in Botany,* 1924, *13*:15–100.

[44] Jens Clausen, David D. Keck, and William M. Hiesey, *Experimental Studies on the Nature of Species, I: Effect of Varied Environments on Western North American Plants* (Washington, D.C.: Carnegie Institution of Washington, 1940).

and Hiesey moved Hall's research program into the mainstream of the modern evolutionary synthesis.[45]

The case of Harvey Monroe Hall provides an interesting contrast with that of John Weaver. Both men were productive scientists, but Weaver had much greater difficulty asserting his independence from Clements. Weaver did important research on the ecology of North American prairies, and to a large extent, Clements's legacy as a grasslands ecologist rested on the later work of his most talented student. But both professionally and intellectually Weaver spent most of his career working in Clements's shadow. Hall, on the other hand, took one of Clements's most suggestive concepts—the idea of an experimental taxonomy—and developed it in novel ways that the ecologist had not considered. But Hall's innovations came at Clements's expense, both institutionally and intellectually. Hall was not ambitious politically, and there is little evidence that he intended to discredit his colleague. However, he found it impossible to develop an independent line of research within the social context of the Clementsian research group. When administrative changes within the Carnegie Institution provided him with the means to explore his new ideas, Hall jumped at the opportunity. Inevitably, this involved making a break with the man who had brought him to the Carnegie in the first place.

III. CONCLUSION

The Carnegie Institution provided Frederic Clements with financial and institutional resources unavailable to most other ecologists of the period. Particularly during his early years at the institution Clements used these resources effectively to promote his ideas. These ideas were influential in his day, and to a considerable extent they shaped the future of ecology. Nearly fifty years after his death, some ecologists acknowledge the important positive influence of Clements's ideas on their work. Another indicator of his success is the common complaint by his critics that Clementsian ideas persist in today's ecology.[46]

One may contrast this success as an individual scientist with Clements's inability to create an effective research group. In retrospect it is easy to see an important weakness in the group. Members were apparently faced with two alternatives: submit completely to the Clementsian research program or break with the team. Clements's domineering personality and dogmatically held views on ecology stifled creativity. He may have been a benevolent dictator, much admired by a devoted group of former students, but he was nonetheless a dictator. The organicism

[45] Hagen, "Experimentalists and Naturalists" (cit. n. 41); and G. Ledyard Stebbins, "Botany and the Synthetic Theory of Evolution," in *The Evolutionary Synthesis: Perspectives on the Unification of Biology,* ed. Ernst Mayr and William B. Provine (Cambridge, Mass.: Harvard Univ. Press, 1980). After Clements's death the Carnegie Institution refused to publish the results of his transplant experiments; see E. S. Clements to H. A. Spoehr, 11 Oct. 1946, and Spoehr to E. S. Clements, 5 Nov. 1946, File "Clements, Frederic—Retirement," CIW. Edith Clements later arranged to have the work published as Frederic E. Clements, Emmett V. Martin, and Frances L. Long, *Adaptation and Origin in the Plant World: The Role of the Environment in Evolution* (Waltham, Mass.: Chronica Botanica, 1950).

[46] For a positive assessment of Clements's influence see F. H. Bormann, "Lessons from Hubbard Brook," in *Proceedings of the Chaparral Ecosystem Research Meeting,* ed. E. Keller, S. Cooper, and J. DeVries (California Water Resources Center Report 62) (Davis: Univ. California, 1985). For criticism see, e.g., Daniel Simberloff, "A Succession of Paradigms in Ecology: Essentialism to Materialism and Probabilism," *Synthese,* 1980, *43*:3–39; and McIntosh, *Background of Ecology* (cit. n. 14), pp. 80–83.

that he saw in nature provided a metaphor for his view of the research group. In Clementsian ecology a community was an organism composed of various plants each of which maintained its individuality, but the overall structure and functioning of the community was determined by one or a few dominant species. For Clements the research group was also an organic entity, and the goals of the group coincided precisely with his own professional goals.[47]

The case of Clements and his coworkers provides an interesting contrast to claims made by other historians. In an important study of research groups in biochemistry, Joseph Fruton argues that the personalities of group leaders are less important than their abilities to identify important scientific problems and channel the efforts of groups toward solving them.[48] Personality cannot always be separated from insight and motivation, however, and the attributes of subordinates may be as important as those of the leader. In his idea of experimental taxonomy Clements identified an important set of problems, and he suggested some innovative approaches to solving them. At first he encouraged Hall's efforts to expand this area of research, but later his domineering style stifled the taxonomist's work. Hall finally broke with his leader and established a rival research group. Both intellectually and institutionally, this split worked to Clements's disadvantage.

Research groups are not a necessary feature of science; isolated scientists are capable of making major scientific contributions. But research groups, particularly effective ones, may greatly speed the conceptual development of a science. David Hull claims that research groups are like demes, the freely interbreeding populations of evolutionary theory.[49] Within the informal social context created by the group, ideas may be modified and transmitted much more rapidly than they can through the formal channels of the more extended scientific community. A research group may also function as an intellectual buffer between a scientist and the larger scientific community. New concepts are often problematic; they contain ambiguities, inconsistencies, and unacknowledged assumptions. Through the everyday give-and-take that occurs within a group, errors can be detected and eliminated before the concept faces scrutiny from a skeptical public. When controversies arise, the group can rally to its support. As Pamela Henson shows in her article in this volume, such cooperation within a research group may play a crucial role in establishing a research tradition. Like Clements, John Henry Comstock put forward ideas that were potentially fruitful, but controversial. Unlike Clements, Comstock recruited a large group of students who successfully expanded and perfected these ideas.

Without an effective research group, Clements was deprived of this important mechanism for developing his ideas. Many of his original ideas had an enormous impact on the future intellectual development of ecology: on theories of succession, on ideas concerning the structure and classification of plant communities, and on the ecosystem concept. But none of these later intellectual developments

[47] Clements described the research group as a kind of organism on a number of occasions; see, e.g., Clements to R. S. Woodward, 25 April 1918, Box 62, Clements coll.; and Clements to J. C. Merriam, 12 Aug. 1929, File "Plant Biology: Investigations of Dr. Clements, 1927–1929," CIW.

[48] Joseph S. Fruton, *Contrasts in Scientific Style: Research Groups in the Chemical and Biochemical Sciences* (Philadelphia: American Philosophical Society, 1990), p. 3.

[49] David Hull, *Science as a Process: An Evolutionary Account of the Social and Conceptual Development of Science* (Chicago: Univ. Chicago Press, 1988), pp. 22–23.

were the products of his research group. Rather, they were the creation of outsiders, who sometimes reacted against Clements's original ideas.[50] The Carnegie Institution provided Clements with an effective platform for disseminating these ideas, but the Clementsian research group did not provide an environment conducive to nurturing and developing them. Clements lacked the necessary characteristics of intellectual leadership, and many of his subordinates lacked the necessary characteristics of discipleship. The legacies of some influential scientists derive from the research traditions that they establish, but it is difficult to draw an extended "family tree" rooted in Frederic Clements. Philosophical organicism notwithstanding, he remained the quintessential individualistic scientist.

[50] See Joel B. Hagen, *An Entangled Bank: The Origins of Ecosystem Ecology* (New Brunswick, N.J.: Rutgers Univ. Press, 1992), Chs. 4–5.

Sir George Darwin and a British School of Geophysics

By David Kushner

A STUDY OF SIR GEORGE DARWIN illuminates many issues in the history and historiography of science, and of research schools in particular. Darwin played a crucial role in the emergence of a new discipline, modern geophysics. The problems he attacked and the methodologies he used were interdisciplinary in nature. He developed his own personal "style" of applied mathematics and contributed to the peculiarly British style of geophysics that subsequently emerged. Finally, and a significant point for this volume, he held a pivotal position in a large social network—as research leader, teacher, correspondent, and friend to a growing number of geophysically inclined scientists around the turn of the century.[1]

George Howard Darwin, the second son of Charles and an elder brother of Francis, was born at Down on 9 July 1845.[2] By the time of his death sixty-seven years later, he was recognized as one of the most eminent scientists of his generation. He was the world's leading authority on the tides. His cosmogonical theories

* Department of History, North Carolina State University, Raleigh, North Carolina 27695–8108.

I would like to thank Gerald L. Geison, Frederic L. Holmes, Frances Coulborn Kohler, and Arnold Thackray for careful readings of earlier versions of this paper, as well as my fellow participants at the Yale Conference on Research Schools, New Haven, 30 November–1 December 1990, for comments.

[1] For a thorough analysis of the emergence of modern geophysics in Britain and for Darwin's centrality in those developments see David Kushner, "The Emergence of Geophysics in Nineteenth-Century Britain" (Ph.D. diss., Princeton Univ., 1990; University Microfilms 9104334 [1991]). Other important, if tangential, studies include Stephen G. Brush, "Nineteenth-Century Debates about the Inside of the Earth: Solid, Liquid, or Gas?" *Annals of Science,* 1979, *36*:225–254; Joe D. Burchfield, *Lord Kelvin and the Age of the Earth* (New York: Science History Publications, 1975); Mott T. Greene, *Geology in the Nineteenth Century: Changing Views of a Changing World* (Ithaca, N.Y.: Cornell Univ. Press, 1982); Walter Kertz, "Die Entwicklung der Geophysik zur eigenständigen Wissenschaft," *Mitteilungen der Gauss-Gesellschaft, Göttingen,* 1979, *16*:41–54; Crosbie Smith, "Geologists and Mathematicians: The Rise of Physical Geology," in *Wranglers and Physicists: Studies on Cambridge Physics in the Nineteenth Century,* ed. Peter M. Harman (Manchester: Manchester Univ. Press, 1985), pp. 49–83; Smith, "William Hopkins and the Shaping of Dynamical Geology: 1830–1860," *British Journal for the History of Science,* 1989, *22*:27–52; and Smith and M. Norton Wise, *Energy and Empire: A Biographical Study of Lord Kelvin* (Cambridge: Cambridge Univ. Press, 1989).

[2] George was the fifth child of Charles and Emma, the third of those who survived childhood. Family sketches include those by Francis Darwin, "Memoir of Sir George Darwin," in George Howard Darwin, *Scientific Papers,* 5 vols. (Cambridge: Cambridge Univ. Press, 1907–1916), Vol. V, pp. ix–xxxiii; Gwen Raverat, *Period Piece* (New York: W. W. Norton, 1953); and Margaret E. Keynes, *A House by the River: Newnham Grange to Darwin College* (Cambridge: Darwin College, 1976). The most valuable obituary is by Darwin's former student S. S. Hough, "Sir George Howard Darwin, 1845–1912," *Proceedings of the Royal Society,* Series A, 1914, *89*:i–xi. See also Zdeněk Kopal, "George Howard Darwin," *Dictionary of Scientific Biography (DSB),* ed. Charles C. Gillispie (New York: Scribners, 1970–1980), Vol. III, pp. 582–584; and the other sources cited there.

concerning the evolution of the earth-moon system were widely accepted. And he held a central position in the scientific aristocracy of late Victorian and Edwardian Britain. Darwin became a Fellow of the Royal Society in 1879; he was elected to the Plumian Professorship of Astronomy and Experimental Philosophy at Cambridge in 1883; and he was made a Knight Commander of the Bath in 1905 after his successful presidency of the British Association for the Advancement of Science (BAAS) on its tour of South Africa following the Boer War. His list of honors is as diverse as it is lengthy. He was awarded the medals of several societies, including the Copley Medal of the Royal Society, the country's highest scientific award. He was also at various times president, vice-president, or council member of numerous organizations. Darwin liked to joke with the astronomer Sir David Gill about their "race" to see who garnered the most honors, and at the time of his death in 1912 he had just edged Gill out with his doctorates from nine universities, foreign memberships of eighteen academies, and correspondentships of ten foreign academies. If such honors and titles give any measure of the man, then in the eyes of his contemporaries Darwin's importance was considerable.

What did George Darwin actually do, and why was it important? To answer that question requires an appreciation of the main concerns and scientific approaches that shaped the prehistory of modern geophysics. Three central interdisciplinary problems were crucial to the coalescence of a nascent community of scientists in Victorian Britain concerned specifically with questions about the nature and history of the earth as a physical body. These were the structure of the earth and the thickness of its crust; the age of the earth; and the astronomical and physical causes of glacial epochs, or ice ages. There were also three ways, broadly categorized, to treat these interdisciplinary problems. One way involved the techniques and concerns of the disciplines of mathematics and physics, and a second way was similarly rooted within the discipline of geology.

But the third approach, the scientific center of Darwin's life, as it is the focus of this essay, was the explicit attempt to apply the techniques and methods of mathematical physics to the concerns of geology. The result was a new strand of applied mathematics and physics of the earth that was variously called physical geology, terrestrial physics, even telluric physiology, and only later geophysics. In this study I will illustrate the ways in which this new, highly interdisciplinary strand, born in the early Victorian period, was transformed in the remarkable hands of George Darwin through his own brand of applied mathematics. I will also explore the nature of this emerging specialty and its peculiarly British national style to ask whether there existed a school of British geophysics headed by Darwin.

I. THE STATE OF GEOPHYSICAL SCIENCE BY THE 1870s

The early history of the geophysical sciences in Britain was shaped by two major figures in the mid-nineteenth century, William Hopkins and William Thomson. In 1835 Hopkins coined the term *physical geology* in an explicit attempt to apply mathematical analysis to the mechanical and physical principles that must underlie the general laws of certain geological phenomena.[3] Hopkins's three-part series

---

[3] William Hopkins, "Researches in Physical Geology" (read 4 May 1835), *Transactions of the Cambridge Philosophical Society,* 1838, 6:1–84, on pp. 1, 9. On aspects of Hopkins's physical geology

of articles "Researches in Physical Geology" (1839–1842) was a conscious attempt to institute his new branch of science, physical geology—to realize Charles Lyell's desideratum that geology become a physical science, emulating physical astronomy.[4] Indeed, Hopkins's memoirs may have seemed to be more astronomy than geology, for they chiefly involved a specific investigation of the phenomena of precession and nutation. In the past these phenomena had been studied by mathematicians and astronomers who assumed the earth to be a solid, rigid body. But no body is perfectly rigid, and most geologists thought the earth was primarily liquid, being covered by a crust less than 50 miles thick. Hopkins treated the problem from a geologist's perspective, but he analyzed it with the tools of higher mathematics. Somewhat to his surprise he found that the minimum thickness of the crust must be 800 to 1,000 miles, otherwise the precessional constant would differ significantly from what it was known to be. Geologists were generally not at all pleased with this result, for a thinner crust had enabled them to explain surface phenomena such as volcanoes, geysers, and hot springs, as well as elevatory pressures, as due to direct communication with a vast lava ocean only a few miles down. But some of those mathematically trained were not satisfied either, arguing especially with Hopkins's initial assumptions.[5] Despite the disagreements, Hopkins's work represents a direct attempt to elucidate questions about the nature of the earth for its own sake, with the tools of mathematics and physics but not with those disciplines' concerns.

The second major contributor to physical geology was William Thomson (Lord Kelvin). Thomson is well known for his central role in the development of thermodynamics and for his attempt at basing physics on energy principles instead of force. He also played a key part in mathematical physical geology, a part scarcely recognized except for his notoriety in the debates over the age of the earth.[6] As that traditional story goes, it was the quick arithmetic of Charles Darwin's singular attempt at estimating geological time in the *Origin of Species*—300 million years for the denudation of the Weald—that provoked Thomson into devising

---

see Smith, "Geologists and Mathematicians," and Smith, "William Hopkins" (both cit. n. 1). For biographical details on Hopkins see W. W. Smyth, "Anniversary Address of the President," *Quarterly Journal of the Geological Society of London,* 1867, *23*:xxix–lxxiv; [R E A], "William Hopkins," *Dictionary of National Biography* (1960), Vol. IX, pp. 1233–1234; and Robert P. Beckinsale, "William Hopkins," *DSB,* Vol. VI, pp. 502–504.

[4] William Hopkins, "Researches in Physical Geology: On the Phenomena of Precession and Nutation, Assuming the Fluidity of the Interior of the Earth," *Philosophical Transactions of the Royal Society,* 1839, *129*:381–423; Hopkins, "Researches in Physical Geology—Second Series: On Precession and Nutation, Assuming the Interior of the Earth to be Fluid and Heterogeneous," *Phil. Trans.,* 1840, *130*:193–208; and Hopkins, "Researches in Physical Geology—Third Series: On the Thickness and Constitution of the Earth's Crust," *Phil. Trans.,* 1842, *132*:43–55. The series is analyzed in detail in Kushner, "Emergence of Geophysics" (cit. n. 1), Ch. 1.

[5] See, e.g., Henry Hennessy, "The Figure and Primitive Formation of the Earth, or Researches in Terrestrial Physics—Part I," *Phil. Trans.,* 1851, *141*:495–510 (read 17 Dec. 1846); Hennessy, "Researches in Terrestrial Physics—Part II," *ibid.,* pp. 511–547 (read 15 Mar. 1849); and Samuel Haughton, "On the Original and Actual Fluidity of the Earth and Planets," *Transactions of the Royal Irish Academy,* 1852, *22*:251–273.

[6] See Joe D. Burchfield, "Darwin and the Dilemma of Geological Time," *Isis,* 1974, *65*:301–321; Burchfield, "Presuppositions and Results: The Age of the Earth in Late Victorian England," *Actes du XIIIe Congrès Internationale d'Histoire des Sciences, 1971* (Moscow: Nauka, 1974), Vol. VI, pp. 91–96; and Burchfield, *Lord Kelvin* (cit. n. 1). Smith and Wise, *Energy and Empire* (cit. n. 1), also devotes considerable attention to Thomson's role in the age of the earth debates.

three arguments to limit the age of the earth based on the secular cooling of the earth, the age of the sun's heat, and the tidal retardation of the earth's rotation.[7] Taking them together, Thomson claimed that the age of an inhabitable earth was around 100 million years—geologists were wont to suppose from 10 to 20 billion years, or even more—and so evolution by means of the principle of natural selection would have to go. But the picture of Thomson I wish to portray is significantly different from this one of spoiler.

Thomson, a student of Hopkins's at Cambridge, had long been attracted to earth-centered physics, from his well-known early interest in Joseph Fourier's work and his inaugural essay at Glasgow on the motion of heat in the earth to his special advocacy of geothermic surveys and experiments on underground temperature. Thomson also actively presided as president of the Glasgow Geological Society for twenty-one years. His abiding interest in this related science was further supported by his fundamental belief in the unity of nature and, by extension, in the unity of the sciences. In 1862 he presented to the Royal Society two highly influential papers, one on the rigidity of the earth and a more theoretical one on dynamical problems in the theory of elastic solids. The latter introduced special tools of harmonic analysis to mathematical physical problems, and the former showed that the earth's figure itself must yield to the distorting forces of the sun and moon, just like the ocean, unless the earth is at least as rigid as steel.[8] Thomson used this notion of tidal effective rigidity to extend Hopkins's thickness of the crust to at least 2,500 miles, and, indeed, unlike his former teacher, he believed the earth was essentially solid throughout.

By the mid 1870s Hopkins's precession-based argument for the structure of the earth was largely overturned—and this after Thomson had become convinced of its invalidity.[9] But Thomson's own results were under attack. A solid, rigid-as-steel earth presented serious problems to geologists, who also found it difficult to accept his limited geochronology when the integrity of geological evidence pointed to vaster stretches of geological time. This period also saw renewed interest in astronomical and physical causes of glacial epochs. Geologists had long labored to explain the existence of extremely cold glacial conditions in now-temperate latitudes as well as the remains of subtropical flora in polar regions. A new, and largely successful, explanation was put forth by the Scot James Croll. Croll argued that global weather patterns would be indirectly affected by the periodic changes in the eccentricity of the earth's orbit about the sun, for a winter occurring when the earth was in the aphelion of its most eccentric orbit would be bitterly cold, and this would set in motion a chain of large-scale climatic

[7] The three arguments are first put forth in, respectively, William Thomson, "On the Secular Cooling of the Earth," *Philosophical Magazine,* IV, 1863, *25*:1–14; Thomson, "On the Age of the Sun's Heat," *Macmillan's Magazine,* 1862, *5*:288–293; and Thomson, "On Geological Time" (1868), rpt. in his *Popular Lectures and Addresses,* 3 vols. (London: Macmillan, 1889–1894), Vol. II, pp. 10–64. For the Weald calculation see Charles Darwin, *On the Origin of Species* (facs. of 1st ed.; Cambridge, Mass.: Harvard Univ. Press, 1964), on pp. 285–287.

[8] William Thomson, "On the Rigidity of the Earth," *Phil. Trans.,* 1863, *153*:573–582; and Thomson, "Dynamical Problems Regarding Elastic Spheroidal Shells and Spheroids of Incompressible Liquid," *ibid.,* pp. 583–616.

[9] William Thomson, "Review of Evidence Regarding the Physical Condition of the Earth" (Presidential Address to the Mathematics and Physics Section), *Report of the British Association for the Advancement of Science,* 1876, pp. 1–12.

changes resulting in large tracts of glacial land ice—an ice age. Indeed, Croll believed, and many followed him, that if enough land ice formed, the earth's center of gravity could shift, making the ensuing climatic changes even more severe. Croll's theory was quite influential, but there were many unanswered questions in this new branch of physical geology, physical climatology. Some geologists went further and asserted that the formation of such land ice was not the cause of the glacial period but the result. They argued that if large enough tracts of dry land were elevated, and if others subsided, then this itself could shift the earth's axis in space and serve as a physical cause of the ice age.[10]

Out of the various controversies and varied approaches to mathematical physical geology of the 1870s, one synthesis emerged that proved quite successful in the short term of the 1880s. This was Osmond Fisher's *Physics of the Earth's Crust* (1881), the first book of the nascent field.[11] Fisher treated nearly every aspect of mathematical geology, but he was particularly concerned to prove the insufficiency of the contraction theory of mountain formation, in which the crust becomes wrinkled and plicated as the cooling nucleus contracts beneath it. He advanced instead his own novel conception of a liquid or plastic substratum between a thin, hydrostatically supported crust and the very large solid nucleus beneath, which gives the earth its great rigidity. Fisher then attempted to base orogeny and volcanology upon his new hypothesis, being particularly careful to conform to the results of William Thomson's terrestrial physics. His geological conceptions were clear and showed the fresh alternative mathematical geology could offer to the geological community. Fisher's *Physics* thus marks what British geophysics might have been like had the field not been entirely transformed by the much more sophisticated approach developed simultaneously by George Darwin.

By the mid 1870s, then, terrestrial physics was largely fractured, as competing factions debated the physical structure, age, and past history of the earth—and the methods by which these issues should be attacked. It was against this background that George Darwin first launched the remarkable researches, beginning with his early work on tidal friction, that remade mathematical physical geology into modern geophysics.

II. GEORGE DARWIN AND TIDAL FRICTION

Darwin graduated second wrangler and second Smith's Prizeman from Cambridge in 1868 and subsequently became a fellow of Trinity College. As was customary, he studied for the bar, but his health turned bad, like his father's; he gave up the law and settled back in Cambridge in late 1873, gradually turning to scien-

[10] For Croll's chief arguments see James Croll, "On the Influence of the Tidal Wave on the Earth's Rotation, and on the Acceleration of the Moon's Mean Motion," *Phil. Mag.,* IV, 1864, *27*:285–293; Croll, "On the Physical Cause of the Change of Climate during Geological Epochs," *ibid., 28*:121–137; Croll, "On the Excentricity of the Earth's Orbit," *ibid.,* 1866, *31*:26–28; Croll, "On the Physical Cause of Submergence and Emergence of the Land during the Glacial Epoch," *ibid.,* pp. 301–305; and Croll, "On the Excentricity of the Earth's Orbit, and its Physical Relations to the Geological Epoch," *ibid.,* 1867, *33*:119–131. For their summary in book form see Croll, *Climate and Time in Their Geological Relations* (1875; rpt. New York: D. Appleton, 1897). On Croll himself see H. C. Burstyn, "James Croll," *DSB,* Vol. III, pp. 470–471; and Christopher Hamlin, "James Geikie, James Croll, and the Eventful Ice Age," *Annals of Science,* 1982, *39*:565–583, and the sources cited there. For further details on the debate and on Croll see Kushner, "Emergence of Geophysics" (cit. n. 1).

[11] Osmond Fisher, *Physics of the Earth's Crust* (London: Macmillan, 1881).

tific pursuits. His father occasionally consulted him on scientific subjects, including the positions of Thomson and Croll concerning the age and structure of the earth,[12] and George seemed to keep well abreast of the literature. When John Evans, in his presidential address to the Geological Society of London in 1876, renewed interest in the physical causes of glacial epochs by setting a distinct mathematical question, Darwin's appetite was whetted. As he began to attack the problem, he could hardly contain his enthusiasm, writing to his father that he was "bursting with delight . . . [and] with ideas." The result was his first major paper, and one that proved quite influential, titled "On the Influence of Geological Changes on the Earth's Axis of Rotation."[13]

Here Darwin proved analytically that "the obliquity of the ecliptic [the 23°.5 angle between the planes of the earth's equator and its orbit] must have remained sensibly constant throughout geological history." Even if enormous polar ice caps had been created, "the position of the arctic circle cannot have been shifted so much as half an inch."[14] He did find, however, that changes of position of the earth's axis of symmetry as a result of geological deformations were possible, although limited, for even large-scale deformations could produce a geographical displacement of the pole of at most 1° to 3°. But unlike Thomson, who believed the earth behaved as if perfectly elastic even for long-term stresses, Darwin thought that the earth exhibited plasticity by making rough readjustments to a figure of equilibrium, perhaps through earthquakes, so that the pole might actually have wandered indefinitely some 10° or 15°. Since Darwin had proved that the obliquity of the ecliptic itself could not have shifted, here he had found a way to explain the geologists' problem of the glacial epoch: The glacial period may only *appear* to have been a period of great cold, for if the north pole were in Greenland, then Europe and much of North America would have been glaciated.[15]

As Darwin had guessed, it was Thomson who reviewed his paper for the Royal Society. Whether by subject matter, the mathematical talent shown, or the surname of the author, Thomson was quite struck, writing a very positive sixteen-page report.[16] Soon thereafter, in the spring of 1877, Thomson invited Darwin to Glasgow to discuss the issues at hand. That dialogue profoundly altered George Darwin's life. It was the beginning of an intimate friendship between him and Sir William and Lady Thomson. Given the traditional picture painted of the confrontational relationship between Thomson and Charles Darwin, George's position is all the more surprising.

The scientific outcome of that initial discussion was a remarkable series of papers, startling in its inventiveness and in the ultimate effect it had on the applied mathematics of the earth, that catapulted Darwin into the scientific elite. Darwin was dissatisfied that he had been unable to explain the obliquity of the ecliptic.

[12] See, e.g., DAR 210.1.1 D68.12.9., Cambridge University Library.

[13] See George Howard Darwin, *Scientific Papers*, 5 vols. (Cambridge: Cambridge Univ. Press, 1907–1916), Vol. III, pp. 1–46 (hereafter **Darwin,** *Scientific Papers*). The address that sparked Darwin's initial interest in the subject is John Evans, "Anniversary Address of the President," *Quart. J. Geol. Soc. London,* 1876, *32*:53–121. For more details see Kushner, "Emergence of Geophysics" (cit. n. 1). George's letter to his father is DAR 210.2 D76.4.25, Cambridge University Library.

[14] Darwin, *Scientific Papers,* Vol. III, pp. 15–17.

[15] *Ibid.,* pp. 25–39. Also see the abstract, G. H. Darwin, "On the Influence of Geological Changes on the Earth's Axis of Rotation," *Proc. Royal Society,* 1877, *25*:328–332.

[16] RR.8.14, Royal Society Archives, no date but internally dated on p. 15 as 7 Mar. 1877.

But he thought that if he treated the earth as a viscous body instead of an elastic one, as Thomson had done (mathematicians and astronomers before had treated it only as rigid), then an analysis of tidal reactions, especially of the frictional resistance to the tides, might prove illuminating.

Darwin was the first to find that Thomson's own path-breaking work on the strain of an incompressible elastic sphere could be adapted to the flow of an incompressible viscous fluid; he was the first to treat the earth as a wholly viscous body; and he was the first to develop a theory of viscous tides in the body of the earth.[17] He began to develop the consequences of such tides in his seminal paper "On the Precession of a Viscous Spheroid, and on the Remote History of the Earth," which he worked on throughout 1878.[18] The paper is ostensibly an investigation of how the rotation of a homogeneous viscous spheroid is altered by the tides raised in it by external disturbing bodies. But it is really about tides in the earth's body caused by the moon and sun and the reaction of such tides on the moon—tidal retardation and tidal reaction—for it was Darwin's desire to fathom the physical history of the earth that led him to apply his mathematical talents along this vein in the first place.

Tidal retardation was William Thomson's third argument to limit the age of the earth, and it was born out of a unique set of historical circumstances. If the earth were completely covered with water, the moon, whose attraction causes the tides, would create a tidal protuberance directly in line with the moon's center. The earth rotates faster than the moon revolves around it, and the oceans, as part of the earth, rotate with it. But the oceans are not rigidly attached to the earth, nor does the earth rotate freely within its waters. The result is that the nearer protuberance, now ahead of the moon, forms an acute angle with the line to the moon, and, because of the friction between the water molecules and the earth's surface and among themselves, the moon's attraction on the tidal protuberance acts like a friction brake on the earth's rotation, tending to slow it down. The reaction on the moon is to accelerate its motion linearly which causes it to recede. The question is, what is the *rate* of tidal retardation?

It happened that just as Thomson was beginning to argue with the uniformitarian geologists, a long-standing international controversy surrounding the secular acceleration of the moon's mean motion was being resolved. It was noticed in the eighteenth century that ancient eclipse observations showed what appeared to be an acceleration of the moon over time, but this was inexplicable theoretically. Laplace finally showed that it could be accounted for by the variation of the eccentricity of the earth's orbit. But in 1853 the English astronomer John Couch Adams found that, through a subtle technical error, Laplace's theoretical explanation could only account for about half the observationally determined effect, and a major controversy ensued.[19] It began to be resolved in 1866 when the French astronomer C. E. Delaunay hypothesized that the difference was due to oceanic tidal retardation of the earth's rotation. Because the earth was rotating slower, the

[17] See esp. Darwin, "On the Bodily Tides of Viscous and Semi-elastic Spheroids, and on the Ocean Tides upon a Yielding Nucleus," *Scientific Papers,* Vol. II, pp. 1–32.

[18] See Darwin, *Scientific Papers,* Vol. II, pp. 36–139.

[19] For an analysis of this controversy and bibliographical references see David Kushner, "The Controversy Surrounding the Secular Acceleration of the Moon's Mean Motion," *Archive for History of Exact Sciences,* 1989, *39*:291–316.

moon appeared to be moving faster. Thomson asked Adams what this rate of retardation would have to be to make up the difference, and Adams estimated that it was around 22 seconds of time per century.

Thomson used the whole episode to illustrate to the uniformitarians that things do not remain in a steady state. Then he took this rate of retardation and calculated that more than 1,000 million years ago the earth would have been rotating so much faster that its figure of equilibrium would be more oblate. If the earth had solidified then, that additional oblateness would be apparent in the earth today. Since it is not, the earth must have solidified more recently.[20]

George Darwin's investigation—and intent—was somewhat different. Thomson himself had shown that there were bodily tides in the earth, and Darwin was treating the tidal friction due to these tides. But Darwin found that the rate of tidal retardation was entirely dependent on the degree of viscosity or of elasticity of the earth, and so no estimate of the present rate of tidal friction would be accurate. Furthermore, he believed that the earth behaved plastically to long-term stresses so that there would be no reason to expect evidences of the faster rate of rotation at solidification. Thomson's third argument to limit the age of the earth would have to be thrown out.[21] Darwin was in a unique, but awkward, position as son of Britain's greatest biologist and protégé of Britain's greatest physicist, and he attempted to set himself above the partisan fray. He vigorously argued in favor of the biologists and geologists against Thomson's strict limits, eventually convincing Thomson to widen the limit based on this argument to 5,000 million years.[22] But just as strongly he argued on Thomson's side for the great rigidity and solidity of the earth. Indeed, Thomson called his friend "the chief guardian of the Rigidity of the Earth."[23] As in the public sphere, George Darwin maintained a delicate balance in the private sphere as well, debating with Thomson over natural selection while agreeing with his criticisms of the uniformitarians.

But if this marked the effective demise of Thomson's tidal retardation argument to limit the age of the earth, Darwin reincarnated the principle in his theory of the tidal evolution of the earth-moon system, resulting from the effects of tidal reaction. If the earth is now being retarded and the moon receding, then in the remote past the earth must have been rotating much more swiftly and the moon must have been much closer. Darwin set up a system of differential equations giving the rates of change of four variables: the sidereal day, the sidereal month, the obliquity of the ecliptic, and the moon's distance. He found, with some difficulty, but tremendous mathematical insight into the process, that a *minimum* of 57 million years ago, the day was as short as 6 hours, 45 minutes; the month as short as 1 day, 14 hours; the obliquity was 9° less; and the moon's distance, currently 240,000 miles, was then 36,000 miles. Darwin did not believe this whole process had to be pregeological, and he saw much to aid the geologist: The change in obliquity could affect climate, the trade winds would be augmented and the ocean

[20] Thomson, "On Geological Time" (cit. n. 7); and William Thomson, "Of Geological Dynamics" (1869), *Popular Lectures* (cit. n. 7), Vol. II, pp. 73–127.

[21] Darwin, *Scientific Papers,* Vol. II, esp. pp. 68–78, 122–124.

[22] This limit is given in William Thomson, *Mathematical and Physical Papers,* 6 vols. (Cambridge: Cambridge Univ. Press, 1882–1911), Vol. V, pp. 212–213. For how Darwin convinced Thomson see Kushner, "Emergence of Geophysics" (cit. n. 1), Ch. 8.

[23] Kelvin Papers, D23, 9 Feb. 1881, Glasgow University Library.

currents affected, the shorter days and nights would lead to more violent storms, and the higher and more frequent tides would increase oceanic denudation.[24]

From dynamical principles it is clear that as long as the day and month are not equal, tidal friction must act, and Darwin was determined to find the initial condition of the earth and moon. Using the principle of the conservation of moment of momentum, Darwin altered his analysis to find a day-month equal to 5 hours, 36 minutes; but this was a position of dynamically unstable equilibrium, for if the month were ever less than the day, then the moon would fall into the earth. Since the moon exists, something caused the equilibrium to tip in the other direction. At first Darwin suggested that the contraction of the earth as a cooling body may have been the deciding circumstance. But with a day-month of 5 hours, 36 minutes, only 6,000 miles separated the surfaces of the two bodies. This clearly indicated to Darwin a rupture into at least two bodies of a primeval planet rotating in about 5 hours. But what caused the breakup? Thomson had shown that a fluid spheroid of the earth's mean density undergoes a complete gravitational oscillation in 1 hour, 34 minutes. Darwin hypothesized that a nonhomogeneous earth would have such a period of about 2 to 2½ hours. But this would be the same period as the solar semidiurnal tide, that is, one half of 5 hours. Resonance might cause the already enormous solar tides to rupture the primeval planet.[25] And with this Darwin gave birth to the fission theory of the genesis of the moon, a theory largely accepted for the next fifty years, and one that still finds its proponents today.

This brought to a close the essential portions of the mathematical analysis contained in the paper "Precession." It is clear that Darwin had begun to construct a significant achievement. While the earlier mathematical physical geologists had important things to say about the (more or less static) structure of the earth, Darwin had begun to develop a theory of the dynamical physical history of the earth, and at a level of mathematical sophistication previously attained only by Thomson. But Thomson, although the only other scientist concerned with the element of time in a way at all like George Darwin's, had been sidetracked by other issues, and he never applied his mathematical sophistication to his concern with geochronology in the same investigation to elucidate the history of the earth specifically, as did Darwin. Darwin's attempt at explicating an evolutional history seems to have reflected the concerns of the geological community, and especially those of his father, but the methods of his highly mathematical approach clearly owe more to astronomy and theoretical dynamics. He had begun to recast mathematical physical geology and to transform it into a new hybrid—geophysics—cleanly conceived in one tradition but effectively executed in another. The significance of George's achievement was not lost on his father, Charles, although it astonished him, for he commented, "I should as soon have expected that a man should have composed a sonata by a fluke."[26]

By the time this early series of Darwin's researches was completed in 1882, he was recognized by the scientific aristocracy as a scientist of the highest caliber who did unquestionably good work as a matter of course. Indeed, by the early

[24] Darwin, *Scientific Papers,* Vol. II, pp. 78–100, 124–129.
[25] *Ibid.,* pp. 101–105, 129–134.
[26] DAR 210.1.3, 17 [prob. Aug.] 1878, Cambridge University Library.

1880s Darwin had himself become a member of those upper echelons of the scientific establishment—aided at first by familial ties, abetted by the powerful patronage of Thomson, but ultimately propelled there by the significance of his contributions.

III. THE TRIUMPH OF DARWIN'S APPLIED MATHEMATICS IN BRITISH GEOPHYSICS

By the mid 1880s George Darwin was well on his way to becoming a central figure of the scientific aristocracy of late Victorian and Edwardian Britain. In 1883 he succeeded James Challis as Plumian Professor at Cambridge and won the Telford Medal of the Institution of Civil Engineers. In 1884 he married Maud du Puy of Philadelphia and was awarded the Royal Medal, which he jokingly referred to as a wedding present, and the couple soon moved into Newnham Grange (now Darwin College) at the end of the Backs. And in 1887 the Darwins gave birth to a future fourth wrangler, Charles Galton Darwin, named for George's illustrious father and for his cousin Sir Francis Galton.

Darwin now exerted considerable influence both before and behind the scenes in several fields. By the 1890s he was considered Britain's leading geodesist. He successfully urged his country's membership in the International Geodetic Association (IGA), for which he typically reported on studies on the tides and on variations in gravity. More important were his pushes for cooperation with the Geological and Seismological Congresses and especially for the completion of the great triangulation of Africa, to which undertaking he offered personal financial assistance, and for the joining of the Russian and Indian triangulations through Pamir. In 1907 he was elected vice-president of the IGA, and it was on his urging that Britain hosted the sixteenth General Conference in 1909 at London and at Cambridge, where he and his wife personally entertained the foreign savants at Newnham Grange. In the subfield of seismology Darwin published only one article, a popular one on earthquakes, but he again exerted much influence behind the scenes, especially within the British Association. He was likewise an influential member of the Seismological Congress and a good friend and major proponent of the views of the leading British seismologist John Milne. According to a lengthy account by Sir Napier Shaw, director of the Meteorological Office, Darwin also greatly affected the direction of British meteorology. He apparently wrote some of the reports of the Meteorological Council to the Royal Society, although they were unsigned. Again Darwin published only one work, according to Shaw, on the evaluation of velocity equivalents of the Beaufort Scale. Shaw also stated that Darwin, in one year in which Shaw was overworked, created a course of lectures on dynamical meteorology at Cambridge; though Darwin "professed the utmost diffidence about it," Shaw attributed "the progress which we have made in recent years in [meteorology to] those lectures and the correspondence which arose upon them."[27]

---

[27] See the accounts in F. Darwin, "Memoir" (cit. n. 2), on pp. xxviii–xxix, by the IGA secretary, the Dutch geodesist H. G. van de Sande Bakhuyzen, and pp. xxii–xxvi, by Napier Shaw. The seismological article was George Darwin, "Earthquakes," *Fortnightly Review*, n.s., 1887, *41*:262–275. For further details on this and other material in this section see Kushner, "Emergence of Geophysics" (cit. n. 1), Ch. 9.

One striking aspect of Darwin's scientific work during this period is the commonality of its themes, especially on the subject of tides. These range from a series of experiments with his brother Horace, founder of the Cambridge Scientific Instrument Company, to measure the lunar disturbance of gravity and to confirm in another way the tidal effective rigidity of the earth—this series leading to George's interest in seismology—to his work on oceanic tidal theory, through which he became the government clearinghouse for the organization and reduction of tidal observations throughout the British Empire. He also wrote the standard reference articles (*e.g.,* "Tides," in the *Encyclopaedia Britannica*), assisted foreign governments, and developed a tide predictor and a tidal abacus. By the turn of the century he was recognized as the world's leading authority on the tides, and his book *The Tides and Kindred Phenomena in the Solar System* (1898)—a semipopular account of nearly the whole compass of his scientific work, based on the Lowell Lectures he gave at Boston in 1897—rapidly became a scientific bestseller; it was soon translated into several languages, including German, Hungarian, Spanish, and Italian.[28]

While the inherent connections between this work on oceanic tides on a rigid nucleus and his earlier work on bodily tides in a viscous earth are clear, some of Darwin's most important work and certainly the most mathematically sophisticated grew directly out of that earlier work on tidal friction. Indeed, Darwin's theory of tidal evolution subsequently led to three other important series of researches. In the first of these the changes in the earth-moon system led him to consider what the figure of the earth must have been in past times, and this in turn led him later to consider the whole theory to the second order of small quantities. It is this work, the astronomer and former Darwin student F. J. M. Stratton claimed, that "contributed to [Darwin's] being the foremost English geodesist of his day."[29]

In the second series Darwin considered the initial conditions of stability of a primeval planet preceding rupture. These studies of the figures of equilibrium of rotating fluid masses brought him into a close relationship with Henri Poincaré. Darwin's researches elucidated the pear-shaped figure of equilibrium Poincaré had shown to exist, and Darwin's determination of stability added even greater weight to his own fission theory. (Darwin in fact determined that the figure does not really look like a pear, but the phrase proved convenient and stuck.)[30]

[28] On the company see M. J. G. Cattermole and A. F. Wolfe, *Horace Darwin's Shop: A History of the Cambridge Scientific Instrument Company, 1878–1968* (Bristol: Adam Hilger, 1987). Most of the important papers on oceanic tides and the problems of tidal observation and reduction fill Volume I of Darwin, *Scientific Papers,* dedicated to Sir William Thomson; some later papers appear in Volume IV. *The Tides and Kindred Phenomena in the Solar System* (Boston: Houghton, Mifflin, 1898) was Darwin's only book. See also G. H. Darwin and S. S. Hough, "Bewegung der Hydrosphäre," in *Encyklopädie der Mathematischen Wissenschaften,* Vol. VI (1B), Pt. 1, pp. 1–83 (1908); and G. H. Darwin, S. S. Hough, and E. Fichot, "Marées océaniques et marées internes," in *Encyclopédie des sciences mathématiques,* Vol. VI, Pt. 2.1 (1916).

[29] See Darwin, *Scientific Papers,* Vol. III, pp. 69–118; and F. J. M. Stratton, "Obituary Notice of George Howard Darwin," *Monthly Notices of the Royal Astronomical Society,* 1913, *73*:204–210, on p. 207.

[30] Darwin's important papers on this subject fill Volume III of his *Scientific Papers.* Brief historical accounts of the large and important literature on this subject are given in R. A. Lyttleton, *The Stability of Rotating Liquid Masses* (Cambridge: Cambridge Univ. Press, 1953), and S. Chandrasekhar, *Ellipsoidal Figures of Equilibrium* (1969) (New York: Dover, 1987). See also Hough, "Sir George Howard Darwin" (cit. n. 2), for a sound analysis of Darwin's contribution; and Henri Poincaré, "Sur

In the third series Darwin began by attempting to discover how a Laplacian ring could coalesce into a planet, but he was quickly diverted to a study of periodic orbits. In these papers, also involving the work of Poincaré as well as that of the American astronomer G. W. Hill, Darwin calculated numerous classes of orbits by a complex numerical procedure and attempted to determine their stability. J. J. Thomson declared Darwin's achievement here "a kind of apotheosis of Arithmetic. Mathematicians have not as yet discovered any general method of dealing with these orbits, Darwin calculated them, so to speak, inch by inch." His friend and former student S. S. Hough remarked of his achievement:

> However much one may admire Poincaré's skill and insight in dealing with abstruse mathematical analysis, to many readers the abstract process of reasoning will be found unsatisfying, and more concrete presentations of the problems will appear to possess greater lucidity.... Many will share Darwin's own distrust, based on experience, of the possibility of correctly reasoning without fear of ambiguity about solutions which have not been definitely found, but his own results cannot fail to carry conviction. Darwin's orbits give clear and tangible illustrations.[31]

The whole of this work, as with Darwin's entire scientific *oeuvre,* stands as a tribute to applied mathematics and numerical analysis before the advent of computers.[32]

In his last paper on the subject in 1912, shortly before his death, Darwin attempted to find a member of a particular librating class of orbits; he failed but instead found a different class in which the satellite ultimately falls into the planet. His concluding paragraph is highly revealing:

> My attention was first drawn to periodic orbits by the desire to discover how a Laplacian ring could coalesce into a planet. With that object in view I tried to discover how a large planet would affect the motion of a small one moving in a circular orbit at the same mean distance. After various failures the investigation drifted towards the work of Hill and Poincaré, so that the original point of view was quite lost and it is not even mentioned in my paper on "Periodic Orbits." It is of interest, to me at least, to find that the original aspect of the problem has emerged again.[33]

As Ernest Brown, another Darwin student, very justly noted, "Thus Darwin's work on what appeared to be a problem in celestial mechanics of a somewhat unpractical nature sprang after all from and finally tended towards the question

---

l'équilibre d'une masse fluide animée d'un mouvement de rotation," *Acta Mathematica,* 1885, 7:259–380, for Poincaré's crucial paper.

[31] J. J. Thomson, "Sir George Howard Darwin, KCB, FRS," *Cambridge Review,* 16 Jan. 1913, pp. 183–184, on p. 183; and Hough, "Sir George Howard Darwin" (cit. n. 2), on p. xi. This comparison seems to confirm the French-abstract–British-concrete dichotomy that Mary Jo Nye argues for as the basis of national styles in her essay in this volume.

[32] Darwin's celebrated paper "Periodic Orbits" (1897) is reprinted in *Scientific Papers,* Vol. IV, pp. 1–113, as are two other papers on the subject: *ibid.,* pp. 140–181, and Vol. V., pp. 59–75. See also Ernest W. Brown, "The Scientific Work of Sir George Darwin" (1916), *ibid.,* pp. xxxiv–lv, and Hough, "Sir George Howard Darwin" (cit. n. 2), for brief analyses by students of Darwin who made their own valuable contributions to the study of periodic orbits.

[33] Darwin, *Scientific Papers,* Vol. V, p. 72.

which had occupied his thoughts nearly all his life, the genesis and evolution of the solar system."[34]

This tie back to his earlier work illustrates well Darwin's single-mindedness and is crucial to an understanding of both Darwin the scientist and Darwin the man. But single-mindedness is only one of Darwin's defining characteristics, characteristics that are crucial to examining his leading role in the emergence of a new discipline, his shaping of its style, and the issue of whether he founded a research school.

IV. THE DEFINING CHARACTERISTICS OF DARWIN'S SCIENCE

Four areas characterize Darwin's science: his scientific methodology, the evolutionary framework of his ideas, the nature of his applied mathematics, and his centrality in the emergence of geophysics.

The very essence of Darwin's inquiries rendered his work at once analytical and numerical-computational—arithmetical in the highest sense of the word—and almost always technical and laborious. Schematically his scientific methodology is this: Define the problem and set its boundary conditions. Make two sorts of simplifications: (1) approximate the complicated physical world with the best possible mathematical model; and (2) reduce the number of parameters to facilitate the first analysis. Now investigate the simplified problem as analytically and generally as possible and interpret the results so as to give them a physical meaning. If this last stage cannot be completed satisfactorily, treat the problem specifically by entering numerical data into the parameters, and then arithmetically compute the results. Go back and increase the number of parameters. Repeat until the real-world situation is approximated. Go back and compare with other mathematical models. This method is apparent not only within individual papers but is clearly suffused throughout the various series of investigations Darwin undertook throughout his career.

Darwin's method is essentially a flow chart whose terminus, in keeping with his notions of how and why science is done, is the best possible general analytical description of some physical world problem, often one of direct concern with the nature of the earth. But in the case of intractable analytical formulæ, it is better to have at least some specific quantitative result than none at all—this at least tells one something useful about the physical world—and so numerical quadratures, for example, must sometimes be resorted to. Darwin did not generally put much stock in the exact numerical value so attained; rather, it pointed to trends or set off extrema that later analysis, he hoped, would confirm. Unfortunately, few others respected the limitations this method necessarily imposed, and thus it was open to misinterpretation. Still, Darwin greatly preferred even the imperfectly quantitative to the lowly qualitative, which he evidently disdained. While the resulting hierarchy—analytic, quantitative, qualitative—emerges clearly enough, it seems too simple to refer Darwin's accordance of scientific respectability to the general nineteenth-century trend toward quantification in nearly all fields. Rather, the roots of his preference must lie in his scientific background and train-

[34] Brown, "Scientific Work" (cit. n. 32), p. lv.

ing, his general mathematical competence, the nature of his scientific work, and his rare ability to squeeze such results out of that work.

Darwin's method is also nicely modular. He used it to work on problems within problems. In this way he was able to overcome hurdles that would have stopped other mathematicians. Clearly, the success of his methodology rested on his mathematical ability and willingness, regardless of how undesirable the task may have been, to have recourse to these numerical methods. But Darwin was no number cruncher. His method required a keen sense of order and symmetry, as well as a powerful capacity for mental organization and an intuition of where and how his various flow chart steps should be applied. Darwin once confessed his procedure was like "a housebreaker who blows in a safe-door with dynamite instead of picking the lock."[35] In truth, Darwin was an applied mathematician of the first rank, recognized as such by his peers when elected president of the Fifth International Congress of Mathematicians in 1912. Through his scientific methodology, he elevated applied mathematics to its highest plane before the advent of computers. Indeed, his approach—flow chart–like, modular, algorithmic to the point where "people computers" could be hired to perform the more tedious calculations—mirrors well the operational strategy of machine computers and signifies the ultimate human element in machine computer organization.

Finally, it must be admitted that Darwin's method is plainly intimidating to the mathematically illiterate, and its pages of formulas forbidding even to the mathematically sophisticated: even highly qualified referees such as Thomson and Lord Rayleigh often read through Darwin's dense mathematical prose in a cursory manner. Darwin recognized this and, with a keen eye to the applications of his results—indeed his investigations were originally undertaken specifically for such applications, particularly to physical geology and cosmology—accordingly conglomerated them and endued them with physical meaning in nonmathematical summaries. He occasionally went even further, presenting qualitative physical reasoning in his abstracts to demonstrate that his mathematical results were conformable to common sense. Nevertheless, with such phrases as "bodily tides" and "viscous spheroid" in his titles he was unlikely to attract the audiences for whom his results might have been most relevant at the time. And even when he did, these readers did not necessarily take away with them what he may have intended.

Darwin's singleness of purpose had at least three interrelated components: an interest in tides, an abiding concern with the history and structure of the earth, and a third aspect, as yet unmentioned—an evolutionary world view that suffused his scientific writings and often revealed itself in his public addresses. George was an impressionable youth of fourteen when his father's *Origin of Species* was published, yet this is not sufficient to explain why, as Charles's life work was to understand the evolution of life on earth, his son George's would be to understand the evolution of the earth itself. A partial explanation must also take account of his mentor, Sir William Thomson, who was himself deeply concerned with questions of the structure of the earth and geochronology.

Darwin's concern with the history and structure of the earth and his evolutionary world view, although intimately connected, are not synonymous. Darwin was concerned not only with the evolution of the earth but with the evolution of

---

[35] Darwin, *Scientific Papers,* Vol. V, p. 79.

planetary and solar systems as well, indeed with some of the deeper problems of cosmogony. Yet this distinction is only superficial. More important, in fact crucial, is that while deeper knowledge about the earth was a scientific end, Darwin's evolutionary world view embodied philosophical commitments of his that affected the means to that end. A good example comes from his address on geological time to the British Association in 1886. Using a biological analogy his father would have approved of, it makes clear that even his view of scientific development and progress was itself evolutionary in character. Darwin painted a picture of facts nourishing the theory-branches of the tree of science, with some theory-branches becoming more vigorous than others in the struggle for scientific acceptance, although while still in their early stages they give little idea of how the final theory-branches will look.[36] By the end of the address Darwin had used the analogy and his view of scientific development to argue against Thomson's position in two of the arguments to limit the age of the earth. It is to Darwin's credit that, even as his argument supported the evolutionary views he and his father advanced, both geologists and physicists felt he treated the matter fairly and reasonably.[37]

Another defining characteristic of Darwin's work cannot be stressed too highly. It is the nature of his mathematics, and, like other characteristics, it has more than one component: the "appliedness" of his mathematics; and his relentless pursuit of quantitative results, discussed above. These two aspects taken together are largely responsible for the transformation in Britain of the earlier mathematical physical geology into modern geophysics. S. S. Hough stated that it was Darwin's influence that "did much to maintain the traditional reputation of Cambridge as a school of applied mathematics" at a time when pure mathematicians such as Bertrand Russell, Alfred North Whitehead, and G. H. Hardy were pulling one way while experimental physicists such as J. J. Thomson were pulling another.[38] Despite the increasing specialization, Sir Joseph Larmor called Darwin the "*doyen* of the mathematical school at Cambridge" and implied that this appellation was widely recognized.[39] Darwin for his own part was often modest about his mathematical skill. In his address as president of the Royal Astronomical Society, awarding the society's Gold Medal to Poincaré, he belittled his own approach to difficult problems, insisting that the "power of grasping abstract principles is the mark of the intellect of the true mathematician; but to one accustomed rather to deal with the concrete the difficulty of completely mastering the argument is sometimes great. To the latter class of mind the easier process is the consideration of some simple concrete case, and the subsequent ascent to the more general aspect of the problem."[40]

Darwin's applied mathematics is firmly rooted in the nineteenth-century

[36] *Ibid.,* Vol. IV, pp. 499–509.

[37] His presidential address on cosmical evolution, delivered during the British Association's tour of South Africa in 1905, is equally revealing: *ibid.,* pp. 520–551.

[38] Hough, "Sir George Howard Darwin" (cit. n. 2), on p. xi.

[39] Joseph Larmor, "Obituary Notice of Sir George Howard Darwin, KCB, FRS," *Nature,* 1912, *90*:413–415.

[40] Darwin, *Scientific Papers,* Vol. IV, p. 519. Although Darwin himself contrasts abstract and concrete here, his use of the dichotomy nevertheless differs in important ways from the distinctions in "national styles" that Nye attempts to explicate in her essay in this volume, despite the coincidence that both involve nationality.

Cambridge tradition of mixed mathematics.[41] The character of his work is chiefly that of mathematical physics, but in its application it is even more specific. Darwin never undertook problems because he thought there was a neat mathematical solution; instead, he attacked specific problems using the most appropriate mathematical tools because he wanted to understand the underlying phenomena, and those phenomena he principally wanted to understand were the physical evolution and the structure of the earth. The insight of his former student, Ernest Brown, on this matter is on the mark:

> [Darwin] was an applied mathematician in the strict and older sense of the word. In the last few decades [before 1916] another school of applied mathematicians, founded mainly by Poincaré, has arisen, but it differs essentially from the older school. Its votaries have less interest in the phenomena than in the mathematical processes which are used by the student of the phenomena. . . . Darwin belonged essentially to the school which studies the phenomena by the most convenient mathematical methods. Strict logic in the modern sense is not applied nor is it necessary, being replaced in most cases by intuition which guides the investigator through the dangerous places.[42]

Brown's is not the retrospective view of a scientist of today, but the understanding of a well-respected mathematician and astronomer of the time, one personally involved in many of these developments.

Perhaps more than any other "applied" mathematician of his day Darwin possessed that peculiar intuition which aids the very best scientists. Certainly it and his steadfast resolve—and ability—to obtain quantitative results were responsible for much of his success. But if that older school of applied mathematics in the "mixed" sense seems to have been superseded by the newer school of Poincaré, it is only because one is looking in the wrong place; for if Darwin were one of the greats of the last generation of applied mathematicians in the nineteenth-century sense, he was also one of the greats of the first generation of the new geophysics and astrophysics. Indeed it is because he so doggedly applied himself and his mathematical tools to the earth, the moon, and the solar system that he so greatly shaped and influenced the nature of these new disciplines.

Even at the time it was recognized that the appliedness and quantitativeness of Darwin's work were responsible for his wide influence and might perhaps actually be his legacy. Brown affirmed that his Darwinian model had become ascendant:

> The influence which Darwin exerted has been felt in many directions. The exhibition of the necessity for quantitative and thorough analysis of the problems of cosmogony and celestial mechanics has been perhaps one of his chief contributions. It has extended far beyond the work of the pupils who were directly inspired by him. While speculations and the framing of new hypotheses must continue, but little weight is now attached to those which are defended by general reasoning alone. Conviction fails, possibly because it is recognised that the human mind cannot reason accurately in these questions without the aids furnished by mathematical symbols, and in any case language often fails to carry fully the argument of the writer as against the

---

[41] On a Cambridge style of mathematics, especially in the early Victorian era, see the essays in Harman, ed., *Wranglers and Physicists* (cit. n. 1).
[42] Brown, "Scientific Work" (cit. n. 32), on p. xxxiv.

exact implications of mathematics. If for no other reason, Darwin's work marks an epoch in this respect.[43]

Although, as Brown noted, Darwin's influence "extended far beyond" their work, that influence was communicated perhaps most tangibly to his students. Among those who came under his tutelage at some point were A. B. Basset, Arthur Berry, E. W. Brown, G. H. Bryan, Charles Chree, P. H. Cowell, F. W. Dyson, S. S. Hough, J. H. Jeans, A. E. H. Love, R. A. Sampson, F. J. M. Stratton, H. H. Turner, and E. T. Whittaker—an impressive list of astronomers and applied mathematicians, many of whom made important contributions to geophysics. It has been seen above how Darwin exerted weight—chiefly behind the scenes—in government-directed scientific undertakings. But there also remains that frequently ineffable type of influence that exists within personal friendships, and Darwin developed close relationships with many of the leading scientists of his day. Besides Thomson, J. C. Adams, and Gabriel Stokes, some of the more notable British names include J. W. Strutt (Lord Rayleigh), J. J. Thomson, Joseph Larmor, Arthur Schuster, J. H. Poynting, Osborne Reynolds, Horace Lamb, R. S. Ball, H. F. Newall, A. S. Eddington, Napier Shaw, Archibald Geikie, John Joly, W. J. Sollas, and John Perry—a veritable who's who of leading British scientists, not to mention again those former students with whom he maintained close ties. Among his distinguished foreign correspondents and friends Darwin could number Poincaré, E. von Rebeur Paschwitz, Edouard Reyer, Otto Hahn, August Ritter, Emil Wiechert, F. R. Helmert, Otto Hecker, Antoine d'Abbadie, Phillip Hatt, and H. G. van de Sande Bakhuyzen on the continent, and Simon Newcomb, G. W. Hill, T. C. Chamberlin, George F. Becker, Cleveland Abbe, Asaph Hall, and R. S. Woodward across the Atlantic. Fully half of these were at some point involved in researches related to geophysics, and it was frequently on such subjects that they would correspond with Darwin.

Darwin's own thoughts on what the enterprise of applied mathematics was all about and its distinction from pure mathematics give significant insight into how he viewed his own career. In his presidential address to the Fifth International Congress of Mathematicians held at Cambridge in August 1912, his last public appearance before his death, he said:

> Both the pure and the applied mathematician are in search of truth, but the former seeks truth in itself and the latter truths about the universe in which we live. . . . [W]hile in pure mathematics every new discovery is a gain, in applied mathematics it is not always easy to find the direction in which progress can be made, because the selection of the conditions essential to the problem presents a preliminary task, and afterwards there arise the purely mathematical difficulties. Thus it appears to me at least, that it is easier to find a field for advantageous research in pure than in applied mathematics. Of course if we regard an investigation in applied mathematics as an exercise in analysis, the correct selection of the essential conditions is immaterial; but if the choice has been wrong the results lose almost all their interest. . . .
>
> The appropriate formulation of the problem to be solved is one of the greatest difficulties which beset the applied mathematician, and when he has attained to a true insight but too often there remains the fact that his problem is beyond the reach of mathematical solution. To the layman the problem of the three bodies seems so

[43] *Ibid.*, p. xxxvi.

simple that he is surprised to learn that it cannot be solved completely, and yet we know what prodigies of mathematical skill have been bestowed on it. My own work on the subject cannot be said to involve any such skill at all, unless indeed you describe as skill the procedure of a housebreaker who blows in a safe-door with dynamite instead of picking the lock. . . .

I appeal then for mercy to the applied mathematician and would ask you to consider in a kindly spirit the difficulties under which he labours. If our methods are often wanting in elegance and do but little to satisfy aesthetic sense, . . . yet they are honest attempts to unravel the secrets of the universe in which we live.[44]

There could hardly be a neater or humbler summary of this aspect of Sir George Darwin's life work.

V. DARWINIAN GEOPHYSICS AND BEYOND

By the 1890s Darwin's researches were widely acclaimed and internationally known, especially in Germany, and there was a new breed of investigators, some Darwin's students and some inspired by him, trained to handle the mathematical demands of a rigorous study of the physics of the earth. It was around this time that the enterprise of terrestrial physics came to be recognized as a distinct scientific discipline—denominated geophysics—and not just as a branch of theoretical geology or of physical astronomy. *Geo*-prefixed words relating to the new field made their way into English, usually from German. The German heritage of geophysics was a strong one and this was partly responsible for its coalescence there at an earlier date, although there were significant differences in the character of the British and German fields that also explain their distinct origins.[45]

German *Geophysik* concentrated its pursuits on studies of terrestrial magnetism, meteorology, and earthquakes on the one hand and geodesy and physical geography on the other. These are chiefly studies of large-scale surface phenomena, in marked contradistinction to British work on the constitution of the interior of the earth and the thickness of its crust; the age, evolution, and cosmogonical origins of the earth; and the astronomical and physical causes of glacial epochs. German developments were largely influenced by the pioneering work of C. F. Gauss, F. W. Bessel, and Alexander von Humboldt in the first half of the century, the first two widely acclaimed for their work on terrestrial magnetism and geodesy and the third for the elaboration of his own program, geographically based, of accurate measurement and quantification of terrestrial phenomena—"Humboldtian science," as S. F. Cannon called it.[46] By the 1880s the leading German-speaking geophysicists, including Darwin's friends and correspondents F. R. Helmert, Edouard Reyer, August Ritter, Otto Hahn, Emil Wiechert, and Otto Hecker, routinely used the term *Geophysik* to embrace work within such subfields as seismology and geodesy. It comes as no surprise then that the first journal devoted to the nascent discipline, *Beiträge zur Geophysik,* was founded in 1887 by a physical

[44] Darwin, *Scientific Papers,* Vol. V, pp. 78–79.

[45] See Kertz, "Die Entwicklung der Geophysik" (cit. n. 1). Kertz believes the term *Geophysik* probably gained some currency quite a few years before the first dictionary definition in 1848, although he is unable to attribute its origin to any one person.

[46] Susan F. Cannon, *Science in Culture* (New York: Science History Publications, 1978), esp. pp. 73–110.

geographer, Georg Gerland of Strasbourg, who continued editing "Gerland's Journal" until his death in 1919.[47]

In Britain, as noted, William Hopkins coined the term *physical geology* in 1835, while Henry Hennessy opted for *terrestrial physics* in 1846. Many later investigators used these two terms interchangeably, although a background in physics or geology seems to have led to a slight preference for the one or the other: Thomson, for example, used "terrestrial physics." Despite the well-established examples of *geo-logy, geo-gnosy, geo-desy,* and *geo-graphy,* it did not occur to any Anglo-American to transmute either the Hopkins or Hennessy terms into *geophysics.* In fact, according to the *Oxford English Dictionary* (second edition, 1989), the related words *geodynamics* and *geodynamical* edged their way into English just ahead of *geophysics* and *geophysical. Geodynamics* first appeared in a report in *Nature* in 1885 that matter-of-factly categorized it as a subfield of terrestrial physics along with seismology and vulcanology.[48] George Darwin was the first to use *geodynamical* publicly, in his February 1887 article on earthquakes for the *Fortnightly Review.*[49] *Geophysical* appeared without fanfare a year later in an article in *Science,* and the first English-language dictionary definition of *geophysics*—"physics of the earth, same as physiography" in the American *Century Dictionary* (1889)—shows the word's German origins.[50] There can be no doubt that *geophysics* was adopted from the German, as it proliferated in Germany in the 1880s in articles about the time that Gerland founded his *Beiträge.* Indeed, any well-read British researcher in the field could hardly fail to be aware of the term's growing use long before its first documented appearances in English. Darwin, for one, kept well abreast of the latest German scientific literature, and it is certain he was familiar with the term several years before its first documented English usage.[51] *Geophysics* and the related terms were probably used in conversation—by Darwin and his circle—before their first actual appearances in print, as had probably been the case in Germany for the term *Geophysik* earlier in the century.

Institutionalization of the field in Britain, however, was slow, despite the explosion of interest and research I have alluded to. Darwin certainly lectured on geo-

---

[47] Less is known about developments in France. Reports on "physique du globe" in the *Comptes Rendus de l' Académie des Sciences,* appearing from the 1830s on, are concerned almost entirely with meteorological issues. One major exception is Édouard Roche, a professor at Montpellier known to astrophysicists for the Roche limit and Roche ellipsoids, who published primarily in the *Mémoires* of the Montpellier academy, worked most of his life in virtual isolation from the scientific and intellectual center of Paris, but gained worldwide recognition after his death in 1883. Roche made important contributions in several areas that mirror Darwin's work intriguingly: figures of equilibrium of fluid masses, the interior state and structure of the earth, and the constitution and origin of the solar system. See M. J. Boussinesq, "Notice sur la vie et les travaux de M. Édouard Roche," *Mémoires de la Société des Sciences, de l'Agriculture et des Arts de Lille,* IV, 1885, *14*:17–35; and Kushner, "Emergence of Geophysics" (cit. n. 1).

[48] *Nature,* 1885, *32*:609.

[49] Darwin, "Earthquakes" (cit. n. 27), on p. 271.

[50] *Science,* 1888, *11*:181–182; and *Century Dictionary* (New York, 1889), s.v. *geophysics.*

[51] Indeed Hugo Hergesill, a colleague of Gerland's in Strasbourg, wrote Darwin in 1886 following Karl Zöppritz's death to request assistance with the yearly "Bericht über Geophysik" for the *Geographisches Jahrbuch.* See Hugo Hergesill to George Darwin, 4 Sept. 1886, Unclassified G. H. Darwin Correspondence File 2, Cambridge University Library. Gerland himself sent Darwin a complimentary copy of the first issue of his *Beiträge zur Geophysik:* see Georg Gerland to George Darwin, 29 Feb. 1888, File 5, *ibid.*

physical subjects, and his students, in turn, often went out and did the same, so that there was a growing base of trained investigators. Darwin and his colleagues at Cambridge also exerted influence by selecting the essay topics for such awards as the Smith's Prize and the Adams Prize and by electing the holders of such scholarships as the Isaac Newton Studentship and the Sheepshanks Astronomical Exhibition.[52] But the field was not formalized within the English universities at this time, Darwin's own lectures at Cambridge being authorized through the Special Board for Mathematics. Government recognition was also slow in coming, it not even being clear what role Britain should take in such international bodies as the Geodetic Conference and the Seismological Congress. Support came for the most part from the Royal Society and especially from the British Association, which played the leading role in organizing seismology. Only several years after Darwin's death was institutional support for geophysics broadly conceived made permanent in Britain. In June 1917 informal meetings at New College, Oxford, chaired by H. H. Turner, Savilian Professor of Astronomy at Oxford, with J. H. Jeans as secretary—both former Darwin students—resulted in a strong geophysical committee being appointed by the British Association to arrange for meetings and discussions and to foster communication among the various branches of the umbrella field. In 1919, largely through the actions of Jeans, Harold Jeffreys, and Sir Frank Dyson, then the Astronomer Royal, it was decided that ultimate responsibility should be passed from the BAAS to the Royal Astronomical Society, and the new RAS Geophysical Committee was formed with representatives from the Royal Geographical, the Royal Meteorological, the Geological, and the Physical Societies as well as the British Astronomical Association. Although the RAS had been publishing geophysical papers for years in its *Monthly Notices,* in 1922 it began issuing the *Geophysical Supplement* (usually twice a year). This was the first British journal devoted exclusively to geophysics, and in 1958 it became the *Geophysical Journal.*[53]

These extremely close ties between astronomy and geophysics are somewhat

[52] Among Darwin's many students, some of the more prominent and geophysically inclined did very well in these competitions. Among Smith's Prizemen were H. H. Turner (1883), A. E. H. Love and Arthur Berry (1887), G. H. Bryan (1888), R. A. Sampson (1890), F. W. Dyson (1891), S. S. Hough (1894), E. T. Whittaker (1897), G. W. Walker (1899), J. H. Jeans (1901), and F. J. M. Stratton (1906). Isaac Newton Studentships, essentially postbaccalaureate scholarships in astronomy, were awarded to Sampson (1891), Dyson (1892), P. H. Cowell (1894), Hough (1895), G. W. Walker (1899), Jeans (1900), and Stratton (1905). Holders of the Sheepshanks Astronomical Exhibition included Turner (1882), Dyson and G. T. Walker (1888), Cowell (1891), and Whittaker (1894). The Adams Prize, a prestigious national competition, was won by former Darwin students G. T. Walker (1899), E. W. Brown (1907), Love (1911), and Jeans (1917). See J. R. Tanner, ed., *The Historical Register of the University of Cambridge* (Cambridge: Cambridge Univ. Press, 1917), pp. 272, 279, 301, 321; and *The Historical Register of the University of Cambridge Supplement, 1911–20,* preface by G. V. C. (Gordon Vero Carey) (Cambridge: Cambridge Univ. Press, 1922), p. 39.

[53] J. L. E. Dreyer *et al., History of the Royal Astronomical Society, 1820–1920* (London: Wheldon & Wesley, 1923), pp. 227–228 (by Dreyer); Harold Jeffreys, "Geophysics and the Royal Astronomical Society," *Monthly Not. Royal Astr. Soc.,* 1936, 96:384–387 (signed H. J. and contained within the "Report of the Council to the Hundred and Sixteenth Annual General Meeting," pp. 273–387); R. J. Tayler, ed., *History of the Royal Astronomical Society 1920–1980,* Vol. II (Oxford: Blackwell Scientific for the RAS, 1987), pp. 24–25 (by Dingle and Tayler), vii (by Jeffreys), 149 (by Allen). These accounts do not quite square, but the most authoritative appears to be that by Jeffreys in the *Monthly Notices.* Additional institutional support came in 1926 when Jeans, then president of the RAS, endowed with £1000 the RAS's first named lectureship, the George Darwin Lecture, which Jeans specifically indicated should embrace geophysical subjects from time to time.

peculiar to Britain, although in the United States George F. Becker did claim that geophysics properly developed would be seen as a subfield of astrophysics.[54] The connections in Britain between astronomy and the new terrestrial physics have been apparent from the very beginning, with Hopkins's precession-based argument for the structure of the earth, through the debates surrounding astronomical causes of large-scale climatic change, to Darwin's theory of tidal friction and cosmogonical speculations concerning the evolution of the earth-moon system. But this did not necessarily make the new field a part of astronomy proper. Even as late as 1892, when Darwin was awarded the Gold Medal of the Royal Astronomical Society, some members of the RAS Council questioned whether what Darwin did was "astronomy."[55] Perhaps Darwin's holding the premier astronomy chair in Britain helped to convince some. It does seem that Darwin's title as Plumian Professor served to foster the ties between the two fields in the ensuing decades.

As seen above, it was in Germany, where the term *geophysics* originated, that geophysics was first recognized as a distinct, new discipline. But once the term was introduced into Britain, there was a veritable explosion of research and development in the new field, albeit differing in style and content from its German counterpart. Before that time, however, there was such a multitude of approaches and methodologies that there was much epistemic confusion over the enterprise of mathematical physical geology. This, I believe, has led some to see the interdisciplinary debates of the time as much more hostile than they really were, whereas instead they should be viewed as negotiations over the domain of the new field. Out of this muddle Darwin transformed the nascent science with his own brand of applied mathematics. A striking anomaly of both the physics and geology of the time is that in the end the speculations of both had to rely on qualitative indications, and it is very easy to disagree over such indications. For physics this occurred when the mathematical analysis proved too intractable and quantitative data were ambiguous or resisted application. For geology this resulted from faint understanding of large-scale processes and reliance on relative, not absolute, measuring posts—and this despite the trend toward increasing quantification in the field. But to Darwin, when it came to the earth, such qualitative indications were useless, and worthwhile knowledge about the structure and history of the earth could only be gained through a rigorous program of applied analysis that persisted through the intractable parts to obtain "hard" quantitative results.

To some extent it is a historical accident that the coalescence of geophysics as a distinct discipline in Germany was contemporaneous with Darwin's early work, for the two bear little direct relation. But it is no accident that, in the mid 1880s, as Darwin's achievement was beginning to be recognized and to exert influence and as the term *geophysics* was being adopted into English, the transformed enter-

---

[54] The juncture is today commonly referred to as planetary science; cf. Stephen G. Brush, *The Temperature of History* (New York: Burt Franklin, 1978); and Stephen G. Brush, "Planetary Science: From Underground to Underdog," *Scientia*, 1978, *113*:771–787. George Becker wrote a position paper to help secure support for the Geophysical Laboratory of the Carnegie Institution; see "Remarks on Geophysics," typescript, 21 Mar. 1902, Unclassified G. H. Darwin Correspondence File 27, Cambridge University Library.

[55] See H. H. Turner to Darwin, 11 Jan. 1892, Unclassified G. H. Darwin Correspondence File 9, Cambridge University Library.

prise should be identified with the new term and rapidly recognized as a distinct discipline. With these fundamental changes under way and working together, the ensuing explosive increase in interest and research begins to make sense within a new context.

The following half century saw the discipline's consolidation into a vibrant and vital aspect of twentieth-century science. The second and third generations of geophysicists could look back on their field's history with admiration and respect; they knew well the guiding influence of Darwin. Appropriately, Sir Harold Jeffreys—the father of twentieth-century British geophysics if anyone was—dedicated the first great classic in the field, *The Earth,* to the memory of Sir George Howard Darwin, "Founder of Modern Cosmogony and Geophysics."[56]

VI. WAS THERE A DARWINIAN SCHOOL OF GEOPHYSICS?

This study of Darwin and his central role in the emergence of British geophysics raises many interesting issues, such as how controversy relates to scientific development; the manner in which new disciplines "emerge"; what the distinct character of British geophysics was; and, naturally, the question that heads this section.

While controversy was a standard feature of the chief interdisciplinary problem areas that are central to the emergence of geophysics, Darwin did not meet the same immediate resistance as many of his colleagues, although he did encounter some. Charles Chree, a former Darwin student, criticized his method in one important paper, although the results were unaffected.[57] And many years after their original publication, some of his results were shown to be incomplete and his more speculative conclusions improperly drawn, although the investigations themselves were technically unimpeachable as far as they went. The "Darwin pattern" thus consisted of considered judgment and general acceptance without contest, followed by (much) later appropriate criticism. This Darwin pattern may be explained chiefly in terms of the nature, orientation, and sophistication of his mathematical arguments. There were few capable of disputing him on technical grounds, and those who were capable were not inclined to do so. The result was that the emerging community of "geophysicists" generally accepted his theories and only began to criticize them after it had gained a greater maturity and sophistication and attempted to move beyond Darwin's science. Darwin's work thus forms a natural boundary; a new plateau has been reached. Thereafter developments in geophysics began to take on a different cast, one that was quite complex, rapidly changing, and international in character.

A second general point to consider concerns the emergence of disciplines. When I have spoken in this study of the emergence of geophysics, I have meant in

---

[56] See Harold Jeffreys, *The Earth* (Cambridge: Cambridge Univ. Press, 1924), dedicatory page. While Darwin's immediate successors well appreciated Darwin's pivotal role, modern earth scientists seem only vaguely aware of Darwin, and few recognize his fundamental importance to their field. A partial explanation, much like those advanced in this volume by Kathryn Olesko to account for the demise of Kohlrausch's "school," and by Steven Turner to account for Helmholtz's not having a school as clearly demarcated as Hering's, is that Darwin's "style" of geophysics became so dominant in Britain, that that is what geophysics simply was. Its total success annihilated other traditions and eventually erased the memory of its own.

[57] The paper, with corrections, is Darwin, *Scientific Papers,* Vol. II, pp. 459–514. Darwin met with nothing like the controversy described by Turner in this volume.

one very important sense the prehistory of geophysics. Thus throughout, the subject has been a new field of scientific inquiry without many of the formal trappings of a discipline as construed by sociologists, such as a standard course of study in a university department or specialized societies or journals. By the turn of the century a distinct new entity or "discipline" of British geophysics had clearly "emerged," but it required the next quarter century to become really consolidated. In Germany, however, the consolidation of the discipline was an integral factor in its emergence as a recognized scientific activity. This difference may be ascribed to the more general one between the university-based German tradition of "professional" science and the relatively "amateur" setting of the British scientific enterprise for much of the nineteenth century. The case of geophysics in general is also greatly complicated by its being an umbrella field, from its very early stages, comprising numerous specialties, each with unique histories, that only eventually come to be recognized as related.

Thus it is not clear to what extent the emergence of geophysics can be generalized or serve as a model for the emergence of other disciplines or specialties. And unfortunately historians and other practitioners of science studies have yet to devise adequate frameworks for such theoretical discussions. In the case at hand, and more fully elsewhere, I have delineated the development of the core of British geophysics, that mathematical-physical-geological approach to the chief interdisciplinary problems of the "earth sciences" of Victorian Britain. Yet once this core was firmly established as a new field, the related specialties of seismology, volcanology, and geodesy were quickly aligned and allied with it, creating the umbrella field. In an important sense these specialties were the special province of problem-centered communities of scientists. It is in part because the membership of these communities frequently overlapped that the scientists in them were able to pull together into a geophysical community. Yet this all seems curious given that one might expect new specialties to branch off from a common core of approaches, techniques, and assumptions about one's own science, as new fields of inquiry are discovered, and not the other way around (although this is not to say that new specialties did not later develop out of the new umbrella field). Perhaps the problem, or charm, of British geophysics is that it did not strictly originate within a particular discipline and then develop on its own, borrowing what it needed from other fields, but with its parentage always apparent. Rather it was always a hybrid, interdisciplinary subject, perhaps one of the first of its kind. Its ties with geology were particularly loose, despite the twentieth-century trend to urge greater cooperation. And it never did become a proper subfield of astrophysics, as the American George Becker believed it ought, although its filial and institutional ties in that direction were particularly strong. I therefore have argued, in part, that we must conceptualize the emergence of a distinctly British geophysics in terms of certain technical-conceptual demands made by and upon the scientists, albeit with an eye to the broader social dimension. Indeed, it was George Darwin's pioneering work that played the fundamental role in the transformation to a modern geophysics, characterized by Darwin's own style of applied mathematics and evolutionary epistemology. Perhaps, then, the fairest way to approach our subjects is to recognize that we might have to conceptualize the emergence of different fields in different social contexts in different ways.

This discussion of the field's unusual "emergence" naturally points to a consideration of the distinctive character of British geophysics. Even though it was never properly a subfield of astronomy, the two were closely related. The earth, as a planet, could be viewed and treated as any other planet. The relationship between the two fields owes as much to this fact as to any similarity of approaches. This astronomical influence or bias can be seen throughout the development of the field of terrestrial physics. Nearly every major problem of concern to the scientists discussed here bears it: Hopkins's precession-based argument for the thickness of the crust, the tides and tidal effective rigidity of the earth, the age of the earth, the astronomical causes of glacial epochs, and Darwin's tidal theory of the earth-moon system and related cosmogonical speculations. No doubt the high esteem in which Newtonian physical astronomy was held in Victorian science colored the matter—indeed, geology proper strove to emulate that paradigm. With this history, the new discipline of geophysics found its first institutional linkages with astronomy: Darwin held the nation's premier astronomy chair; many geophysical papers were published in the *Monthly Notices of the Royal Astronomical Society;* and the RAS became home to geophysical meetings, lectures, and the first disciplinary journal in English, the *Geophysical Supplement,* precursor to the *Geophysical Journal.* Such close connections between the two fields may have been peculiar to Britain, but they were not peculiar within the British context. To British scientists, still standing in the long shadow of Newton, who had become "institutionalized" at Cambridge and "canonized" by John Herschel, William Whewell, George Biddell Airy, and others, the development of their sciences—including geophysics and the types of problems early "geophysicists" were inclined to attack—seemed perfectly natural.[58]

Consideration of the special circumstances in which British geophysics emerged leads eventually to the question of whether Darwin founded a research school. As Gerald L. Geison has argued, historians usually depend on particularities and contingencies in answering such questions, whereas sociologists of science tend to abstract from the case study and devise general theoretical structures. Geison further argued that historians choose to focus on research schools, while sociologists emphasize emerging specialties. While I am naturally sympathetic with the historian's emphasis on particularity, the emergence of British geophysics seems to have little in common with research schools as loci of scientific change, at least those studied to date.[59] Although the three major figures, Hopkins, Thomson, and especially Darwin, could all be said to have personal research programs in physical geology or terrestrial physics and all three were associated with Cambridge, it would be stretching things to say there was a Cambridge school of terrestrial physics. Darwin's vast correspondence network and institutional connections cannot be so characterized. S. F. Cannon and Crosbie Smith

---

[58] Indeed, British geology seemed no less peculiar to foreigners for its emphasis on stratigraphy, as Mott Greene has urged; see Greene, *Geology* (cit. n. 1). For that matter, to foreigners the British seemed peculiarly concerned with evolution and with making mechanical models of the ether.

[59] See Gerald L. Geison, "Scientific Change, Emerging Specialties, and Research Schools," *History of Science,* 1981, *19*:20–40, for a thorough discussion of the literature on research schools and emerging specialties. See also J. B. Morrell, "The Chemist Breeders: The Research Schools of Liebig and Thomas Thomson," *Ambix,* 1972, *19*:1–46; Joseph S. Fruton, "The Liebig Research Group: A Reappraisal," *Proceedings of the American Philosophical Society,* 1988, *132*:1–66; and Joseph S. Fruton, "Contrasts in Scientific Style: Emil Fischer and Franz Hofmeister, Their Research Groups and Their Theory of Protein Structure," *ibid.,* 1985, *129*:313–370.

are quite persuasive on the notion of the "Cambridge Network," but while that network may have exerted strong influence on the development of research schools in Britain, it cannot itself be labeled a "research school." Furthermore, the studies of the Cambridge Network have concentrated on the early Victorian period, and little has been done to extend the notion to the later Victorian or Edwardian periods, although Darwin's own network meshes well with such a notion.[60]

Yet if one considers the characteristics ascribed to research schools, in either J. B. Morrell's well-known "ideal" model or Geison's checklist, then Darwin does not fare too badly. Indeed on Geison's checklist, of whose value he admits being skeptical, Darwin scores on 11 of the 14 points, failing on (7) "simple and rapidly exploitable techniques," (13) "institutionalization in university setting," and (14) "adequate financial support."[61] This places Darwin just behind the "successful" schools of Justus Liebig, Arthur A. Noyes, and Michael Foster, just ahead of the temporarily successful Arcueil School and Enrico Fermi's group, but well ahead of the failed schools of Thomas Thomson, John Scott Burdon-Sanderson, and Ira Remsen (the anomaly being W. D. Bancroft).

Although such a formulaic approach is problematic, Darwin's failure on only three key features may well be enough to vitiate the notion that there was a Darwin-led research school of geophysics. Perhaps the most important point is Darwin's lack of transmittable experimental techniques. Undoubtedly this is because analyses of "schools" to date have concentrated on laboratory-based research schools, especially on schools of chemistry. Within the context of a laboratory, with its instruments and standard procedures, the actual content of the science prosecuted becomes almost reified, so that it is easier to explain how and why scientists associated with the laboratory share common scientific assumptions, methodologies, and goals within a unified research program. Outside of a laboratory environment, especially in a largely theoretical research program, the task of explicating what binds a research "school" or "group" of scientists together becomes much more difficult and problematic, leaving the historian to fall back on other common institutional, cultural, and social factors. In the case of Darwin and British geophysics, the situation is further complicated because Darwin's research program was essentially one of applied mathematics, and, since historians and sociologists often treat mathematics distinctly from the rest of science (when they treat it at all), the question of whether there can be research schools in mathematics has yet to be broached—and this notwithstanding Larmor's belief that Darwin was the "*doyen* of the mathematical school at Cambridge," as mentioned above.[62]

Darwin's case is perhaps most saliently contrasted not with the leaders of research schools studied to date but rather with that of his own Cambridge col-

---

[60] Cannon, *Science in Culture* (cit. n. 46); and Smith, "Geologists and Mathematicians" (cit. n. 1).

[61] Geison, "Scientific Change" (cit. n. 59), on p. 24. Darwin does seem to possess the following eleven characteristics, taken numerically from Geison's chart: (1) "charismatic" leader; (2) leader with research reputation; (3) "informal" setting and leadership style; (4) leader with institutional power; (5) social cohesion, loyalty, *esprit de corps,* "discipleship"; (6) focused research program; (8) invasion of new field of research; (9) pool of potential recruits (graduate students); (10) access to or control of publication outlets; (11) students publish early under own names; (12) produced and "placed" significant number of students.

[62] Larmor, "Sir George Howard Darwin" (cit. n. 39).

league, J. J. Thomson. Thomson's school of experimental physics—or if a longer perspective is desired, the Cavendish School of Physics, headed in turn by James Clerk Maxwell, Lord Rayleigh, Thomson, and Ernest Rutherford—would meet very well historians' criteria for a research school, whatever fate the science produced by that school met.[63] This parallel of course exposes the bias in the exclusionary notion of a laboratory-based research school.

The two other features Darwin conspicuously lacked, university institutionalization and adequate financial support, are connected. Geophysics, which only just became recognized as a distinct discipline with Darwin, was hardly likely to gain immediate institutional support, financial or otherwise. In fact, the interdisciplinary nature of the new specialty hindered rather than aided such support, for in the British context the discipline's recognizable constituent parts were separately institutionalized: in separate scientific societies; in separate government offices, where the study of the tides, geodesy, and meteorology were administered by the Admiralty, Ordnance Survey, and Meteorological Council (later Meteorological Office), respectively; and in the universities themselves, where the separate, endowed professorships were in astronomy, mathematics, and geology.

Indeed it is Darwin's pivotal role as Plumian Professor of Astronomy that most tellingly handicapped the university institutionalization of the emerging discipline, yet linked it with its sister science of astronomy, giving that peculiar British twist to geophysics. As Plumian Professor, Darwin was expected to lecture upon astronomical topics, and given his own research interests, it was not hard for him to do so—and to skew them towards his own hybrid theoretical astronomy-cum-geophysics. Darwin lectured not only on dynamical astronomy and the theory of potential and attractions, themselves integral elements of his own work, but also on figures of equilibrium of rotating fluid, orbits of planets, and the figure of the earth and precession, all major components of his scientific research program, as examined above, imbued with his applied mathematical methodology.[64] The problem for Darwin came, however, with placing his advanced students. There was no geophysical laboratory in which to place them as demonstrators (as J. J. Thomson could do at the Cavendish). Indeed there was no professional career path for a "geophysicist" at all. But as the nation's preeminent professor of astronomy, Darwin did have tremendous placement power in the astronomical observatory system, one of the most stable professional careers for scientists at the time. Many of Darwin's brightest students, with little practical or observational experience (for Darwin was never much interested in observational astronomy), thus came to be assistants at the Cambridge Observatory, the Royal Observatory at Greenwich, the Royal Observatory at the Cape of Good Hope, and other observatories. From these and similar positions, Darwin's students came to dominate the leading astronomical positions and professorships, carrying with them their

[63] For background on the Cavendish Laboratory see Romualdus Sviedrys, "The Rise of Physics Laboratories in Britain," *Historical Studies in the Physical Sciences,* 1976, 7:405–436; and J. G. Crowther, *The Cavendish Laboratory, 1874–1974* (New York: Science History Publications, 1974). Gerald L. Geison, *Michael Foster and the Cambridge School of Physiology* (Princeton, N.J.: Princeton Univ. Press, 1978) briefly compares Foster's school and the Cavendish school at pp. 112–115.

[64] The *Cambridge University Reporter* contains the list of lectures given by Darwin and his colleagues each term.

interests in geophysics and Darwin's brand of sophisticated mathematical analysis, and in this way geophysics eventually eased its way into institutional footholds.[65] And for such hybrid scientists it was a good thing, too, for it really was not until several years after Darwin's death in 1912 that direct nonuniversity institutional support was forthcoming, primarily from the Royal Astronomical Society. More surprising is that there was no direct, unambiguous support for geophysics at Cambridge until 1931, when Harold Jeffreys was appointed the first University Reader in Geophysics.

Finding direct public financial support for science was always a tricky matter in nineteenth-century Britain, where the laissez-faire attitude of the Victorians favored private patronage. Darwin could occasionally get small sums from the government to hire computers for his tidal reductions or for work on the *Admiralty Scientific Manual*—but that was government work, not associated with his own research program. Small sums (less than £50) were also occasionally forthcoming from the Royal Society and the British Association. But much came out of Darwin's own pocket; indeed he even paid for the completion of the triangulation of Africa. Even at Cambridge, where the coffers seemed more open to science than anywhere else in the British Empire, reliance was placed on the patronage of its benefactors: the Duke of Devonshire paid for the Cavendish Laboratory and Rayleigh's Nobel Prize money paid for a major addition to the lab, while on the astronomy side the University Observatory, Newall Telescope, and solar physics instruments benefited from the bequests of Richard Sheepshanks and his sister Anne, R. S. Newall, and Frank McClean, respectively.[66] Darwin was perhaps fortunate that the type of theoretical, mathematical geophysics and astronomy he pursued did not require vast sums for buildings, instruments, or other equipment. But as geophysics matured and consolidated, subspecialties such as seismology and geomagnetism required bigger bucks for the bang, and the international prosecution of geophysics, especially after World War I, was as much a part of the proliferation of big science in the twentieth century as any other field.

There are then a number of problems in forcing Darwin's case into categories designed for other contexts. The advantages gained from focusing on laboratory-based research schools can prove to be liabilities when the scope is enlarged to include nonexperimental, nonobservational, theoretical, or even mathematical

[65] E.g., Charles Chree was at first an assistant at the Kew Observatory and later Superintendent there from 1893 to 1925; Chree was also the assistant director of the Meteorological Office, headed by Napier Shaw, another Darwin student. P. H. Cowell was chief assistant at the Royal Observatory, Greenwich, from 1896 to 1910, and afterwards the Superintendent of the Nautical Almanac Office from 1910 to 1930. F. W. Dyson started as the chief assistant at Greenwich from 1894 to 1905, moved on to become the Astronomer Royal for Scotland for five years, and then in 1910 became Britain's ninth Astronomer Royal. S. S. Hough was chief assistant at the Royal Observatory, Cape of Good Hope, from 1898 to 1907, and subsequently Royal Astronomer at the Cape from 1907 to 1923. A. E. H. Love was Sedleian Professor of Natural Philosophy at Oxford, 1898–1940. F. J. M. Stratton assisted first at the Cambridge University Observatory from 1906, became the assistant director of the Solar Physics Observatory at Cambridge in 1913, and afterwards Director and Professor of Astrophysics in 1928. Finally, H. H. Turner began as chief assistant at Greenwich from 1884 to 1893, then became the Savilian Professor of Astronomy and Director of the University Observatory at Oxford from 1893 to 1930. From J. A. Venn, *Alumni Cantabrigienses, Part II,* 6 vols. (Cambridge: Cambridge Univ. Press, 1940–1954).

[66] Tanner, ed., *Historical Register* (cit. n. 52), pp. 216–220, 232 (see pp. 214–245 *passim* for other major private gifts benefiting the sciences at Cambridge during this time).

research groups, circles, teams, or schools. I am hopeful, however, that there will be characteristics shared across the various boundaries of time, institutions, nations, and disciplines, beginning with research leaders who do innovative science in important problem areas and who foster a common sense of purpose among students, colleagues, and the wider scientific community. If we allow for the differing contexts of emerging disciplines *vis-à-vis* established fields, interdisciplinary studies *vis-à-vis* subspecialties of mature sciences, and theoretical constructs *vis-à-vis* experimental techniques, then the number of attributes consistently shared will no doubt be fewer, but they are more likely to get at the heart of the role of research schools in scientific change.

There can be little doubt that Darwin was the head of something—so influential a figure that Jeffreys called him the founder of modern geophysics. If the prejudices we as historians have attached to research schools can be set aside, if the notion of a research school can be weaned from its laboratory base, and if our semantic meanings of such terms can be broadened without eviscerating their explanatory power, then I should have no problem placing George Darwin at the head of the British School of Geophysics.

But perhaps in the end our best efforts on this tricky enterprise of elucidating the nature of research schools really ought to be tempered by a healthy skepticism. This enterprise will, I believe, be best prosecuted if we remember the lesson Geison taught us a decade ago: "Further analyses of research schools . . . ought to be welcomed even though (or perhaps precisely because) their most likely outcome would be to expose as illusory any effort to develop a magic formula for organizing innovative and successful groups of scientists."[67]

[67] Geison, "Scientific Change" (cit. n. 59), on p. 37.

CONCLUDING REFLECTIONS

The two "chemist breeders." **Left:** *Justus Liebig, 1803–1873.* **Right:** *Thomas Thomson, 1773–1852. Both courtesy of the Edgar Fahs Smith Collection.*

Research Schools and New Directions in the Historiography of Science

By Gerald L. Geison*

DESERVEDLY HIGH TRIBUTE is paid in this volume to the influence of J. B. Morrell's pioneering article of 1972, "The Chemist Breeders: The Research Schools of Liebig and Thomson." The deep impress of Morrell's essay is visible in two of my own works: the book of 1978 on the Cambridge school of physiology, which also drew on Jerome R. Ravetz's striking if more abstract insights into research schools; and the synoptic article of 1981, "Scientific Change, Emerging Specialties, and Research Schools," which developed Morrell's "conjectural model of an 'ideal' research school" and extended it to several other laboratory-based research schools, including examples from physiology, physics, and physical chemistry as well as chemistry.[1]

A substantial body of related scholarship has appeared in the meantime, as this volume makes abundantly clear. Much of that recent scholarship, and nearly all of the essays in this volume, refer to my article of 1981, and I like to think that I have helped spread the Morrellian gospel to some of the heathen who had not yet fallen under its spell. In any case, Morrell's model of the research school has now been widely deployed, extended, and criticized, and this volume should draw still further attention to its virtues while also allowing us to see some of its limitations.

This essay consists mainly of reflections on topics discussed or alluded to elsewhere in the volume, with special attention to their implications for Morrell's model and other current historiographic concerns. Section I is devoted to "merely" terminological issues, precisely because I believe that some words matter a lot—including *model, school,* and *research school.* Section II examines the utility of Morrell's model in contexts very different from the laboratory schools on which it was originally based. Section III addresses the vexed questions of conceptual change and success or failure in research schools. Finally, in Section IV, I suggest that studies of research schools and "scientific styles" might reinforce the emerging links between history of science and cultural history in general.

* Department of History, Princeton University, Dickinson Hall, Princeton, New Jersey 08544.

[1] J. B. Morrell, "The Chemist Breeders: The Research Schools of Liebig and Thomson," *Ambix,* 1972, *19*:1–46; Gerald L. Geison, *Michael Foster and the Cambridge School of Physiology: The Scientific Enterprise in Late Victorian Society* (Princeton, N.J.: Princeton Univ. Press, 1978); Jerome R. Ravetz, *Scientific Knowledge and Its Social Problems* (New York: Oxford Univ. Press, 1971); and Gerald L. Geison, "Scientific Change, Emerging Specialties, and Research Schools," *History of Science,* 1981, *10*:20–40.

I. ON MATTERS OF WORDS AND WORDS THAT MATTER

Happily, this volume includes a contribution by Morrell himself. It consists almost entirely of a lively empirical account of the younger William Henry Perkin's
research schools of chemistry at Manchester and especially at Oxford during the
first three decades of this century. In his concluding paragraphs, however, Morrell
returns to his essay of 1972, partly to assess the applicability of his model to this
new empirical material but also to remind us of the historiographic concerns that
motivated his essay in the first place. Morrell concedes that his account of Justus
Liebig's school now seems "sketchy" in the light of more recent scholarship by
Frederic L. Holmes and Joseph Fruton,[2] but he expresses greater concern about
the extent to which his 1972 article lapsed into "prescriptive" language on the way
to a "normative" model of the research school. It would be better, Morrell now insists, if we deployed his model "heuristically" rather than prescriptively.

This shift in Morrell's tone goes a long way toward meeting a reservation I
voiced in my article of 1981. As I put it then: "Morrell's schema . . . is not really a
'model' in any very deep sense of the word. It is rather a usefully systematic catalogue of the factors to be considered when examining a research school."[3] What
made me uneasy about applying the word *model* to Morrell's analysis was my impression, perhaps reinforced by his prescriptive language, that he meant thus to
imply that his scheme had causal explanatory power. In an essay of 1986, James
A. Secord captured much of what I had in mind more directly and more forcefully: "In adopting and refining concepts like the research school, it is important
to keep in mind that such categories cannot serve as final arbiters of explanation. . . . [I]n the end, a research school, like a discipline, is essentially a descriptive category for charting patterns of changing and contingent social
relations. Although it cannot explain those patterns in a causal sense, it does suggest fruitful ways of exploring them."[4] This quotation comes very close to expressing my own point of view. It would have come closer still had Secord emphasized
that a research school is fundamentally a *unit of analysis,* of which one can have a
concept, though it is not itself a "concept" and most assuredly not an "explanation" of anything. The research school is, I believe, an uncommonly fruitful unit
of analysis for historians of modern science, and Morrell's categories are very useful indeed in the investigation of particular cases—as the contributions to this
volume fully attest.

But it is always an empirical question whether the list of attributes or features
in Morrell's "ideal" model is appropriate to the case at hand. The absence of one,
two, or even several of Morrell's criteria does not automatically exclude a group
of scientists from the category of research schools, while some research schools
may have important features undreamt of in Morrell's model. Other seemingly
cohesive groups of research scientists may scarcely conform to Morrell's model at

---

[2] See Frederic L. Holmes, "The Complementarity of Teaching and Research in Liebig's Laboratory," *Osiris,* 1989, *5*:121–164; and Joseph S. Fruton, *Contrasts in Scientific Style: Research Groups in
the Chemical and Biochemical Sciences* (Philadelphia: American Philosophical Society, 1990), Ch. 2
("The Liebig Research Group in Giessen"), pp. 16–71.
[3] Geison, "Scientific Change" (cit. n. 1), p. 26.
[4] James A. Secord, "The Geological Survey of Great Britain as a Research School, 1839–1855,"
Hist. Sci., 1986, *24*:223–265, quoting from p. 261.

all. But if Morrell's categories are deployed heuristically, as he now recommends, I see no danger, and a good deal of convenience, in using the term *model* as a covering term for his scheme. In any case, analysts of research schools can and have profited from systematic attention to Morrell's categories, even when they doubt or deny the full-fledged applicability of his model to a particular group of research scientists.[5]

A second major terminological issue runs through several of the chapters in this volume: Is *research school* the most appropriate term for the small scientific collectivities with which we are concerned? Fruton thinks not, preferring instead the term *research group*. In the first footnote of his important recent book, *Contrasts in Scientific Style,* he writes as follows: "The term *research school* has also been used to denote what I describe as a *research group*. . . . I prefer the latter term because *research school* has also been applied to a community of scientists, not necessarily located at a single institution, or even in the same country, who are united solely by a common interest in a particular direction of research."[6] More pointedly, during the Yale conference that helped bring this volume to fruition, Fruton asked whether "research school" might not be a phrase created by historians rather than one used by the actors themselves. When the other conference participants pondered Fruton's question, we realized that almost none of us had paid close attention to the specific terms used by our historical actors in their references to research units. We quickly agreed on the need for a systematic historical investigation of the ways in which such terms have actually been used at different times and in different places.

In his contribution to this volume, John Servos takes a large step toward that goal by examining the way in which the phrase *research school* entered the vocabulary of historians of science. He finds clear traces of the notion almost a century ago in J. T. Merz's monumental *History of European Thought in the Nineteenth Century,* especially when Merz applied the otherwise ambiguous word *school* to laboratory-based research groups in German-language universities. Indeed, Servos notes in passing that Merz may even have coined the term in the form "school of research"—though he is quick to add that *research school* itself did not become common currency among historians of science until after 1969, when Owen Hannaway used it in a remarkably influential book review as a label for the early nineteenth-century group of French physical scientists that Maurice Crosland had called the Society of Arcueil.[7] In the two decades since then, as Servos shows in his admirable survey of the shifting meanings and valuations of these terms, the sometimes derogatory connotations once associated with the

---

[5] In this respect, there is a striking similarity between Morrell's "ideal" model of research schools and Talcott Parson's equally "ideal" model of the professions, which has exerted a powerful influence on American sociologists and historians since its formulation in the 1950s, despite increasingly vigorous critiques. In 1983 I wrote of the Parsonian model in terms very similar to those I have just applied to Morrell's: "Despite its limitations, the Parsonian conception of the professions does have value and utility in certain contexts, especially when its categories are deployed as heuristic devices rather than as central elements in a rigid and universal model of the professions." Gerald L. Geison, introduction to *Professions and Professional Ideologies in America,* ed. Geison (Philadelphia: Univ. Pennsylvania Press, 1983), pp. 3–11, quoting from p. 5.

[6] Fruton, *Contrasts in Scientific Style* (cit. n. 2), pp. 1–2 (note 1).

[7] Owen Hannaway, review of Maurice Crosland, *The Society of Arcueil: A View of French Science at the Time of Napoleon I,* in *Isis,* 1969, *60*:578–581.

term *school* have been largely replaced by neutral or even positive connotations in recent scholarship on research schools.[8]

What also emerges from Servos's account—and several other contributions to this volume—is that some of our historical actors did indeed explicitly refer to small, geographically localized groups of research scientists as schools—in other words, they used the term in settings like those where Fruton prefers "research group." The immediate answer, then, to Fruton's question is that the term *school* (if not, to my knowledge, the full term *research school*) for such local collectivities is decidedly not an artifact introduced by historians.

At some point, of course, such close attention to matters of terminology can become an obsession, and there is much to be said for Secord's point that "the idea underlying the historical study of research schools" is more important than the label. What matters most, Secord insists, is that this approach "focuses attention on small groups within the scientific community, and the social and intellectual ties that bind them together"—and such an approach, he continues, "is the only way that the history of science will go beyond studies of innovation, to see how ideas become embodied in the concrete practice of specific individuals and groups."[9]

Secord is surely right about the relative unimportance of labels. Even so, I want to insist on the advantages to be gained from the continued use of the research school—rather than, say, the research group—as an analytic category in studies of the sort found in this volume. For one thing, the term *research school* now enjoys wide currency in the historical and sociological literature, and it has acquired a reasonably clear and consensual meaning among those engaged in analyses of small scientific collectivities. More important, the term has the distinct advantage of focusing attention on the role of pedagogy and training in such groups.

In my book on the Cambridge school of physiology, I tried to convey some sense of the crucial pedagogical dimension of the interaction between Michael Foster as research director and the investigators he trained. No small part of the "teaching" in Foster's school, I suggested, had to do with the transmission of "tacit" or "craft" knowledge—both in guiding students toward promising problems for investigation and in ensuring that they became proficient in the most effective techniques for the pursuit of those problems.[10] Now that Kathryn Olesko, among others, has begun to show us just how much can be done to uncover and specify the hitherto tacit features of pedagogy[11]—that is, to illuminate the once mysterious process by which research skills are acquired and transmitted—I need say little more about this issue here, except to note an important difference in emphasis among analysts of research schools as to the most salient features of tacit knowledge.

Servos, for example, in his essay here, suggests that "tacit knowledge of technique constitutes but a small part of what masters transmit to their disciples" in research schools. "Far more important," he continues, "may be the guidance that

[8] Mary Jo Nye also emphasizes this point in her essay in this volume.

[9] Secord, "Geological Survey" (cit. n. 4), p. 264.

[10] Geison, *Michael Foster* (cit. n. 1).

[11] See her essay in this volume, and Kathryn M. Olesko, *Physics as a Calling: Discipline and Practice in the Königsberg Seminar for Physics* (Ithaca, N.Y./London: Cornell Univ. Press, 1991).

they offer on the problem-structure of their disciplines and the enthusiasm and inspiration to persevere that some inspire through informal exchanges and example"—a suggestion that is, I think, basically consonant with the message of Fruton's *Contrasts in Scientific Style*. Servos even asks whether the transmission of tacit (or "hard-to-specify") knowledge might not be accomplished all apart from personal contact—specifically, through textbooks, a possibility that Olesko's work also invites us to consider. The issues thus raised by Servos, Olesko, and others about the relation between pedagogy and the acquisition of research skills are crucial and obviously deserve further attention. But the basic thrust of the most exciting recent scholarship, it seems to me, is precisely to show that the "enculturation" of experimental techniques, practices, and skills through direct personal interaction in research schools is more important than the transmission of "impersonal" knowledge through textbooks or other relatively distant forms of communication.[12]

There is, finally, one other point to be made on behalf of continued reliance on the research school as an analytic construct. We should, of course, always be alert and sensitive to the specific terms our historical actors actually used at different times and places. But whether or not they explicitly used the term *research school,* we should not allow ourselves to be conceptually enslaved by their linguistic choices, however "historically correct" such an approach may be. Consider, in this connection, Thomas S. Kuhn's famous term *paradigm*. Surely few, if any, of Kuhn's historical actors thought of themselves as representatives of a paradigm. But that historical reality does not vitiate the analytic power of Kuhn's celebrated category. The term *research school* has not yet achieved anything like the status of Kuhn's *paradigm* and perhaps never will, but it does have discernible advantages over such related terms as *research group* or Kuhn's own *communities*. Compared to these flat descriptive terms, *research school* resonates with meaning, no doubt partly because of the very ambiguities that surround it.

II. RESEARCH SCHOOLS OUTSIDE THE LAB: MATHEMATICAL GEOPHYSICS AND THE FIELD SCIENCES

Morrell's ideal model of the research school grew out of his investigation of nineteenth-century chemical laboratories, and almost all efforts to extend his model to other cases have likewise been restricted to laboratory-based research schools. That includes my article of 1981, where I simply ignored the question of how far, if at all, Morrell's model could be applied to small groups of scientists whose interactions took place outside the laboratory. If the scholarship then available gave me some warrant for ignoring the issue at the time, that is no longer the case. Indeed, one major virtue of this volume is that it includes three valuable case studies of more or less cohesive groups of scientists who interacted in

---

[12] Frederic L. Holmes has made several major and deeply informed contributions to this literature. See, e.g., Holmes, "The Complementarity of Teaching and Research" (cit. n. 2); Holmes, "The Formation of the Munich School of Metabolism," in *The Investigative Enterprise: Experimental Physiology in Nineteenth-Century Medicine,* ed. William Coleman and Holmes (Berkeley/Los Angeles: Univ. California Press, 1988), pp. 179–210; and Holmes, "Manometers, Tissue Slices, and Intermediary Metabolism," in *The Right Tools for the Job: At Work in Twentieth-Century Life Sciences,* ed. Adele E. Clarke and Joan H. Fujimura (Princeton, N.J.: Princeton Univ. Press, 1992), pp. 151–171.

settings outside the laboratory: David Kushner's chapter on George Darwin and British geophysics, Joel Hagen's study of Frederic Clements's school of ecology at the Carnegie Institution in Washington, D.C., and Pamela Henson's essay on John Henry Comstock's schools of entomology at Cornell and Stanford.

Kushner offers a detailed account of the emergence of geophysics as a discipline in Victorian Britain, culminating in the work of George Darwin. In his exegesis, Kushner rarely uses the term *research school* or the associated Morrellian categories, and some readers may wonder why his chapter is included in the volume at all. But quite apart from its intrinsic merits, Kushner's essay draws attention to the limitations of Morrell's model in the case of such mathematically based domains as theoretical geophysics. When the tools of the trade are readily transportable mathematical techniques and abstract theoretical concepts rather than locally constructed experimental systems, including site-specific instruments, techniques, and materials, Morrell's model of research schools does seem to lose at least some of its force and salience. On Kushner's account, historians in search of a fruitful unit of analysis within the emerging disipline of theoretical geophysics would do well to look not for localized research schools but rather for geographically dispersed *correspondence networks.* That advice surely applies to research collectivities in other disciplines, especially but not only in other mathematical and theoretical domains.[13]

The essays by Hagen and Henson also take us outside the laboratory setting in which Morrell's model was forged. These authors deal instead with two "field" sciences, plant ecology and evolutionary entomology. Both explicitly discuss the applicability of the Morrellian model to their case studies—with very different, almost divergent results. In his study of Frederic Clements's school of plant ecology at the Carnegie Institution from 1917 to 1941, Hagen gives special attention to the personal dynamics within the school, notably the tension between Clements and his most talented students, while spinning a tale of a research school that failed to flourish. In Hagen's view, this case study reveals a basic flaw in Morrell's model, or at least that version of it represented by my article of 1981. For Hagen, as we shall see below, my "top-down" (or elitist) model of the research school is at odds with the story he wants to tell.

Henson, in striking contrast, finds a remarkably close fit between my version of Morrell's model and John Henry Comstock's highly successful research schools of entomology at Cornell and Stanford between 1880 and 1930. The most obvious reason for the disparity between Henson's and Hagen's results is that Comstock's schools were university-based, while Clements's school of ecology was located outside a university, at the Carnegie Institution in Washington, D.C. But this institutional difference, however important, cannot fully account for the divergence in results. For there is at least one major study of a research school in yet another field science, namely geology, that also (like Clements's school of ecology) had its institutional base outside a university but that nonetheless proves

[13] The crucial role of correspondence networks in nineteenth-century British geology and natural history is now abundantly clear from a rich and impressive body of recent scholarship. See, e.g., Secord, "Geological Survey" (cit. n. 4); Martin J. S. Rudwick, *The Great Devonian Controversy: The Shaping of Knowledge Among Gentlemanly Specialists* (Chicago: Univ. Chicago Press, 1985); and Anne Larsen, "Not Since Noah: The English Scientific Zoologists and the Craft of Collecting, 1800–1840" (Ph.D. diss., Princeton Univ., 1993), esp. Ch. 7.

amenable to a Morrellian analysis. This case study is James Secord's 1986 essay on the British Geological Survey in the mid-nineteenth century, the earliest and still most extensive attempt known to me of the application of Morrell's model to a field science. In Secord's words, "the [Geological] Survey's first director, Henry De la Beche, was intent on creating what can best be described as a research school in geology: a group of established investigators and young trainees united in a common approach, and distinguished (both socially and intellectually) from the scientific community as a whole."[14]

Neither Secord nor Henson adopts Morrell's model *tout court* and neither applies it in a mechanical way. Almost by definition, research collectivities in such field sciences as ecology, entomology, or geology are different in several important respects from the laboratory-based schools on which Morrell's model was initially based. In the latter the research director and his apprentices worked cheek by jowl in the same physical and instrumental setting, day in and day out. In the field sciences, by contrast, the members of a research school were and are perforce spatially dispersed at least part of the time. A priori, this difference, which receives pointed attention from Henson and Hagen as well as Secord, might seem to discourage any effort to apply Morrell's model to the field sciences. Yet Secord's study of the British Geological Survey, like Henson's essay in this volume, shows that the model can yield important insights outside its original domain. Even Kushner's essay on George Darwin and British geophysics, for all of its reservations about the applicability of Morrell's model to this particular case, does not deny the heuristic value of Morrell's categories.

Against this background, Hagen's objections to Morrellian models can perhaps be traced partly to the relative failure of Clements's school—as compared, say, to Comstock's highly successful schools of entomology. Morrell's model does seem to work best in the case of successful research schools. In fact, Morrell himself expressed concern from the outset that his model "suffers from the limitation that it tends to be an idealizing rationalization of Liebig's success."[15] Precisely for that reason, Morrell also gave close attention to Thomas Thomson's relatively unsuccessful, indeed previously obscure, school of chemistry at the University of Glasgow. It is to this issue of success and failure in research schools that I now turn—beginning, however, with the more general question of the relationship between research schools and conceptual change.

III. CONCEPTUAL CHANGE AND SUCCESS OR FAILURE IN RESEARCH SCHOOLS

How to measure success and failure in science? And how much can either result be ascribed to institutional circumstances? In their contributions to this volume, both Steven Turner and Joel Hagen suggest that research schools are privileged sites of conceptual innovation. As illustrated mainly by his impressive case study of Hering's school of physiological optics, Turner argues that at least some research schools can be seen as distinctive "linguistic communities." Turner is bold enough to compare and contrast the results of his investigation

[14] Secord, "Geological Survey" (cit. n. 4), p. 224.
[15] Morrell, "Chemist Breeders" (cit. n. 1), p. 45.

with Kuhn's famous views on scientific change: "Thomas S. Kuhn, who first insisted on incommensurability as a necessary correlate of all deep change in science, has increasingly emphasized the semantic and linguistic aspects of conceptual incommensurability. On that Kuhnian position, research schools may be the only real nuclei of radical scientific change, because they are the only adequate loci of semantic innovation." Turner and Hagen also draw on evolutionary models to illustrate the connection between research schools and conceptual change, both citing David Hull's 1988 book *Science as a Process,* arguably the subtlest effort yet made to develop an evolutionary epistemology of scientific knowledge.[16] (As we learn from Kushner's essay here, such efforts can in fact be traced back at least as far as Charles Darwin's own son, George Darwin, whose modest attempt at an evolutionary epistemology did not, however, refer explicitly to research groups or schools.) Hagen borrows from Hull to suggest that "research groups are like demes, the freely interbreeding populations of evolutionary theory" within which "ideas may be modified and transmitted much more rapidly than they can through the formal channels of the more extended scientific community." For his part, Turner compares the research school to a "genetic variant" that can "become the nucleus of a new specialty or subdiscipline," or "succeed by imposing its new direction on the entire existing field of which it was a part."

Yet modern evolutionary theory also teaches us that the usual fate of genetic variants, or at least major mutations, is failure—that is, extinction. But precisely because research schools are collectivities or "populations," their conceptual innovations have a better chance of surviving and flourishing in the crowded environment of modern intellectual life than do the ideas put forth by individual "mutant" scientists, whether cranks or geniuses. Even so, some research schools are bound to lose out in competition with others. The point here is to identify which factors are responsible—and to what extent—for these differential outcomes.

My article of 1981 includes a table or chart, developed from Morrell's model, that summarizes some of the basic features that may account for success or failure in research schools. A version of that chart appears in Henson's essay, and I direct further attention to it here only because Hagen objects to the use I make of it. Specifically, he complains that it fails to indicate the differential weight that each of the listed features actually carries in the rest of my analysis. If my chart were revised along these lines, Hagen continues, it would be clear that my version of the Morrellian model represents a top-down approach in which the role of a school's leader or director is exalted at the expense of other factors, including institutional circumstances and the characteristics of subordinate members of the research schools.

In one sense, Hagen is right on the mark. To a degree that even I had not appreciated at the time, my analysis does indeed emphasize the role and characteristics of the school's leader—and not only in the case of such obviously personal factors

[16] David L. Hull, *Science as a Process: An Evolutionary Account of the Social and Conceptual Development of Science* (Chicago: Univ. Chicago Press, 1988). For another recent attempt at evolutionary epistemology see Robert J. Richards, *Darwin and the Emergence of Evolutionary Theories of Mind and Behavior* (Chicago: Univ. Chicago Press, 1987).

as the leader's "charisma" or prior "research reputation." For, as now seems obvious to me, a school's leader also bears major responsibility for such superficially "institutional" features as "access to or control of publication outlets" and "adequate financial support." When a research school is led by a talented, effective, and charismatic individual, these and other so-called "institutional" advantages are vastly more likely to come its way.

Leaders of research schools do, of course, face very different constraints under different circumstances, and sometimes institutions do go a long way toward making the man or woman. That point is in fact nicely illustrated by some studies of relative failure in research schools—including, in this volume, the study of Blas Cabrera's school of physics at Madrid. The sometimes crucial role of institutional circumstances emerges even more tellingly in cases where the same leader enjoyed variable success in different settings, as in Morrell's account here of Perkin's schools at Manchester and Oxford.

Even so, most studies of failure in research schools ultimately assign major responsibility or blame to their directors—whether because of the sterility of their research programs (as in Alan Rocke's impressively detailed account in this volume of Hermann Kolbe's schools at Marburg and Leipzig) or perhaps more often because of defects in their personal leadership styles. Current historiographic fashion may wish it were otherwise, but I am repeatedly struck by the crucial role of individual human agency, personality, and leadership in the fate of research schools as in other institutions and forms of life.[17]

Ironically, Hagen's own account of Clements's school seems to me a striking vindication of just this position—of precisely that top-down approach to which he objects. For in the end, his attempt to explain the relative failure of the Clementsian school points directly toward the "dictatorial" personality of Clements himself. In Hagen's own words, "Clements's domineering personality and dogmatically held views on ecology stifled creativity." And though Hagen makes a valiant effort to shift attention from Clements to his students, who (Hagen suggests) lacked the requisite qualities of "discipleship," it is hard to see why any creative research scientist would choose to become a "disciple" in Clements's school. Even in the case of Clements's most notable student, the plant taxonomist Harvey Monroe Hall, Hagen repeats the point that Clements's "domineering style stifled [Hall's] work." Hagen would have us believe that "the case of Clements and his coworkers provides an interesting contrast to claims made by other historians," including notably Fruton. In fact, however, it seems to me that Hagen's otherwise valuable case study actually confirms what I take to be the central point of Fruton's *Contrasts in Scientific Style:* Nothing is more important to success or failure in a research school than the intellectual and personal qualities of its leader. Indeed, why else are research schools so often referred to in eponymous terms; why else do we read so often of Liebig's school, Foster's school, Ludwig's school, or even Clements's school itself?

[17] For an explicit expression of this "elitist" position see Gerald L. Geison, "International Relations and Domestic Elites in American Physiology, 1900–1940," in *Physiology in the American Context, 1850–1940,* ed. Geison (Bethesda, Md.: American Physiological Society, 1987), pp. 115–154.

IV. LOCAL KNOWLEDGE, DISPERSED RESEARCH SCHOOLS, AND NATIONAL STYLES

In my synoptic article of 1981, I mentioned but did not seriously address two major gaps in Morrell's model of the research school. First, I warned that we would eventually need "to recognize and take account of the extent to which the members of a research school may extend its geographic scope by moving else-where." Second, I noted that we could not properly evaluate the success or failure of local research schools unless at some point attention was shifted "back to the level of the discipline as a whole."[18] What links these observations is a concern that Morrellian models tell us little or nothing about the crucial process by which the products of a research school, whether human or technical, move beyond it and become incorporated into larger social units, ranging from subspecialties through disciplines to the scientific community at large.

This concern is brought into focus and given empirical content in several con-tributions to this volume, including at the least the essays by Olesko, Rocke, Henson, Turner, and Mary Jo Nye. All draw attention to the existence and signifi-cance of what Turner calls "dispersed research schools." Perhaps most directly pertinent here is Nye's brave attempt to show how research schools in French and English chemistry served as carriers of "national styles" at the end of the nine-teenth century. She relies partly on the essays by Olesko and Turner to urge that we go beyond the local level—whether Fruton's research groups or research schools as I define them—in order to examine the history of more expansively de-fined research schools and to follow the fate of their "styles" as they are extended to other sites and later generations.

At stake here are two of the deepest issues in recent science studies: "How does local knowledge become universal?" and "What should be the proper unit of anal-ysis for scientific styles?" The notion of scientific styles, although sometimes dis-missed as a hopelessly vague and outmoded idea borrowed from a passé version of art history, has clearly gained ground of late. I have already referred several times to Fruton's 1990 book *Contrasts in Scientific Style,* and a 1991 issue of the journal *Science in Context* is devoted entirely to "Style in Science."[19] Nye begins her essay here by rightly insisting that conceptual and social styles really do exist in science. "Style," she writes, "plays a role in the emergence and perpetuation of scientific ideas, institutions, and ideologies. Style is invoked in order to explain success or failure of individual, institutional, and national scientific endeavors."

Not surprisingly, distinctive scientific styles are most evident in small, local units. That is because, as Holmes put it elsewhere, "personal influences and styles have the most powerful effects on people working in physical proximity to one another."[20] Also crucial to the style—and indeed the very identity—of some research schools are site-specific techniques, instruments, and materials. To confine attention here only to examples from the history of American neuro-physiology in this century, Louise Marshall has suggested that what I would call research schools coalesced around the cathode-ray oscilloscope in Joseph

---

[18] Geison, "Scientific Change" (cit. n. 1), pp. 34–35.

[19] The questions quoted here are from Lorraine Daston and Michael Otte's introduction to the special issue "Style in Science," *Science in Context,* 1991, *4*:230–231.

[20] Holmes, "The Formation of the Munich School" (cit. n. 12), p. 180.

Erlanger's group at Washington University in Saint Louis, the stereotaxic in-strument in Stephen Ransom's Institute of Neurology at Northwestern, and the microelectrode in Ralph Gerard's laboratory at the University of Chicago. Other examples will readily occur to those who have followed the recent effloures-cence of scholarship on instruments, techniques, and materials in the history and sociology of science.[21]

The distinctive conceptual, technical, and social features of local research schools perforce tend to fade as their personnel migrate to other sites and as their conceptual innovations are incorporated into larger social units in the scientific community. Perhaps, indeed, every successful research school eventually under-goes diaspora. At least some junior members of these schools will move on to po-sitions at other research centers, where they will often modify or even forsake their mentor's programmatic vision in order to assert their newly independent status and to accommodate themselves to different local circumstances. Like the constituents of other diasporas more familiar to us, once-distinctive local schools thus face the possibility of dilution through "assimilation."

That point emerges most explicitly here in Olesko's essay on Kohlrausch's school of physics at Göttingen and in Henson's essay on Comstock's schools of entomology at Cornell and Stanford. In these cases, the once-distinctive ap-proaches of local research schools became so dominant in their disciplines that there were eventually no viable alternatives. By swamping the competition, so to speak, these "genetic variants" became part and parcel of a larger and more ho-mogeneous disciplinary "gene pool" whose products came to be seen as items of consensual or "universal" scientific knowledge.

Put another way, the distinctive styles of local research schools tend to disap-pear as controversy fades and scientific consensus is achieved. This conclusion is in keeping with the emphasis in Turner's chapter on the role of controversy in the very creation and existence of distinctive research schools in the Hering-Helmholtz dispute over issues within physiological optics. It also confirms, less directly, a suggestion made by Kushner in his chapter on George Darwin and geo-physics: If it is hard to identify distinctive local schools within this emerging dis-cipline, perhaps that is partly because George Darwin's work never did arouse much controversy.

Nonetheless, I would insist that many scientists, even after they leave their mentors and migrate from their "ancestral" research schools, carry with them a more or less deep impress of that prior experience and training—not only in their general conceptual orientation, but also in their preference for specific modes of organizing scientific work and their choice of particular research problems, meth-ods, techniques, and materials. Eventually, of course, all such connections with past training will fade, but many scientists, even now, proudly trace their career path back to one or another of the leading "fathers" of their discipline or spe-cialty. Even now, scientists can and do produce "intellectual genealogies" of the sort constructed by Karl Rothschuh long ago for research schools in German

---

[21] Louise H. Marshall, "Instruments, Techniques, and Social Units in American Neurophysiology," in *Physiology in the American Context,* ed. Geison (cit. n. 17), pp. 351–369. For a full and rich intro-duction to this scholarship see Clarke and Fujimara, eds., *Right Tools for the Job* (cit. n. 12), esp. pp. 3–44.

physiology or by Fruton in his exhaustively detailed recent book on research groups in chemistry and biochemistry.[22] Such genealogies should not be cynically dismissed as attempts to "legitimate" the scientist or his discipline; they also attest to the persistent influence and appeal of local research schools that may no longer exist in anything like their original institutional form. Even in modern science, that is to say, ancestral local traditions sometimes matter deeply to their dispersed descendants.

Nor, finally, should we ignore the surprising resilience of *national* styles or traditions in science—as Nye argues in her essay here on French and English chemistry. Quite obviously, national styles have lost some of their salience in the face of the powerful homogenizing forces of an ever-more-interconnected international scientific community—forces that were, indeed, already evident to Merz himself nearly a century ago. But Nye's essay shows that national styles persisted well into this century in the case of English and French chemistry. Even Kushner's chapter on George Darwin and geophysics, which finds little evidence of local research schools, nonetheless points toward the existence of a peculiarly British style of work in the emerging discipline, marked above all by a link with astronomy that seemed curious to geophysicists in Germany or the United States. Elsewhere, I have emphasized the differences between "Anglo-Saxon" and German or Russian styles of physiology as late as 1950 or so. And in presumably the "hardest" case of all, modern theoretical physics, S. S. Schweber has persuasively argued for the existence of different national styles at least into the 1930s and 1940s.[23]

No serious student of modern science will deny that it represents the closest thing we have to consensual, objective, international, "universal" knowledge. The claim to a special epistemological status for modern science—dare we call that an ideology of its own by now?—has been under assault for a generation or more, but no better alternative is yet in sight. Perhaps, however, in the post-Enlightenment world we are ready to acknowledge some degree of multiculturalism even in the case of science itself. Such a position may seem disturbing just now, when we see all about us the consequences—sometimes inspiring but too often horrific—of ethnic, religious, racial, and other cultural divides. Yet for good or ill, we are nowhere near "the end of history," despite the fall of the Berlin Wall and the expanding hegemony of multinational corporations.[24] And if the history of science has any relation to cultural history in general, as surely it must, we are also nowhere near the end of the history of science. Few if any topics in our field illustrate that point more forcefully than the study of culturally distinctive research schools and national styles in science. This volume thus represents a valuable and timely contribution to new directions in the historiography of science.

[22] Karl E. Rothschuh, *History of Physiology,* trans. and ed. Gunter B. Risse (Huntington, N.Y.: Krieger, 1973); and Fruton, *Contrasts in Scientific Style* (cit. n. 2).

[23] Geison, *Michael Foster* (cit. n. 1), esp. pp. 331–355; and S. S. Schweber, "The Empiricist Temper Regnant: Theoretical Physics in the United States, 1920–1950," *Historical Studies in the Physical Sciences,* 1986, *17*:55–98. See also Jonathan Harwood, *Styles of Scientific Thought: The German Genetics Community, 1900–1933* (Chicago: Univ. Chicago Press, 1992).

[24] The briefly famous but already absurd case for "the end of history" was made by Francis Fukuyama, *The End of History and the Last Man* (New York: Free Press, 1992).

Notes on Contributors

Gerald L. Geison is Professor of History at Princeton University. In addition to his work on research schools in British and American physiology, he has long-standing interests in national styles in science, the relation between basic science and medical practice, and the career of Louis Pasteur.

Joel Hagen, Associate Professor of Biology at Radford University, is the author of *An Entangled Bank: The Origins of Ecosystem Ecology* (Rutgers, 1992). Aside from his research in history of ecology, he is involved in a project to develop historical materials for use in teaching undergraduate biology courses.

Pamela M. Henson is Historian at the Smithsonian Institute Archives. She received her doctorate in history and philosophy of science from the University of Maryland and specializes in the history of entomology and evolutionary biology.

Frederic L. Holmes is Professor and Chair of the Section of the History of Medicine at the Yale University School of Medicine. The author of books on Claude Bernard, Antoine Lavoisier, and Hans Krebs, he is at work on a book about Justus Liebig and his school and on a history of the Meselson-Stahl experiment on DNA replication.

David Kushner received his doctorate in history of science from Princeton University in 1990. He has since taught at Duke University and at North Carolina State University, where he is now Visiting Assistant Professor of History. One of his long-term projects is a scientific biography of George Darwin.

Jack Morrell was Reader in History of Science at the University of Bradford, England, until 1991, when he took early retirement. He is now at work on a book about Oxford science from 1914 to 1939, while not entirely ignoring his long-standing interest in John Phillips, the Victorian geologist.

Mary Jo Nye is George Lynn Cross Research Professor of the History of Science and Chair of the History of Science Department at the University of Oklahoma. Her new book, *From Chemical Philosophy to Theoretical Chemistry: Dynamics of Matter and Dynamics of Disciplines,*

1800–1950, will be published by the University of California Press in fall 1993.

Kathryn M. Olesko is Associate Professor of History at Georgetown University. The author of *Physics as a Calling: Discipline and Practice in the Königsberg Seminar for Physics* (Cornell, 1991) and editor of *Science in Germany* (*Osiris* 5, 1989), she is writing a book on the scientific, political, economic, and cultural meanings of precision measurement in Germany from 1780 to 1870.

Antoni Roca-Rosell is a member of the Working Group on History of Science of the Institut d'Estudis Catalans and Associate Professor in the School of Industrial Engineering at the University of Barcelona, Spain. He is interested in the history of the physical sciences in Spain in the nineteenth and twentieth centuries.

Alan J. Rocke teaches in the Program for History of Technology and Science at Case Western Reserve University in Cleveland. He is the author of *Chemical Atomism in the Nineteenth Century* (Ohio State University Press, 1984) and *The Quiet Revolution: Hermann Kolbe and the Science of Organic Chemistry* (California, in press).

José M. Sánchez-Ron is *profesor titular* of theoretical physics at the Universidad Autónoma de Madrid. A former physicist, he now works on the history of nineteenth- and twentieth-century mathematics. His latest book is *El poder de la ciencia* (Madrid, 1992); at present he is finishing a biography of Blas Cabrera.

John W. Servos is Professor of History at Amherst College, where he teaches the history of science and medicine. He is the author of *Physical Chemistry from Ostwald to Pauling: The Making of a Science in America* (Princeton, 1990) (Pfizer Award, 1992), and he is now engaged in a history of the industrial sponsorship of scientific research in American universities.

R. Steven Turner teaches the history of science and technology at the University of New Brunswick in Fredericton, Canada. His research deals with the history of the German universities of the nineteenth century, the development of sensory physiology and psychology, and the careers of Hermann von Helmholtz and Ewald Hering.

Index